The Websters
of Kendal

A North-Western Architectural Dynasty

Francis Webster by James Ward, 1823
(Kendal Town Council Picture Collection)

The Websters
of Kendal

A North-Western Architectural Dynasty

by

Angus Taylor

edited by

Janet Martin

CUMBERLAND AND WESTMORLAND
ANTIQUARIAN AND ARCHAEOLOGICAL SOCIETY

Record Series Volume XVII
2004

George Webster,

Eller How

Contents

Angus Taylor at Burton, 28th October 1999 (Janet Martin)

Angus Taylor – a Memoir

ANGUS Taylor was born in Sedbergh in 1928 and retained a love of the area throughout his life. After attending the local primary school and Queen Elizabeth School, Kirkby Lonsdale, he became a day boy at Sedbergh School at the age of thirteen. There his artistic talents were nurtured by Sandy and Alice Inglis and in 1945, encouraged by Harold Holden, a relation who was Principal of Birmingham College of Arts and Crafts, he became a student at Leeds College of Art, specialising in painting. There he gained his NDD and ATD before completing two years' National Service in the Royal Engineers.

Between 1956 and 1962 Angus taught at the James Mackinlay Secondary Modern School in Redcar. Then, after a one-year temporary post at St John's College, York, he moved to the High Melton College of Education in Doncaster where he remained until its closure as a teacher training college in 1984.

From an early age Angus was interested in architecture. A thesis of 1950 was entitled 'Some Buildings of Architectural Interest in Upper Lonsdale'. His visual recall of architectural detail was acute and, allied to a strong streak of intellectual curiosity, led to the writing of articles for a variety of publications and research into the work of architects such as William Lindley and Joseph Pocklington.

His principal interest, however, from his student days, was in George Webster and the work of the Webster family of stonemasons and architects. During a sabbatical from High Melton in 1973 he, with Jeffrey Haworth, organised an exhibition at the Abbot Hall Art Gallery in Kendal of the Websters' architectural legacy in Kendal and elsewhere. It was the first public recognition of the family's achievements.

Retirement in 1984 brought the opportunity to widen and deepen Angus's Webster researches. He drove many thousands of miles, took and developed hundreds of photographs, and amassed a great deal of material. He was fortunate later in enlisting the help of Janet Martin who undertook the work of editing it all. When he died in August 2000 he had the satisfaction of knowing that the book was nearing completion; since then, Janet has worked unstintingly to bring it to publication. Angus's family is very aware of the debt of thanks which we owe to her for realising his life's work.

Mary Taylor

Preface

WHEN Angus Taylor died in August 2000 he had almost completed the work on the Websters of Kendal which he had planned more than thirty years ago. In 1997, through the good offices of the late Oliver Turnbull of Titus Wilsons, he asked me to collaborate with him, realising that a great deal still remained to be done, and that it was not all to his taste. We spent the next three years chasing and standardising references and revising each section until we could agree a final form. It was a collaboration which gave us both much pleasure.

Since Angus died I have continued the work, though missing his wry comments and patient acceptance of what I hope was positive criticism, and am most grateful to Mary Taylor and her family for continuing his trust in me. I have had very positive help from a great many people and between us we have made some further discoveries and alterations, which I believe Angus would have been happy to accept. The inventory of the contents of George Webster's house at Eller How in 1864 was discovered at a late stage and is included here in full as it was clearly important. I am especially grateful to Angus's friends Jeffrey Haworth and John Martin Robinson. Both read the whole text and made valuable suggestions as to the rearrangement of Chapter IV and the exclusion from the gazetteer of a small number of buildings which both they and I agreed were unconnected with the Websters. Jeffrey in particular has given much time to helping me; my debt to him is very great. Michael Bottomley and the late John Satchell contributed most generously from their encyclopaedic knowledge of Kendal and its buildings. We, and others, have smoothed the text in various places without, I hope, detracting from Angus's style. My daughter Sophia and my husband have lived patiently with the Websters throughout; both deserve much more than formal thanks.

It gives me great pleasure to be able to thank two of George Webster's great-grandchildren. George Bartlett sent me copies of George's passports and has kindly given permission for Richard Stirzaker's watercolour of Eller How to be used for the dust-jacket, and Vicky Elmitt showed me some family memorabilia and provided a copy of Eleanor Webster's will.

Had he lived, Angus would have added to these acknowledgments. He would undoubtedly have first wished to thank all the owners of Webster houses who displayed their homes and their documents. We both owe a great deal to members of staff at the Cumbria Record Office, especially to Richard Hall at Kendal, and at the Lancashire Record Office, and elsewhere. During the course of his work Angus visited a great many libraries. I can only single out Kendal, Accrington, Lancaster, the Brotherton Library at Leeds University, and the library of the Yorkshire Archaeological Society; other people and organisations will, I am sure, take his, and my, thanks on trust. I am also grateful to the Georgian Group for permission to reprint Appendix III.

Wherever possible all references have been checked and where necessary augmented, corrected, or better ones substituted, as much of Angus's earliest research lacked adequate references. Most of the illustrations are from photographs taken by Angus himself, in many cases as much for a record of what he saw on his visits as for particular illustrations for the book. With such a variety of material and sources it has been difficult to deal exhaustively with copyright. In continuing Angus's work I have done my best to trace the origins of pictures and plans. If some anomalies remain I should be pleased to hear of them. Place-names are throughout assigned to their historic counties as they existed before the Local Government Act of 1972.

Angus Taylor's notebooks, indexes, working papers, and photographs have been deposited, as he wished, at Cumbria Record Office, Kendal.

Janet Martin
Finsthwaite, 2004

The Published Works of Angus Taylor

'Kirkleatham', *Architectural Review*, 124, no. 74, October 1958, 247-50

'Thomas Harrison and Stramongate Bridge, Kendal', *CW2*, lxix, 1969, 275-9

'A Bank and its Buildings: Ulverston Trustee Savings Bank', *CW2*, lxxiv, 1974, 146-58

'Paper Houses: an Anglo-Irish Interlude', *Leeds Arts Calendar*, no. 77, 1975, 25-32

'Compulsive Lakeland Builder: Joseph Pocklington 1736-1817', *CL*, 5 September 1985, 614-7

'Francis Goodwin's *Domestic Architecture* and two Cockermouth Villas', *Architectural History*, 28, 1985, 125-35

'"More Vile Taste . . .": The Pocklington Brothers and their Buildings', *CL*, 1 May 1986, 1184-8

'The Dukery of Carlisle', *CL*, 31 August 1989, 92-7

'Denison Hall, Leeds: a Postscript to Richard Hewlings', *Yorkshire Archaeological Journal*, 63, 1991, 220-21

'The Bank of Westmorland Lion', *Quarto*, xxix, January 1992, 16-19

'George Webster (1797-1864): the Education of an Architect; a Proposal', *Quarto*, xxxi, April 1993, 13-16

'The Wordsworths, the Websters and Chantrey's Quillinan Monument', *Quarto*, xxxii, July 1994, 12-14

'William Lindley of Doncaster', *Georgian Group Journal*, iv, 1994, 30-42

'The Lowly Dwelling of William Wordsworth Esqre.', *Georgian Group Journal*, vii, 1997, 43-55

Notes and letters in various journals

List of Illustrations

Frontispiece
Francis Webster by James Ward, 1823 *(Kendal Town Council Picture Collection)*

Angus Taylor at Burton, 28 October 1999

Houses

Industrial and Commercial Buildings

Hotels

Bridges

Monuments

Abbreviations

Annals = C. Nicholson, *Annals of Kendal*, 2nd ed., London and Kendal, 1861

Boumphrey and Hudleston = R. S. Boumphrey, C. R. Hudleston, and J. Hughes, *An Armorial for Westmorland and Lonsdale*, CWAAS, Extra Series xxii, 1975

Burke, *Visitations* = B. Burke, *A Visitation of Seats and Arms of the Noblemen and Gentlemen of Great Britain and Ireland*, 2 vols, London, 1852-3; 2nd series, 2 vols, London, 1854-5

CL = Country Life, various dates

Colvin = H. M. Colvin, *Biographical Dictionary of British Architects, 1600-1840*, 3rd ed., New Haven and London, 1995

CRO = Cumbria Record Office, Carlisle

CRO B = Cumbria Record Office, Barrow-in-Furness

CRO K = Cumbria Record Office, Kendal

CRO K, *Annals* = J. F. Curwen's annotated copy of *Annals*

Curwen, *KK* = J. F. Curwen, *Kirkbie-Kendall*, Kendal, 1900

Curwen, *Rec. Kendale*, iii = J. F. Curwen, *Records relating to the Barony of Kendale*, iii, CWAAS, Record Series vi, 1926

CW2 = Transactions of the Cumberland and Westmorland Antiquarian and Archaeological Society, new series, 1901-2000; also *CW1*, to 1900; *CW3*, from 2001

CWAAS = Cumberland and Westmorland Antiquarian and Archaeological Society

Gunnis = R. Gunnis, *Dictionary of British Sculptors, 1660-1851*, 2nd ed., London, n.d.

Kelly = Kelly's *Directories* [of Cumberland and Westmorland], various dates

Local Chronology = Local Chronology, Kendal, 1865

Lons. Mag. = J. Briggs (ed), *Lonsdale Magazine*, 3 vols, Kirkby Lonsdale and Kendal, 1820-22

LRO = Lancashire Record Office

Mannex = Mannex's *Directories* [of Westmorland and Lonsdale], various dates

Mannix and Whellan, 1847 = Mannix and Whellan, *History, gazetteer and directory of Cumberland*, Beverley, 1847

NYRO = North Yorkshire Record Office

Parson and White, 1829 = W. Parson and W. White, *History, directory, and gazetteer of Cumberland and Westmorland*, Leeds, 1829

Pevsner, *Cumb. and Westm.* = N. Pevsner, *Cumberland and Westmorland*, Buildings of England, London, 1967; also *N. Lancs.*, 1969; *S. Lancs.*, 1969; *W. Yorks.*, 1959

Quarto = Quarto, Abbot Hall Art Gallery, Kendal, various dates

Robinson, *Country Houses* = J. M. Robinson, *A Guide to the Country Houses of the North-West*, London, 1991

Twycross = E. Twycross, *Mansions of England and Wales: County Palatine of Lancaster*, 3 vols, London, 1847

VCH *Lancs.* = W. Farrer *et al.* (eds), *Victoria History of the County of Lancaster*, 8 vols, London, 1906-14

Websters of Kendal = The Websters of Kendal, Abbot Hall Art Gallery, Kendal, 1973

WG = Westmorland Gazette, 1818 to date

Whitwell = J. Whitwell, *The Old Houses of Kendal*, Kendal, 1866

Introduction

ARCHITECTS have often emerged from building-trade dynasties. One thinks of John Carr of York and his family, the Smiths of Warwick, and especially of the Wyatts, who numbered over twenty kinsmen involved in building or architecture or the decorative arts. George Webster of Kendal, who died in 1864, a cultivated gentleman, with a connoisseur's collection at his country seat, was the product of such a family. It was his father, Francis, who added architecture to his mason's skill which, with a good head for business, paved the way for George's architectural achievements and acceptance into the ranks of the provincial gentry.

Too little is known of the eighteenth-century Websters, Thomas, Robert, his son Robert, and his grandson, yet another Robert, to make confident generalisations – with one exception: they were all master masons. They acquired their skills from other masons, in this case through four generations of one family, working with the obdurate stones of south Lakeland – slate and carboniferous limestone. Son carried on his trade in much the same unselfconscious way as father, using the same materials, the same methods, the same plans, to meet the plain, unchanging needs of yeomen, statesmen, tenants, and cottagers for houses and ancillary buildings – barns, stables, shelters. This strong vernacular tradition carried on well into the nineteenth century. In remoter areas features were retained where elsewhere fashion ousted them. Thus the mullioned window persisted in the mason's repertory where elsewhere the snugger sash window had taken over. Again, scraps of 'polite' architecture attached themselves and a mason would see that a pediment of sorts could be affixed over an entrance door. Such details would perhaps be picked up when the mason worked for an architect on a 'designed' building.

Some masons had special skills. Robert Webster senior provided elaborately carved chimneypieces of imported marble to the house at Hollow Oak, Haverthwaite, between 1760 and 1774. No doubt he also carved monumental tablets, perhaps including some of the unsigned examples at Cartmel Priory. Those skills he passed on to his youngest son Francis. Robert worked with John Hird at Sizergh Castle in 1777. Hird was described variously as house-carpenter (1763) and joiner (1767, 1771, 1775), but by 1777 his designs were inscribed 'architect', as early

1

as 1765 at Leighton Hall. Nor is there anything of the vernacular about his Witherslack church of 1768.

Francis Webster followed a similar pattern from his move to Kendal about 1787. In his early works he was often described as a mason together with his partner William Holme. However, he was clearly the designer when required and he possibly performed this function at Hawkshead where he was part of the team building the Assembly Rooms and Market Hall in 1790-91, a team which included his father and/or brother. His designs for Lowther Hall about 1800 were in both scale and ambition the work of an architect, not a mason. William Green knew him in 1813 as 'Mr. Architect Webster'.

Before Francis's death in 1827 his son George had already designed several of his finest houses. They followed the pattern of great classical and Elizabethan houses. In the same years he came under the influence of Wordsworth and his ideas of how houses in the Lake District should be built, as propounded in his *Guide*, first published in 1810. The poet asked him to design a house and even the first version shows vernacular features. In the second such features are even more emphatic and in the specification for the masons' work Webster gave the instruction that 'for better examples reference must be had to some of the old houses in the neighbourhood', some of which could have been built by his ancestors. To a degree the wheel had come full circle.

I

Master Masons
Thomas Webster (fl. 1725-1760)
Robert Webster (1726-1799)
Robert Webster (1758-1805)
Robert Webster (1785-1828)

THE Webster family may have had its roots in Kendal but by 1754 it had migrated to Cartmel. There the next three generations were engaged in either building or architecture, or were mariners or fishermen, until about 1787 when Francis Webster (1767-1827) moved back to Kendal and prospered there.

The first record of a payment to a Webster mason was one of £4 10s. to Thomas Webster of Kendal[1] in 1749 for repairing 'the 300 feet at the west end' of Kirkby Lonsdale bridge, whereupon he petitioned the council, pointing out that he had made an engagement with the High Constable of Lonsdale to make the repair for £35. He complained that the people of Kirkby Lonsdale were supposed to have provided sixty horses and carts and men to carry 'proper materials' but that had not happened. He had to do it himself and was to be paid £4 10s. for 'carrying the said materials' on 7 April 1749.[2] There is no record of further payments.

Thomas Webster and his wife Mary lived in Stricklandgate, Kendal, until about 1730 when they moved to the Market Place. They had five children between 1726 and 1739. The eldest was Robert (1726-99) who became a mason and married Ann Crosfield at Cartmel Priory in 1754. They were living at Cark Hall in 1755 but in the following year moved to Quarry Flatt on the Holker estate, where there was one of the few quarries of fine freestone in the district – a great asset to a mason.

Recent discoveries reveal that Robert was providing chimneypieces of imported marble as early as 1760. He probably built houses and appears to have had a working relationship with John Hird (fl. 1760-96), sometimes referred to as house-carpenter, sometimes as architect. Hird was 'of Kendal' when awarded the freedom of Lancaster in 1763. No building either there or in Kendal is known to be by him but he did produce a design for a new Stramongate bridge in 1793, although that of

Thomas Harrison was preferred.[3] Amongst others, he made designs for Leighton Hall and probably built Ponsonby Hall near Gosforth about 1775, a copy of James Paine's design for St Ives, Bingley, in the West Riding of Yorkshire, published in his *Plans* of 1767 to which Hird was a subscriber. He lived at Green, Cartmel, and as a neighbour of the Websters and the only 'architect' in the area is the man most likely to have interested Robert Webster's son Francis in becoming an architect himself.

In 1767 Hird was paid twenty guineas by James Machell of Hollow Oak, Haverthwaite, for 'sundry repairs at my house' where Robert Webster was also paid for at least two marble fireplaces.[4] It seems that the two were already a team.

On 17 February 1773 Cecilia Strickland, guardian of the infant Thomas Strickland, agreed with various workmen to alter and repair the 'Mansion house of Sizergh'. 'Robert Webster of Quarry Flatt in Cartmel, mason', was one of them and was 'to provide good and sufficient freestone and execute all such mason's work necessary to complete and finish all alterations etc. according to the plans of John Hird, architect'.[5]

There are few records of Robert Webster's building activities. He received eighteen guineas for paving the church at Finsthwaite in 1771.[6] He was paid twelve guineas in 1787 'for Maysons work' at an unidentified building possibly in Cartmel Fell,[7] and either he or his son Robert (1758-1805) of Flookburgh supplied 'extra mason work Deliver'd at the Markett House' in Hawkshead, including the datestone and cornice, for £10 2s. 11d. in 1790. His youngest son Francis was the mason and possibly the designer at Hawkshead.[8] Robert of Flookburgh had a son, yet another Robert (1785-1828), of Quarry Flatt. This Robert, who was also a mason, was paid £5 12s. by the churchwardens of Cartmel in 1820 for 'Freestone work for the West window' of the priory, and 10s. for unspecified work in 1823.[9]

Robert Webster senior was a man of some means, as his will of 1793 shows. Apart from Quarry Flatt, he had property at Mitchelland, between Bowness and Crook, a 'parcel of land' called Quarry Parrock, including a house or cottage and other buildings, at Hawcoat near Dalton-in-Furness, and a house and barn in Ulverston. This and other real estate was to be held in trust by his executors, his son Robert and his friend James Stockdale junior. His eldest son Thomas had died before the will was drawn up but Thomas's eldest son and five other grandchildren received small legacies. Son Robert was left not only his quarry tools but his cows, horses, and 'husbandry gear'. The furnishings of Quarry Flatt which he left to his wife, including the best bedstead and hangings, best table and china, and his mahogany table, suggest a comfortable existence.[10] Francis is not mentioned so perhaps he had had his portion when he left Cartmel for Kendal about 1787.

After Francis went away his elder brother Robert and his son Robert carried on a mason's trade much as their father had done. It was no doubt his position as a youngest son that obliged Francis to move away from the valley and establish himself in Kendal, rather any particular manifestation of the ambition, inventiveness, skill, or industry to which his obituary would attest forty years later.

Notes

[1] He was probably the son of Robert Webster and baptised in Kendal on 18 July 1707: information from Dr Blake Tyson, who kindly provided other details of the family history.

[2] Curwen, *Rec. Kendale*, iii, 284.

[3] For Hird, see Colvin, 498-9; A. C. Taylor, 'Thomas Harrison and Stramongate Bridge', *CW2*, lxix, 276-9; LRO, DDCa/153 (mention of John Hird of Green, joiner). Some of his various dealings with Robert Webster are in LRO, DDCa/154 and 254.

[4] LRO, DDMc/28/1; one fireplace at £3 10s. on 4 Sept. 1766, and another at £3 on 18th May 1767. He had provided one earlier at 9s. on 18 Feb. 1760. Further payments were made to Webster in 1774, 'on account 3 gns', and 1775 'his bill in full £5. 11. 6'.

[5] Sizergh Castle archives: information from Miss S. Macpherson; H. Hornyold, *Genealogical Memoirs of the Family of Strickland of Sizergh*, 1928, 260. Only a fraction of the work was carried out. The designs are at Sizergh. Hird's saloon was badly compromised in 1969 when not only the plate glass in the three east-facing windows but their pointed gothick heads were removed.

[6] CRO K, WPR 101/W1, 31.

[7] *Ibid.*, WDY 462.

[8] But see p. 153; B. Tyson, 'Francis Webster and the Market House at Hawkshead, 1790', *Quarto*, Oct. 1993, 8-11. This is one of the 'new erections' so hated by Wordsworth (and Coleridge): *Prelude*, ii, 31-40. An earlier version spoke of the 'smart Assembly-rooms that perked and flared with wash and rough-cast'.

[9] Information from Dr Blake Tyson.

[10] LRO, WRW/F, will of Robert Webster, proved 1800. He, or more probably his son, Robert of Flookburgh, had bought eight acres of land on Newton Fell in 1798 when the Cartmel common lands were enclosed after 1796: J. Stockdale, *Annals of Cartmel*, 1872, 334. Robert also built some of the new sluices in 1797: *ibid.*, 332. The heirs of Robert senior were allotted two acres on Winder Moor and had some old enclosure at Flookburgh: CRO K, WPR 89/Z3.

II

Francis Webster (1767-1827)
Mason to Architect

FRANCIS Webster's transition to Kendal was easy – perhaps because he had relations there, perhaps because a partner was found for him. From the beginning he joined up with William Holme, mason.

Holme had built a large house in Stricklandgate, Kendal, for Joseph Maude who moved to Kendal from Sunderland in 1773 and was one of the founders of the Kendal Bank. The first indication of the work is in a letter from Maude to Thomas Fenwick of Burrow Hall, near Kirkby Lonsdale, of 26 July 1776 in which he informs Fenwick that he has just bought a house in Kendal for £1,450 and intends to rebuild it immediately, as a preliminary to reminding Fenwick that he owes him £1,000. Before this, Maude's account book shows that on 14 February 1776 he had bought a freehold estate at Holmescales, Old Hutton, for £3,480. Three days later he paid William Holme five guineas for work at the Bull Coppy there and there are further payments of six, five, and four guineas in April and May.[1] Then on 23 July is a payment of £4 10s. 3d. for the new house but on 17 August come three guineas for pulling down the old house. Three days later drink for workmen laying foundations cost 8s., and on 30 August William Holme was paid ten guineas 'on account of New house'. Several payments for stone, wood, timber, and so on are followed in September and October by further payments to Holme of £58 12s., making a total to him of £82 7s. 3d. On 14 November a John Richardson was paid £12 18s. 6d. 'for Cornice'. There is no sign of any payment to an architect, but it seems very unlikely that William Holme could have been the designer of what was later described as the 'largest and best [house] in the town'.[2] There is no evidence that he ever stepped out of his role of mason/waller, but he was clearly an experienced man, and senior enough in 1777 to be called in as arbitrator at Flookburgh chapel which John Hird designed in that year.[3] It is tempting to award the architect's work at the Stricklandgate house to Hird who, a few years later, may have brought Francis Webster and Holme together.

From 1780 to 1786 Holme was repairing houses on Fellside in Kendal for the portrait painter, Daniel Gardner,[4] and in 1785 he was involved with work at the new

House of Correction there.[5] A James Pennington was the carpenter and probably the designer at Fellside.[6] Work there went on in most years until 1808, and in 1798, 1801, and 1803 it involved Francis Webster.[7] In 1793 Holme and Webster repaired the House of Correction 'agreeable to a plan exhibited at the last assizes at Appleby',[8] but in 1801 it was no longer large enough and 'great additions' were planned by Webster.[9] In 1817 it was enlarged 'or nearly rebuilt', it was said,[10] and along with designs for a House of Correction at Appleby plans of 1824 were presented to the governors of Lancaster Prison for advice. The work was carried out in 1825 from 'the plans already prepared'.[11]

To a degree the work overlapped with Appleby, but Appleby was more than a gaol. It was also the seat of the county assizes and a greater challenge. Francis Webster presented three sets of designs in 1812, 1818, and 1824. The first was to 'remedy defects'[12] and Webster brought many familiar craftsmen from Kendal, like John Fisher the joiner. The design shows an awareness of the ideas of Jeremy Bentham for the improvement of prison building – the Panopticon principle. In 1818 Webster, by careful additions, achieved a symmetrical classical front of two storeys of 2+3+2 bays, the centre three carrying a pediment.[13] It is of the same proportions, but in a simplified version, as Robert Adam's design for a court house at Appleby which was formerly at Lowther and so known to Webster.[14] He sent the designs to Lord Lonsdale with a letter on the back explaining the colouring and the cost (£1,140). The earl was no doubt the patron. The third set of plans of 1824 was sent to Lancaster for approval and again Bentham's ideas were used. Webster was paid, posthumously, £70 in 1828.[15]

The first work at the prison after Webster's death was by William Coulthard of Lancaster, who was paid £20 in April 1830 and who was linked with the Websters in ways not yet clear.[16] Holme's name does not appear after 1808 and Webster's fellow mason at Lowther in 1800-02 was Ben Proctor and at Shaw End, Patton, in 1796-1802 Robert Snibson.[17] The days of partnerships outside the family are over. From now on separate trades are tendered for. The transition from master mason to architect is complete. Whatever the exact date, Francis Webster is credited with being the 'first to introduce the public profession of architecture into Kendal'.[18]

The date of Webster's move to Kendal is generally accepted as 1788, but since his first known work with his new partner is of that year – the obelisk on Castle Howe celebrating the centenary of the Glorious Revolution – he probably arrived a year or so earlier.[19] He settled in the New Inn Yard off the west side of Highgate and married Janet Slater of Spital Farm near Kirkby Lonsdale in 1793. Their first child, Robert, was born the same year, to be followed by George and four daughters, and finally Francis in 1805 whose birth caused the death of his mother.[20] The widower was married again in 1808 to Margaret Lowry, the widow of an Ulverston sail-maker, George Lowry, who also owned a slate quarry at Kirkby Ireleth.[21] There were no further children.

In 1790 Webster was part of the team which built the new Assembly Rooms and

Market Hall at Hawkshead. He also provided chimneypieces from his enterprise in Kendal and may have been the designer. One of the principal design motifs is an arched window set in a shallow recess of the same form, a device which he used elsewhere, but it has recently been suggested that John Carr of York designed the building and introduced Webster to the possibilities of the arched device.[22] In 1796 Webster and Holme built Beck Mill, north of Kendal, for the Levens Hall estate.[23]

In Kendal itself, Webster designed the building in Stricklandgate, now demolished, to which John Wakefield moved his bank in 1797. Part-office, part-house, it had a handsome if severe façade of five bays and two-and-a-half storeys of ashlar masonry with a rusticated ground floor of arched doors and windows. A vellum foundation document in Latin and English recorded the name of the architect and his client and that of William Holme as the mason.[24]

In the last years of the century Francis Webster began to work at Lowther Hall and at Whitehaven and elsewhere for Lord Lonsdale,[25] a powerful patron who unfortunately for Webster died in 1802. However, commissions from the new earl continued at Lowther and Appleby, even after Smirke's appointment as principal architect. With William Holme Francis built the gunpowder works at Lowwood, Haverthwaite, in 1798, and they provided slate for the inscription on the castellated tower, originally of three storeys, on a hill top at Finsthwaite for James King of Finsthwaite House in 1799.[26] At the same time the firm was involved in building a house in Ulverston for William Strickland of Whitestock, Rusland.[27]

So by 1800 Webster had an established architectural practice in north Lancashire and Westmorland. He had few rivals. A Richard Pedder was paid two guineas for plans and a model for the new workhouse on Kendal Fell in 1767 and he made additions in 1776, but if he worked on into Webster's period there is no record.[28] John Richardson (1774-1864) designed the New (Shakespeare) Theatre in 1828, the Infants' School in All Hallows Lane (1829), the White Hart Hotel and Shambles (1828-30), and Town View (1831), the latter very Websterian. He is not known to have worked outside Kendal.[29]

William Coulthard of Lancaster (d. 1833) was rather a competitor than a collaborator and his independent designs and detailing depend on George Webster's work. John Hird's known works were complete by the early 1790s. He was possibly the unknown architect of the gothicising of Broughton Tower in 1777, prompted by Batty Langley's designs and other pattern books. We know that Francis had a 'library' of architectural books. Soon afterwards pattern books would be advertised in the Carlisle and Kendal papers. Lovell's *Builder's Assistant* and others were mentioned as being for sale in a Kendal bookshop in the first issue of the *Westmorland Gazette* in 1818. Hird's surviving drawings are certainly competent and it may be that he gave Webster instruction, or at least encouragement, in draughtsmanship, but Francis's grasp of perspective always remained unsure, an aid to identifying his hand noted by the editors of *Architectural Drawings from Lowther Castle* in 1980.[30]

It was at Lowther that Francis Webster was about to start his greatest project so far. The west wing of Lowther Hall had survived a devastating fire in 1718. Many of the greatest names in British architecture, including Colen Campbell, Matthew Brettingham, James Adam and others, had provided designs which never left the drawing board. Just before 1800 Webster made a sketch of the site[31] and the west wing on which Harrison of Chester based seven inventive designs for a new house incorporating the existing building. Nothing was built and here it seems that Lord Lonsdale handed the task to Webster who made several designs of his own and began work. Lord Lonsdale died in 1802 and the new lord began taking advice on building an entirely new house. Eventually Robert Smirke was chosen but Webster was retained, and kept the title of architect. And he could not have been in a better place to study the designs of the old masters – many of his own are reductions and simplifications of theirs, particularly those of Robert and James Adam.[32]

Webster worked for the Howards of Levens in many capacities. Architecturally, he built the Howard Tower (1807-20), in which the ceilings are miniature imitations of the drawing room design. Further imitation occurs in several rooms – the library, the smoking room, and elsewhere. All this is attributed to Francis Webster and was apparently the earliest Jacobean copying in the Webster *oeuvre*, so important in the career of his son George from about 1820. Indeed he may have advised his father at Levens.[33]

Francis Webster was a prominent Kendalian. He was a member of the Kendal Union Lodge in 1791 and seems to have attended until 1800.[34] He became an alderman and in 1823 was elected mayor for the coming year. He was an officer in the Kendal Volunteers and his absence at camp near Penrith was mentioned in a letter from Richardson, the Levens agent, to Richard Howard in Surrey on 19 May 1808.[35] In 1826, late in his life, he was one of the signatories of a handbill circulated by the Kendal banks stating his 'perfect confidence' in them.[36]

He was a friend of William Green of Ambleside, the landscape draughtsman and former surveyor. Green's diaries record a visit to 'Mr. Architect Webster' on 13 December 1813. He was away working at Levens Hall and Milnthorpe workhouse but 'Mrs. Architect' was at home entertaining company. On another occasion the Green family had lunch with the Websters and then heard *Messiah* in the parish church.[37]

Francis Webster's eldest son, another Robert, born in 1794, was naturally and evidently intended to follow his father in the business. He was an extraordinarily precocious draughtsman and rather unexpectedly hundreds of his drawings survive, unlike most Webster documents. He may have gone to school at Mr Gray's Academy at Milnthorpe, Owlet Ash House, of which he made a drawing, and it seems likely that William Green coached him, although his style never became formulaic as Green's tended to be. He drew Green's studio in Ambleside and very few of his works are without some architectural content. Between 1806 and 1809 are sheets labelled 'architectural studies', two of the orders and two of picturesque cottages, one classical and one a rustic gothic design reminiscent of John Plaw. All have the air of a diligent student with his pattern books open before him. As can be seen from the dates, all are drawn by a boy; indeed he died in 1810 aged fifteen or sixteen.[38] It does look as though architectural training was to have been his lot.

The third turning point in Francis's career, after the move to Kendal and the patronage of Lord Lonsdale, was the creation of a new commercial area across the river Kent from the town. The occasion for this was the extension northwards of the Lancaster Canal in 1818 after a lengthy interval. It would terminate in a basin in Kendal and Webster was involved from the start. The work included his new marble yard and showroom and a new bridge to connect the whole enterprise with the town, and it ended the use of the yard in Highgate. The new yard had direct access to water transport to the south and to Liverpool where another showroom would be opened.[39]

When it became clear to Webster that his eldest son would not take his place as head of the firm, the second son George was the next choice. Francis must have realised that his own route to architectural practice was no longer open and that in future a sound professional training was essential. In order to find such training George would need to leave Kendal to work in the office of an established architectural practice like that of John Foster I of Liverpool, and there was a link there as Francis had supplied a chimneypiece for Foster's Union News Room of 1801.[40] Another possibility was Harrison of Chester. Webster and Holme had carried out his design for Stramongate bridge in Kendal in 1793-4.[41] An alternative would be to become a student at the Royal Academy Schools in London. George did not take that route (but what was his elder brother doing there drawing from casts in 1807?).[42] However, William Atkinson in Manchester seems the most likely candidate.

There is a group of small country houses in north Lancashire and Westmorland which, though not documented, have similarities of style and may be attributed to the Websters. In the second volume of the *Lonsdale Magazine* an article on Lunefield, Kirkby Lonsdale, was expanded into an analysis of the planning of local houses. Lunefield itself was cruciform, the transepts rounded. It was small but carefully planned, had deep eaves, and was built in 1815-16.[43] The writer compared it with Cark Villa, which had square transepts and the offices underground, whereas Lunefield had them at the north end. Many 'throw' them behind. Examples given were Crowtrees (Melling), Penny Bridge Hall, Belfield (Bowness), Coniston Waterhead, and Stoney Dale (Field Broughton), and one can add Fair View (Ulverston), Shaw End (Patton), Heaves Lodge (Levens), and Bigland Hall to the list. Some incorporated the offices in the design so as to be indistinguishable from the living rooms, as at Springfield, Ulverston.

The third group, where the central house is symmetrically connected by short links to smaller wings, includes Sedgwick House,[44] Broughton Lodge, Longlands and Aynsome (Cartmel), Burton House, Beetham House, Plumtree Hall (Heversham), Island House (Barrow), and Leighton Hall. The Websters and Maudes were friends so that Blawith Cottage, Grange-over-Sands, also cruciform, was probably by Webster too. Plumtree Hall was built for Joseph Braithwaite, mayor of Kendal in 1820. Allithwaite Lodge was part of the estates of Richard Winfield of Kendal. Many of the houses have, or had till recently, fine groups of Webster fireplaces and there are several decorative themes that link some of them. Springfield, Allithwaite Lodge, and Longlands have a Palladian motif between hall and stairs, and Bigland and suburban Belle Vue, Ulverston, have openings of coupled fluted columns, the latter Palladian. A curious method of decoration by hanging short rows of dentils on a narrow moulding is used at Springfield, Bigland, and Belle Vue. Most of the houses have simple porches, at Shaw End and Plumtree with feathered capitals.

Almost all use Palladian or tripartite windows freely, without and within. Leighton Hall is of the right type, but too early, as it is of 1765 and probably by Hird.[45] Broughton Lodge, the largest and perhaps unlikely to be by Francis Webster, is of 1791, two-and-a-half storeys with two-storey wings.[46] Few have designers' names attached, few have even a reliable date, but most are c.1790-1815. Shaw End is known to be by Webster. How many others could be?

There is a group of buildings in Settle, by or attributable to Francis and George Webster. The earliest, probably by Francis, is not unlike the Morecambe Bay group. Ashfield House in the main street is a plain seven-bay house with wings attached directly to it and a semi-circular porch, which was built for William Birkbeck about 1800. Just south of the town in a small park stands Anley, built for John Birkbeck and completed in 1818. This has a Grecian portico and interior detail that resembles Esthwaite Lodge of the same period. The Birkbecks had moved out of Westmorland about 1700 and were merchants and then bankers, like many Kendalians at this period. Some married into Kendal families – Wilsons, Braithwaites, Goughs, and Wakefields – and with the Fells of Ulverston. William Birkbeck had an account with his cousin John Wakefield's bank in 1780-85. Later Susannah Birkbeck married E. W. Wakefield of Birklands, and when Low Mills at Kendal was sold on 2 May 1805 those involved were James Gandy, John Ireland, Isaac Wakefield, several Wilsons, and William Birkbeck of Settle. It is not difficult to see that the Birkbeck cousins might well borrow their architects from Kendal. The Birkbeck Bank joined Alcock's Skipton Bank and that of Chippendale, Netherwood, & Carr in 1834. George Webster thereupon designed Aireville, Skipton (1836), for Alcock and Cliffe House, Keighley (1833), for Netherwood.[47]

Notes

[1.] CRO K, WD/K/182, letter and bill book, 1774-1803.

[2.] Whitwell, 19; CRO K, *Annals*, 304.51.

[3.] J. Stockdale, *Annals of Cartmel*, 1872, 286, 288. Holme died in 1824 at the age of 86 and was buried at Kendal parish church on 10 June.

4. CRO K, WDX 398/E5/2-43, E8/1-3, 8.

5. See p. 154.

6. CRO K, WDX 398/E5/8, 10, 16; in 1793 Pennington was paid for planning a house.

7. *Ibid.*, E5/25, 32, 36.

8. CRO K, Quarter Sessions Minute Book, 1780-1804, *sub* 1793.

9. Curwen, *Rec. Kendale*, iii, 95.

10. Curwen, *KK*, 337.

11. B. Tyson, 'An Architectural History of the Gaols and Court-Houses at Appleby', *Trans. Ancient Monuments Soc.*, xxxii, 1988, 101-139.

12. *Ibid.* 120.

13. *Ibid.* 121, and plan on 122.

14. H. Colvin, J. M. Crook, and T. Friedman, *Architectural Drawings from Lowther Castle*, Society of Architectural Historians of Great Britain, 1980, no. 149.

15. Tyson, 'Architectural History of the Gaols . . . at Appleby', 126.

16. Colvin, 273.

17. M. H. Port, 'Lowther Hall and Castle', *CW2*, lxxxi, 127; CRO K, WD/SE.

18. *Annals*, 246.

19. Curwen, *KK*, 85-6.

20. See family tree, p. 300. There is a memorial tablet to Janet Webster by her husband in Kirkby Lonsdale church.

21. It may have been slate which brought them together. The slate quarry was certainly important to George Lowry when he made his will in 1805: CRO B, BD/L/3/208.

22. B. Tyson, 'Francis Webster and the Market House at Hawkshead', *Quarto*, Oct. 1993, 8-11; B. Wragg, *The Life and Works of John Carr of York*, ed. G. Worsley, 2000, 113.

23. Information from Dr Blake Tyson.

24. Reproduced in J. Satchell and O. Wilson, *Christopher Wilson of Kendal*, 1988, 3.

25. Colvin, Crook, and Friedman, *Architectural Drawings from Lowther Castle*, *passim*.

26. A. Palmer, *The Low Wood Gunpowder Company . . . 1798-1808*, Gunpowder Mills Study Group, 1998, 13, 14, 23. Robert Webster also had some involvement with both the gunpowder works and the tower and probably provided local masons.

27. CRO B, Z62. This document, in which arrangements were made for dealing with the debts of William Strickland, includes payments to Francis Webster, mason, and to the firm of Webster & Holme, 9 April 1800.

28. *Annals*, 291.

29. Colvin, 811.

30. Colvin, Crook, and Friedman, *Architectural Drawings from Lowther Castle*, nos. 110-112.

31. *Ibid.*, no. 113.

32. *Ibid.*, nos. 107-112, castellated designs for Lowther attributed to Francis Webster, which are reductions of designs by James Gibbs, nos. 87-91.

33. *Lons. Mag.*, iii, 1822, 369-70; *The Websters of Kendal*, no. 4.

34. Information from Dr Blake Tyson.

35. Letter from William Richardson to Richard Howard, 19 May 1808: Surrey RO, Howard papers; information supplied by Miss S. Macpherson.

36. Curwen, *KK*, 37.

37. M. E. Burkett and J. D. G. Sloss, *William Green of Ambleside*, 1984, 23, 66.

38. The drawings survive in CRO K, WDX 1315 and in private collections. Robert is said to have attended Kirkby Lonsdale grammar school: M. Hall, *Artists of Cumbria*, 1979, 95. He was not buried locally and may have died in London, but it is strange that he is not commemorated with his mother and sister on the tablet in Kirkby Lonsdale church.

39. See below, pp. 50-51.
40. Gunnis, 418.
41. A. C. Taylor, 'Thomas Harrison and Stramongate Bridge', *CW2*, lxix, 275-9.
42. CRO K, WDX 1315; and see below, p. 21.
43. *Lons. Mag.*, ii, 1821, 161-164, elevation facing 161, and plan 162.
44. A survey of 1796 shows the house with a block plan like Longlands: CRO K, WD/W. Another of the 1820s shows an elaborated version: *ibid.*, WDB/22, plan vii.
45. There are two designs at the house, one of which is signed by Hird, though not the one used.
46. CRO K, WD/W, box 15, sale particulars.
47. For the Birkbecks, see R. Birkbeck, *The Birkbecks of Westmorland*, privately printed, 1900, and CRO K, WD/AG, boxes 62-3.

III

Francis Webster
Executant Architect

IT was the practice of metropolitan (and other) architects when a design of theirs was building in a remote part of the country to appoint a trusted intermediary to carry the work through to completion. The designer/architect would visit the executant on the site from time to time, perhaps making changes in the design and checking the quality of the work. At Lowther Hall, after collecting designs for a new house from many of the first architects of the day, Lord Lonsdale eventually turned to Francis Webster, the local man who worked for him at Whitehaven and Appleby, and Webster began to rehabilitate the wing that survived the fire of 1718. Lowther died in 1802 and was succeeded by a Yorkshire cousin who became Earl of Lonsdale of the second creation in 1807. The new earl inherited a vast fortune, was persuaded that he needed a new house to match, and eventually chose the young Robert Smirke to design it. The 23-year-old architect was probably glad to find Webster with his experience and local connections, and kept him on as architect as well as mason and supplier of marble chimneypieces.[1]

This question of local connections may well have been a factor in other cases also. Only in one instance did the experience of building to another's design directly affect the later development of the Webster firm and that was at Storrs Hall, Bowness, details from which appeared in Webster buildings well into the 1860s. And in view of the fact that George Webster based his first complete house, Read Hall, on William Atkinson's Clapham Lodge (1814) it is possible that his father was executant there and also at Broughton Hall (1809-11).

Francis Webster's experience as executant architect at Storrs Hall in 1808-11 was to be of value to the firm for the next fifty years. The designer was Joseph Michael Gandy (1771-1843), one of the most extraordinary figures in English architecture. Much of his life was spent as a draughtsman and he was largely employed by Sir John Soane.[2] His actual buildings are few, a surprising number of them in Liverpool and Lancashire. He followed Thomas Harrison in the reconstruction of Lancaster Castle between 1802 and 1823, and was in Liverpool between 1809 and 1811, when he acted as tutor to Soane's son.[3] He came to the notice of John Bolton, perhaps when working at Lancaster Castle, for Bolton, amongst other things, raised and equipped a regiment of 600 men for the French wars, and his friend George Canning, a Liverpool MP and later Prime Minister, no doubt persuaded the king to accept this gesture.

Storrs was not the first of Bolton's houses to be remodelled by Gandy. In 1808 he bought the manor of Bolton-by-Bowland and a reconstruction of the hall began. The man chosen to carry out Gandy's designs was Francis Webster,[4] doubtless through the influence of Bolton (1756-1837), who was born in Ulverston, the son of an apothecary, Abraham Bolton. That is very close to Webster country, in that remote part of Lancashire cut off by the sands of Morecambe Bay, and in a town with many Webster connections. Even more remarkably, it was Francis Webster who built Storrs Hall immediately after Bolton Hall. There are other links. John Bolton was one of the committee which commissioned John Foster I in 1801 to build a News Room in Liverpool which had a chimneypiece of Westmorland marble by Webster.[5] It seems that Bolton may have pressed Webster's interests in the first decade of the nineteenth century. Webster was also an officer in the militia, another of Bolton's enthusiasms.

The rebuilding of Bolton Hall was, naturally for a house in which Henry VI sheltered in 1464, gothic, and much old masonry was retained.[6] Unlike Storrs, Bolton seems not to have had an effect upon Webster's style. Storrs, however, provided him, and later his son and still later Miles Thompson, with a repertory of structural and decorative motifs in a way that no other building ever did. A comparison of later Webster houses with Storrs does not perhaps prove that Francis was its builder, but an article of 1881, ostensibly on the Harrington tomb in Cartmel Priory, does.[7] The author mentions that an elderly lady could still remember the small carts taking the stone from the quarry where 'workmen were employed for two years . . . chiselling under sheds the ornamental stonework for that handsome building [Storrs]' about fifteen miles away. It was understood at the time of writing that Francis Webster, 'the originator of the well known marble works at Kendal', was the architect, suggesting that Gandy was not often on site. The quarry was on the Holker estate, one of the scarce sources of freestone in the area, and near the Websters' family house at Quarry Flatt.

Storrs was not a new building. There was a square house on the site with a canted bay facing the lake, built by Sir John Legard, Bt, a fanatical sailor. Gandy had worked for him, designing a boathouse and perhaps the simple octagonal temple standing at the end of a jetty. Sir John Soane's Museum holds a notebook of Gandy's sketches made at Storrs about 1806 before he began his transformation of the house for John Bolton. A sketch of Legard's house from a boat on the lake shows it to be of two storeys and three bays with a single canted bay on the south-west front. Behind, on the summit of a hill, is a large classical temple. Was it Bolton's intention to build such a temple or was it a fantasy of Gandy's? Other sketches are for offices – cowhouse, stables, a lodge, and a gardener's cottage. Another shows the causeway to the Temple of Heroes, walled with widely-spaced openings.[8]

Francis Webster would have been surprised to have heard that he was the designer. Gandy's idiosyncratic Grecian design must have shocked him, at least in its detailing. Gandy added long wings at either side of the old house, filled in the entrance side with a colonnade, and wrapped a verandah round the lake front. It is the cresting of these and some of the windows with unique fleshy lotus flowers or leaves of Egyptian inspiration that can still surprise. The Websters ignored them in their later borrowings, but other features of the exterior soon appeared, not so much in the work of Francis as in that of his son and of Miles Thompson. Francis had perhaps retained some designs.

The part-fluted columns, the giant angle pilasters, base- and capital-free, with their sunken moulded panels, the crisp tripartite windows with elegant long consoles, the verandah with its pattern of intersecting circles, and above all the window architraves of the upper floor – these sit immediately under the entablature of the house and are framed by pilasters with sunken centres and rudimentary 'capitals' with a single rosette. The sills are similarly hollowed out. Perhaps in order not to obstruct the view of the lake, Gandy required glazing bars so fine that they could not be made of wood, but were cast in metal with a woodgrain texture.[9]

Inside there is some unconventional plasterwork like the distorted acanthus frieze in the music room, all writhing stalk, and the windows with typical frames of ribbing with angle circles, here given pointed ribbed projections above the corners. There is a good deal of Greek fretting. In the staircase hall a two-storey screen of columns, Corinthian over Grecian Ionic, has its end pilasters turned through forty-five degrees, a grave solecism which is probably Webster's. He would be familiar with the Roman Ionic where such an error could not occur.[10]

Across Lake Windermere, only a few miles from Storrs, lies Esthwaite Lodge, begun in 1819 for Thomas Alcock Beck. It owes more to Storrs than any other house. Smaller than Storrs, it not only has panelled pilasters and a verandah of the same pattern but also key and fret patterns, tripartite windows with long consoles, a domed staircase, and a part-fluted Greek Doric order in the porch. No doubt George Webster was at least in part responsible for Esthwaite. The year before he had started his first independent commission, Read Hall, which has the Storrs pilasters, as does his own house in Kendal, no. 4 Thorny Hills of about 1822, where they are confined to the upper floor. They can also be seen at Rothay Bank (now Manor) and Scale How, both at Ambleside and of about 1826. At Masongill, near Ingleton, the new wings of c.1830 have them, and at Summerfield, Tunstall (1841) they were again of full height.[11] They appear in the similar lodges at Eden Hall and Broughton Hall of the 1830s and in the upper stages of Italianate towers at Belsfield, Bowness (1845), Flasby Hall, Gargrave (1840),[12] at Rigmaden Park, Mansergh, on a design of 1852 by Miles Thompson, and as late as 1859 on the tower of Kendal Town Hall, in this case coupled. There are also innumerable minor examples on chimneypieces, window and door architraves, porches, and sideboard recesses.

The Storrs verandah pattern was used not only at Esthwaite but also at Scale How (Ambleside), Blawith Cottage (Grange-over-Sands, demolished), Boarbank (Allithwaite, demolished), Cliffe Hall (Keighley, later radically altered), Field Head House (Hawkshead),[13] and on the undated (*c*.1835) Italianate design at Downham.[14] The virtues of the verandah were soon apparent in this damp corner of England and many designs appeared in the early nineteenth century.

Tripartite windows with long consoles are seen at Esthwaite, Croft Lodge (Ambleside), Stockbridge (Ulverston), and Heaves (Levens); at Townhead (Staveley-in-Cartmel) they are short. Incised lines and frets are used at Esthwaite, Croft Lodge, and at Beezon and Aynam Lodges, Kendal, and in a multitude of smaller houses.

The drum of the dome at Storrs has glazing in which circles are held in suspension by straight bars, a pattern which occurs in Webster buildings at Ormerod House, Cliviger (demolished), Broughton Hall, Eller How, and Belsfield, in the turret of the White Hall, Kendal, and the Savings Bank, Ulverston, in bookcase doors in the library at Read Hall, and in the design for Rigmaden. The unusual upper windows at Storrs are used with slight variations at Broughton Hall, Slyne Lodge, the Lancaster Bank and a shop on the east side of King Street, Ulverston. Rigmaden has a version of the design without the 'capital'. The curious motif of the pointed extension upwards of the inner window frames at Storrs is repeated at Beezon and Aynam Lodges, in George Webster's own house at Thorny Hills, and on the exterior of nos. 24-28 Highgate, all in Kendal.

In the Storrs music room is a fine chimneypiece with female musicians in the supports, probably by Gandy's friend Richard Westmacott. There is a similar design by him and of much the same date for Milton Abbey, Dorset, and others are scattered across England and Ireland.[15] Geographically closest of all, a direct copy, at least of the musician supporters, is at Croft Lodge, Ambleside. The carving is softer but there can be no doubt of its origins. Croft was remodelled *c*.1828, almost certainly by George Webster, so could the chimneypiece have been carved in the marble yard at Kendal? It seems unlikely in view of the lack of sculptural expertise there at the time. The frieze at Storrs has a tablet of Leda and the swan, but at Croft the entire length of the frieze is given over to a lively chariot race.

If Colonel Bolton did support Francis Webster in these early years, did he also encourage the opening of a showroom in Liverpool in 1829? In 1835 he agreed to replace the old school at Bowness. At the opening ceremony in April 1836 Wordsworth spoke of the 'elegance of the architecture' and a toast was drunk to the architect.[16] He was George Webster.

Notes

[1.] In the *Lancaster Gazette*, 24 May 1806, is an advertisement for masons: 'Liberal wages and constant employment' may be had by applying 'to . . . Mr. Francis Webster'.

[2] See Colvin, 388-389. Gandy's designs were exhibited at the R.A. in 1808 and 1811. John Summerson compared him with Wordsworth: 'The Vision of J. M. Gandy', *Heavenly Mansions*, 1949, 119-22.

[3] He was briefly a partner of George Bullock of Liverpool who supplied doors, lanterns for the entrance, and furniture for Storrs: Colvin, *loc. cit.*; Gunnis, 68-9.

[4] *Gentleman's Magazine*, 1841, i, 581: 'carried into effect by Webster of Kendal'.

[5] Gunnis, 418.

[6] Pevsner, *W.Yorks.*, 115.

[7] H. F. Rigge, 'The Harrington tomb in Cartmel Priory Church', *CW1*, v, 114-15.

[8] I. Goodall and M. Richardson, 'A Recently Discovered Gandy Sketchbook', *Architectural History*, xliv, 2001, 45-56. Gandy's design for the boathouse was exhibited at the RA in 1804, but it may not have been built. The temple was probably not by him, and is just as likely to be by, say, Francis Webster: B. Thompson, 'A Naval Temple on Windermere', *CL*, 29 Nov. 1962.

[9] A. Clifton Taylor, *The Pattern of English Building*, 3rd ed, 1972, 396.

[10] One of a set of fine watercolours of 1814 by J. C. Buckler shows the square lodge with angle pilasters and part-fluted columns. This is now a lodge for Yews, nearby.

[11] All the detail has long been removed. Twycross, ii, 26 shows its original state.

[12] A variant design with giant angle pilasters has recently come to light.

[13] D. Foskett, *John Harden of Brathay Hall, 1772-1847*, 1974, pl. xxix, nos. 96-7. Harden lived at Field Head House 1836-1837.

[14] Design at the house; see G. Worsley, 'Downham Hall', *CL*, 5 Oct. 1989.

[15] There are others at Bold Hall, Lancs. (now at Lanhydrock, Cornwall), Laxton, Northants., Womersley Park and Burton Constable, Yorks., and Downhill, Northern Ireland. All derive from Robert Adam's no. 20 St James's Square, London, of 1771-4, itself based on a Piranesi design.

[16] *WG*, 16 April 1836. 'Mr. M. Thompson said Mr. Webster had gone to the Continent for the benefit of his health': *Windermere Grammar School*, 1936, 44; for his journey, see pp. 78-9. Bolton was too ill to attend the opening; he died in 1837.

IV

George Webster (1797-1864)
Architect

Training and an early masterpiece

FRANCIS Webster was a mason who through contacts with professional architects evolved into an architect himself. It would be more difficult for the next generation. Architecture was no longer quite a trade nor yet quite a profession in 1800. Sir John Soane in 1788 defined an architect as 'the intermediate agent between the employer, whose honour and interest he is to study, and the mechanic, whose rights he is to defend' and questioned whether the two roles could be combined 'with propriety'.[1] The architect should make designs and estimates and coordinate all the trades involved in building. Francis Webster remained in this intermediate situation, both designer and mason, but organising the other trades. His son was in no doubt that he should not dirty his hands.

In 1818, at the age of 21, George Webster designed his first independent country house, Read Hall in Lancashire, a neo-classical house which has some claim to be his masterpiece in the style. At the Webster exhibition of 1973 at Abbot Hall in Kendal, Clapham Lodge (now Ingleborough Hall) was attributed to George Webster on the strength of its resemblance to Read. With its similar plan, its columned bow with a saucer dome tweaking the line of the main facade, and its entrance in the return front, it was clearly a variation on a larger scale. So it was, except that Clapham preceded Read by four years, the design being exhibited at the Liverpool Academy in 1814. The architect turned out to be William Atkinson (*c.*1773-1839), a pupil of James Wyatt. He had built up a large country house practice in England and Scotland and is perhaps best known as Sir Walter Scott's architect at Abbotsford. In the north of England he added neo-classical wings to Broughton Hall, near Skipton, for Stephen Tempest in 1809-11. He opened an office in Manchester from which he wrote to the Duke of Devonshire in February 1812, and he exhibited at the Liverpool Academy in 1813 and 1814.[2]

So Read followed Clapham and George Webster was elaborating on William

Atkinson's design which he could have known as a pupil of Atkinson.[3] It is also possible that Francis Webster was the executant architect here as elsewhere; the chimneypieces and polished fossil limestone columns defining the staircase appear to be products of the Kendal marble yard. And Broughton Hall? Could Francis have been Atkinson's builder there in 1809-11? Christopher Hussey, writing on Broughton in 1950 and knowing nothing of George Webster, needed an explanation for his splendid remodelling of the house in 1838 and suggested that he was a young assistant of Atkinson, and perhaps he was not far wrong.[4] In such a way a pupillage could naturally arise and Atkinson's Manchester years are just right – George Webster was fifteen years old in 1812.

Another feature of several Webster designs from 1825 also appears to derive from an Atkinson building, Scone Palace, Perthshire (1803-12), where the Tudor-gothic house stands on a terrace with strongly battered walls which have square and circular bastions.[5] When Webster designed a house for William Wordsworth the excavations into the steep site would have provided material for just such a terrace, to which he gave the form of a strongly battered and buttressed wall with two circular bastions. He used the device again at Thurland Castle, Tunstall (1826), at Whittington Hall (1831), at Ingfield, Settle (1841), and at Wanlass How (1841) and The Knoll (1845), both at Ambleside. At Thurland, Whittington, and Ingfield he varied the shapes of the bastions as Atkinson did.[6]

These four areas of evidence – his father and metropolitan architects in need of a reliable executant of their plans; the presence of Atkinson in Manchester at the right time; the pronounced similarity of Clapham Lodge and Read Hall; and the use of a 'fortified' bastioned terrace as the base for a house do not constitute proof that George Webster learnt his architecture in the office of William Atkinson, but no other explanation has so much in its favour. It is true that Atkinson in the 'battle of the styles' preferred to work in a picturesque irregular gothic and Webster deliberately chose a regular late Elizabethan/Jacobean. That may have been simply to avoid copying, looking for a new field to develop, wishing to be the first to reintroduce the style and combine it with 'modern' planning? Webster could have discovered Elizabethan and Jacobean architecture from his father's work at Levens and his own at Alkincoats, near Colne. The style had appeared occasionally and selectively in the eighteenth century but in small ways and as a relaxation from the prevailing classical models. Webster's revival was serious and he practised it throughout his career.[7]

The Jacobethan and regional vernacular styles

In the early nineteenth century most new houses were built in a classical style based on the architecture of Italy and Greece; others were gothic, derived from medieval buildings. Pavilions, temples, and prospect towers in gardens, however, had long been acceptable in more exotic guise; Sir William Chambers's pagoda at Kew dates from 1761. Then the exotic spread to the house, the Prince Regent's pavilion at

Brighton perhaps the most exotic of all. Soon all the styles of the world were available to the British architect. There was a brief vogue for Egyptian, a longer one for towered Italianate. National styles were resurrected and brought into use again, the Elizabethan/Jacobean revival being sometimes conveniently referred to as Jacobethan.

George Webster was a pioneer in this style, though he neither abandoned Grecian classicism nor ignored the Italianate. He offered the bankers of Ulverston a choice of Italianate or Elizabethan in 1836 and the Asshetons of Downham Italianate or Grecian in 1834. Italian and Greek were chosen respectively. Egyptian barely touched him. Atkinson preferred an irregular gothic; Webster favoured symmetry, reserving gothic for churches.

Webster would know most of his sources only from engravings. The Jacobean houses of Westmorland and North Lancashire were, externally at least, too rustic and irregular for his purposes. One work alone would give most of the finest examples he needed, Kip's *Nouveau Théatre de la Grande Bretagne*, 1715-17, with a supplement of 1728. Webster's library included Loudon's *Architectural Magazine* of 1834 and John Britton's *Cathedrals*,[8] but Britton's earlier *Architectural Antiquities* contains points of architectural detail adopted by him. Smaller houses contributed too; the crestings on the bays of Claverton Manor near Bath were lifted without modification onto the bays of Alkincoats, Underley, and Eshton. At Underley there is a hint of the crazily complex pattern books published in the Netherlands and Germany by engravers such as Dietterlin, Vriedeman de Vries, and others, although Webster may have come to them through houses like Wollaton, Notts., which was already indebted to them at the end of the sixteenth century. The decoration of the metopes with flowers and animal heads are the most striking example. At Eshton there are flowers only, but at Moreton the animals return.[9]

Horace Walpole, praising his friend Lord Dacre's house, Belhus at Aveley, Essex, recently improved in the gothic style in 1745, described the genuine Jacobean work as 'Good King James's Gothic', an expression which Nikolaus Pevsner adopted as the title of his important essay on the style in 1950.[10] He saw it as a symptom of the coming Victorian age with its desire for 'something of a bolder variety, thicker relief, and more restless play of light and shadow and altogether more robustness than could be offered by gothic or classical', and made the point that before the full Elizabethan revival later in the century there were already architects who saw the style 'as more than a variety of gothic or a whim. One example is Eshton Hall, Yorks, by Webster of Kendal'. He went on to quote J. P. Neale and used his engraving as an illustration. In a footnote he added '[Webster] also built Underley Hall in Westmorland, a very successful piece of Elizabethanism'. What Neale actually said was that Eshton was 'a faithful composition from some of the finest specimens of . . . domestic architecture prevalent at the latter end of the reign of Queen Elizabeth'.[11]

When Henry Shaw wrote his *Details of Elizabethan Architecture*, the illustrations engraved in 1834 but not published till 1839, he said: 'Elizabethan architecture has established well-founded claims to public notice, and it is no longer necessary to apologize for a zealous attachment to the pursuit of its characteristic features: it has survived the prejudices which at first embarrassed its revival; and the style with all its exuberance and variety of detail has been adopted with success in the designs of several considerable mansions recently erected'. Of those, he proceeded to single out 'Eshton and Moreby in Yorkshire, Underley in Westmorland, and Harlaxton in Lincolnshire [as] beautiful examples of what may be produced by correct adherence to propriety of design'. Moreby (1828) and Harlaxton (1831) are both by Anthony Salvin who became one of the most successful architects of mid-Victorian England. Webster's Eshton and Underley predate them. Moreby is very similar to Webster's manner and could almost be mistaken for his work, but it is Harlaxton which makes the great leap forward. Webster owned a framed engraving of Moreby.[12]

Eshton and Underley were both started in 1825, but two of George Webster's designs show that their mature completeness did not spring fully fledged from nowhere. Alkincoats was a Jacobean house of the Parker family which had been given some sash windows and altered inside in the eighteenth century, In 1820 Webster was asked to enlarge the house and of course had an incentive to use the original style, though the work was never carried out. He proposed large projecting wings on either side containing drawing and dining rooms, and mullioned and transomed windows enclosing a bay with the balustrading used again at Underley and elsewhere. The gables were to be crowned with elaborate finials which link Alkincoats with Netherside, at Threshfield, of c.1820. This was a new building but the effect, with its recessed centre between projecting wings, is similar, although with the addition of a spectacular arcaded porch projecting across the central three bays and with elaborate cresting – a true Jacobean effect and clearly the forerunner of Webster's later entrance features. It is all the more effective against the rubble walls of the house itself.

The core of Netherside is a large two-storied saloon lit from a massive lantern. The interiors owe much to those of Read Hall. By the time that Underley and Eshton were built, they had become fully Jacobethan, with elaborate ceilings of interlocking geometric ribs with plaster pendants, Tudor roses and *fleurs de lys*.

Netherside was designed for Alexander Nowell who in 1825 laid the foundation stone for his new house at Underley, near Kirkby Lonsdale. Nowell had been a soldier in India and his enthusiasm was for horses. At Netherside the stables are insignificant but at Underley they were magnificent and integral to Webster's design, with curved gables of a style still exemplified in the estate office, a former lodge. At Netherside the Jacobean style was tentative, at Underley fully developed, with gables, mullions, rows of chimneys, crestings, finials, and so on. The main entrance used two storeys of columns and over the centre a towering third storey was intended. Inside, there is rich plasterwork with pendants and good woodwork,[13] all similar to Eshton, of the same period.

Eshton was built for Matthew Wilson IV and replaced a large house on the same site. In comparison with Underley, it is more compact, with no turrets to break the outline. Underley has two fronts of equal weight; Eshton is essentially one front. At Underley the stables are level with and as prominent as the house; at Eshton they turn away from the facade and form no part of the picture. The single turret at Eshton was not part of the original design. It was added after 1836, at Wilson's son's suggestion in a letter to Webster of 20 March in that year:

> We are quite busy here with roads, gates, farm buildings, and gardens. Your plans are much needed as the time for moving shrubs and plants is quickly passed away.
>
> There is something in the elevation of the front of the house, I mean in this room, I mean my father's, which I do not quite like, it seems to belong neither to house or offices and has to my eye a patched appearance – could it not be recast into a tower? The gables and pinnacles do not seem to belong to this front and the roof level with the main house makes it combine too much with the house of which it spoils the uniformity – write me what you think of it.[14]

Webster must have agreed. The tower was duly built and in fact led to further changes from the plan in this part of the house. Another was to move the intended entrance from the west front to the east. The morning room became the hall and the interesting plan for the west front was abandoned. The door here would have had the same plan as that at Holker and have carried the first floor over it.

The interior of Eshton is unlike that of Underley but derives from Netherside, the imperial oak staircase and first-floor galleries filling that space which at Netherside forms the saloon, and which Webster perhaps now recognised as something of very limited practical use. The principal rooms open off, with richly-panelled plaster ceilings and the best fireplaces. The windows look like casements, but are in fact sashes, like those which Webster was about to introduce into Wordsworth's house at Rydal. The service wing and stables are towered, pinnacled, and irregular, in contrast to the Jacobean formality of the house. The clock tower was built as late as 1840, by which time Flasby, with its own tower, was going up across the valley.

A Jacobean feature applied by Webster at Underley, Eshton, and the next house in the series, Moreton Hall, Whalley (1828), is the frontispiece. In it, the entrance to the house is marked by pairs of coupled columns rising floor by floor the whole height of the building, the sturdiest and simplest at the bottom, the Doric order, then the Ionic, Corinthian, and, if need be, the composite. Hatfield House has one of the more successful examples and was probably a model for Webster's three versions.[15]

The frontispieces at Underley and Eshton appear to be of the same design but in fact they are subtly different. Both use the Doric and Ionic orders but at Underley the columns are free-standing; at Eshton the square piers are attached to the building which has a strongly modelled façade. The Underley entrance front is more open and the bays on either side are canted. The frontispiece does not break the skyline whereas at Eshton the porch is crowned by an heraldic achievement as at Hatfield.

Although the planning of Webster's houses was in no manner Elizabethan, his staircases and most of his interiors were enriched with panelling, pilasters (usually with a sunken centre), and ceilings inventively panelled by ribs into quatrefoils, squares, lozenges, hollow-sided squares, or circles, usually intersecting and with heraldic roses and other flowers, *fleurs de lys* and so on at the intersections. Some are recognisably versions of ceilings at Haddon Hall and Penshurst Place, both dating from the early sixteenth century – at Eshton and in Webster's own house at Eller How (1827), for example.

When George Webster decided to exhibit a design at the Royal Academy Summer Exhibition in 1826 he chose Underley. His objective was probably to make his name known beyond the north-west of England. Perhaps he considered leaving Kendal if he was successful but, if that was his hope, it was dashed by the incompetence of academy officials. In the catalogue no. 998 was given as 'Webster, George, painter, of 3 Thanet Place, Temple Bar, Renderley Hall, the seat of Alexander Nowell Esq., in Westmorland' and 'Kendal' as the place of submission. Of course the house is Underley and the designs survive. When Algernon Graves published his *Royal Academy Exhibitors 1769 to 1904* in 1906 he noticed the error: 'this is as catalogue but 998 is evidently the work of an Architect living in Kendal'.[16] It is not hard to imagine Webster's anger and frustration. So far as is known he did not exhibit again.

Could this catastrophe have contributed to radical changes which he made in his next Jacobethan design? Moreton Hall had the strong modelling of Eshton, the bays canted as at Underley, the frontispiece was as Eshton, but the huge change was that the calm level skyline was replaced by a picturesque forest of gables and chimneys and finials which continued into the offices. And here a new finial was introduced – a diapered column on the central gables, a detail more familiar on East Anglian chimney stacks in brick.[17] The return façade here – two gabled projections with canted bays framing a plain centre which carries a smaller gable rising from roof level – became something of a Webster standard and is seen at Aireville, Skipton (1836), Summerlands, Preston Richard (1846), Merlewood, Grange-over-Sands (1853), and elsewhere.

Whittington Hall near Kirkby Lonsdale (1831) is the next development in the sequence. There was a small Jacobean house already on the site and parts of it may have been incorporated at the northern end. In place of the frontispiece we have a projecting gabled porch with octagonal turrets at the corners. The familiar canted bays are brought close to it and have a battlemented finish, linking up with the (apparent) pele tower which rises behind but off-centre. A broad terrace of the kind derived from Atkinson spreads out in front of the house. In the centre of the terrace wall another door leads to a staircase rising to hall level. The main staircase hall is off-centre here and has twisted balusters. It is clear that the intended impression is of a house that has developed over the centuries. Whittington is more deliberately vernacular than previous examples, a characteristic underlined by local details like windows of three lights where the central one is higher, and a doorcase with the lintel carved into bizarre geometric forms. The interior was partly Georgianised in the 1920s but the surviving plasterwork resembles that at Underley and Eshton. Lord Reay's recent spirited redecoration and refurnishing of Whittington demonstrate more than anywhere else why Webster's interiors were so much in demand.

It seems that William Wordsworth was responsible for the ever-increasing use of vernacular features through his contacts with George Webster and the planning of his own house on the Rash Field at this time.[18] Horizontality was for classical designs. In this group of houses there is a certain retrogressive move from the pure Jacobean of Netherside and Underley to the bastions and pele tower of Whittington. Perhaps the next stage should have been a full-blown castle such as Salvin designed at Peckforton in Cheshire in 1844-50. If so no client obliged.

One house, Hornby Castle near Lancaster, came close to imposing a castle style. It had a genuine pele tower on a splendid site above the river Wenning but had been classicised in the eighteenth century. In 1823 the invalid owner, John Marsden, seems to have decided to restore its ancient appearance and to this end Webster produced a design which predates his more mature Jacobethan work. It was undeniably a castle, but its perfect symmetry, large Elizabethan windows, and front door militate against the keep and the multiplicity of castellated turrets and gatehouse in the centre. The gazebo on the keep, with an eagle on its dome, was retained. Marsden's death in 1826 put an end to his plans.

A commission in 1826 to remodel Hutton-in-the-Forest, near Penrith, had more success. This interesting house had a pele tower which was largely concealed by later building which included a richly-decorated Baroque centre built in 1680. Webster's 'castle' additions are more robust than at Hornby and the new 'pele' tower at the south-east angle is convincing. The design was not fully carried out. Some of his interiors survive, including the dining room with its Elizabethan decoration, and several fireplaces were installed.[19]

Soon after his father's death in 1827 George began to enlarge the cottage at Eller How and went on altering and adding to it until about 1850. The style externally was irregular, gabled with individual rooms set at angles to one another – in a phrase, picturesque vernacular. There were, however, sophisticated features, the porch for instance, where a Venetian opening with curious turned columns is set under a barge-boarded gable. He used the idea again at Cliffe Hall, Keighley (1833), with its shaped gables, and at Broughton Hall (1838).

In 1829 Webster enlarged Thurland Castle, adding a low outer wall with a series of bastions. Croft Lodge, near Ambleside, was described by Housman as a 'little white seat' in 1812. Its transformation for James Brancker in 1829-30 taxed Hartley Coleridge's imagination: its style was one 'which neither Vitruvius, Piranesi nor Sir Jeffry Wyatville dreamed of in nightmare or under the influence of opium'.[20] The eighteenth-century structure was gothicised but all within is Grecian with Greek sarcophagi as overdoors.[21] Another hybrid, Ormerod House, Cliviger (demolished), was remodelled in 1833-4. Here Webster's additions were outwardly classical, but the interior and the porch were Jacobethan. A remarkable detail is the 'local' saw-toothed arch linking house and stables.[22]

Penwortham Priory (demolished), on the south bank of the river Ribble near its mouth, must have been one of Webster's most interesting houses. The little we know is tantalising. The name was not just romanticism. There had been a religious house on the site, and what Webster started with was a genuine Jacobean nucleus and an ecclesiastical aura. In 1830 he continued the original brick ranges of the house on a larger scale with more shaped and finialled gables, built an octagonal tower and a gabled chapel-like room with lancets and a 'cloister', an extremely picturesque composition. Not far away stood another red-brick Jacobean house with shaped gables: in 1832 Webster made large additions in the same vein to Bank Hall, Bretherton, long derelict. Clifton Hall, also near Preston and also red-brick but new, and Howick House, like Penwortham a Rawstorne house, are both attributable to Webster.

Webster's Jacobean style was fully developed by 1831 at Whittington, even by then turning back towards the medieval with bastions and tower. There were still many fine houses in the style to come; scarcely a year passed between 1830 and 1853 when one was not started.

Elm Grove (now Croftlands) at Caton, was built for a friend of Webster's, Richard Sparling Berry, or rather 'restored' as an inscription has it although everything of value is of 1833. A small house, elaborately done, it relates to Webster's later work at Conishead Priory and is best seen through the ogee-domed entrance gates down the ghost of the elm grove.

Whelprigg, Barbon, a stone and multi-gabled Jacobethan design of 1834, has a central saloon with the staircase rising round the walls to a gallery. Another very stony small classical house, Hay Carr at Forton, was enlarged by the Duke of Hamilton's agent in 1835 when it was Jacobethanised and given a new wing and a porch which duplicates that at Howick. The Hoghton family had abandoned its eponymous tower in mid-Lancashire in the eighteenth century and it had become dilapidated. Webster's plans of 1835 were not the first to propose improving it – Lewis Wyatt had suggested rebuilding it as a castle in 1816. There are no elevations, so did Webster intend to keep in keeping with the house? The Hoghtons lived at Walton Hall in the eighteenth century but the house burned down in 1830 and instead of altering Hoghton Webster had the task of rebuilding Walton.

At the foot of the Ulverston canal the Rev. Bartholomew McHugh, who laid the foundation stone of the Catholic church in 1822, built Hammershead Hill Villa on the sea wall in 1835. Jacobethan in style, it has largely disappeared, castellated extensions at either end alone remaining. Little is known of it, but George Webster was probably its architect.

Mozergh House, Selside, with initials and a datestone (J. & M. M[achell] 1835), has elaborate barge-boarded gables and has good interiors. It is probably by Webster. Grimeshill, at Middleton in the Lune valley, was remodelled by Webster in 1836. In west Cumberland The Flosh, Cleator, was enlarged in the Jacobethan manner in 1837 for Thomas Ainsworth, almost certainly by Webster who was the architect of the church there (1841-2) and probably of the model village.

It was perhaps through the influence of the Rawstornes that Webster designed the lodges when the Town Moor at Preston was enclosed in 1834 – a third was added two years later. All are Jacobethan, a modest enough commission but public buildings, at least externally, can be as great a subject for display as the private house. The Public Rooms (now the Town Hall) at Settle (1832), are just such an example. On an island site in the market place, with all four walls visible, the building displays its shaped and straight gables, chimney stacks, and the four-centred arches of the once open ground floor, and borrows its octagonal turrets from Whittington Hall of the previous year. Dowker's Hospital, Kendal (1833, demolished) was in a similar style but on a more modest scale.

John Bolton of Storrs wished to provide a new school for the children of Applethwaite and Undermillbeck (Windermere and Bowness). George Webster was his chosen architect and the foundation stone was laid by Wordsworth on 9 April 1835. The Jacobethan building perching on a hill above the centre of Bowness was praised by Wordsworth not only for the facilities to be provided. He considered 'that the building, from the elegance of its architecture and its elevated conspicuous situation, will prove a striking ornament to the beautiful country in the midst of which it will stand'.[23] The benefactor was too ill to attend the ceremony but a toast was drunk to the architect.

In 1834-5 several new 'Jacobean' inns were built in mid-Lancashire towns and can be attributed to Webster from their style. In Accrington he did much for the Hargreaves family and one of his designs must have been for Bank Terrace which ends in the Hargreaves Arms, in Jacobethan style with characteristic detail. This also applies to the Starkie Arms, with Moreton Hall detailing, and to the White Lion, both in Clitheroe, all modest buildings compared with the hotels of ten years later.

Francis Webster's death and George's succession

In the middle of the evolution of his Jacobethan style George Webster's father, 'Kendal's Everlasting Alderman',[24] died. He had left Kendal in 1826 for the country house, Eller How near Lindale which he had bought some years earlier, and died there on 10 October 1827. He was working almost to the end with at least two minor commissions in the year of his death. His obituary appeared in the *Westmorland Gazette* on 13 October:

> At Eller How, near Cartmell, on Wednesday morning last, Mr. Francis Webster, of this town, architect, and one of the Aldermen of this burgh, in the 61st year of his age. More than a common obituary may be looked for to notice the death of one who has for so many years, with credit to himself, moved as a public man. His numerous works in this and the surrounding counties, will long bear ample testimony of the estimation in which he was held as an architect.

The perceptions of his mind were quick, extensive and correct. He was the sole inventor of machinery by which almost every description of mouldings can be wrought in marble or stone with greater accuracy than by manual labour. It is not too much to say, that in his private life his goodness of heart, the simplicity and kindness of his manners, will be generally acknowledged – by none more than the numerous workmen in his employ. To his cottage, near which he was born, he had lately finally retired from the bustle of a town and active life, to spend his closing years in domestic quiet and rural amusements. But, alas! man is frail. Death has put an end for ever to his earthly enjoyments – 'the pictured pleasures of his closing life'.

Francis was taken back to Kendal for burial at the parish church of the town in which he had worked for forty years and which he had served so well. In the churchyard, his memorial echoes its importance in his life: 'Francis Webster, late of this town, architect and one of the aldermen of the burgh, born May 1st 1767, died at Eller How, in Cartmel, October 10th 1827'.

In his will, made in the March before his death, Francis left all his books to his son, together with Eller How and other lands at Lindale, and all his 'stock-in-trade and all my machinery, utensils and implements of trade'. Land 'in or near Ulverston, Cocken and Hutton Roof' was to be held in trust by his friends Robert Graham of Liverpool and Thomas Butler of Dalton. The witnesses were his friend Edward Tatham, and Miles Thompson and Richard Stirzaker from his office. Stirzaker, who had provided views of houses for the *Lonsdale Magazine*, was a fine watercolour artist, associated with the Webster office in the 1820s. He was adept at showing architectural proposals in beautiful landscape settings and some of his work survived at Eller How in 1864.[25]

George Webster married in the year of his father's death. His wife was his step-mother's daughter, Eleanor Lowry (1804-67). There were five children of the marriage: Francis (1829-72), who subsequently worked for his father in the marble works, and four daughters, Margaret (1830), Jane (1832), Eleanor (1834), and Ellen (1840). Francis and his youngest sister were baptised in Kendal, the others at Lindale.

Alderman George Webster served his native town as his father had done. He was mayor in 1829-30 and gave his mayoral feast, the traditional treat for his fellow citizens, on 29 December. One of his duties was to proclaim William IV as king in 1830 and to preside over the wine-drinking in the King's Arms in the evening. He supported the establishment of a Mechanics' Institute and Apprentices' Library at a public meeting in 1824.[26] His pretensions to gentrydom, the months spent travelling – up to three in a year – and his country houses suggest, however, that he was more detached from Kendal than his father, who lived in the town for most of his life. George put up his house in Kendal to be let in an advertisement in the *Westmorland Advertiser & Kendal Chronicle* on 11 September 1830, with the evident intention of living permanently at Eller How, although how he managed to run the business from there is hard to understand. In addition, the journeys he made across Europe between 1828 and 1846 were not professional journeys. They came too late for that except that they did lead to his wide use of the Italian villa style.

The classical buildings

Alongside his neo-Jacobean style George Webster continued to use a Greek classical style. Up river in Kendal from his father's new canal head development and at a suitable distance, land had been opened up for housing in 1823.[27] Here, facing the river he built a house for himself – no. 4 Kent Terrace (Thorny Hills). Nos. 1 and 2 had already been built by his father, probably with George's collaboration, unostentatious three-storey houses with arched doors and bracket eaves, clearly the beginning of a terrace.[28] No. 3 broke the intended line, being of two storeys. No. 4 is also of two floors, but even so it fills the space of the three-storey houses at nos. 5 and 6 with its massive entablature, its pilastered upper floor and its pedimented doorcase. The interior, which was altered when nos. 4 and 5 were combined as an old people's home in 1970, was of the same quality.[29]

No. 4 was probably the first house in Kendal to be built in the Grecian style, and a magnificent advertisement, on a scale and with an assurance about it which had not been seen in Kendal before. At once the gentlemen of Kendal were demanding such houses for themselves, not in the town but on their country estates. Helme Lodge (1824) for William Dillworth Crewdson is a handsome villa just outside Kendal. Rigmaden Park, Mansergh (1825, for Christopher Wilson of Abbot Hall), is a larger house with a bow looking across the Lune. Inside, the idea of a two-storey central saloon has been adapted from Webster's contemporary Jacobethan designs. In Kendal again, Sand Aire House (1827-8, for the wine merchant Daniel Harrison) has a handsome recessed Greek Doric porch and Grecian decoration and, despite tactful as well as tactless additions, it is probably the best-preserved Webster house in the town. The elder Webster died in 1827 and if we compare Sand Aire with the other Grecian houses in this group it is not hard to see the innovating son guiding the firm.

The Greek revival style was also applied to industrial buildings at this time. Kendal was first lit by gas in July 1825 and the gas-works meter house of that year is a temple with a front of two square piers and two columns supporting a pediment. It is usually attributed to Francis but the idea, and the ease with the Grecian language, must be George's.

Meetings of interested parties were held in Kendal in 1824 to discuss the building of new assembly rooms and later to settle on a method of funding such a project. The issuing of £55 shares was agreed and £6,000 was eventually raised. Francis Webster, as mayor, was in the chair and it was agreed that he should be the architect. The site chosen was the junction of Lowther Street and Highgate, with the narrow entrance front to the latter. The name of the architect was sealed under the foundation stone, but again the design must be George Webster's, like the other Grecian buildings of Kendal in the 1820s.[30] It is in effect the design of the meter house with an Ionic order raised on a rusticated basement and a balcony between the columns. Altered by George to form a town hall in 1859, it was treated with respect in 1893 when more additions were made.

Dallam Tower, Milnthorpe, a brick house of about 1710, had in 1826 an untidy cluster of minor buildings around it when Webster was brought in to pull the composition together. He rendered the brick grey, concealed the basement, added a Tuscan *porte-cochère*, and regularised the wings. Inside a new dining room and library were created and a fine pre-Paxton orangery added at the back. The result was successful in much the same way, if less grandly, as his work at Broughton Hall a dozen years later.

A series of related houses in the area have Webster characteristics. Hill Top, New Hutton, was probably built *c*.1795; altered and enlarged *c*.1820 for Ralph Fisher, it is a rich mixture of both Francis and George's styles. Curwen Woods, Holme (*c*.1830), has projecting wings holding between them a loggia of square piers; behind is a top-lit staircase. George Webster was probably the designer.

Graythwaite New Hall (now Silverholme) was a completely new build. John Job Rawlinson of Graythwaite Low Hall, close to the south-western shore of Windermere but hidden from it, decided on a new house with views of the lake. The site is only yards from the old building, the occasion probably his marriage in 1831 to George Romney's granddaughter. Clearly Webster was his architect. The interior is richly done in the manner of Read Hall. The windows are particularly large to take advantage of the views over the lake.

The 1830s saw no other new classical houses, but there were some important remodellings. There are several surviving bills for chimneypieces for Rydal Hall, but many more Webster chimneypieces than bills, and it soon becomes evident that George remodelled the interior, including the staircase, in the mid-1830s, although the south range was perhaps earlier as Gillows of Lancaster provided furniture for the main rooms about 1824.[31] The body of the house was probably designed by John Hird. A smaller house enlarged *c*.1832 is Masongill near Ingleton, which was given attached wings with Webster's favoured panelled pilasters and canted bays.

The Oddfellows' Hall in Highgate, Kendal (1833), has an impressive front which is difficult to see to advantage. It has an arcade of segmental arches across the first floor over a tripartite window between the arched openings to yards behind. Also of 1833 is the Westmorland Bank (now HSBC), one of five classical elevations offered by Webster. The plan was probably common to all. As built it has an attached portico of square piers carrying a straight entablature and a lion couchant.

The next house of this period, Downham Hall, near Clitheroe (1834-5) was a remodelling. There are two sets of designs. The first of 1833 had an Italianate arcaded porch and windows, three years before George Webster's first known visit to Italy. The second, Grecian, design of 1834 was preferred.

The trustees of the Ulverston Savings Bank asked Webster for designs for their new building in 1836 and then chose the Grecian rather than the Elizabethan version. The entrance is flanked by sturdy Tuscan columns reminiscent of

Downham. The Italian tower was added in 1845 but there were already Italianate windows in 1836.

Just what Webster did at Eden Hall is not clear, but it must have included the long east wing. Smirke's rebuilt house was finished in 1825. Who supplied the Grecian chimneypieces like the Doric one in the library? Webster restored the church in 1834 and received bills for iron stoves at Eden Hall and Whittington at the latter house in 1835.[32] The magnificent lodge and cross-roads planning must be of similar date. Lady Musgrave gave Webster her card and an introduction to a Genoese sculptor on his first Italian journey in 1836. The Eden Hall stables of 1842 are probably Webster's. At Penny Bridge Hall the two handsome south rooms date from *c.*1840 and could be attributed to Webster, a view borne out by the chimneypieces.

Flasby Hall, just across the little valley from Eshton, was in 1840 a late-Georgian house with some interesting planning features. In that year Webster was asked to enlarge it and he turned it into a large towered Italianate villa, scarcely disturbing the older work inside. The detail was the most brutal he ever used. Belsfield at Bowness (1845, for the Baroness de Sternberg), was similar but softer and painted white. Coniston Cold, not far from his other Yorkshire houses, was of 1841-4 and heavily classical. Many of the drawings are by Miles Thompson who was in 1845 to become Webster's partner. Graythwaite Hall was remodelled in Jacobethan style *c.*1840 with a loggia between two (different) wings. There was an Italian tower, in this instance with mullioned windows.

George Webster's later mansions – Broughton Hall, Holker Hall, Conishead Priory

At the end of the 1830s Webster took on two of his largest and most successful commissions, Broughton Hall, near Skipton, and Conishead Priory, Ulverston, although neither was a new house. The visible parts of Broughton were a not entirely symmetrical centre of the mid-eighteenth century and attached wings of 1809-11 by William Atkinson. There was a gothick chapel at some remove. Despite the quality of the parts there was little cohesion between them and George Webster was commissioned to transform a rather muddled façade into a masterpiece of picturesque composition. Atkinson's wings were left untouched – indeed Webster may have been his pupil/assistant when they were built – and they provided the order for the grand new portico. Webster transformed the front by extending Atkinson's order in pilaster form and creating a *porte-cochère* and replaced the west wing which ended in a tower capped by a tempietto. The windows were re-framed in 'Storrs Hall' architraves. The result is 'as good an example as one may find of the Picturesque movement's application to the classical style'.[33]

Inside, less was done. Atkinson had designed the red and white drawing rooms; Webster redecorated the white one and formed a new link to the red. He was also responsible for the gates and eastern lodges in the style of the house, one with a portico and one with a Venetian porch.

All this was carried out between 1838 and 1841, the same years as Webster was working at Conishead Priory where Philip Wyatt had started a new house in 1821-2 for Colonel Thomas Richmond-Gale-Braddyll. Wyatt was considered charming but feckless and few commissions came his way. Among them were Conishead and in 1822 Wynyard Park in County Durham for the 3rd Marquess of Londonderry. At Conishead he began with a service wing in expensive Bath stone. Work went slowly and after seven years the house was only half finished. James Losh noted in his diary on 28 May 1828 that 'when the new house is finished it will in all respects be one of the finest places in the kingdom'. Visiting again in 1831 he added 'had the house been completed the place would have been one of the best worth seeing in the kingdom. As it is one can only consider it a monument of expensive and thoughtless folly'.[34]

Braddyll became increasingly frustrated and dismissed Wyatt in 1829. Across England Londonderry carried on for one more year, holding the work together himself. The two men corresponded over their dealings with Wyatt.[35] Nothing seems to have happened until 1839 except that Braddyll was still borrowing huge sums, £50,000 in 1831 for example. In 1839 he brought in George Webster to build a house to his own designs, his largest Jacobethan mansion. From his plans for 'the New Extension' it is clear that Wyatt's work had ended at the east end of the gothic corridor. Webster continued this as a fluid space to the east door with hall and staircase to the north and a regular suite of rooms to the south. Although brick replaced stone, the decoration was richer and more complex than was usual with Webster and on a grander scale. The twin towers flanking the entrance hall are 100ft tall and borrow detail from his Roman Catholic church in Kendal, building at the same time.

Work went ahead at high speed and Lord Burlington of Holker wrote in his diary on 28 August 1839 of 'an immense pile of building at the Priory since I was last there. It will look very well when finished as there will be a fine set of rooms and a very huge hall'. In December he noted: 'The Priory has grown a great deal since we saw it in the Summer. Dining-room ceiling finished and looks v. well. Entrance hall also very handsome'.[36] This is a man used to the spaces of Chatsworth. He was not a disinterested observer; the foundation stone of Webster's rebuilding of Holker was laid in 1838.

Conishead's interiors were indeed on a grand scale, large rooms with elaborate plasterwork and handsome chimneypieces, panelling and wall arcading. The hall has enormous pendants at the intersections of the vaulting, and there is glass by Willement & Wailes. Some distinguished woodwork was imported, including the parclose screen from Samlesbury Hall, another Braddyll property,[37] which was used in the hall gallery. The mannerist panelling of 1623 in the oak room is perhaps from Middleton Hall, near Sedbergh, a house of the Askew family from c.1750 to 1850.[38] It had to be extended to fit, which suggests that it was brought in later by

H. W. Askew who bought Conishead *c.*1850 and made minor alterations in 1853 (datestone).

The gardens at Conishead were already famous. Braddyll commissioned new buildings from Webster, a *cottage orné*, a bridge, and a 'ladies' cottage'. In 1840 Webster designed a delightful gothic alcove, deriving its detail from Elm Grove.

Across the estuary of the Leven from Conishead, and within sight of it, classical Holker Hall was being remodelled and extended at the same time for the 2nd Earl of Burlington. When he inherited the estate in 1834 he decided to build a new Jacobean wing with larger rooms and to dress up the older work in congruent detail, choosing George Webster as his architect, and when Webster wrote to Thomas Greene of Whittington in November 1834 to account for the lack of progress there he said that he was 'at present fully engaged designing for Lord Burlington.[39]

The plan consisted of a suite of rooms with a corridor behind, linking the staircase with the hall. The porch into this was splayed with multi-faceted buttresses, no doubt topped by little ogee cupolas as suggested in the plan which shows the house at this stage.[40] The earl's diaries recorded Webster's visits to the site and his making suggestions for altering the designs – an oriel window was suggested. Burlington rode out to the marble yard at Kendal to choose new fireplaces. He visited Webster at Eller How and thought house and garden very pretty. Paxton provided a greenhouse design, perhaps the ridge and furrow example as built. Plans for library bookcases arrived from Kendal. Webster was taken off to London where at Coade's manufactory he was shown a new material, a cement that polished to a white marble finish. When Lady Burlington died suddenly her widower resolved to carry on 'as she intended'; the house, he wrote, was 'one more memorial of the happy period of my life . . . '.[41] The new house was finished on 13 May 1841, but payments to Webster and his partner Miles Thompson continued to be made.[42]

The offices and old stables are no doubt also by Webster. The cupola on the offices exactly replicates those at Dallam Tower which date from 1826. In 1846 Webster accepted a commission for a 'decorative cottage', now the estate office, to screen new farm buildings.[43]

The later 1830s and early 1840s

Ingmire Hall, Sedbergh, a house of many periods, was enlarged in 1838 in a picturesque manner with a theatrical tower rising behind gables. There were later alterations and it was severely damaged by fire in 1928. At Broughton Tower the original pele tower was fitted up with new rooms in Jacobethan style in 1839 and a new front was made for Tolson Hall, Burneside, at about the same time. A new house for the Rawstornes of Penwortham was begun in 1839 at Heysham, which also had a tower rising from the usual gables. At Kents Bank, Abbot Hall was heavily remodelled for Miss Lambert of Boarbank. This is externally a rustic modified Jacobethan, internally Grecian.

Wansfell at Waterhead, Ambleside, of about 1840, is a handsome Jacobethan house by Webster though it is undocumented. The good chimneypieces, the porch, barge-boards, and gable brackets all indicate his authorship. The same is true of another Waterhead house, Wanlass How (1841). This had a verandah and stood on a rocky site secured by a Webster buttressed terrace and bastion as in the designs for Wordsworth's house in a similar situation. Ingfield at Settle (1841), was designed for the first vicar there and is a reduced Eshton in plan, standing on a bastioned terrace.

Just north of Cartmel is Aynsome Manor, a Machell house which later passed to the Remingtons by marriage. It is likely that the Rev. Thomas Remington employed Webster to remodel his classical house in Jacobethan style in 1842 – externally, that is, for classical was preferred inside. Here much of the eighteenth century remains, but what Remington called the Royal Room is very close to work at Rydal Hall. The porch has a lintel in the form of a figure 3 on its side, a fairly common vernacular device.

The Aspinall family's two seats near Whalley were probably enlarged by Webster at about the same time. John Aspinall bought Little Mitton Hall about 1840 and restored it, adding a new wing and reshaping the approach. The new wing at the back of Standen Hall, Clitheroe, is probably of the same date and has a fireplace in familiar Webster style. The alterations at Little Mitton are, like the original house, Jacobethan; Standen is wholly classical.

After the death of Jacob Wakefield in 1844 'several great improvements and additions'[44] were made to the north end of the Old House, Stricklandgate, Kendal, clearly identified from the street where a large tripartite window lights a fine apsed room. The Wakefields were amongst Webster's most loyal employers.

In preparation for the arrival of Queen Adelaide in the Lake District in 1840 Thomas Ullock decided to rebuild his White Lion Inn (now the Royal) in Bowness. George Webster produced an Italianate design in 1839 with a tower and verandahs to take advantage of the views over the lake, all rather grander than his Lancashire inns. He also built nearby Quarry How for Ullock himself, the friend who would later be a trustee of his will.

The Low Wood Hotel, near Troutbeck Bridge on the shores of Windermere, developed over centuries. An early view shows it as very plain but extensive.[45] Work of about 1824 by its owner, Christopher Wilson of Kendal, is still recognisable and is perhaps by Francis Webster when he was rebuilding the Salutation a few miles away in Ambleside. The alterations of 1843 with their lighthearted mixture of gothic and classical must be by George.

Elemental gothic churches

George Webster's churches were built between 1822 and 1853. Most – there are exceptions – look as though he had very little interest in them. They are almost all the result of the growth of towns and the division of parishes. As Summerson observed of the Commissioners' churches at large: 'They are almost always recognisable. There is a peculiar drabness about them, a slackness in the proportions, a lack of vitality as if their designers had driven themselves to a task for which they had no heart'.[46] In a sense George was a prisoner of his time, trapped between the charm of eighteenth-century gothick and the thoughtfulness of later designs after the rise of the cleansing Camden Society, founded in 1841, and the first appearance of *The Ecclesiologist*. Webster's churches are all spiritually pre-Pugin and where they have been adapted, as in the provision of structural chancels at, for example, St George's, Kendal, the result aesthetically is invariably an unhappy hybrid.

The Websters had done some work at Rydal Hall in 1818 which is probably why Lady Fleming chose George Webster to design a chapel at Rydal in 1822 – his first church and an early use of gothic in his work. Although critical of detail Wordsworth, at whose windows it stood, generally approved.[47] Burneside, with a short spire, followed in 1823, and Levens, also frugally spired, in 1826. In 1828 he built the church for his own village at Lindale, where he also erected a family tomb.

Did George – or his father – design the Roman Catholic church at Ulverston in 1822 at the instigation of the Rev. Bartholomew McHugh? On a severely cramped site adjoining a terrace of houses owned and built by the Websters, it nevertheless has a high plaster vault, quite exceptional at the time and in this place. Other churches include Natland (1825, demolished), New Hutton (1838), and probably Haverthwaite (1824); all were small buildings with towers and called for no great designing skills. Dalton-in-Furness was ancient and large with nave and aisles. The north aisle and gallery were rebuilt in 1825-6 and the three eastern gables and south aisle in 1830. The Cavendishes of Holker were the lay rectors and George Webster was the architect. In 1829 he designed extensions to the church at Mansergh for Christopher Wilson of Rigmaden. Were they ever built? The plan suggests that it was rigorously classical in style.

Webster was not alone in his use of pre-archaeological gothic. In 1833 the Clergy Daughters' School moved from Cowan Bridge to Casterton and new buildings were needed including a church. This was plain and cheap and his experiences in building it persuaded the Rev. William Carus Wilson to publish in 1835 a pamphlet entitled *Helps to the building of Churches, Parsonage Houses and Schools: containing plans, elevations, specifications etc*. It is doubtful if Carus Wilson himself was capable of drawing plans and elevations or of understanding the qualities of materials shown here, and even more in the second edition of 1842. In this Holme church and parsonage appear together with views of Casterton school, parsonage, and village school. In neither edition does he acknowledge an architect or a builder except for the black Dent marble font from Mr Nixon.[48] Carus Wilson chaired the meeting at which Webster was chosen as the architect for the new church at Milnthorpe in 1835.[49]

Holme church was built in 1839 and there is a signed plan of it.[50] The signatory is George Webster so to that degree he was involved. Why should Carus Wilson have chosen Webster? He was a cadet of the Wilsons of Dallam Tower for whom Webster remodelled the house in 1826. He was vicar of Tunstall 1816-28 when Webster was working in the parish at Thurland Castle (1826-9) and rector of Whittington from 1828 when Webster was rebuilding the hall (1831-6). The lay buildings at Casterton are shown in landscape settings in the 1842 edition of the pamphlet and all suggest the hand of Webster, with their barge-boarded gables and mullioned windows. The parsonage has a plan used by Miles Thompson in the 1840s and later, and a treatment of the lower walls was used by him at Staveley in 1859.

One or two of Webster's churches are exceptional. St George's, Kendal (1839-41), with its twin spires buttressed by twin porches, all reflected in the river Kent, must be counted as one. Kendal's Roman Catholic church, Holy Trinity and St George (1835-7), has a good front with sculpture by Thomas Duckett (as has St George's on a smaller scale). The interior is rich with minor sculpture and gothic niches, the altar wall being particularly successful. If anything has been altered it is not apparent: unity reigns.[51] Other churches of the decade need no comment here. The ubiquity of the lancet window is broken in later years when some plate tracery was introduced as at Bardsea and Coniston Cold. One or two have superb sites and became objects in the landscape, like Bardsea above Morecambe Bay and Firbank against the Howgill Fells. A curiosity is the 'chapel' at Penwortham Priory with its tall turrets and trio of lancets which in fact concealed the dining room.

Garden design

George Webster's only surviving garden design is for Nibthwaite Grange, Colton, of 1837,[52] although it is clear that he was involved in planning the gardens at Eshton in 1836. We know from his letters from Europe how much gardening (and farming) meant to him. From the same source we know how constantly his exhortations and instructions reached the gardeners at Eller How and Black Rock by way of his wife. A letter in the *Gardener's Magazine* in 1839 exactly describes the Nibthwaite garden: 'scores of meandering flower beds in the shape of kidneys and tadpoles and sausages and leeches and commas disfigure the lawn'.[53] The style 'gardenesque' was derived from Repton's practice with its taste for formal beds near the house. In 1840 at Belsfield Webster designed a similar garden in the space between elaborate greenhouses.[54] The architect of Holbeck Cottage, Troutbeck, is not known but may have been Webster as its array of cylindrical chimneys suggests. Here too the gardens have areas of gardenesque, and at Larch How, Underbarrow, of 1847 it appears again.[55] Eller How has several small lakes in which the house was reflected and some island beds, but it was the network of paths among the precipitous woods which rise directly from the house that Webster's letters insisted must be swept and trimmed and open. At the top are two follies. Merlewood, like Eller How, had steep woods behind the house. It also once had a serpentine ha-ha in front with island beds.

Black Rock Villa

After his father's death George Webster had a town house in Kendal and the country house at Lindale, Eller How. Probably at the suggestion of his doctor, Dr Longmire, he built an Italian villa on the shore at Grange-over-Sands, then a place of a few cottages. Black Rock Villa with its tower, balconies, and verandah was conspicuous in such company. There was little space between the house and the sea wall for anything but verandahs, paving, and stairs, but planting was trained over trellis work.[56] The intention was to allow Webster, as part of the treatment of his various illnesses, to have hot and cold brine baths in his basement by taking water directly from the bay. He was therefore partly responsible for the growth of Grange as a resort and built another villa nearby in 1849. He seems to have considered Grange to be a northern Torquay,[57] a confusion still found in modern advertising. Later Grange villas may also be by Webster, notably Yewbarrow Lodge. Perhaps he considered developing Grange himself .

What Webster could not have foreseen in 1840 was the effect that railway mania would have on his retreat a few years later. The Furness Railway did not then run as far as Ulverston but in 1845 the decision was taken to build a line from Ulverston to join the main line at Carnforth. Webster himself went to Parliament with Thomas Rawstorne, the solicitor for the company, and others 'on railway business'. The bill went through but the line was incorporated only in 1851. Both the Leven and Kent estuaries were formidable barriers but the line opened finally in 1857. When did Webster realise what effect this would have upon Black Rock? Instead of the sea the windows would look out onto railway lines on the top of an embankment which would cut off his supply of brine. He made a group of drawings of the before-and-after kind which were clearly intended as some form of protest to the company, but as they remained among his papers it may be that no representations were ever made.[58]

A new partnership and retirement

The turning point in the fortunes of the firm was approaching, compounded of the disagreements over the management of the Burlington quarries, George Webster's increasing ill health, and his resulting loss of interest in architectural practice. He lacked a son with the inclination to follow him and the need for a partner had become evident.

An early sign of his malaise was a letter to Lord Burlington on 17 December 1844[59] asking that all questions to do with the quarries be referred to Miles Thompson. Just over a month later, on 1 February 1845, an advertisement was issued in which Webster announced that 'in consequence of the faithful services of Mr. Miles Thompson as his Clerk and Assistant for twenty years he has taken him into Partnership'. The firm would now be Webster & Thompson but 'Mr. Webster may, as usual, be consulted at his residence, Eller How, Lindale, in Cartmel'.

Thompson added the hope that in view of 'twenty years experience and extensive practice in every class of Buildings' he would merit 'by strict attendance to business . . . the patronage so liberally conferred on Mr. Webster'.[60] He could have said much more, for who but he had carried the architectural practice in Webster's long absences abroad? For example, the Ulverston Savings Bank of 1836 was built in one absentee year and its tower of 1844 in another. The superintendence in both years was largely Thompson's as the frequent letters to the bank's trustees show.[61]

Miles Thompson was born in Kendal in 1808, the son of John and Betty Thompson. His father was probably the John Thompson, slate merchant, who was listed in Parson & White's directory of 1829. Another John Thompson was a stonemason and waller, and either occupation might explain Miles's gravitation towards the Websters. From the advertisement of 1845 we get the first indication as to when Thompson joined the Websters which, read together with Francis Webster's will of March 1827 to which Thompson was a witness, suggest that the date was about 1825. George Webster may have early noted a talent for drawing that could be developed.[62]

Lord Burlington's unhappiness over the operation of the quarries at Kirkby Ireleth resulted in Webster and others losing their franchises. The estate itself would manage them. On 31 January 1846 Webster was informed and offered £2,000 in compensation and an offer to design 'a decorative cottage' at Holker to screen the new farm buildings from the gardens. He replied from Grange on 2 February: 'My Lord, I have the honour to accept the receipt of your Lordship's favours of the 31st ult. My only reason for continuing the profession of Architecture since my health has declined was owing to a belief in it materially assisting the sale of our slates and my son succeeding to the working of the quarries held under your Lordship at Kirkby Ireleth. Having no longer connection with these workings I have resolved wholly to abandon the profession further than seeing the works engaged upon brought to a conclusion'. However, the cottage (now the estate office) was designed and an account 'for plans etc' sent to the earl on 3 March. On 21 February, in a letter to the agent acknowledging the receipt of the compensation money, Webster wrote 'I am thankful that this, to me, most unpleasant and harrowing business is at last brought to a close'.

The abandonment of architecture took place without delay. Notice was given on 20 March that the partnership was dissolved by mutual consent and 'the undersigned George Webster retires on 20 March'. He was forty-eight years old. Thompson reminded the firm's patrons that he had 'upwards of twenty years experience in Planning and superintending nearly every class of Buildings'.[63] The firm would now be known as Thompson & Webster. Was the retention of George's name a mere courtesy or in the hope of advice to come or introductions to be made? It was not for continuing involvement in the business although he could be consulted at home and, as he wrote to the Rev. Thomas Remington in March 1862, he designed Merlewood (1853) 'to oblige a neighbour', leaving the 'constructive part' to Thompson. In the same letter he admitted to being a 'house-prisoner for a week concocting some plan' for a house.[64]

As late as 1859, when the White Hall was bought by the corporation of Kendal as a town hall and altered for its new function, George Webster, who 'in conjuction with his father' had designed the original building, stepped out of retirement to design the alterations including the clock tower. Miles Thompson's nephew John S. Thompson was the contractor.[65]

The firm was in the right place when the railway arrived in the Lake District and a branch from the west coast line at Oxenholme was proposed. In the largely empty fields above Bowness a new hotel was built even before the station; tenders for Rigg's Windermere Hotel were invited by Webster & Thompson on 8 November 1845.[66] But when the station was similarly offered to tradesmen on 31 October 1846 it was to Thompson alone they should apply.[67] Thompson bought 36 acres of eligible land near the station which he marked out in plots for villas which would be convenient for the trains to Manchester and Liverpool.[68] He also built a church for the new 'village'.

The changes in the firm leave some uncertainties. Who designed the Jacobethan Summerlands, Preston Richard – Webster, Thompson, or Thompson & Webster? Or Craig Foot, Bowness (1848), for a friend of Wordsworth, or the Italianate extension, with its dignified stone cantilever staircase, to the delightful Palladian hall at Clayton-le-Moors (1846, demolished)? In 1853 Thompson & Webster invited tenders for the building of Rothersyke (Egremont), Merlewood (Grange), and others.

Some clients in need of new buildings acknowledged Webster's retirement at once, including the trustees of the Kirkby Lonsdale Savings Bank and the Rev. Thomas Remington who commissioned a Tudor design for a bank at Cartmel and who wrote directly to Miles Thompson in 1847 and 1846 respectively.[69] However, in Kirkby Lonsdale seven years later the new market hall was by Thompson & Webster. After about 1856 the '& Webster' seems to have been dropped in line with reality. It was at about this time that John Starkey entered Thompson's office where he would remain for twelve years.[70]

Independence did not bring change. Thompson carried on much as before, using the same styles, Grecian, Jacobethan, Italianate, and gothic. The typology shifts a little; public baths are a new addition to the architect's repertoire. Churches disguised as dependent chapels have parishes carved out of the vast ancient ones as the population grows, and new parsonages are needed, Thompson designing many of them across the region. Hotels grow larger – Thompson enlarged many that he had designed a few years earlier. More schools are needed, and old patrons build new stables or new accommodation for servants as at Holker where Thompson obliged with a picturesque village at the hall gates (1861-2), stables (1863), and a school (1864).[71]

New regulations on building embodied in the Boards of Health established by law in 1848 required that designs, however small, must be scrutinised and passed, above all as being hygienic. Thompson's designs for his later works in Kendal therefore survive.[72] He continued to work for many of Webster's old clients, not only for the Cavendishes at Holker but for the Wakefields and Wilsons in Kendal. At the Old House he designed the stables (1865) and added wings to High Park, a Webster villa east of the town.[73] Elsewhere he remodelled Rusland Hall and added substantial wings in 1850, and extended his Prince of Wales Hotel in Grasmere, ten years after it was first designed in 1853. Also at Grasmere, the Hollens and Lowther Hotel, in the Italianate style, was altered in 1849 and again in 1851. The Waterhead Hotel at Coniston was in a thorough-going Webster/Thompson Jacobethan; the Ullswater Hotel, Glenridding of c.1860 is probably by Thompson too.

A large new assembly room was built in Great George Street, Ulverston. The Victoria Hall has one long Grecian front to the narrow street with a pediment on pilasters and wreaths in the frieze and can be attributed to George Webster about 1840. The Lancaster Bank (now the National Westminster) is a noble design of c.1860 facing the descending space of the market place and is no doubt by Thompson. It owes much to Webster's Westmorland Bank at Kendal of fifteen years before. The attached bank house has the peculiar window architraves derived from Storrs Hall.

1854 saw the designs for market halls at both Kendal and Kirkby Lonsdale. That at Kendal (demolished), an anarchic building with restless arched openings topped by a crushing entablature, took the place of the former St George's chapel. It contrasted strongly with that at Kirkby Lonsdale, a subtle design turning a street corner by degrees, each bay quietly arcaded and rusticated.

There was a lot of building in and around Ulverston in the fifties and sixties. At Pennington the church had been partly rebuilt in 1826 and in 1850 Thompson built a true *cottage orné*, Conyger Hurst, and then across the village and ten years later Shannon (now Pennington) House with a complex timber porch. He designed Heaning Wood, Ulverston, in 1863 for George Webster's daughter Ellen on her marriage to Stephen Hart Jackson.

The Grammar School at Cartmel was housed in a plain classical building of 1789. In 1863 Thompson added a contrasting master's house to the west and a 'porch' – a play space – to the east. Here too George came briefly out of retirement to help his former partner with a difficult headmaster.[74] In the same year village schools of similar Jacobethan design appeared at Milnthorpe, Endmoor, and Burton-in-Kendal. In Kendal, the brewery built in 1853 in a garden off Highgate is probably by Thompson, whereas the shop of the same year at the corner of the New Shambles and the Market Place is by Thompson & Webster.

The ancient Sandes Hospital in Highgate was partly rebuilt in 1852 by Thompson as a harsh gothic range behind the gatehouse of 1670 to which he added new wings. In 1852 he made two designs for a new stable block at Rigmaden of which the second has survived. It was to have had a splendid tower based carefully upon Webster's at Broughton Hall. Lakefield, Claife, was enlarged in Italianate style in 1854 by Thompson & Webster and Hawksheads House, Bolton-le-Sands, in rough limestone *c.*1860, presumably by Thompson alone, as was the towered Italianate Borrowthwaite in Stainmore (1862). Like Webster, Thompson designed several churches, St Mary, Windermere (1848), Egton-cum-Newland and Irton (1856), Garsdale (1861), and All Hallows, Kendal (1864). Several have since been enlarged to leave only fragments of Thompson's original buildings.

To return to George Webster and his circumstances after retirement, the census of 1851 describes him as a 'landed proprietor' at Eller How Mansion, owning and working 186 acres and employing eight farm servants. Also living in the house were his wife Eleanor, his son Francis, a law student, his daughters Margaret and Jane, Eleanor Wibberley, a cousin of forty years,[75] Margaret Carradus and Hannah Wilson, house servants, and James Pedder, the groom. At Eller How Farm lived Thomas Birkett, labourer, and at Eller How Cottage George Pattison, gardener. It all sounds very comfortable. The situation was much the same in 1861.

Railway shares seem to have been Webster's preferred investments, from the Hull & Selby line in 1846 to the East Lancashire/Lancashire & Yorkshire, amalgamated in 1860. The *Westmorland Gazette* published a provisional list of directors of the Furness & Windermere Railway on 17 May 1845 with George's name among them. The following week a revised list omitted it. His residuary account shows that his investments in railways alone totalled over £108,000.[76]

George was a great collector, as his will shows, largely of souvenirs brought back from his travels.[77] He had family portraits, a marble bust of himself, and other paintings, amongst them a Romney. He had jewelry and plate, and busts of the great philosophers and poets carved in lava from Vesuvius and bought in Naples. Pictures, engravings, drawings, statues, marbles and bronzes, and other articles of vertu are listed but unspecified. He had a bronze biga, a two-horse chariot from Rome which had been 'mounted there under my directions upon various portions of Roman and Egyptian Antiquity'. Also undetailed were Roman and Egyptian antiquities, cabinets of gems and antiquities 'from my Foreign Travels', Roman coins and medals, and a case of cameo heads.[78] His library included 'Books relating to Architecture with the Book Cases and appendages' and, most precious to any student of his work, the 'large folio volumes containing copies or originals of my Architectural Works with all loose Plans of Buildings contained in portfolios or upon Boards as working drawings and all specifications for buildings'. Not one has survived. Where we have designs by him they are from clients and estate offices. Nor has the 'years Journal of my life' survived.

George Webster died at Eller How on 16 April 1864. Although he had suffered from ill health for at least thirty years, as the letters from his travels show, his death was possibly unexpected. A man who owned relatively few clothes and had been at pains to have parts of his wardrobe 'turned' recently, would perhaps not buy a pair of new 'fancy tweed trousers' three weeks before his death unless he was expecting to get good use from them.[79] He was buried on the 22nd at Lindale in the vault outside the porch which he himself had designed some years earlier. In his will he asked that his funeral should be 'as plain and quiet as possible consistent with decency and in the opinion of my Widow and Executors with my station in life'. No obituaries appeared in the local papers, only the bare announcement: 'On the 16th instant, at his residence Eller How, Lindale-in-Cartmel, George Webster, Esq., aged 66 years'.[80]

No picture of George survives although both his will and inventory mention the portrait by James Ward which went to Kendal Town Hall and which has now most regrettably disappeared. His passports indicate that he was 5ft 6ins. in height, with brown hair and eyes and a presumably regular oval face. He lived well into the days of photography but again no photograph survives, although there were four at Eller How in 1864.

Hoggarth's 1853 plan of Kendal shows that the whole area of the Lound, from the river to the canal was owned by Miles Thompson, including a foundry and his own house at the canal end. Over the canal is the extremely rustic cottage of the change bridge keeper, no doubt by Thompson. At a later date there were houses of several other Thompsons and that of another architect, Eli Cox.[81] Thompson's career seems to have concluded with two very different houses. No. 1 Cliff Terrace, Kendal, has an Italianate tower soaring over the town. The bold decoration of the design[82] has less impact in the actual building. The other, Holeslack Farm on the Sizergh estate, was reconstructed in unimpeachable vernacular in 1868, the year in which he died at the Lound.

As his will of 1866 shows,[83] Thompson had a passion for property, much of it in Kendal. All of it went to his brothers and sister and nephews at his death. His estates at Grange, including the Eden Mount quarries, with land at Burneside and Grasmere were left to his brother Marcellus, who continued to work the quarries. To Robert went the houses and lands near the station at Birthwaite (Windermere) as well as the Old Dungeon Ghyll Hotel in Great Langdale which Miles had bought in 1862.[84] Brother John was bequeathed property in Kendal – yards and cottages, and so on. Brothers and nephews were involved in quarrying or building or worked as marble-masons. They were not, however, left the architectural practice, not even nephew John (1848-?1907) who was Thompson's pupil in the last two years of his life and then continued under Daniel Brade and E. H. Smales who bought the goodwill.[85] John Thompson became an associate of the Royal Institute of British Architects in 1882, proposed by Brade, Ewan Christian, and E. G. Paley. He started independent practice in 1874, but no works are listed in the RIBA records and he was not prolific at home, his known works including St George's Hall (1879, demolished), and the ritual east end of St Thomas's church (1882).[86] Another nephew, John Strickland Thompson, was a builder who announced in 1863 'to the Gentry and Clergy' that he was to sell his 'builder's stock in trade' and 'devote his whole time to the duties of Building Surveyor and architect'.[87] Before this he had built the tower of the new Town Hall for George Webster (1859) and the new vicarage, built to the designs of Bowman and Crowther of Manchester in 1859 and now demolished.[88]

Miles Thompson's assistant for twelve years, John Starkey, who presumably could not find the money for the goodwill, was obliged to set up independently after Miles died. He designed the almshouses at Grayrigg (1869) and the Dean Gibson school (1897).[89]

Notes

[1.] Quoted in Colvin, 45.

[2.] *Ibid.*, 84; *The Websters of Kendal*, no. 16. In order to reduce the number of footnotes, most references for individual buildings mentioned in this chapter are given in the gazetteer.

[3.] A. Taylor, 'George Webster (1797-1864): the education of an architect; a proposal', *Quarto*, April 1993, 13-16.

[4.] C. Hussey, 'Broughton Hall,', *CL*, 14 April 1950.

[5.] Illus. in Taylor, *op. cit.*, 15.

[6.] A. Taylor, 'The Lowly Dwelling of William Wordsworth Esq[re]', *Georgian Group Jnl*, vii, 1997, 43-55; see below, pp. 353-68.

[7.] Simonstone, very near Read, was refaced in a Jacobean style in 1818. Could this be even earlier Webster Jacobethan? There are 18th-century examples at Hampton Court Palace (George II's gate, 1732), and at Audley End, Essex, by Vanburgh, *c.*1730, where the style is used purely decoratively.

[8.] George Webster's copies are in the possession of Jeffrey Haworth and Donald Buttress; and see below, pp. 304-5.

[9.] Underley with its intended tower looks to Wollaton, whereas the even silhouette of Eshton is reminiscent of Longleat.

[10.] N. Pevsner, 'Good King James's Gothic', *Architectural Revue*, cvii, 1950, 163.

[11.] J. P. Neale, *Views of the Seats*, 2nd ser., v, 1829.

[12.] See p. 339.

[13.] By an anonymous carpenter from Skipton, who was recommended by Webster for use at Whittington in a letter of 10 Jan.1834 to Thomas Greene: LRO, DDGr/6/34.

[14.] CRO K, WDX 1315.

[15.] Webster's houses were of two storeys, so the feature did not dominate as at, say, Stonyhurst (1592), the best example in the north-west. There is another at Browsholme, another Parker house, engraved for Britton.

[16.] Graves, *op. cit.*, viii, 189. The Underley designs are in a private collection.

[17.] But seen in stone profusion at Barrington Court, Somerset (1515). A number of engravings from the south-western counties in Webster's albums suggest that he may have made an early journey there.

[18.] Taylor, 'The Lowly Dwelling of William Wordsworth Esq[re]', 43-54; see below, pp. 353-68.

[19.] J. Cornforth, 'Hutton-in-the-Forest', *CL*, 4, 11, 18 Feb. 1965; RIBA Drawings Collection, W8/1/1-2; other designs at the house.

[20.] J. Housman, *Descriptive Tour and Guide to the Lakes*, 2nd ed., 1802, 165; G. E. and E. L. Griggs (eds), *Letters of Hartley Coleridge*, 1956, 114.

[21.] The sarcophagi are interchangeable with those of Webster tablets at Lowther to the Rev. J. Satterthwaite (d. 1821), and at Richmond, to the Rev. C. Goodwill (d. 1822).

[22.] There are 17th-century examples at Barcroft (1636), Martholme (1607), Ordsall, and Shuttleworth, all in South Lancs.

[23.] *WG*, 16 April 1836.

[24.] *Rec. Kendale*, iii, 98.

[25.] LRO, WRW/F, will of Francis Webster, proved 1828. For Richard Stirzaker (1797-1833), see M.

Hall, *The Artists of Cumbria*, 1979, 83-4.

26. *Local Chronology*, 58, 122.

27. P. Barker, 'The Websters' Marble Works in Miller's Close', *Quarto*, Jan. 1991, 10-14; and see p. 67.

28. CRO K, WD/AG, plans and elevations; see below, p. 67.

29. The house is described in detail in 1830: 'A newly erected dwellinghouse, pleasantly situate in the centre of Kent Terrace . . . and fit for the immediate reception of a Family of Respectability, being replete with every convenience and finished in the best manner. The House consists upon the Basement Floor of a Kitchen, Scullery, Wash and Brewhouse, Cellar Pantry and Coal Vault; on the Ground Floor of a spacious entrance and staircase, a Drawing Room 23 feet by 15 feet, Dining Room 17 ft 6 in by 15 ft, Study 12 ft by 10 ft fit up with glazed bookcases also with Storeroom and Closets; on the First Floor of a Sitting Room, Two Bedrooms with Dressing Rooms attached and two without; on the Second Floor of three bedrooms and a large attic capable of being converted into two bedrooms. The back of the House opens upon a Pleasant Garden': *Westmorland Advertiser & Kendal Chronicle*, 11 Sept.1830. The editor is grateful to Michael Bottomley for providing a transcript of this advertisement.

30. At this time designs which are clearly in George's style were signed by his father as head of the firm; sometimes they just have 'Kendal' and a date, but no signature.

31. Information from Jeffrey Haworth.

32. LRO, DDGr 6: the Lune Foundry, Cable Street, Lancaster, presented Musgrave's and Greene's accounts.

33. C. Hussey, 'Broughton Hall', *CL*, 31 March, 7, 14 April 1950.

34. E. Hughes (ed), *The Diaries of James Losh*, ii, Surtees Soc., clxxiv, 1963, 10, 112 n. 10. At Wynyard Park, Co. Durham, Lord Londonderry suffered in a similar way at the same time and almost, but not quite, resorted to dismissal: J. M. Robinson, *The Wyatts*, 1950, 122.

35. Durham RO, D/LO/C141. Braddyll as well as Londonderry had interests in Co. Durham coal. His Haswell estate was sold with other properties: LRO, DDMc 32/58.

36. In Chatsworth Library.

37. R. Eaton, *History of Samlesbury*, 1936, 46.

38. J. F. Curwen, 'Middleton Hall', *CW2*, xii, 109.

39. LRO, DDGr 6.

40. Holker estate office, plan of Holker, 1840. The entrance at Eshton had the same plan, altered in execution.

41. The house as completed by Webster is illustrated in Twycross, ii, 5, and in J. Richardson, *Furness Past and Present*, i, 1880, facing 37.

42. For payments for work on the house, see LRO, DDCa 13/305, 308-38 (bills), and 13/13/262 (accounts); see also C. Aslet, 'Holker Hall', *CL*, 26 June, 2 July 1980.

43. See p. 98.

44. Curwen, *KK*, 335.

45. P. Crosthwaite, *Map of the Grand Lake of Windermere*, 1783, reproduced in A. Hankinson, *The Regatta Men*, 1988.

46. J. Summerson, *Architecture in Britain, 1530-1830*, 1953, 317.

47. A. G. Hall (ed), *Letters of William and Dorothy Wordsworth*, iii, pt. 2, 1978, 301: '. . . when time has softened down the exterior a little it will prove a great ornament to the Village'.

48. Paul Nixson or Nixon of Carlisle who quarried black marble at Dent: Colvin, 707. The iron gutters came from Kendal.

49. R. K. Bingham, *The Chronicles of Milnthorpe*, 1987, 221. For Carus Wilson, see J. Ewbank, *The Life and Works of William Carus Wilson 1791-1859*, 1959. His brother Roger (d. 1839) was vicar of Preston and a great church-builder there: Pevsner, *N. Lancs.*, 194.

50. CRO K, DRC/10.

51. Illustrated in J. Macaulay, *The Gothic Revival*, 1975, figs 149-50.

52. Design at the house.

53. Quoted in L. Fleming and A. Gore, *The English Garden*, 1979, 187.

54. Illustrated in Richardson, *Furness Past and Present*, ii, 1880, 185.

55. For Holbeck, see CRO K, WDB/35, sale particulars, 1886. OS 6" shows the same state in 1863. There is a later plan of the Larch How garden at the house. The garden at Aynsome Manor, Cartmel, now a caravan park, may have been a Webster design: information from Michael Bottomley.

56. CRO K, WDX 1315.

57. *Ibid.*; he had engravings of both places.

58. *Ibid.*

59. *Ibid.* The correspondence with Lord Burlington referred to here and below is in copies, probably preserved for good business reasons. For the slate quarries, see pp. 57-9.

60. *WG*, 1 Feb. 1845.

61. A. Taylor, 'A Bank and its Building', *CW2*, lxxiv, 147-58.

62. A perspective watercolour of Holy Trinity, Ulverston, dated 1828, has been tentatively attributed to him: J. Marsh (ed) *Dear Mr Salvin*, 1999, frontispiece.

63. *WG*, 28 Mar. 1846.

64. CRO K, WPR 89/PR/2704/1.

65. CRO K, *Annals*, 304.58.

66. *WG*, 8 Nov. 1845, plans at the offices of Webster & Thompson, Kendal.

67. *Ibid.*, 31 Oct. 1846, tenders to Miles Thompson, Kendal.

68. *Ibid.*, 22 Sept. 1849.

69. CRO K, WPR 89/PR/2718/10.

70. CRO K, *Annals*, 304.79.

71. In Webster's albums (private collection) are early cuttings from *The Builder*, founded in 1842, of rustic cottages, one block in 1843 bearing a resemblance to Holker village, supplied by 'a correspondent'.

72. CRO K, WSMB/K. The designs are now too fragile to examine.

73. *Ibid.*, Bk 1/44 (1861), High Park.

74. CRO K, WPR 89/PR/2704/1.

75. She was George's first cousin once removed, the daughter of his father's niece Ann (1786-1852), who married George Wibberley (d. 1832), a Liverpool hosier, in 1807. There are memorials to her parents outside the south transept of Cartmel Priory.

76. CRO K, WD/MM/box 113, probate papers.

77. *Ibid.*, will of George Webster. However, see below pp. 303-52 for further details.

78. A funerary urn discovered south of the marble mills was said to be 'in the care of our friend George Webster of Eller How, who fortunately possessing archaeological tastes, was mainly instrumental in the discovery of these sepulchral remains': *Annals*, 12. Twycross described his collections: 'The paintings, and other works of art contained in Eller How, consist of a selection of the first by the old masters, but more particularly of copies of them by Mazzolini of Rome, also of sculpture, busts, mosaic tables, bronzes, Etrurian terra-cotta vases, and relics from Egypt and the Holy Land, all made by the present owner during his different tours through the Continent of Europe. The residence contains a number of warlike weapons, and a good and extensive collection of oak Furniture of the olden time'.

79. CRO K, WD/MM/box 113. George's death certificate stated that he died of 'Fatty degeneration of Heart', a condition not recognised today, but which probably indicated corpulence. He referred in his letters to being overweight, e.g. on 6 June 1836 ('little increase in reducing my bulk') and on 11 Aug.1841, when he felt that his weight had increased. He clearly suffered from severe hemorrhoids,

which caused bleeding, and in 1844 referred to 'Palpitations of the Heart' and 'pain about the lungs and chest'. The presence in his library of a number of medical books argues a preoccupation with his health.

80. e.g. in *Soulby's Ulverston Advertiser*, 24 April 1864. The funeral cost £270 16s. 11d. The probate papers show that 27½ yards of crepe at 4s. a yard and 106¾ yards of black silk were bought, with 27 pairs of gloves for the mourners. The silk was made up into four dresses and four mantles, for Eleanor, her two unmarried daughters, and Eleanor Wibberley, by Parker & Head of Kendal who also acted as undertakers. After the funeral Francis Webster was paid for '2 Blue Yorkshire Tombs' at £8 10s. each, for inscribing a tablet, refixing the old family tablets in Lindale church, and repainting their inscriptions: CRO K, WD/MM/box 113.

81. For Cox, see 1851 Census, The Lound, Kendal; Kelly, *Cumb. and Westm.*, 1873, 956.

82. CRO K, WSMB/K/Bk 2/177; ibid., *Annals*, 304.79.

83. CRO K, WDX 708/T46.

804. He had bought a half share in the hotel in 1862 and bought out his partner, John Hurst Taylor of Windermere, in 1865: CRO K, WDX 40.

85. CRO K, *Annals*, MS note facing 304.79. Brade seems to have done most of the designing. Pevsner called his church of St John, Bassenthwaite, 'pretentious', which is perhaps more encouraging than the 'wilful and irresponsible' which he applied to Old Hutton: *Cumb. and Westm.*, 64, 281.

86. CRO K, WSMB/K/Bk 4/499 (St George's Hall), 590 (St Thomas's).

87. *WG*, 31 Jan. 1863. Another nephew, Marcellus, became the cashier of the Kendal Gas Co., and was imprisoned in 1893 for the 'defalcation' of £3,600: R. K. Bingham, *Kendal: A Social History*, 1995, 337.

88. Curwen, *KK*, 175; *Annals*, 160.

89. LRO K, *Annals*, 304.79; *Victorian Kendal* (picture chart), Abbot Hall Art Gallery, 1990.

V

Marble and Slate

MARBLE and slate between them provided a large part of the income of the Webster firm. Francis first went to Kendal to work the local marble and foreign marble was imported. It was sold only when sculpted into chimneypieces, funerary tablets, even furniture, of some aesthetic quality, however slight. Slate quarried for landowners and to cover the buildings designed in the architectural department of the firm was also sold directly to anyone who needed it. As George Webster wrote to the Earl of Burlington in later life, he would have given up architecture were it not for the fact that it sold slate.

Marble

If Francis Webster designed his first work in Kendal, the obelisk on Castle Howe, in 1788, he must have arrived in the town by then. Already a master mason, he settled in the New Inn Yard off Highgate and established his marble yard there with a water-driven mill at Helsington Laithes on the river Kent, south of the town. He would stay there for the next thirty years.

In 1790 Webster and his partner William Holme were described as 'builders and marble cutters'[1] and soon afterwards the Rev. John Hodgson[2] noted a 'marble manufactory employs several hands . . . The marble is of great variety . . . in 1793 a very beautiful kind interspersed with white red and other tints was discovered on both banks of the river Kent'.[3] By 1828 Francis Webster & Sons were 'Architects, Sculptors and manufacturers of Italian and British chimney-pieces by machinery'.[4] A year later a more comprehensive account was given:

The Marble Works in the town and neighbourhood . . . are very extensive, and were first brought into repute by the late Mr. Webster, architect, who about 30 years ago, constructed machinery . . . for sawing and polishing the marble. This machinery is brought to such a state of perfection, that every description of mouldings, whether straight or circular, is now wrought by it with more accuracy than manual labour; and the flutings of diminishing columns are furnished by it in a most beautiful and regular style. In the town Messrs. Webster have their splendid show-rooms for manufactured chimney-pieces, &c. The surrounding mountainous district supplies the finest black and other marbles; and the advantage possessed by Kendal of sea and inland navigation facilities facilitates the importation of Italian marble to be here manufactured and re-shipped to most of the principal towns in the kingdom.

Twenty years later Mannex had little to add.[5]

Webster, however, was not the first to give local stone a high polish. In 1698 Celia Fiennes reported seeing at Lowther Hall 'chimney pieces . . . of a dark-coulloured marble which is taken out of the ground just by, and its well polish'd'.[6] Half a century later Bishop Richard Pococke wrote: '. . . to Grange . . . a most delightful situation commanding a view of the strand . . . The hilly part . . . consists of a sort of rock, which seems to be a limestone marble, but is full of flaws . . . and is used for small bridges, shambles, and the like'.[7]

The earliest known reference to Francis Webster's chimneypieces is of the five, at least one of Kendal Fell limestone, which he supplied for the new Assembly Rooms and Market House at Hawkshead in 1790.[8] The next is one for John Foster's News Room in Liverpool in 1801.[9] Four years later the 3rd Earl of Egremont ordered a group, since removed, for his rehabilitation of Cockermouth Castle.[10] The fireplaces provided by Webster for his own rebuilding scheme at Lowther Hall and then for Smirke's fresh start brought him the remarkable sum of £1,293. They were gothic, and of coloured marbles in the best rooms.[11]

Another house with early chimneypieces is Shaw End, Patton, with at least three, one a very pretty white one with inlaid fluting and honeycomb-pattern tablet (1796-1801).[12] The chimneypieces at Hill Top, New Hutton, bear enough resemblance to examples elsewhere to suggest that they are from the Webster showroom. One, with Doric columns in black and coloured marbles, is repeated at Aynam Lodge, Rydal Hall, and Clapham Lodge (Ingleborough Hall). Hill Top had two main building periods, c.1795 and c.1820, and its builder, Ralph Fisher (d. 1837) has a Webster tablet in the church. Enough houses in Kendal itself have similar pieces to indicate how many more there must have been before drawing rooms became shops and offices, and central heating prevailed.

Work on the Lancaster canal was suspended in 1797 about twelve miles south of Kendal, resuming in 1812 and completed when it reached the town in 1819. Francis Webster saw what was coming and that he must make the most of the development and move his marble yard as near as possible to the canal. In anticipation of the new port the corporation decided to rebuild the mill bridge over the Kent and Webster was appointed architect on 13 April 1818. He designed a handsome structure of three eliptical arches of limestone. The masons were Edward Gibson and James Harrison who often worked with the Websters. The foundation stone was laid on 20 May 1818 and the bridge completed in the following November at a cost of £888. It was named Kent Bridge but is now better known as Miller Bridge.[13] Simultaneously Webster designed another bridge of three arches to cross the mill race and here the basins, wharves, and warehouses of the canal head were constructed at 58 degrees to the line of the canal.[14]

No doubt everyone in Kendal was calculating the value to them of this new wonder. For the Websters, dealing in weighty matters of stone, slate, marble, timber, and lead, it would allow loading and unloading within feet of their new marble yard, for on 26 October 1818 the corporation committee agreed to let Webster that part of Miller's Close between the new bridge and the canal basin for twenty-one years at £15 a year. The committee also agreed to pay £400 towards the total cost of £500 for new buildings. Letting the work was delayed but on 14 December the joiners' work went out to tender, followed the next month by those for masons and glaziers. Webster designed a shop (perhaps the showroom), a wheelwright's shop, and a row of cottages for £620.[15]

In June 1819 it was reported that a 'young man named W. Atkinson employed in Mr Webster's marble manufactory in the New Inn Yard' had been swindled, and in the same edition of the *Westmorland Gazette* the opening of the canal was described.[16] The New Inn was put onto the market in the same year together with 'extensive premises behind in the occupation of . . . Francis Webster and others'.[17] For the opening of the canal 'a Corporation Flag [was to] be immediately made with proper Emblems', and Mr Alderman Hodgson and Mr Burgess Webster got the job. The flag, which was flown from the castle, carried a view of the marble works alongside the Genius of Commerce. Ingenious Mr Webster.[18]

In order to keep up a steady flow of chimneypieces and memorial tablets as required the yard recruited both apprentices and mature masons. In 1809 the fourteen-year-old Thomas Lindsay of Ravenstonedale was apprenticed to Francis Webster, 'mason and marble cutter', and he was still there in 1841.[19] In 1826 'Six or Eight Stout Active Youths' of about fourteen were offered apprenticeships of seven guineas, and the firm also advertised for 'a number of Marble Masons who have served an apprenticeship to stonemasons [to] find immediate and constant employment at very liberal wages'.[20]

Mature craftsmen also joined the firm from time to time, and it was perhaps an indication of the Websters' ambitions that they took on a full-time sculptor. Thomas Duckett (1804-78) of Preston, after an apprenticeship to a plasterer, joined Messrs. Franceys in Liverpool, and exhibited a bust at the Liverpool Academy in 1828.[21] He moved to Kendal to manage the Websters' sculpture department and carved the figure of St George in the gable of the church of Holy Trinity and St George, designed by George Webster in 1835, and the headstops of the door. Interior work in the church is also probably his. Figurative sculpture was largely absent from the firm's output and it is likely that Duckett was responsible for what little there is. That includes the eloquent heads on the west windows of St George's church, Kendal (1838), as well as the mourning soldier on the monument to Captain Considine in Chester Cathedral (1841), and the weeping figure and urn in memory of Francis Webster which was once in the garden of Eller How. Duckett returned to Preston about 1844 and became a reasonably well-known sculptor in his own right. His statue to Sir Robert Peel in Winckley Square, Preston, no doubt his *magnum opus*, is of Kendal Fell limestone. Even after he left Kendal the firm seems to have relied on Duckett for busts, profiles, and figures. A bust signed by him forms the monument in Crosthwaite church to William Pearson (d. 1856), and that to James Thompson (d. 1850) at Clitheroe may well be his, though it bears the name of Francis Webster junior as head of the firm.

The archives of Lambton Castle, Co. Durham, give the best insight into the workings of the marble yard from about 1822 onwards.[22] Ignatius Bonomi had stayed on in the north to complete his father's work at Lambton Hall. In a letter to his employer, the 1st Earl of Durham, in 1822 he wrote: 'we have a manufacturer and importer of marble at Kendal whose concerns are carried out upon the largest scale and his work is both cheaply and superiorily done by the use of machinery. I mention this because you may perhaps be desirous of employing him'. As indeed he was, almost at once. Bonomi must have asked for estimates for two chimneypieces and a matching door architrave for the dining room and George Webster supplied his no. 14 marble for the task.

The two men met at Marton House, near Appleby, which Bonomi was building in 1822-3.[23] In a letter of 24 December 1822 Webster wrote of having

> no idea of the size or massiveness [of the work] or should not have spoken of the Marble No. 14 as one proper to execute the work in, not but that Blocks or Slabs sufficiently large can be procured but that in so large a surface it is impossible to have the marble clear of flaws or soft places containing a clay substance which is not capable of receiving an equal Polish with the other parts besides the nature of the stone or serpentine or green marbles which renders the working of minute members of carving very precarious being so liable to splinter. I consider it almost impossible to execute the carved mouldings in Green Marble: for the Door Architraves should not consider marble No 14 sufficiently strong for 6 ft hollow Bearing unless considered on a back of some other stone as it is not always free from faults almost imperceptible at first working; to which the green is also liable; under these circumstances after having given the Designs every consideration could not with the hopes of giving perfect satisfaction for Mr. Lambton or yourself undertake the execution of them on <u>M.14</u> it being best adapted to such as are of plain or simple forms. Should this kind be adopted will use my endeavours to procure it as free from flaws as possible.

George Webster did his very best to press his reservations home. He went further and suggested either a fine dark-veined dove or the black and gold, no. 11, as alternatives.

The Lambton chimneypieces were evidently of a Greek Doric order since 'the carving of the 5 crests upon the metopes' would be a problem with no. 14. Webster's estimate was for £117 10s. for each one and £44 for the door, dearer than Bonomi had expected. On 16 February 1823 he wrote to Lambton 'the marble mason from Kendal has not yet sent his estimate of the bases of the gallery columns. If the cost of the 4 columns in porphyry scaglioia is to be 150£s without the capitals I am inclined to think the charge high'. In an undated covering letter he sent Lambton 'two letters of Webster the Kendal Master-mason [whose] estimate for the marble bases of the gallery being considerably above the Scagliolists they should be ordered of the latter immediately . . . I have written to Webster and told him . . . but that you might . . . allow him to revise his proposal for the chimney[piece] of the gallery which appears rather high'.

Further light is shed upon the yard in the 1820s. Bonomi built or remodelled many houses in the north-east, much as Webster was doing in the north-west, and it is clear that there was further collaboration with the marble yard. A group of chimneypieces for the Earl of Darlington at Newton Hall, Bedale, was 'finished and awaiting orders as to how to be sent' in 1822 and 'the workman we had at Mr. Shafto's' [Richard Shafto of Whitworth Hall] 'has brought the dimensions of one of Sir Robert Eden's chimneypieces respecting which I wait your command'. The Eden house was Windlestone Hall, Co. Durham, rebuilt between 1822 and 1824. Working for Bonomi was altogether a laborious business, full of the possibility of misunderstandings and made possible only by the use of numbered samples, turnpike roads, and a regular public coach service daily from Kendal to Newcastle.

It was easier for clients who lived nearer to Kendal. The diary of the 2nd Earl of Burlington[24] for the end of the 1830s makes many references to Holker, then being enlarged by Webster. Not only was the architect in constant attendance on site, but the Burlingtons could drive into Kendal for the afternoon and choose chimneypieces from the showrooms at the yard. This they did on 15 November 1839, as the earl wrote in his diary: 'To Kendal, saw over Webster's marble yard and liked some of the Westmorland Marble very much and have ordered several chimneypieces for our new rooms'. No doubt this was common practice for the local gentry and the Kendal merchants could drop in at any time.[25]

In about 1816 Lewis Wyatt designed a virtually new house for Robert Townley-Parker at Cuerden Hall, south of Preston.[26] A letter in the family papers shows that Wyatt ordered a chimneypiece to his own design from the Websters. The letter shows the young George very much in control. He dealt with the order, not his father, as he would do later in the firm's dealings with Bonomi. He proposed a meeting as he would be in Preston the next day.[27]

At Haverthwaite a new vicarage, now demolished, was built in 1842 with no named architect but a mason, William Smith, to make the plans and certify all expenditure including chimneypieces from Webster's yard. One was of Italian vein marble at £8, the other Kendal Dark Imperial at £5.[28]

After the death of their father George Webster and his brother Francis seem to have decided to set up showrooms for marble products in other towns. In 1829 they opened a showroom in Bold Street, Liverpool, one of the city's finest streets and near Thomas Harrison's Lyceum. The ten-year lease ran from 1 October 1829 at £78 a year.[29] There was a house and stabling for the manager, George's cousin John Webster, the son of his father's elder brother, who died in Liverpool and was buried in the Necropolis in 1843. According to Cornelius Nicholson in 1861 they had another showroom in Preston[30] and the distribution of their tablets south of

Manchester offers some support to the claim that there was also one in that town.[31]

The opening of the canal made transport of the firm's output very much easier. Cornelius Nicholson drew attention to the 'works of art, scattered throughout the kingdom, with numerous sepulchral monuments and specimens of architectural skill, which adorn this town and neighbourhood in particular [which] will long bear honourable testimony to his [Francis's] merit'.[32] However, the tiny port of Milnthorpe remained of use, and 'grates paints whiting and marble for George Webster' were arriving there as late as the 1840s.[33]

The Webster firm had competitors in Kendal, some of whom may have been trained in their yard. In 1830 Edward Bayliffe set up as a marble merchant.[34] He may have been the son of Francis's elder sister Sarah, who married a mason, William Bayliffe, in 1799, and could have been trained by his uncle. In business for only a short time, he had a most distinguished client, the King himself. Sir Jeffry Wyatville remodelled Windsor Castle between 1824 and 1840 and ordered two chimneypieces from Bayliffe which were installed in 1831. One was of Kendal Fell limestone for the guardroom; the other, of Italian Dove marble, for St George's Hall. It is not known how Bayliffe attracted the architect's attention.[35]

The Websters, long established, would naturally be piqued. Revenge of sorts came later. George's son Francis wrote to his father in Wiesbaden in the summer of 1836 of the failure of Bayliffe's business. His reply, in a letter to his wife, was vindictive in tone. 'Francis, in his letter to me mentioned Bayliffe is going to give up the Marble Business and that his stock was to be sold shortly. Take not the least notice of the sale or purchase one iota of his goods, let them get out of the scrape as best they can. Our Business must be kept in a small compass – pray inform Francis'.[36] Oddly no work by Bayliffe is known locally and indeed only one other is documented, two chimneypieces for a house in York by Peter Atkinson, one of black Kendal marble, the other of Italian.[37]

There were other marble masons in and around Kendal. Thomas Airey, active c.1815-34, was perhaps related to the John Airey who was Webster's mason at Helme Lodge and the canal head. He was no doubt an apprentice in the yard and his monuments, found as far away as Skipton, are readily confused with the Websters'. His mill was at Park End, Preston Patrick, about five miles south of Kendal, 'where the marble, chiefly brought from Dent, in Yorkshire, is cut and polished by machinery, propelled by water power'.[38] Airey seems to have been in financial trouble by 1834. The mill was to be sold for creditors in that year, and later mill, tools, and marble were to let. By 1849 it was a bobbin mill.[39]

A Kendal ironmonger, Thomas Braithwaite (1773-1822), with premises first in Highgate and then Kirkland, and his sister Margaret manufactured marble chimneypieces at their workshop in Capper Lane, and presumably also supplied the iron fireplaces to complement them. Margaret was said to have been in charge of this part of the business. 'Arrayed in her quaint Quaker dress and cap, with a basket of provisions on her arm . . . she would trudge off to Hawes Wood to attend to the getting of the marble'.[40]

In 1843 another Thomas Airey informed the readers of the *Westmorland Gazette* that he had opened a marble manufactory at Battlebarrow, Appleby, making chimneypieces, headstones, and monuments, but by July 1845 he was at new premises in Blackhall Yard, Kendal. In 1850 he advertised for an apprentice.[41] Meanwhile, Richard Fawcett of Skerton and Scotforth marble mills, just outside Lancaster, 'Begs leave to announce . . . that he now has in his Show Rooms, at Skerton, a number of elegant Marble Chimney Pieces of Various Orders and Designs, composed of British and Foreign Marbles, suitable for Houses of all characters'. He also had a showroom in Preston where an 'S. Fawcett, Builder, &c.' was the agent.[42]

Most interestingly the advertisement tells us that Fawcett had at his showroom 'Design Books [which] may . . . be inspected' before ordering monuments, tombs, and gravestones. Presumably his was not the only yard where this could be done. As the largest yard in a wide area one would expect the Websters to have this facility but if they had it was nowhere mentioned. In 1805 Francis Webster erected a pretty tablet to his first wife in Kirkby Lonsdale church and soon after one of the same design at Bolton-le-Sands to John Park (d. 1819). In Cartmel Priory is another similar tablet to James Newby (d. 1824) but here signed by Fawcett. Had he been trained in Webster's yard, or were both working from the same pattern book? Ryelands Park, Skerton, is a Grecian villa of 1836 without a known architect. It has chimneypieces matched in several Webster houses – Bay Villa, Grange, Thorny Hills, Kendal, Trinity House, Ulverston, Hawksheads House, Bolton-le-Sands. So are they from Webster's or Fawcett's yard?

The chimneypieces in George Webster's early Jacobethan houses, Underley and Eshton, are very classical, their coupled fluted pilaster supports exactly echoing the porticos outside.[43] At Read Hall, Netherside, and Rydal Hall is a design with panelled supports ending in an apse-like motif at both ends and with studs in the resulting spaces. There is another at Quernmore Park, Lancaster, where one of the Websters' favourite designs using a fluted Ionic order also appears.[44] A design with pilaster supports ending in flattened Ionic capitals which was used at Read is seen again in George's own Kendal house and elsewhere.

Many of the firm's marble products, chimneypieces and monuments, were repeated, often far apart. For instance, a tablet at Lowick church, north of Ulverston, was repeated at Garstang, near Preston. Tablets were often signed, a way of advertising, and where a house is known to have been designed by the firm it is safe to assume that the chimneypieces are theirs also.

The earlier monuments and chimneypieces often have panels of colour inset in white or black surrounds. In the north transept of Cartmel Priory is a group of monuments in such a form dating from 1788 to 1809, none of which is signed but which are perhaps by Francis Webster or more probably by his father Robert.

Monuments had their own repertoire of symbols to incorporate in designs and were carved in discrete units for assembly – sarcophagi, lamps, inverted torches, draped urns, wreaths, all denoting ripeness or death. Chimneypieces run from plain slabs to those with geometric insets, supports for shelves, flowers, architectural orders with or without their entablatures, acanthus scrolls, palmettes, and so on. There was little figurative sculpture.

John Bolton of Storrs died before the completion of the school at Bowness which George Webster designed for him. He was buried in a vault outside St Martin's church but his real monument is the tablet with wreathed profile erected at the school by the grateful inhabitants of the village.[45] Another tablet with more than usual interest is that to Jemima Quillinan in Grasmere church. She and her husband Edward came to live in Rydal in 1821, but the following year she was badly burnt and in spite of nursing by the Wordsworth ladies she died. Wordsworth approached Chantrey[46] about a memorial and in the ensuing correspondence there was talk of 'profiles', 'a sketch by Mr Chantrey', a 'model to be sent to Webster', and then 'the Monument to be sent soon from [Chantrey's] warehouse'. And suddenly, in February 1824, it is in place, fixed by a 'competent person sent by Webster'.[47] The tablet is wholly uncharacteristic of Chantrey, to whom one went for busts or figures. The chief ornament here is an ivy wreath much admired by Mary Wordsworth. The tablet is unsigned. So is this a new addition to the Chantrey canon, merely fixed by Webster, or did the firm have some hand in the design?[48]

The memorial in Kendal parish church to George Romney (d. 1802) is a black marble urn with a fluted base and key-pattern rim. It is clearly a version of the freestone urn which Francis Webster placed as a memorial to his father in a pedimented niche on the outside of the south transept of Cartmel Priory in 1799. The Romney example is itself repeated in Beetham church to the Rev. William Hutton of Beetham House who died in 1811.

Many tablets are Grecian in decoration; gothic apparently had less appeal except to certain families, the Musgraves of Eden Hall for one. In spite of Smirke and Webster's stern Grecian house the chancel of the church, seen through Webster's chevroned Norman arch, is a vision of buttresses, crockets, pinnacles, and cusping. There is a less claustrophobic effect at Slaidburn where the Wilkinson family is celebrated in gothic. Examples at Preston (1822) and Lancaster (1832) have exceptionally rich carving.

Webster tablets also appear in relatively distant places. In Northallerton is one to Susannah, wife of Fletcher Rigge of Cark Hall, near Cartmel, who was appointed to the Northern Circuit. His wife found the landscape of Lancashire-over-Sands rough and oppressive and persuaded her husband to exchange it for the Vale of York. When she died her tablet was nevertheless transported to Northallerton in 1828 from the Websters' yard.[49]

In theory George Webster retired completely in 1846, and his brother Francis, who was in charge of the sculpture department, not until 1880, but after 1870 very few tablets are signed by a Webster. In 1873 the Helsington part of the marble yard was bought by Charles Jackson who, to judge from his tablets, had been a Webster apprentice, but he was only there for three years.[50] There was no Webster to carry on the business after Francis retired, though Miles Thompson did sustain a marble business of sorts in a rather quiet way. Two of his nephews carried on an architectural practice in Kendal (John S. Thompson) and a quarrying business employing five men and two boys (Miles S. Thompson).[51] Miles senior was very attentive to his younger brother Robert for whom he designed buildings between Collin Croft and Beast Banks.[52] The Eden Mount quarry at Grange-over-Sands was run by Marcellus Thompson, marble mason and landowner, with seven men and two boys in 1871, and was sold by another Miles Thompson to Albert Nelson of Kendal in 1905.[53]

Slate

Francis Webster was working for the Levens estate at least as early as 1799 when he and William Holme rebuilt the mill at Helsington Laithes for which they were paid £210.[54] They then rented it from the estate as a marble mill at £35 a year. The weir may well have been rebuilt at the same time.[55] From *c*.1805 Webster was working at the hall itself in his role of architect and in 1814 he paid £100 as rent for the Wrangle Gill quarries at the head of Longsleddale where Fulke Greville Howard of Levens was lord of the manor.[56] Payments were still being made in September 1824 but in 1827 the Levens steward, J. B. Toozey, wrote to Howard at his Surrey house about problems at Wrangle Gill, accusing 'those who rented it under lease . . . your architects . . . of villainy towards you in past times (though not of ancient date)'. *Inter alia* they had opened another quarry 'very near . . . and did all they could to destroy yours'.[57] It is probably significant that two years later Wrangle Gill was being worked by Sinkinson, Wilson, & Walker, whereas in the same year the Websters were operating the largest of three quarries at Kirkby Ireleth, north-west of Ulverston, for the Cavendishes of Holker.[58]

In 1750 Bishop Pococke 'went near Kirkby, and there they have a light slate which is esteemed the best in England'.[59] In later years it was the vast chasms left by the extraction of slate which were considered picturesque and capable of producing an authentic *frisson* and they joined other sites visited by tourists. Wrangle Gill, for example, appeared alongside abbeys and castles in T. Rose and T. Allom's *Westmorland, Cumberland, Durham, and Northumberland Illustrated*, of 1832.

The 2nd Earl of Burlington inherited the Holker estates in 1834 and came from London to take possession the following year. Almost at once he decided to rebuild the hall and George Webster claimed in a letter to Thomas Greene at Whittington in the same year that he was 'fully engaged in designing for Lord Burlington' there.[60] However, Burlington was made aware that one of his chief sources of income, the slate quarries at Kirkby Ireleth, were inefficiently run. When the Websters began to operate the largest of the three quarries is not clear but by 1829 they were established as 'slate quarry proprietors' with a depot at the Canal Head in Ulverston and an agent, John Winram.[61]

Lord Burlington kept a diary from January 1838 to which he confided his thoughts and feelings about the quarries[62]. In January he wrote, 'I have two large extra drains for money, the additions at Holker and the new slate works', whatever 'new' means here. In April 1838 he records that he has 'borrowed £3,400 . . . part for the slate works'. On 5 July he spent a day at the quarries, encouraged by methodical business practices and a stock of four hundred tons of roofing slate. After almost a year abroad he noted on 13 June 1839 that he could not expect good news when Curry, his London lawyer, visited him, yet on the 27th he wrote 'slate quarries better'. He was always comforted by progress at the house – 'altogether much pleased' (30 July). By March 1840 he reported 'much change' – whatever that means – but by August the workings were again 'a source of great uneasiness', which by February 1842 had deepened to a 'very anxious concern' and he noted men out of work. On 15 February he was 'almost in despair'. By April he was pondering on having the quarries valued, presumably with the idea of selling, but on 10 May he was hopeful that they would succeed after all. 1842 showed a profit of £650, 1843 of £623, and by 1844 it had risen to £723.[63]

Domestic incidents show the day-to-day business of the quarry as opposed to the negotiations of the principals. In 1840 the parishioners of Cartmel Fell agreed to reslate St Anthony's chapel 'with new slates on the south side from Mr. Webster's quarry at Kirkby and on the north side with the old slate. The work to be done between Haytime and Harvest'.[64] Here the slate is bought directly from the quarry, a practice borne out in 1842 when the Websters begged to inform their friends and the public of 'a regular assortment of the dark Blue Lancashire Slates in the Marble Yard at Kendal . . . at the Canal Head, Ulverston; and at the Quarries, Kirkby Ireleth'.[65]

Soon afterwards letters[66] from Curry and from Lord Burlington himself demonstrate their determination to reorganise the quarries, Burlington always careful of Webster's feelings, Curry blunt and practical. It was the earl who explained the threat from Welsh slates in the great market of south Lancashire (14 December 1844), Curry who felt 'assured that you will assent to Lord Burlington's wishes. I have left all the necessary directions for carrying [the changes] into effect . . . after Christmas unless in the meantime I hear you to forbid it'. He followed this on 19 December by 'Lord Burlington is taking the questions into his own hands'.

More delays followed. Curry was still being 'persuasive' in his letter of 24 April 1845: 'Lord Burlington feels that without an entire change in their management and mode of working he cannot look for any improvement . . . our slates driven out of nearly every market . . . must throw into one concern . . . Coward to manage . . . proper agents for sale', a greater yield with 'considerable profit to divide . . . Lord Burlington will make all the changes and find the capital'. On 1 May the earl wrote to Webster regretting that 'he had been distressed by the proposed changes', repeating the Welsh threat, and trusting that a combination of interests will be to 'great advantage'. He identified the 'discretion to the workmen' as a central reason for poor performance although 'your quarry has maintained its ground'.

All this makes sense only when seen with a 'Memorandum of Agreement' dated 1845. It must have been early that year, certainly before April. It specified that Lord Burlington should have sole management, with no interference, and that he should receive a royalty before there was any division of profits. Such profits would be divided as seven tenths to the earl, one fifth to Webster, and one tenth to Edward Coward who would manage the quarries under the agent. Proper account books were to be kept, the agreement to run for twenty-one months, and George Webster to advise.

Webster continued to write letters which look like delaying tactics. On 22 November 1845 he pointed out to Curry that he did not consider his son Francis to be 'a strong boy', and asked for a receipt for his fifth share of the profits. Four days later a similar letter was sent to Burlington who replied the same day that he thought the terms satisfactory. Also on 26 November another letter went to Curry telling him that he, George, was 'harassed and totally unfit for business'. A day later Curry replied, covering old ground and hoping that 'on further reflection [Webster] will see that the Draft is exactly what was arranged'. On 1 December Curry allowed payment to Webster's agents against his anxieties and on 4 March it was up to Lord Burlington to determine the agreement. After further quibbles, the earl wrote on the 11th that Curry would be at Holker soon 'finally to arrange the quarry matters' and on the same day Edward Coward, who was in an unenviable position, wrote hoping that 'he will be free of anything unpleasant with my friends and neighbours'. In a letter to Webster on 10 October 1845 Curry had revealed that Coward had formed 'a very favourable opinion of Mr Thompson, if he wishes to take up the position at £100 p.a.' What position is not exactly made clear. Thompson continued to design for Burlington into the 1860s.

Among all these irritable letters is a formal notice from Burlington to Messrs Webster dated only 1845: 'I hereby give you notice to quit and deliver up at Christmas'. Whenever it was sent it had its effect early in the new year when Webster gave up the quarry. He was compensated for the loss with £2,000 together with £500 for equipment and good will by agreement, which seems, according to George's own figures, to have swollen to a total of £3,277.

George's decision to take a partner must have arisen out of all these problems. From here on the quarry ceases to be a matter of possession, management, and profit and moves into the history of the firm.

Notes

1. *Universal British Directory*, 1790-91, 476.
2. J. Hodgson, *Topographical and Historical Description of the County of Westmorland*, 1820, 191.

3. At Hawes Wood; '. . . above the village of Sedgwick a vein of marble . . . runs across the river and is worked at both sides': J. Housman, *A Descriptive Tour*, 2nd ed., 1802, 190. In 1799 the editor of the 7th edition of Thomas West's *Guide to the Lakes* described it more particularly: 'A quarry of marble has lately been discovered . . . which produces quite a new variety. It is of different colours beautifully variegated and takes the highest polish. When inlaid in statuary marble it has the best effect and is equal if not superior to any imported from Greece or Italy. Chimneypieces and other ornamental works are made from it and of the common limestone of the country which also polishes very fine in a good stile by Webster & Holme, masons, in Kendal who have erected a mill for sawing and polishing the same'. There are examples of chimneypieces at Sizergh Castle and Dallam Tower: *Lons. Mag.*, ii, 1821, 284.

4. Pigot, *Directory of Cumberland and Westmorland*, 1828, 848.

5. Parson & White, 1829, 638-9; Mannex, 1851, 288; see also *Annals*, 246-7.

6. C. Morris (ed.), *The Journeys of Celia Fiennes*, 1949, 200.

7. J. J. Cartwright (ed.) *The Travels through England of Dr Richard Pococke*, Camden Soc., N.S., xliv, 1889, 4. 'Shambles' are marble slabs for butchers' stalls.

8. B. Tyson, 'Francis Webster and the Market House at Hawkshead, 1790', *Quarto*, Oct. 1993, 8-11.

9. Gunnis, 418.

10. G. Jackson-Stops, 'Cockermouth Castle', *CL*, 18, 25 July 1974.

11. M. H. Port, 'Lowther Hall and Castle', *CW2*, lxxxi, 136 n. 87. In the same accounts Webster and Proctor received £14,560 13s. 4d. 'for masons work done by contract'.

12. CRO K, WD/SE, building accounts.

13. P. N. Wilson, 'Canal Head, Kendal', *CW2*, lxviii, 138-40; CRO, D/Lons/L11/9/35 is the design for a bridge of three arches by Francis Webster, n.d.

14. Wilson, *op. cit.*, 141; CRO, D/Lons/L9/34. The bridge eventually had four arches.

15. P. Barker, 'The Websters' Marble Works in Miller's Close', *Quarto*, Jan. 1991, 10-14; see also J. Satchell, *Kendal's Canal: History, Industry and People*, Kendal Civic Society, 2001.

16. *WG*, 19 June 1819.

17. Curwen, *KK*, 141.

18. CRO K, WSMB/K/Box 4, canal management committee minutes, *sub* 10 June 1819.

19. CRO K, WPC/8; He appears in the 1841 Census living in Beast Banks, still a marble mason, as was his son, another Thomas.

20. *WG*, 29 April 1826.

21. Gunnis, 133. A bust of Vitellio at Abbot Hall, Kendal, has more vitality than any of his contemporary sitters, which suggests that it is a copy of a Roman bust. On 3 May 1834 the *WG* commented on an 'Ecce Homo, a very fine head of Christ in marble from the chisel of Mr. Duckett in the employ of Messrs. Webster' and compared him with 'those who stand higher in the Hall of Fame'.

22. All information on Webster's involvement in Bonomi's houses in north-east England has been kindly contributed by Mr Peter Meadows.

23. Colvin, 138.

24. In Chatsworth Library.

25. J. O'Connor, *Memories of Old Kendal*, 1961, 162, shows a Webster fireplace set in panelling of 1651 in Thomas Sandes's house in Elephant Yard. The same design is found at Bigland Hall.

26. Lewis was cousin to Philip Wyatt who was later dismissed from Conishead Priory.

27. LRO, DDX 1564, building accounts.

28. CRO K, WPR 90/79.

29. CRO K, WD/MM/box 45; Pigot, *Directory of Lancashire*, 1834, 367: 'Webster, George and Francis, Sculptors and Marble Masons'.

30. *Annals*, 246.

31. Chester Cathedral, Holmes Chapel, and Prestbury (Ches.), Ledbury (Heref.), and Market Drayton

(Salop) have been noted.

32. *Annals*, 246.

33. R. K. Bingham, *Chronicles of Milnthorpe*, 1987, 54.

34. J. Somervell, *Water-power Mills of South Westmorland*, 1930, 57.

35. N. Cooper, 'Growth of a Lakeland Town', *CL*, 27 Sept. 1973; W. H. St John Hope, *Windsor Castle*, 1913, ii, 567 and plate cxviii. The fireplace in St George's Hall survived the fire of 1992: A. Nicholson, *Restoration: the Rebuilding of Windsor Castle*, 1997, illus. on 43, 127, 256.

36. CRO K, WDX 1315.

37. Gunnis, 42. A Richard Bayliffe, mason, was at the opening of the Harrington tomb in Cartmel Priory in 1832: J. Stockdale, *Annals of Cartmel*, 1872, 546. A William Bayliff was working at Hutton Roof quarry c.1870: *WG*, 16 Dec. 1916.

38. Parson & White, 1829, 684.

39. *WG*, 14 June 1834; Somervell, *Water-power Mills of South Westmorland*, 80.

40. CRO K, WD/PD, J.S. Campbell (ed.), *The Braithwaite Will Case and the Black Drop*, 1872, 5; Curwen, *KK*, 99, 165.

41. *WG*, 18 Nov. 1843, 5 July 1845, 10 Aug. 1850.

42. *Ibid.*, 23 July 1842. *Soulby's Ulverston Advertiser*, 31 Aug. 1848 advertised: 'G. H. R. Young, Sculpture Carving and Masonry, Fountain St., Ulverston, chimney pieces, tombs, headstones in stock, made to order Busts from life, Marble chimney pieces etc.'. There were some doubtful entrepreneurial forays into the marble business. In 1863 a Kendal grocer, John Matthews, advertised 'a large assortment of Marble Mantelpieces from Manchester for sale at Colwith Bridge, Brathay': *WG*, 26 Sept. 1863.

43. The lower half of the drawing room chimneypiece at Levens Hall may well have influenced Webster. Unlike the overmantel it is severely classical.

44. The house is probably by Harrison of Chester, c.1795-8, then rebuilding Lancaster Castle nearby (1788-99): unsigned designs in LRO. Others of this design at Heaves Lodge, Taitlands, Boarbank, and Derwent House, Cockermouth.

45. Re-erected on the wall of Wordsworth Court, below the site of the school.

46. Sir George Beaumont had commissioned Chantrey to carve a head of Wordsworth, a cast of which had been delivered to Rydal Mount two years earlier: M. Moorman, *William Wordsworth: the Later Years*, 1965, 443.

47. A. Taylor, 'The Wordsworths, the Websters and Chantrey's Quillinan Monument', *Quarto*, July 1994, 12-14. Wordsworth is thought to have been involved in writing the inscription.

48. The only other Chantrey monument in Cumbria is that of 1830 to Edward Hasell at Dacre. However, the *Lons. Mag.*, ii, 1821, 284, reports in an article on Dallam Tower the 'present Mrs. Wilson cut in fine Parian marble' by Chantrey on an 'elegant column of Granite made by Mr. [Francis] Webster'.

49. Stockdale, *Annals of Cartmel*, 466-7.

50. Somervell, *Water-power Mills of South Westmorland*, 68.

51. *WG*, 31 Jan. 1863; Census 1881.

52. J. Satchell, 'The Evolution of Collin Croft', *History of Kendal*, 1998, 27-34; see p. 70.

53. Information from J. Beckett; Census 1871; W. E. Swale, *Grange-over-Sands*, 1969, 52.

54. Levens Hall MSS, box 7, receipt from Lady Andover.

55. Somervell, *Water-power Mills of South Westmorland*, 68.

56. Levens Hall MSS, box 12/1.

57. Surrey R. O., Howard papers, 203/30/128. Whatever the villainies, they coincided with the death of Francis Webster.

58. Parson & White, 1829, 672, 719. For the Kirkby Ireleth quarries, see R. Stanley Geddes, *Burlington Blue-Grey*, 2nd ed., 1991. In 1851 it was said that Wrangle Gill 'was noted about seventy years ago

for its extensive quarries of fine blue slate, but owing to the difficulty of getting to the veins, and the consequent expense of carrying on the works, they have not been wrought for several years': Mannex, 1851, 304.

[59.] Cartwright (ed), *Travels through England of Dr Richard Pococke*, 15.

[60.] LRO, DDGr 6, George Webster to Thomas Greene in Paris, 18 Nov. 1834

[61.] Parson & White, 1829, 728.

[62.] In Chatsworth Library.

[63.] CRO K, WDX 1315. This was not the first time quarrying was threatened. In 1795 Thomas Rigge wrote to Lord George Cavendish at Holker that a tax on slate proposed by William Pitt's government had brought 'almost total stagnation in the trade which your Lordship will find by the returns from Kirkby': LRO, DDCa/22/12.

[64.] J. F. Curwen, 'St Anthony's Chapel, Cartmel Fell', *CW2*, xii, 289.

[65.] *WG*, 23 April 1842.

[66.] CRO K, WDX 1315, in which copies of the whole correspondence were preserved.

VI

Domestic Building in Kendal

This chapter surveys the houses built in Kendal during the Websters' time. Churches, parsonages, schools, and other buildings appear in their respective sections of the gazetteer. Numbers in heavy type refer to the illustrations on pp. 253-61.

TOWN planning received scant attention from the citizens of Kendal. There were no grand schemes, not even a square, a favourite innovation throughout the Georgian period and one adopted by many Cumbrian towns. They were included in the grand plan for Whitehaven in the late seventeenth century. Even small towns laid out squares: Broughton-in-Furness in 1764, Workington about 1775, Burton-in-Kendal about 1810, Kirkby Lonsdale in 1822. In north Lancashire, Lancaster's Dalton Square of 1783 was on a grander scale as was Winckley Square in Preston on its dramatic site. Nor are there any substantial terraces unless one includes the 'Ladies' College' in Stramongate, and New or Lowther Street, which was driven through from Highgate to the river like a gloomy canyon in 1782. Kendal largely retained its medieval plan, a main street running south to north, forking at the top of the town and lined by the characteristic yards at right-angles to it, and one has, in searching for newer work, to look for single or paired houses without any formal setting.

Two books dominate any attempt to dissect the fabric of Kendal in however limited a way, Cornelius Nicholson's *Annals of Kendal*, published in 1832 (2nd ed. 1861), and J. F. Curwen's *Kirkbie-Kendall* of 1900. They follow very different methods, Nicholson choosing areas of interest, the church and so on, and Curwen proceeding geographically, following the streets of the town and noting anything of interest on the way. Nicholson produced his second edition when George Webster and Miles Thompson were still alive and some of his details probably came from them.[1] Curwen, although an architect himself, rarely mentions others of his profession. He had a copy of Nicholson's work which he annotated – another valuable source.[2] Neither Nicholson nor Curwen provides a proper model for a selective survey and both were confused about the domestic work of the Websters and Miles Thompson. Indeed very little of that has documentation; traditional and stylistic attributions must be relied on. To their work may be added *Local Chronology*, a book of excerpts from the *Kendal Mercury* and the *Westmorland Gazette*, issued in 1865. Another valuable work is John Whitwell's *Old Houses of Kendal* of 1866. Again, the author was reluctant to name architects and anticipates Curwen in choosing to follow the pattern of the streets. Kendal is, however, fortunate in having three well-spaced and invaluable town plans, by John Todd (1787), John Wood (1833), and Henry Hoggarth (1853).

The early period

Thomas Webster (fl. 1725-60) has no known work in Kendal, nor is anything known of his son Robert (1726-99) before he left the town for Cark in 1754. He came near when he acted as John Hird's mason at Sizergh Castle in 1773. If Hird designed part of the old Kendal vicarage, then Robert was probably the mason there too. His youngest son Francis came to Kendal about 1787 as William Holme's partner and their first recorded work is the monument on Castle Howe of 1788.[3]

The first houses considered here were largely of pre-Webster construction. The former vicarage in Kirkland had good work of at least two periods. Old illustrations show something of what was lost when part of it was demolished in 1860. The vignette on Todd's map of 1787 shows the west front of the early eighteenth century with its rows of cross-windows and a horizontal oval in the ball-finialled gable.[4]

Facing the river a wing projected, bearing a pediment, the base of which was open, allowing the super-arch of a Venetian window to project into it. This is a motif much used by James Paine (1717-89) but he seems not to have worked in the north-west. However, John Hird did and he not only subscribed to Paine's first volume of *Plans* (1767) but probably reproduced that for St Ives, Bingley, at Ponsonby Hall on the Cumberland coast about 1775. Hird also worked at Hollow Oak, Haverthwaite (1767) and at Sizergh Castle (1772), on both occasions with Robert Webster. Moreover, he was described as 'house-carpenter of Kendal' in 1763-4.[5] The two men may well have introduced this Painesque look to Kendal in what may have been the drawing room added to the vicarage about 1770 for Dr Thomas Symonds (vicar 1745-89). More work was done about 1815 when a library was added, probably by Francis Webster.[6]

Between the vicarage and Kirkland were noisome tanneries until in 1825 'Mr [Francis] Webster architect and William Fisher joiner' were asked to 'survey the tanyards . . . all buildings to be removed and the land to be added to the vicarage'. A faculty of 1826 provided for a garden round a new carriageway from an entrance lodge near Nether Bridge. This latter was in George Webster's finest Jacobean style in spite of Nicholson's description of it as 'in conformity with the classical taste manifested throughout'. The planting was of lime, birch, elm, and acacia.[7] Miles Thompson's schools were built on the site in 1861.

At the other end of Kendal the grandest town house of its period is Stricklandgate House (1776), the seven-bay, three-storey home of the Maudes, 'the largest and best in town'.[8] The designer is unknown but a few Painesque details like the framing of the central window suggest Hird again, and the builder was Francis Webster's future partner William Holme. The staircase is lit by a Venetian window under a super-arch. About 1850 plans to convert the house into a market were drawn up by H. P. Horner of Liverpool, the architect of Wray Castle. However, in 1854 it became the town's museum and the home of the Literary and Scientific Society, until 1914.[9]

Another large town house is Blindbeck House, no. 151 Highgate. It has few architectural pretensions. Long and narrow, turning its windowless end to the street, it is L-shaped, of three storeys and irregular bays, with two bays quoined and rendered. Said to have been rebuilt by Christopher Wilson in 1785,[10] it seems rather the vernacular work of a mason than the designed work of an architect. Perhaps Wilson remodelled rather than reconstructed the whole building. It should be compared with Stricklandgate House of ten years earlier.

Francis Webster

Francis's earliest recorded work in Kendal is the Castle Howe obelisk of 1788. In 1787 the Rev. John Wilson, fellow and bursar of Trinity College, Cambridge,[11] rebuilt Bank House (nos. 112-14 Highgate) so that it is just possible that Francis was the builder. He was not the designer; Wilson brought plans by Robert Furze Brettingham.[12] The house has exceptionally good plasterwork with roundels until recently filled with paintings in the style of Angelica Kauffmann.

Webster may well have designed the Maude/Wilson/Crewdson bank of 1792 (no. 69 Highgate) and if so what is now the Milne Moser offices (no. 100 Highgate). Both are of three bays and three storeys, rendered, with quoins. The ground floor of no. 100 has been altered recently. One of the problems with street houses is that the ground floors are frequently replaced and really telling architectural evidence is therefore lost.

A pair of stately limestone ashlar houses, nos. 134-6 Highgate (**139**), of six bays and three storeys with arched doors and good joinery is traditionally attributed to Francis Webster for John Davison, in or just after 1797.[13] The interiors are akin to those of Shaw End, Patton. No. 117 Highgate of 1811, for Samuel Greenhow[14] is similar in detail, has a good marble chimneypiece, and so may be attributed to Francis. Grandy Nook on Low Fellside is said to have been altered by Francis Webster in 1795.[15]

The New Shambles linking the Market Place and Finkle Street dates from 1803-4.[16] The row of shops on the west side is articulated by broad wooden pilasters with discs in the 'capitals'. They are probably by Francis Webster, with William Fisher as his joiner. No. 99 Stricklandgate was built about 1804 but was partly demolished for the construction of Sandes Avenue after 1886. It has semi-circular twin balconies which are probably original and is attributed to Francis Webster who may also have been responsible for the sash windows and cylindrical chimneys (perhaps replacing original ones) of Black Hall, *c.*1810 and *c.*1820.[17]

No. 41 Highgate is a druggist's shop with a pestle and mortar over the coupled pilastered door. It was by William Fisher, *c.*1812, and was 'considered a shop of exceeding excellence and architectural pretensions'.[18] Was Francis Webster perhaps involved? No. 132 Highgate is similar and probably by either or both men.

Nos. 48-52 Stramongate (**140**), sometimes called the Ladies' College, is a terrace of thirteen bays in all, which must have been designed of a piece, although it is clear from the back that it is not all of one build. John Whitwell gives the 'close of the last century, the one to the north . . . about 1802'.[19] The latter part still has its arched windows set in an arcade and there are tripartite windows over the two entrance arches with their handsome doorcases. There are excellent chimneypieces and Francis Webster was probably the designer. No. 56 nearby is of three storeys with even quoins and survives intact. Inside are good chimneypieces and plasterwork; again, probably by Francis Webster, *c.*1820. No. 58 has recessed windows comparable with Thorny Hills and is probably by Webster.

Union Terrace in Longpool, 'a large range of houses just built' in 1821, is a terrace of thirty-one modest cottages but before the railway was brutally pushed through in 1846-7 it had several more. Wood's map of 1833 shows it as symmetrical, with its inn in the centre. It was built for James Gandy in 1820; a sketch of just such a terrace in Francis Webster's hand suggests that he was the architect.[20]

Further out, off the Shap road, is Mint Cottage built in 1821 (datestone) for the Long family of nearby Mint House. It is of three bays and two storeys, with the ground-floor windows segment-headed and set into similar recesses such as Francis Webster liked. Some plasterwork and a marble fireplace remain inside.[21]

No. 40 Stramongate, a house with a double flight of steps to the entrance was built in 1786. The first Crewdson bank was established there in 1788. In 1824 William Fisher, then working for the Websters at Helme Lodge, repaired a house in Stramongate for the Crewdsons, possibly this one.[22] The house was demolished in 1963 for the construction of Blackhall Road.

At the foot of Lowther Street, no. 31 was described as 'A Genteel House' advertised to be let in October 1826, 'in good Repair, and now in the occupation of Mr. Francis Webster, Architect, who will show the Premises'.[23] It appears to be later than its neighbours but was refaced in 1906 (datestone). In 1826 the owner was Richard Simpson of Far Cross Bank, from whom Francis rented it as his Kendal home and perhaps his office.

There must be other houses by Francis Webster in Kendal. There are plenty of candidates, especially in Highgate, like no. 60, attached to the former Bank of Westmorland, of three bays and three storeys in fine ashlar above the later shop fronts and with bracket eaves, or nos. 73-5, also in ashlar, of five bays and three storeys.

Francis and George Webster

Having finished his work on the construction of the Canal Head Francis Webster had the foresight to see that the ground called Thorny Hills to the north, rough, hilly, and facing the river, was a site where superior houses might be built. The land belonged to Thomas Cookson, a woollen manufacturer, who was persuaded to sell the first plots at 2s. a square yard in January 1823. 'When finished, the Thorney-Hills will be the most elegant promenade in this neighbourhood'. No uniformity was to be imposed, though it might have been felt to be desirable, but arrangements were made for a road, front gardens or 'courts', and pallisades in front of the houses.[24] The row was at first called Kent Terrace. Plots 1 and 2 were sold to Isaac and William Wilson, no. 3 to Samuel Bromley. No. 4 was George Webster's own house, no. 6 Nathaniel Bateman's, bought in 1852 by George's brother Francis.[25] Each purchaser presented his chosen plan (**141**).

The surviving plan for no. 2 is signed 'Kendal 1823' which as usual suggests father and son working together.[26] Of three storeys with arched door and windows set into segmental recesses, no. 1 is referred to as the standard for the masonry of Helme Lodge in the specifications of 1824.[27] George built his own house, no. 4 (**142-4**), in very much the grand manner with a treatment he usually reserved for large country houses; indeed the plasterwork derives from Read Hall and Storrs and is equally grand. Of three bays and two storeys, the ground-floor windows are framed and the door is pedimented on panelled pilasters which also appear on the upper floor. The outside is finished in stucco, unlike the ashlar of the other houses.

No. 5, built for George Hinde, has a tripartite window on the ground floor and no. 6 has a window in a recess flanked by arched doors. No. 7 is similar with later alterations. The plot of no. 8 was still empty on Wood's plan of 1833 with the name Thompson across it, but the house built on it in 1838 was designed by George Webster for George Gibson, woollen manufacturer[28] and it was the most ambitious of all. Of three bays with a central door, it is symmetrical; the centre bay projects and the façade is flanked by pilasters. The ground-floor windows are tripartite and there are deep bracket eaves. No. 9 has the lower windows set in shallow arches. Nos. 10-11 are a pair with broad angle pilasters and canted bays; 11a is a later replica. No. 12, of three bays, has interior reeded doorcases with angle roundels. From no. 14 there is a gradual loss of quality until Thorny Hills merges into Castle Crescent.

Aynam Lodge, which relates to the earliest houses in the terrace, was built for Thomas Harrison, surgeon, who bought the land in 1825. His consulting room, in the south-west wing, was approached along a verandah from a rear entrance.[29] The house is of three bays with lower wings, of limestone ashlar but with yellow freestone dressings. The interior has good chimneypieces and plasterwork based on Storrs Hall. Beezon Lodge, for Richard Rawes, 1825,[30] is a smaller version and also has good interiors and chimneypieces.

The Canal Committee had some idea of selling building plots itself. At its meeting on 5 March 1821 Francis Webster presented plans for 'a Range of Houses' to be built on the waste ground between Miller Bridge and Aynam Bridge and was asked to take levels of the ground and make specifications. A year later, on 4 March 1822, it was 'resolved that Mr F. Webster mark out the ground'. On 15 March he placed a plan of the site before the committee which decided that 'this plot shall be offered for sale . . . Proposals and Plans of Buildings intended to be erected . . . will be received by the Corporation . . . further particulars may be seen by applying at Mr Webster's Office, Millers Close'. There is no indication that any of the land was sold at this time,[31] but Aynam Lodge may have been built on part of it.

Other Kendal buildings may be joint designs by father and son. No. 8 Highgate (formerly no. 12) was a handsome shop, more architectural than those noted earlier, as is the row of overhung buildings, nos. 13-17 Stricklandgate, renovated in 1822-3 for Thomas Miller of which Farrer's, no. 13 (**145**), remains unchanged and was said to have been 'a sensation' at the time.[32] Again, the work probably involved both the Websters and William Fisher.

George Webster

No. 23 Stricklandgate, designed for Wilson Marriot in 1826, 'one of the best in the town'[33] is of hammered limestone with angle pilasters and a segmentally arcaded ground floor, recently and pointlessly destroyed. It clearly belongs with the group that includes Sand Aire House and Helme Lodge and can be attributed to George Webster. Almost opposite is another five-bay ashlar building with angle pilasters and a destroyed ground floor, probably by George. Relating to these two is a handsome shop, no. 163 Highgate (**146**), with the door on the boldly projecting curved corner. It has panelled pilasters coupled for the door with wreaths in the course and bracket eaves.

Sand Aire House at the bottom of Stramongate is the finest classical house in Kendal (**148-9**). It was built for the wine merchant Daniel Harrison in 1827-8, in ashlar limestone, of three bays with two more in a slight projection and angle pilasters. The ground floor windows are set into a shallow arcade. The entrance is a three-bay porch of the Greek Doric order *in antis*, surprisingly of wood painted to resemble stone. The interior is perfectly preserved with excellent chimneypieces and plasterwork very like that at Rigmaden and the designer was George Webster who had the working drawings at Eller How in 1864.[34] The building has twice been enlarged, sensitively about 1926, rather less so in 1969-70. In 2000 the whole complex was sold for development into flats.

The trio of shops in Highgate, nos. 24-8 (**147**), was altered in 1828 when it was given the curved windows between three doors for which a design from Storrs Hall was again used, suggesting George Webster as its architect.[35] Over the doors there were originally little timber pediments supported by scrolls which acted as signboards, and in front, to door height, there was a pentice supported on pillars.[36]

Town View at the north end of Stricklandgate is a terrace of three houses displaying a full Webster repertory of design motifs but has been attributed to John Richardson, 1831-2.[37] No. 172 Highgate has a plain front to the street but the entrance in the yard is of sturdy Greek Doric design. There is good joinery behind it and there can be no doubt that it is by George Webster, perhaps about 1830.

In 1830 part of the marble works at the Canal Head was converted to a house, now no. 3 Bridge Street, for George's brother Francis, who was in charge there. A new doorway was inserted and the design must have been made by George.[38]

Nos. 34-6 Kirkland were rebuilt for John Yeates as what John Whitwell called 'a modern built house in the Elizabethan style'.[39] The first floor timbering may well have been inspired by spinning galleries. There is a projecting gable with barge boards and a reset datestone, Y 1563. The windows were mullioned with drip-moulds and some nineteenth-century ironwork survives over the door. The work is attributed to George Webster about 1840. The Yeates family and the Websters were connected.

At the north end of Stricklandgate is the Old House, the larger part of which was originally a mill of three floors converted by the Wakefields into a house with a pretty door of about 1810. 'Several great improvements' at the north end of the house were made after the death of Jacob Wakefield by his daughters, c.1844.[40] Classical, and on a larger scale than the old building, the extension has a large segment-headed window to the street which lights a grand apsidal room with characteristic George Webster plaster- and timberwork. Miles Thompson designed a coach house and stable in 1865.[41]

High on Kendal Fell is a wholly irregular *cottage orné*, Cliffside Cottage, with a porch of cyclopean limestone blocks, barge-boarded gables, and mullioned windows. It was built between 1833 and 1853, probably c.1845, and Francis Webster, George's brother, lived there in 1865.[42]

Two further works by George Webster are indicated in the lists of the plans and drawings at Eller How in 1864. There were elevations and working drawings for a farm at Murley Moss for Alderman Thompson (now Murley Moss House, with a datestone of 1844), and plans for cottages in the Angel Inn Yard.[43]

George Webster and Miles Thompson

As with Francis and George Webster in the early 1820s it is impossible to separate the work of George in the late 1840s and 1850s from that of Miles Thompson. One must assume that Miles must have done a great deal of, if not all, the work after George retired in 1846. He certainly continued to work in the styles that he was familiar with from his twenty years as draughtsman to the firm.

The last building on Summer Hill shown on Hoggarth's map of 1853, now nos. 38-40 Greenside, a fine pair of semi-detached houses with canted bays and a combined entrance, may be by Thompson alone. No. 42, built after 1853, has a doorway and other details which also suggest that he was the architect. However, the designs for alterations to a house and shop in the Market Place at the corner of the New Shambles for Allan Birkett were signed by Thompson & Webster and dated 1853.[44]

In 1787 Monument House, Beast Banks, was a dissenters' meeting house. By 1833 it was Bank House and in 1853 Monument House. It was bought by Edward Burton, auctioneer,[45] and remodelled about 1860 by Miles Thompson into a picturesque classical composition. The open court to the street was flanked by Italianate pavilions derived from the designs for the hall at Coniston Cold, NY, made by Webster & Thompson in 1841 and 1849. To the house he added an open porch carrying a balcony between oriels and false wings surmounted by a lion and a unicorn, since removed.[46]

Collin Croft, the yard running from Highgate to Beast Banks, has buildings at the top designed by Miles Thompson for his brother Robert and marked by a three-light Italianate window. Nearby on Beast Banks is a house by John S. Thompson with a bay window rising into a gable. Until 1998 the figure of an architect, thought to have been Miles Thompson himself, stood on the apex. It was blown down in a storm but a copy has been replaced by the Kendal Civic Society.[47]

At the end of Stramongate, now nos. 82-8, near the bridge, Thompson designed a large shop in 1863, Italianate, with paired arched windows, for J. Harrison, Kendal's leading grocer.[48] Above Kendal to the west soars Cliffside Terrace, not quite regular in either height or design. Much of the detail is solid plain Websterian and several of the houses are probably by Thompson, perhaps nos. 3 and 9. All were built between 1851 and 1853 except for no. 1 Chapel View, another matter altogether. It was not designed until 1866, for Thomas Garnett by Miles Thompson, whose designs show the house much as built, a towered Italian villa with a varied plan and outline. Many of the windows and the door are tripartite, and the quoining and rustication are especially telling on the north elevation.[49]

Much of no. 29 Lowther Street is probably of the same date as the street itself, c.1782. It is the 'large house, with the bold flight of steps at the south-east corner' built for a Captain Haygarth.[50] The steps are set into the building behind a rusticated arch. The superimposed dining and drawing rooms with their heavily moulded chimneypieces and plasterwork are of a type seen in George Webster's house on Thorny Hills and elsewhere. They were refurbished for Samuel Gawith, the snuff-manufacturer, who lived there between about 1842 until his death in 1865. This will be the work of Thompson who had his office in the street.[51]

He also had a house-cum-office at the Lound where he bought the site of the iron foundry there about 1848.[52] By 1853 he owned land on either side of Garden Street up to the canal where there was a wharf and a small rustic house. He added a larger block to this, tall and narrow, the entrance bay projecting slightly. Other members of the family lived in cottages nearby as the census of 1881 indicates. Several short terraces around Kendal Green are also by Thompson, including nos. 14-16 Horncop Lane, built in 1863.[53]

In Highgate, nos. 104-6 are two houses for which there are elevations made in 1868, the year of his death, by Thompson for R. F. Thompson, where he takes advantage of the sudden broadening of the street[54]. Some of this work is still visible, but the building was later extended by the addition of a large square bay and an oriel window to Highgate. The upper room in the bay has luscious plasterwork. Presumably all this is due to John Thompson in 1881.[55]

The Villa

Joseph Gwilt's definition of a villa in 1842, the period of many of the houses considered here, was 'a country-house for the residence of opulent persons' and he cited bankers and merchants as such.[56] Perhaps Aynam and Beezon Lodges and Monument House should be included here? Sand Aire House, however, was from the beginning a place of business as well as a residence.

Aikrigg End (**150**) is a small villa developed out of a cottage facing the Burneside road which was advertised to be let by William Geldert in 1819.[57] A George Geldert was living there in 1849 when he owned Humphrey Head near Cartmel with its summerhouse and holy well.[58] He seems still to have been there in 1861 when he subscribed to Nicholson's *Annals of Kendal*. He probably added the east wing in the 1840s as it appears on Hoggarth's map of 1853. The entrance was moved to the new work and made tripartite and there is a canted bay window. Thompson was probably the architect.

Spital (**151**), on the site of the medieval St Leonard's hospital, is a three-bay Elizabethan-style farmhouse, built for the Earl of Lonsdale in 1836,[59] probably to the designs of George Webster. Fowl Ing, built for John Gough about 1812,[60] is distinguished by its fine iron verandah behind which is a plain three-bay front. Inside there are good cornices and marble chimneypieces. Francis Webster was probably Gough's architect.

Castle Green, Sedbergh Road, was built in 1848 (datestone) for Thomas Bindloss, twice mayor of Kendal and an ironmonger. The original house was of three bays, the two outer ones gabled with barge-boards, the centre recessed. It had cross windows above and there was a delicate iron balcony; to the north a wing with an Italianate window, and further on a large greenhouse. The designer was almost certainly Miles Thompson, perhaps still with George Webster. The house was much altered in 1896, for J. H. Jeffreys by Stephen Shaw, and again on conversion to offices in the 1950s and to an hotel in the 1990s.[61]

Singleton Park was built for the town clerk of Kendal, Thomas Harrison of Sand Aire House, in 1848-9 (datestones). It essentially repeats the front of Castle Green – two gabled projections, a recessed centre, and bay windows linked by a wooden verandah. The large central hall has the staircase climbing the outer walls. The house is by George Webster who had two working drawings at Eller How in 1864; the lodge and gates of 1857 were probably by Thompson, who certainly designed a pair of cottages in 1863.[62]

Broom Close (**152**), perhaps built for James Bousfield, who was living there in 1861 when he subscribed to Nicholson's *Annals,* and demolished in 1997, was clearly a Webster/Thompson Italianate villa with a tower entrance with arched windows and a pyramid roof. It bore a strong resemblance to St Andrews, Bowness (1843), which suggests a date of *c.*1845.[63]

Birklands (**153**)was built for E. W. Wakefield by George Webster in 1831-2 and is one of the more eccentric and elaborate of his houses. It is Jacobethan and in ashlar, but everywhere there are gables and gables branching from gables, rendered and slate-hung. The chimneys and dormer windows clearly derive from his plans for Wordsworth's house. The windows are mullioned and transomed, there is a glazed verandah, and inside good chimneypieces and plasterwork.[64]

High Park, Oxenholme, was built about 1835 for William Wilson, the fourth son of Christopher Wilson of Abbot Hall and Rigmaden, of freestone with a central canted bay and broad eaves. There can be no doubt that it was by George Webster following the success of Rigmaden which Wilson later inherited. In 1861 he added wings to the designs of Miles Thompson, in a heavy Italianate style.[65]

Notes

[1.] He referred to George Webster as 'our friend': *Annals*, 12.

[2.] In CRO K.

[3.] See above, pp. 7-8.

[4.] A design of *c.*1715 for the school at Sedbergh engraved by J. Kip is similar.

[5.] Colvin, 488-9.

[6] *Annals*, 159.

[7.] CRO K, WDRC/10; Leeds City Archives, RD/AF/2/2/47; *Annals*, 160; illus. in *Then and Now*, i, 1984, 6.

[8.] Whitwell, 19; see above, p. 7.

[9.] CRO K, WD/K/182; Curwen, *KK*, 331; R. K. Bingham, *Kendal, A Social History*, 1995, 415.

[10.] J. Satchell and O. Wilson, *Christopher Wilson of Kendal*, 1988, 43, 55. The rainwater heads are initialled C. and M. W.

[11.] John Wilson, *c.*1748-91, son of Isaac Wilson of Lambrigg, held various livings *in absentia*, including Helsington, 1770-81. The house was named from the Cross Bank on which it stood. For Wilson's purchase, see CRO K, WD/AG/box 117, T20-21.

[12.] Curwen, *KK*, 159; Whitwell, 11; plans in CRO K, WD/AG/box 117. The upper floors were converted to become the Conservative Club by John Thompson in 1881: CRO K, WSMB/K/Bk 4/568. Before that it was John Whitwell's own house: Curwen, *op. cit.*, 145.

[13.] Whitwell, 9. Curwen, *KK*, 150 gives 1797 as the date of purchase by Davison.

[14.] Curwen, *KK*, 110.

[15.] G. Williams, *Life on Old Fellside*, 1991, 53; it was restored by John Fisher in 1864: Curwen, *KK*, 314.

[16.] *Annals*, 292.

[17.] A. Nicholls, 'The Story of Sandes Avenue', T/S, 2000, 3, 53-4, although it is ambiguous about where the railings came from; the illus. on 3 clearly indicates two on the part of the house that remains; Curwen, *KK*, 351-2 (no. 99), 346 (Black Hall).

18. Whitwell, 15.

19. *Ibid.*, 26. The Ladies' College was apparently the girls' section of the Friends' School, a little further down the road: information from Dr John Satchell.

20. *Lons. Mag.*, ii, 1821, 405; CRO K, WD/RG (acc.303), T1-5; *ibid.*, WDX 362, T1-4.

21. Dept. of Environment listings.

22. Whitwell, 26; Curwen, *KK*, 398-9; CRO K, WD/Cr/4/203/11; *WG*, 23 Jan.2001.

23. *WG*, 21 Oct.1826.

24. *Ibid.*, 11 Jan. 1823.

25. *The Websters of Kendal*, no. 44. The plans for no. 4 and working drawings for another house were at Eller How in 1864: see p. 342. George bought his plot on 13 Feb.1823: CRO K, WD/MM/box 113, trust account book.

26. CRO K, WD/AG, loose plan.

27. *Ibid.*, WD/Cr/4/, mason's specification.

28. *Ibid.*, WD/MG.

29. Information from Michael Bottomley; a document at the house records the purchase of the land.

30. *WG*, 23 Jan.1981.

31. CRO K, WSMB/K/Box 4, canal management committee minutes; P. Barker, 'The Websters' Marble Works in Miller's Close', *Quarto*, Jan.1991, 10-14.

32. Whitwell, 16. Once the Wagon and Horses inn: *A Walk round Kendal*, Kendal Civic Society, n.d., no. 16.

33. *Ibid.*, 17.

34. Curwen, *KK*, 406; see p. 342.

35. *Ibid.*, 76; *Annals*, 123-4..

36. Illus. in Curwen, *KK*, 76, and in J. Sharp, *Kendal. A Photographic Record*, 1974, 23. Their appearance before 1828 was recorded from memory by John Richardson in 1845: Curwen, *op.cit.*, 31.

37. *Annals*, 298.

38. J. Satchell, *Kendal's Canal: History, Industry and People*, Kendal Civic Society, 2000, 26.

39. Whitwell, 8.

40. *Ibid.*, 22-3; Curwen, *KK*, 335.

41. CRO K, WSMB/K/Bk 1/114.

42. Wood's map, 1833; Hoggarth's map, 1853.

43. See p. 342. For Alderman William Thompson, who bought the Underley estate in 1840, see Boumphrey and Hudleston, 293.

44. CRO K, WSMB/K/ Bk 1.

45. *WG*, 12 Jan.1850. It was also known as Hill House: Mannex, 1851, 319.

46. Todd's map, 1787; Wood's map, 1833; Hoggarth's map, 1853; Curwen, *KK*, 84.

47. J. Satchell, 'The evolution of Collin Croft', *History of Kendal*, 1998, 29-30, 33. Thompson's connection with the yard dated from 1842 when he bought what is now nos. 14-16 from his father John: information from Dr John Satchell. His own house was in the yard before he moved to the Lound: e.g. Mannex, 1851, 318.

48. CRO K, WSMB/K/Bk 1/71; Curwen, *KK*, 409. The original timber pilasters to the windows were removed in the 1970s: information from Michael Bottomley.

49. *Annals*, 149; CRO K, WSMB/K/Bk 2/177.

50. Curwen, *KK*, 381.

51. Information from Michael Bottomley. Thompson's office was no. 8 Lowther St and both Brade and J. S. Thompson succeeded him there until the property was replaced by an extension to the Town Hall in the late 1890s: information from Dr John Satchell.

52. *WG*, 29 Jan., 29 April 1848; but see Satchell, *Kendal's Canal*, 87. The house was left to his brother Marcellus: CRO K, WDX 708/T46.

53. CRO K, WSMB/K/Bk 1/76.

54. *Ibid.*, Bk 2/218.

55. *Ibid.*, Bk 4/567.

56. J. Gwilt, *An Encyclopaedia of Architecture*, 2nd ed., 1867, 1274.

57. *WG*, 29 Aug.1819.

58. *Sketches of Grange*, 1850, 41-2.

59. Whitwell, 28; *Annals*, 81. Earlier farms for the Lowther estate, including Spital, Lupton, the home of Janet Webster's family, are examined in P. Messenger, 'Lowther Farmstead Plans', *CW2*, 1975, 327-51.

60. Whitwell, 28; *Annals*, 81. It was completed by 1814: CRO K, WD/K/219-20.

61. C. R. Hudleston and R. S. Boumphrey, *Cumberland Families and Heraldry*, 1987, 384; CRO K, WDB25/85.

62. See p. 342; Curwen, *KK*, 406; CRO K, WSMB/K/Bk 1/74.

63. Worked stone from Broom Close has been built up into 'features' in the housing estate opposite the cricket ground in Parkside Road: information from John Marsh.

64. *Annals*, 298.

65. CRO K, WSMB/K/Bk 1/44.

VII

The Journeys of George Webster for 'Pleasure and Health' (1828-58)

IN the eighteenth and nineteenth centuries it was quite usual for newly-trained architects to travel abroad before they settled to a practice, particularly if they could find a patron. Their destination was Italy and, in due course, Greece as well – and France was on the way; their objective to study classical architecture at source and to return with notebooks full of sketches and heads full of new ideas.

George Webster pursued a similar course, or rather courses, the difference being that his journeys began in mid-life and his objectives were at least nominally 'health and pleasure'. Nonetheless they were planned to take in the same classical sites. Many of his finest designs were already built, although he did acquire a taste for towered Italian villas. The extent of his travels was exceptional for an early nineteenth-century provincial architect: not just Italy, Germany, and France, but Austria, Portugal, Spain, Gibraltar, Greece, Egypt, and the Holy Land.

We know of these journeys, which took Webster from home for up to three and a half months in one year, through his letters to his wife Eleanor,[1] for he always travelled alone. Unfortunately we do not have Eleanor's half of the correspondence. Almost from the start bulletins on his health are prominent; symptoms are described but no specific illness is ever mentioned. Eleanor did not need to be told. He carried medication, 'strong pills' from Dr Longmire,[2] wherever he went.

The content of the letters is that of an informed traveller rather than a professional architect – for Eleanor's benefit no doubt. Naturally a 'marble man', he visited quarries such as those at Carrara. He was excited and impressed by the great Doric columns of Paestum, which he had been using in his designs for years, and was enthusiastic about Rome, at least as much for papal ceremonial as for architecture.

There are commonplace complaints – undrinkable wine, uneatable food, beds, diligences, heat, fleas, roads, and so on; grumbles about his fellow travellers and caustic and witty comments on the behaviour of many, particularly on board ship. Scenery constantly impressed him, and his envy of the variety of fruit and flowers reveals the dedicated gardener. The stream of instructions for the gardeners at Eller How, about training creepers, cleaning the lake, doctoring trees to keep paths open, is a constant thread running through the letters.

Other home thoughts obtruded upon him: his son Frank's progress at school – he exhorts him to study and to practise drawing at home; an outrageous business move his brother Francis seems to have made; and business in general, stimulated by the English papers he saw. Miles Thompson's inferred part in all this is extraordinary. In theory his brother would have been in charge, but he was not an architect, and George's thought that the firm was 'carrying' Francis kept surfacing. Even if one supposes that George designed in the winter months and left what he called 'the constructive part' to Thompson in the spring and summer, it was a huge burden for a man who was still only the chief draughtsman. The partnership, when it came in 1845, was long overdue.

Not all Webster's journeys are documented by letters. He had been to Belgium as early as 1828 as a remark in a letter from his journey there in 1846 indicates, but not one letter from 1828 survives. Perhaps the idea of keeping them had not yet occurred to anyone. One sign of a journey is the existence of a collection of engravings. There is such a group from the West Country, around Bristol, but nothing more from England.

The letters are pasted into three albums. Some are clearly missing; there are none from Florence, for example. Others are so damaged as to make them illegible. They are not all in the right order, not even in the right year. Webster speaks of the White Sea and Kronstadt when near Constantinople. Engravings of the Black Sea ports of Varna and Odessa and of the Crimea make one wonder if he went there, but no letters survive and he may have picked them up in Constantinople. Did he extend his journey in 1841 beyond Munich to Nuremburg and Marienbad as engravings if not letters suggest?

As arranged here, the letters do make one kind of sense. Their value is not so much for themselves but for the only real evidence we have of George Webster the man, our only means of standing close to a human being who also happened to be an architect.

Of Webster's visit to Ireland about 1830 only a fragment of a letter survives, but there are references to Killarney in letters from later journeys in 1836 and 1841. The fragment was written in the Victoria Hotel, Killarney, and dated 9 December, but it lacks the year. It must have been before 1836 and after his father's death. It tells us that he had kissed the Blarney Stone and been to Cork. The weather is such that it 'does not allow fair comparison with home'.

He was able, however, to express his feelings about some action of his brother's at home: 'with all the changes of scenery I cannot get out of my head what has happened in Kendal, sleeping or awake. The event is first and foremost in my imagination. To be driven first from taking an active part in the business, secondly from the Business itself which I can safely say was one of . . . [here it becomes partially illegible] . . . bringing to notice or perfection and this by a younger Brother holding only 1/3 of the concern . . . quite sure my nerves have got a shake . . .' [here the letter crumbles away]. It rather looks as though the junior partner had exceeded his powers without any consultation and brought about a crisis. Nominally he was in charge of the sculpture department, but there are signs that George at least attempted to keep control here too. The practice shows no sign of falling away in the 1830s. Had Francis sprung the 'event' when George was away in Ireland? Perhaps it was soon after their father's death before the division of responsibilities had settled down. Subsequently Francis seems to have had a minor role to George's major one.

In the early spring of 1836 Webster must have written to several friends and patrons about travel in Italy – what he should see, where he should go, and possibly suggesting commissions. Those whose replies survive certainly provided commissions. None of them complained that he would not be able to supervise the work that he had planned for them. They no doubt knew Thompson as well as they did Webster and trusted him in the same way. Eshton Hall was still unfinished, twelve years after its inception, if only in the matter of driveways and planting. Matthew Wilson wrote on 20 March 1836 recommending Galignani's library in Paris where 'you will find every information', in particular 'an Historical Essay on Architecture by the late Thomas Hope published by Murray (in two volumes, 1835) – if you have not got it already it is well worth room'. Wilson was very up-to-date in his reading. Hope's forte was decoration and furniture and when it came to architecture he employed William Atkinson to execute his ideas, the same Atkinson who may have been Webster's tutor. Wilson concluded, 'if we do not meet until you are Italianised, believe me, yours truly, Matthew Wilson' and added an invitation to dine at Great Cumberland Street on 5 April.

John Taylor of Moreton Hall wrote on 9 March that he was 'delighted with your intended tour – my mother joins me in our best respects to Mrs Webster and you'. The Rev. John Maude,[3] brother of George's close friend Thomas Holme Maude of Kendal, gave advice on diligences, luggage allowances, hotels, and so on, tells him that another unnamed brother will be at the Palazzo Mastiani in Leghorn, and suggests that in Rome his name should be given to 'young Frantz' at the Frantz Hotel in order to secure Webster a room. He gives a route from Geneva to Rome and mentions 'a very pretty shop for alabasters' in Florence. Del Vecchio in Naples is good for 'imitation Etruscan vases and little figures . . . harp strings are very good . . . and . . . gold and silver filigree work is in great perfection' in Geneva.

Richard Sparling Berry of Bolton Lodge, Bolton-le-Sands, and Elm Grove, Caton, wrote to Webster on 26 March about work going on, probably at both houses, and then asked his architect to 'get a worthy edition of Palladio, I will gladly put £100 into your hands if you will accept the commission'. Vicenza is a 'glorious feast . . . but many of his finest things are almost smothered by vile squalid houses'. Other 'curious things' would be welcome, perhaps to include 'a bronze group for the marble table from Leghorn'.

The vicar of Kirkby Lonsdale, J. H. Fisher, wrote cordially on 5 April on travel, hotels, sites of interest, and cheap marble, and his own vicar at Lindale, James

Statter, was concerned entirely about Webster's health with hopes that the 'bland airs of a southern climate, purer as they are', would prove beneficial.

Webster carried with him a card from 'old Lady Musgrave' of Eden Hall which had written on the back 'Guisseppe Gaggini, Sculptor and Marble Dealer, Genoa', and a list of mainly English sculptors in Rome: Wyatt (Richard James Wyatt who spent most of his life there); Gibson (John, who trained in Liverpool but spent much of his career in Rome); Gott (Joseph, of Leeds but much in Rome after 1824), and the Italian, Tadolini.

Overland to France, Italy, and Germany, 1836

On 9 April, from the Tavistock Hotel, London, George wrote to his wife: 'on return [I] must endeavour to keep my mind much more free of the anxiety and Cares of Business'. Already he feels so improved that he 'cannot but attribute the chief cause of the bilious attacks to the confines of leaning on a desk'. Then he brings up business, asking that his attorney Moser[4] should complete the sale of the Star as delay has left him 'in a pretty predicament'.

Reaching Rouen he 'is in raptures at the old buildings', but was tired of Paris on the 22nd, having 'severe bleeding and pain in the side'. From Chalons his journey to Marseilles was by river, and then by sea to Leghorn. Moser was again irritating him by bungling the collection of rents from George's property in Liverpool.[5] From Naples he visited Pompeii and Herculaneum and climbed Vesuvius. He crossed desolate country to spend two and a half days at Paestum inspecting 'the Ruins of the most Perfect Temples of Greek origin that now exist'. In Rome he met an acquaintance from England, a Mr Woodcock, who warned him of cholera in Venice and suggested the lakes as an alternative. George hopes 'that Miles [Thompson] has been from home and got most of the outstanding debts collected' and that his brother Francis 'feels no great want of me and that he is making money <u>fast</u>'.

From Rome he probably went directly to Florence, but at this point letters are missing. We know he was there for he parted from John Knowles[6] at Florence, as he wrote from Milan on 17 June. After Pisa and Lucca he was in Leghorn again on 6 June, planning a stay of a week, determined to know all about Carrara. At the quarries he noted that they were in mountains 'higher than Skiddaw' and so precipitous that visitors were 'let down by ropes from rock to rock, exposed to the burning sun'. 'The difficulty of getting and transporting the marble is much greater than I could have formed any idea of', no doubt comparing it with the quarries in Garsdale or at Hawes Bridge. He found the Italians 'entirely without system, working the same now as 100 years ago'.

Then he moved north again, via Milan to the lakes, Lugano, Como, and Maggiore, but looked forward to being at Eller How – 'the gardens here are nothing'. Five hundred men were repairing the Simplon as he passed through on the way to Chamonix to visit the Mer de Glace and climb halfway up Mont Blanc. Lake

Geneva disappointed him, as did Voltaire's house at Ferney. He arrived in Baden-Baden by way of Lausanne, Berne, and Basle where he drank the 'waters of this most fashionable Watering Place for the English, especially the younger ones, and enjoying good health, old Dowagers in most public places gambling to an extent I had no conception of'. Here he met John Maude, who was 'quite astonished at what I have seen'. They explored the town together. 'J. Knowles will now be settled down to business', he exclaims in his next letter, meaning perhaps the building of Heysham Tower, though that was not his work.

Eleanor must have told him that Longlands near Cartmel was to be occupied by one of the Machells who is to marry Miss Rigby[7] which led him to muse that there is 'no place like England or its climate'. 'Jno Maude and I left the gay and unholy scenes of B-B for Mannheim by way of Carlsruhe, a most beautiful city, and Heidelberg'. At Weisbaden he had news from home that a Kendal rival in the marble business, probably his kinsman Edward Bayliffe, had been forced to sell up his business. George was very angry and was insistent that Eleanor and Francis should 'take not the least notice of the sale . . . let them get out of the scrape as best they can'.[8]

Embarking at Mainz he continued down the Rhine and reached London on 21 July where he got news of his sister Margaret's illness. Francis was told that any cases arriving from Liverpool should not be touched. They perhaps contained his commissioned purchases as well as some of the antiquities which would later appear in his will. On 26 July he was shocked to hear that Margaret had died. He set off for home.

Overland to France, Italy, Sicily, and Germany, 1841

Webster's journey in 1841 began in the same way. Again, he crosses to France, reaching Paris on 17 May and finding the city 'much improved' in five years. Napoleon's coffin is lying in state until his tomb, 'a gorgeous affair', is ready. From Lyons he asks that Miles Thompson should see the letter and 'tell young Gandy of Heaves that I have had the works he asked me to get for him at Galignani's packed up to see if they would squeeze into my boxes but to no purpose . . . The bookseller further said I would have great difficulty in getting them through Italy and Austria . . . had I returned via Paris I would have managed it'.

He used the Rhone again, but this time to see the antiquities at Nîmes and Arles. He asks that Eleanor have 'the lower ponds' at Eller How cleaned out and 'if the Church Commissioners should pay any money in my absence it should be paid into the bank'. The Commissioners were established to assist in the building of new churches; this payment would be for St George's, Kendal, completed in 1844, which had a grant of £878. When he reached Marseilles he found that his boat had left and so was able to enjoy hot sea-water baths as he waited.

Naples (10 June) was *en fête* for the king's birthday. Everything was illuminated and George enjoyed the opera at San Carlo in the presence of the royal family. Vesuvius was climbed again and he then followed the coast, crossing to Messina to explore Sicily where he visited Palermo, Stromboli, and Lipari. The cities 'were once fine and the country is extremely beautiful . . . Eller How uppermost in my thoughts and all comparisons drawn from it and I assure you no disparagements of its Beauties of Seclusion . . . A kiss to all the children from Papa'.

His Rome letter of 19 June describes the end of his Naples visit and a 'coastal trip to Capri, Amalfi and Castelmare not leaving out my favourite Pompeii'. He stays in Rome for the 'ceremonies in St Peter's when the saint's tomb is illuminated for the last days of Corpus Domini when the Pope walks in procession . . . also St John Lateran for St John's Day', the Pope officiating. 'I hear no good news from England as regards trade - slate will be dull as possible – hope Miles in my absence exerts himself both in getting of orders and money – when he takes Frank back to school . . . he must make a Business Journey of it . . . tell Frank [aged 12] I hope he pays great attention to his French which I now so feel the want of – his drawing too I shall hope to see much improved – I mean specimens he has done at home not those brought from school of which I cannot judge!'

On St Peter's Day he visits Albano, '30 years older than Rome', and its beautiful lake, Frascati, and a villa of Cicero's. From a high hill are 'splendid views of the Campagna and the winding Tiber. The air here is like swallowing fire – I fancy it agrees with me'. St Peter's tomb is open and the splendid sarcophagus exposed to view . . . the Pope is carried on a chair of state on men's shoulders – the music indescribable. Next day he watched the fireworks at the Castel San Angelo from the balcony of St Peter's.

Webster, the sick man, after five days and four nights of 'incessant travel' reached Ferrara, then moved on to Loreto, Ravenna, and Padua. Presumably referring to the villas, he considered the route thence to Venice 'the finest yet'. Climbing a hill which reminded him of Dixon Height behind Eller How, he was rewarded by 'perfect views with the Adriatic on one side, the Alps the other, turrets and convents between, the road one long avenue to Mestre'. He took a gondola the last six miles to the Grand Canal and for some time sailed the 'water streets'. The hotels were full until he found one 'near Byron's and Countess Guiccioli's palace' and the Rialto. 'A long-formed wish in some measure is gratified – I am in that most singularly beautiful city'.

He saw the Doges' Palace, St Mark's and other churches, and the Bridge of Sighs, moving on to Istria only to be dissuaded from going on to Constantinople by stories of plague. Returning to Venice he goes from church to church, palace to palace, gallery to gallery. Vicenza, although Palladio's city goes unremarked, came next, then Verona, Garda, Brescia, Bergamo, and Lake Como. A fine new road led up the Val Tellina to a spa with water tasting like 'Shap Wells though not so strong',[9] then over the Brenner Pass to Innsbruck. He confesses to being 'tired of cities, painting and sculpture', refusing to go to Milan again – 'after all what are the productions of Art but poor imitations of Nature?'

By devious routes he reached Lake Constance and Schaffhausen, where he dined 'with Mr Postlethwaite who married Miss Losh'. But at Lucerne on 10 August he was 'disappointed to find all Mr Grigg's family from home'. Near 'pretty Lake Zug' he was robbed and abandoned on a mountain by his guide. Lost in the dark and encumbered by his cloak he was suddenly back at his starting point. 'So much for Swiss guides'. Lucerne, 'the most famous Lake in the world', he found 'not as fine as Killarney'.

Webster was 'determined to go to Munich' and was glad he did, having 'no idea of what had been going on and what is now doing in the way of architecture and every branch of the fine arts – the 'style of Decoration different to what I had been accustomed to! The new Palace defies all description, my only fear is that the climate is not the thing for it, indeed in all directions I detect decay although quite new . . . the English Garden a perfect paradise'. What was new in Munich at this time were buildings like Gartner's National Library of 1831, in an Italian Renaissance style, the Rundbogenstil, the equivalent of Charles Barry's work in England. Much of the work was stuccoed – hence the reference to climate.

At Frankfurt he saw the Yeateses in their 'pretty house, furnished . . . a good plan to retire thither'. Mrs Yeates had just given birth to a son, which identifies the father as John R. Yeates, mayor of Kendal in 1836.[10] Webster was related to the family and their house at Levens, Park Head, has evident Webster improvements. Back in London a letter from Thompson awaited him, giving 'a very gloomy account of Business . . . I am now determined not to sit over a Desk as has been the case for some years past . . .'.

By steamship to Greece and the Middle East, 1843

For the next journey in 1843 a cruise in the Mediterranean was chosen; perhaps the overland journey had been too taxing after all. George Webster booked a cabin (£100) on the Peninsular & Orient Steam Navigation Company's SS *Tagus*. The boat to Lisbon from Millwall was the *Liverpool*. The trip began not in April or May but on 7 January – an easier journey, a cooler season. Almost at once gales forced the *Liverpool* to shelter in Portland harbour. She put to sea again the next day but was obliged to take shelter again in Tor Bay, from sixty miles south of the Lizard. In the morning, Falmouth was the refuge. They tried again but sixty miles out they could go no further after eight hours steaming. Nor could they retreat. It seemed that the *Liverpool* would not survive; it was 'little more than a log in the water'. However, 'thanks to the crew and Providence', they put into Falmouth again on 14 January, a week after leaving London.

Nine passengers, including Webster, wrote to *The Times* at once about the unsuitability of the *Liverpool* for the Lisbon run. P. & O. rejected the criticism, claiming that the boat was fit 'in every way for her duties', but offered a refund of £36, holding the remainder 'against your travelling again this year'.

The nine had by now dispersed and it was easy for P. & O. to increase their pressure on individuals. On 18 January they informed Webster, and no doubt the others, that they considered 'the offer of a refund suspended', the secretary claiming to be 'surprised that you signed a letter in such strong and authoritative language . . . [I am] . . . awaiting your further explanation'. Suddenly poor George is in the wrong. In a fragment of a letter of 24 January the company is assured that he had 'nothing to do with the drawing up of the letter'. They now know – two others have said so – that Lt. Wise, an Admiralty agent, was the writer. The letter discussed horsepower, a highly professional matter. As an honest man the secretary should not fail to answer the question, presumably posed in the missing part of the letter, did Lt. Wise write the letter of complaint? P. & O. replied on the 26th that they were perfectly satisfied. It is not difficult to fill in the gaps and the complete picture does not show Webster in a heroic light, nor P. & O. in a very honest one or worse – 'as regarding yourself . . . I had been much hurt at seeing your name attached to a letter so uncalled for'. Mendacious is perhaps a better word. George's refund was restored and he did undertake a further journey later the same year. What, one wonders, happened to Lt. Wise?

After 1840 it was possible to travel directly from Lancaster to London by train and that was probably the reason for George's change of base from the Tavistock to the Euston Hotel. Before he sailed, he protested to Eleanor of the 'impertinence and officiousness' of James Statter, the incumbent of Lindale. 'He has already caused me to take a dislike of Eller How by his being at Lindale . . . Mr Rawstorne said I ought to have returned his letter'. George breakfasted with Mr Greene (of Whittington Hall) and dined with Mr Rawstorne.

He had 'a bad bleeding fit' and took pills, but the boat reached Lisbon without incident on Easter Monday. There was more bleeding and pill-taking and already he is asking for Black Rock Villa to be 'well aired against my return for Baths are sure to be in great request'. He was spending 'much time' at Cintra, referring to Byron's description, and saw 'the most beautiful paeonies', longing to take some. The architecture was 'nothing to compare to Italy'. He had been to the opera with the king and queen. He sent a 'Lisbon kiss' to Ellen. At Cadiz he was 'glad to find an 'English dinner' and 'clear the Abominable Imposters at the hotel, the customs and boating'. He went on to Gibraltar and thence to Seville, where he saw 'some of Murillo's finest paintings' and greatly admired the cathedral and Moorish palace, 'almost equal to the Alhambra'. But his attitude changed abruptly and it became a 'wretched place [when he saw] the ground covered with carcases of horses killed at bull fights'.

In Gibraltar itself he mentions 'the beautiful Cheltenham Villas high on the fortifications' – his own Black Rock Villa would have transplanted happily to the Rock. 'Oh! The delicious gardens with every flower and fruit almost that Nature has provided', he exclaimed. He had been pain-free since Lisbon – 'Sea breezes are doing wonders for me'. However, five days later with the heat at 80 degrees in sun and shade, he had a few severe attacks of bleeding and biliousness, decreasing without pills, and thanked the fine, dry air for the improvement.

Off Algiers he observes that the *Tagus's* 'saloon is as big as the ballroom of the White Hall Buildings' in Kendal which he and his father had designed in 1825. Off the coast of Africa he notices that there are now four doctors on board but turns away from any meaning in that to give Eleanor instructions for the garden at Black Rock, 'particular attention to be paid to the Training of the plants to the Verandah, pillars and trellis work'. She is not to let the 'Greenhouse grow wild'. George hopes that she will be able to get 'some cash from Thomas Bigland previous to my return otherwise I shall be out of humour with him'. A. Akister is to be told 'that the Pedestal be made and set up for Sir Geoffrey . . . [the letter is torn away here].[11] Malta (18 May) displayed the 'finest crops of Barley, wheat, Cotton, melons, and potatoes I ever saw' and he visited the place where St Paul was shipwrecked. The blood 'oozed through my Stockings from the flea bites'.[12]

Webster had a 'complete quarrel' with a doctor with whom he shared a cabin and who 'ranged his medicines and physic bottles' on the shelves with their 'savoury smells' and left to sleep elsewhere. And he was 'tired with sail, a Monotonous Life'. However, he was looking forward to seeing the Acropolis and the Parthenon 'and to those splendid remains of Greek Magnificence which since my first visit to Rome I have more then ever long'd to see'. This was immediately followed by instructions for Joseph to have 'plenty of lettuce, turnips, radishes against my return – am convinced vegetable diet does no harm to me or anything my stomach seems to relish – I have had long conversations with an MD!'

As they neared Athens he noticed the snow-covered Parnassus and rose one morning at 3 a.m. to visit Mount Pentelicus with its white marble. Surprisingly, he has nothing to say about the temples of Athens and it seems likely that a letter is missing except for a remark that 'it is not Rome – have not the least wish to come near it again'.

The boat entered the Sea of Marmora on 26 May, the strait, he points out, being about the width of Windermere. Part of the cargo caught fire. The journey 'is not without its dangers', he wrote. From the Hotel Angleterre in Constantinople, he writes of his amazement that what appear to be marble buildings are in fact whitewashed – 'Bronzes and gilded bronzes all covered with this curse to the Antiquary and Architect!' Webster is also amazed to meet 'Mr Warren Maude from Blawith Cottage', another brother of Thomas Holme Maude. The *Tagus* then (30 May) takes them into the Black Sea and there are engravings of the Crimea including Sevastopol and of Varna in Bulgaria. Perhaps a complete letter has been lost, for we are next off Africa having avoided Smyrna.

In an undated letter George claims that 'no consideration will ever induce me to become again a Prisoner in a steamship for three weeks', a pledge forgotten by the following August. One of his objections to this form of travel was having children on board. He counted fourteen. Another was to the 'Young Bloods, exquisites of the first water'. He makes a further allusion to the life of a farmer, seeing 'no prospects but to turn Farmer as I fear Rents will be out of the question' and hopes 'cows will be in milking order on my return'.

In the Bay of Biscay he was again irritated by the exquisites, in particular 'Mr. Clarke, son and heir to Sir James Clarke MD to the Queen – a fop, Mr Drummond-Hay – a fop, all know how to coin others money at cards'. Finally, 'George Webster – a nondescript', and home at the end of June.

By Steamship to Greece and the Middle East, 1844

Having forgotten his resolution of the previous year, George Webster left Blackwall Dock on 22 August 1844. His departure seems to have been a secret for before sailing he wrote to Eleanor 'you may now tell who you choose where I am gone. Aunt Ashburner[13] in particular who I daresay never dreamt she should have a Nephew voyaging to Jerusalem for pleasure and health'. He also advises Eleanor on what to do 'if mishap befall me', which is to 'send for Mr Moser or Mr Harrison . . . to arrange affairs . . . the one who will take Frank on as a clerk . . . my intention is that he should practise as an attorney and succeed to my 2/3 of the slate quarry. Mr Moser has a deed though unsigned'. Was Webster thinking of a possible accident to himself or of his poor health? He was always anxious about Frank's future. Frank was a law student in 1851 and eventually became an attorney but never inherited his father's two thirds of the Kirkby slate quarries since within two years Lord Burlington would repossess them.[14]

Once at sea his 'nerves improved though the pain in [his] side had not gone if the palpitations had'. He had less pain in his lungs or chest and the bleeding and pain of piles was less violent. Two days later, at Gibraltar, he was 'a little surprised by the pain in my chest' and blamed the sirocco.

In Athens he spent the first day 'looking over the whole of the ruins' and was 'able to act as cicerone to some of the party . . . several like myself in search of health'. An 'attack of a species of cholera [had] nearly gone off' by 13 September when he arrived in Constantinople. He took a caique up the Bosphorus, scrambled up a hill, and saw 'the most sublime scenery blended with the most awful Phenomena of Nature. In front was gathering a mass of dense Black clouds discharging vivid forked lightening accompanied by Raging Thunder when one of the clouds opened, an immense Water Spout descended with Balls of Fire . . . of course our descent was as quick as possible . . . The velvet collar of my coat has turned green where the ice struck – caused by sulphur'.

The Sultan granted George a passport to visit Egypt (apparently including Jerusalem) on the *City of Zion* which also stood off Smyrna for two days – 'this most abominable place'. One hundred pilgrims 'cover the decks with provisions and beds and all was <u>filthy</u> . . . but these poor people have a great zeal in their religious feelings we cannot boast'.

He travelled by way of Rhodes, where he admired the splendid architecture of the fortresses and palaces left by the Knights of Malta, and the Bay of Macri, 'where Mr. Fellowes[15] has for so long been engaged by the government to send antique marbles to the British Museum'. Reaching the Turkish coast he catalogued the variety of plants, commenting 'the natives are wretched in the midst of plenty – but so it is wherever the Turk rules'. From Cyprus the boat crossed to the Lebanon and down the coast; then the party went inland where George found the going very trying – 'everywhere there are mountains & rocks and lava and hard limestone'. Reaching the gates of Jerusalem at two o'clock he has 'a thrilling sensation' despite the guard of 'abominable Turks'. His hotel was 'full of every abomination of filth' but on the other hand 'every step I take in this Sacred place may have been trod by him who gave up his life'. The steps he took were to the sites of the Crucifixion and burial, Solomon's temple, the Mount of Olives, and so on. He is shown 'the footprint of Christ as he left the Terrestrial for the Celestial – I could see the marks of the chisel'. He recognised that other sites 'may be fictitious but if not then very near'.

Webster moved on to Bethlehem, Bethany, the Dead Sea, and so back to the ship, armed with the certificate proving that he had made the pilgrimage to Jerusalem. Off Alexandria the view reminded him of Heysham point 'by refraction cut as it were, into islands'. There was 'Syrian' fever on board but a party, including George, sailed up the Nile to Cairo 'where my miseries continue': the crowding, 'every horrid insect for which Egypt is so famed, the exhalation of this immense mass of Waters of Mud'. Presumably he was in search of sphinx, pyramids, and tombs, but if so there is neither mention nor comment. Suddenly he is at Malta, in quarantine; there have been several deaths from typhus, whether on board or on the island is not made clear.

Not for the first time George criticises letters from home on grounds of brevity or lack of information and pops into his next some jobs for the staff. 'Robinson and John . . . are to take up dead trees from the new plantation in front of Akisters and all weeds from the Walks, all the dead trees to the last seat towards Buck Crag – I expect all has been done to the Tower on the Hill – tell Aaron Akister I should like the wall between his house and the Hartleys built this winter if he could be making preparations'. He had brought with him some water from the Jordan which he would be soon 'forced to part with . . . because of the smell . . . it is already too much to be near'.

'I must have a long letter sent to me at the post office at Southampton, Miles might as well write to me there also but no bad news!!' The next letter picked up at Gibraltar told of the death of Aunt Ashburner, which did not surprise him. He asked for the address of R. Ashburner, presumably a relation, and two or three Kendal papers.

The *Montrose* anchored off Falmouth on 13 November and Webster felt 'a want of winter clothing particularly my leather waistcoat'. He asked if 'Mr Thompson is settled to the Island'. This would be John Thompson who bought Holme Island in Morecambe Bay, became a neighbour of the Websters, and completed the *cottage orné.* 'You say nothing of our new Clergyman and his wife and family'[16] – again a shortage of information from home. And he has to ask 'how are Frank and Maggie going on at school' and where are the Sinkinsons going to live?[17] He looks forward to a week at Grange, in Black Rock Villa.

Overland to Belgium and Germany, and to Scotland, 1846

In the *Westmorland Gazette* of 17 May 1845 George Webster's name appeared in a provisional list of directors for the new Furness Railway promoted by his patron the Earl of Burlington and the Duke of Buccleuch. It was not there the following week. Nevertheless, he was one of a party which gathered in London on 1 April 1846 to consider the Bill for the line, soon to be before Parliament. Webster's friend and patron Thomas Rawstorne seems to have been its leader and Curry, Lord Burlington's lawyer, a member. A viaduct over the Kent near Milnthorpe would alter the channels of the river and probably destroy that town as a port. Did Webster realise that there would be trouble ahead for his villa on the shore at Grange?

He seems not to have been much engaged in discussions, writing to Eleanor 'I am at a loss how to dispose of myself, I think I shall go into France from Dover'. But the next letter was written from Ghent on 14 April – 'you will wonder what has become of me'. He had met the Baron and Baroness de Sternberg at Dover and spent a day with them. He had been their architect at Belsfield in Bowness.

Webster established a headquarters in Brussels to visit those 'cities all over the country if I have not previously visited them . . . [on my] . . . first visit to Belgium eighteen years ago'; the itinerary to include Aix, Cologne, Dusseldorf, Elberfeld, Hanover, Dresden, Berlin, and Hamburg, and thence by sea to London, a German rather than a Belgian list. 'As usual I have left myself little rest – at Aix I shall have a sulphurous bath or two'. And as usual instructions were sent home, here about matting to be cut away 'for the bust to stand on the flags – I daresay you will have to send for Dobson to fit it properly'.

Travelling by way of Liège and up 'the beautiful Meuse with its precipitous limestone rocks like Witherslack Scar', he feels 'slight benefit from such a short stay at Aix and decides that Berlin and Dresden 'must wait for more railroads' before he visits them. Instead he went up the Moselle, to Strasburg to see the cathedral, and down the Rhine to Rotterdam. Back in London on 6 May he found the railway bill had been thrown out. 'For some time to come our district will remain clear of prospectors', he noted optimistically, and bought a piano for £95.[18] This was George's last foreign journey supported by letters home. Visas show that he at least stayed at Aachen and Cologne.

A letter of 22 August 1846, with an engraved heading of the Royal Exchange, marks Webster's arrival in Glasgow after 'a pleasant sea voyage, a much finer city than I had any idea of'. There is a 'great press of tourists' which he will swell on a visit to Loch Lomond in the morning. He hopes for a fine week at home so that Birkett may get on with some illegible task which involved getting stone to Ulverston.[19] He enjoyed a trip down the Clyde through the Kyle of Bute and went north through the Crinan canal to Oban. He wrote from Inverary on 27 August that he had 'made acquaintance with Lord Maidstone and Lady, late Lady Constance Paget[20] en route for Skye'. He went out to Staffa and Fingal's Cave through 'Islands quite equal to the Greek Archipelago'. He was worried about his eyesight, being 'scarcely able to write in spite of strong gaslight' and thought 'a sort of cholera' responsible for his langour. But he was in good spirits. On 3 September, writing from Inverness, he complained of 'a bed in a filthy lodging house at 7/6d a night' and of only climbing half way up Ben Nevis.

Turning south, he saw Taymouth Castle, Dunkeld, the tomb of the Wolf of Badenoch, Perth, Stirling, and the Highland games at Blair Atholl before arriving in Edinburgh on 9 September. There follows the cryptic remark that 'on my return shall have to go to Bowness and bring back the Baron [de Sternberg]'. After Edinburgh he went to Dryburgh and Abbotsford, reaching Melrose on 13 September. His instruction from there was that Harrison was to 'dress the ponies in case he needed the gig' to collect his master wherever his journey should end. He concludes that he had 'every reason to be much pleased with this Trip and thankful that it has been of <u>Service to my Health</u>'.

Recently discovered evidence in the form of passports in the possession of a descendant show that he made further journeys and confirm an indication in a letter of May 1846 that he had been to the Low Countries eighteen years before, in 1838. There is a gap of six years before his visit to Hamburg and Berlin in April 1852. No letters have survived from the last three journeys, merely the passport evidence, which also covers those of 1836, 1841, 1843, and 1844. He visited Paris in April 1854 and France, Austria, Dresden, and Leipzig in August 1858. It is possible that Eleanor travelled with him in these post-retirement years when he could forget instructions to the firm now that he was no longer responsible.

Notes

1. They are preserved in CRO K, WDX 1315. References to individual letters will not be made in this chapter. George also found time to sketch things that he saw; some of his drawings survive in private collections.

2. William Longmire, surgeon, was listed in Highgate, Kendal, in 1829 and 1851.

3. John Barnabas Maude (1781-1851), fellow of Queen's College, Oxford. In 1803 he became a victim of the Napoleonic Wars in some unknown way and spent the next eleven years interned at Verdun. In 1816 he revisited the place and noted a local man's gravestone 'in the ground allotted for my countrymen during our long captivity': *Local Chronology*, 7, 13.

4. His solicitor, Roger Moser. The 'Star' is unexplained.

5. Nothing is known of the extent of this Liverpool property. It is possible, however, that Eleanor had inherited the houses in Williamson Square which her father had left to her mother: CRO B,

BD/L/3/208. They are not mentioned in George's own will, although he did own some land at Oxen Park which had belonged to George Lowry, but it was sold before the will was proved.

6. John Knowles or Knowlys, for whom Edmund Sharpe designed Heysham Tower in 1836: J. Price, *Sharpe, Paley and Austin*, 1998, 68.

7. John Machell (1755-1845), of Springfield, Ulverston, married Charlotte Rigby (d. 1860).

8. See p. 54.

9. The medicinal springs at Shap Wells were developed in the 1830s when the Earl of Lonsdale built an hotel for visitors coming to take the waters: Mannex, 1851, 222-3. George must have been an early visitor. The spa was never a great success. Murray's *Handbook to the English Lakes*, 1889, 91, remarked 'Certainly nothing but sanitary objects could induce a sojourn in so dreary a spot'.

10. The son was George Henry Brettargh Yeates (1841-75): Boumphrey and Hudleston, 335.

11. Aaron Akister, farmer and master mason, was recorded in Lindale in the 1851 Census. He worked for George as a waller and slater at Whittington Hall in 1831-6. For 'Sir Geoffrey' see pp. 304, 345.

12. Can he have meant phlebitis? The words are quite clear and such a play on them not uncommon. It is hard to imagine flea bites bleeding so badly.

13. George Webster's step-mother had been an Ashburner before she married George Lowry. Aunt Ashburner was perhaps her first husband's sister or sister-in-law.

14. See p. pp.57-9.

15. Sir Charles Fellowes (1799-1860).

16. James Statter, whom Webster so much disliked, retired from Lindale in 1844 and was replaced by James Pollitt: R. H. Kirby *et al.* (eds), *The Deanery of Cartmel*, 1892, 72.

17. Perhaps the family of Edward Sinkinson, wine merchant of Kendal, whose daughter Eleanor married George's brother Francis in 1837.

18. Presumably the Broadwood which was in the nursery at Eller How in 1864: see p. 316.

19. Thomas Birkett of Eller How Farm, which was built by George and bears his and Eleanor's initials.

20. In 1846 Lady Constance Paget, daughter of the 2nd Marquess of Anglesey, married George, Lord Maidstone, who succeeded as 11th Earl of Winchelsea in 1858.

Gazetteer

The following abbreviations are used: C = *Cumberland;* L = *Lancashire;* W = *Westmorland;* YNR = *Yorkshire North Riding;* YWR = *Yorkshire West Riding. For houses in Kendal, see pp. 63-74. Numbers in heavy type are those of the illustrations on pp. 175-297.*

HOUSES

Accrington (L)

The houses of the Hargreaves family: *c.*1815-48, attributed to Francis and George Webster. The Oakenshaw textile printing company of Taylor, Fort, & Bury was founded in 1792 at Clayton-le-Moors. Bury retired after two years and Taylor in 1801 when the property was divided. The partnership was dissolved in 1811 when Broad Oak Mills, Accrington, were taken over by Thomas Hargreaves, formerly a manager at Oakenshaw.

As the Hargreaves sons came of age they needed houses of their own. The eldest, John, had the examples of the sons of his father's former partners, John Fort and John Taylor: Read Hall for the former, Moreton Hall for the latter, neither far away, and both designed by George Webster. It seems that Webster built new houses for John, Benjamin, and Robert Hargreaves. They are mostly long since demolished, but there are photographs in Accrington Library.

Accrington House: *c.*1800, a Peel family house. Ashlar, five bays with shallow bays at once on both return fronts, the *in antis* porch quadripartite and pedimented. The window above has decoration which links it with Bank Hall, Burnley.

Arden Hall (**1**): 1846, for Benjamin Hargreaves, a Jacobean, barge-boarded and gabled house with mullioned windows and grouped, tall chimneys.[1] Demolished.
[1.] Burke, *Visitations*, ii, 1853, 250.

Bank House: conversion *c.*1840, for Robert Hargreaves. The original house dated from before 1800 and was made into an Italianate villa with two towers of different heights and tripartite windows. Demolished.

Broad Oak House: 1834-5, for John Hargreaves,[1] a hill-top three-bay villa with a recessed centre and flanking bays with tripartite windows. Originally of plain ashlar, it was elaborated and extended in 1902 for Sir George MacAlpine. The lodge was very similar to lodges by Webster at Eden Hall (1834-5) and Broughton Hall (1838-41), with Greek Doric columns *in antis* and Italianate windows. Demolished.

1. R. S. Crossley, *Accrington Captains of Industry*, 1930, 45. John Hargreaves also owned Hall Barn, Beaconsfield, one of the great Buckinghamshire houses: Burke, *Visitations*, ii, 1853, 37.

Hyndburn House: extensions for F. Steiner, another member of the firm, by George Webster.[1] Demolished.

1. Burke, *Visitations*, ii, 1853, 249.

Oakhill: for Thomas Hargreaves, 1815, traditionally attributed to Francis Webster. A modest five-bay house with a porch of slim, fluted columns, it has good plasterwork inside. George Webster may have been the architect of the later library wing.[1]

1. *CL*, 13 Dec. 1979; Robinson, *Country Houses*, 224.

Aldingham (L)

Colt Park: an Elizabethan-style farm of 1830 (datestone), for the 2nd Earl of Burlington, with mullioned windows, square chimneys, and arched porch, and no doubt one of the improvements by George Webster who inspected the Holker farms in Furness. William Brockbank, Salvin's builder at Holy Trinity, Ulverston, noted in a letter to the architect, 19 Feb. 1831, that Webster was on his rounds.[1]

1. J. Marsh (ed.), *Dear Mr Salvin*, 1999, 30.

Allithwaite (L)

Abbot Hall (Kents Bank): for Miss Mary Lambert of Boarbank Hall, 1840, by George Webster.[1] Built on the shore of Morecambe Bay with a sea wall and castellated tower, the house is rustic Jacobethan and was surrounded by verandahs. Surprisingly, the interior is Grecian, the plasterwork resembling that at Rydal Hall and Aynsome. The house has two lodges in the same style. On the hill behind is a 'folly' tower with castellations contrived from water-worn limestone blocks and rubble. Mary Lambert was the granddaughter of Thomas Lambert of Kendal and London, who inherited Burrow Hall in 1801 from his cousins the Fenwicks. He left her a rich woman on his death in 1837.[2]

1. D. C. Mycock, *Eighty Years Onward, 1916-1996*, Methodist Guild Holidays, 1996, 21.

2. Boumphrey and Hudleston, 181. She inherited Abbot Hall from an aunt: J. Stockdale, *Annals of Cartmel*, 1872 , 505-6.

Allithwaite Lodge (2): for Edward Barrow. One of a group of similar houses in the area of *c*.1800 and attributable to Francis Webster. The entrance front is of three bays and two storeys with a porch and tripartite windows, with a canted bay on the garden front; hall with Venetian screen; good plasterwork, marble chimneypieces by the firm. There is a tablet to Barrow (d. 1814) in Cartmel Priory.

Boarbank Hall (3): *c*.1837, by George Webster, begun for Richard Winfield of Kendal but completed for his granddaughter Mary Lambert, who moved from Allithwaite Lodge *c*.1835 and whose monogram appeared over the entrance and remains on the lodge of 1837. The south front had a two-bay pedimented centre with lower one-bay links to two taller wings, the whole held together by a verandah of the Storrs Hall pattern. The front was rebuilt in 1857 after a fire; the house was again destroyed by fire in 1870 and rebuilt in a formal Italianate style, probably by a Kendal architect.[1] Of the old house an excellent Webster fireplace remains. The stables were built by Grundy of Ulverston in 1876-8.[2]

[1] R. Stevens, *History of the Parish of Allithwaite*, 1990, 29-39; P. Makin, *Boarbank Hall*, n.d. (*c*.1970).

[2] Designs in CRO B, Z1153.

Ambleside (W)

Croft Lodge (Clappersgate) (**4-8**): alterations 1829-30, for James Brancker, a Liverpool sugar merchant, attributed to George Webster. In about 1820 Croft Lodge was a three-bay, three-storey house with two-storey wings with canted fronts, Housman's 'little white seat . . . of Miss [*sic*] Pritchard'.[1] It is essentially unchanged except that the west wing is now of three storeys with a veneer of monstrous gothic detail. What happened was that the centre was given overhanging eaves on deep brackets ending in grotesque heads. The wings were castellated and vast chimney stacks carried castellated octagonal pots. A gothic iron verandah ran between the wings and a new entrance was protected by a three-bay gothic porch.

In complete contrast the inside was made heavily Grecian, with fluted Doric columns, wreathed friezes, incised ornament, and pedimented door cases akin to many Webster memorial tablets. The chimneypieces are no doubt from the Webster yard. One is a variation on the music room fireplace at Storrs, replacing the lintel tablet with a chariot race. The sequence of rooms was spatially impressive, some being of two storeys and top-lit, others low and oppressive. The house suffered from neglect after 1945 but has since been converted into flats.

[1] J. Housman, *A Tour of the Lakes*, 2nd ed., 1802, 165; watercolour by James Wilson (private collection). There is a tablet to Laetitia Pritchard (d. 1827) in Grasmere church, unsigned but clearly by the Websters. For Brancker, see Boumphrey and Hudleston, 49.

The Knoll: 1845-6, for Harriet Martineau, either by the Webster firm or by herself, as she claimed, with the advice of Wordsworth.[1] The great circular bastion derives directly or indirectly from Webster's design for the poet's house at Rydal, as do the cylindrical chimneys.

[1] H. Martineau, *Autobiography*, 3rd ed., 1877, ii, 228.

Lesketh How: 1844 (datestone), for John Davy, son-in-law of Mrs Fletcher of Lancrigg, possibly by George Webster; a fine display of cylindrical chimneys and an extraordinary balcony of cantilevered slate slabs. The marble chimneypieces have been removed.

Rothay Bank (now the Rothay Manor Hotel): *c*.1825 and probably by Francis Webster, with panelled pilasters and an iron balcony of intersecting arcs as in many early Webster houses; traceried gothic door.

Scale How (now part of the Charlotte Mason College): a remodelling, probably of 1824-5, of a square house of *c*.1775 for Benson Harrison, the ironmaster who married Wordsworth's cousin. A wing with a bow was added and a verandah of the Storrs pattern wrapped round the building; other Webster details and chimneypieces. At the foot of the drive stands *Low Nook*, a small house with larger additions. That to the north-west has windows with hood-moulds and varied chimneys and was perhaps by Webster or Thompson for James C. Wilson, 5th son of Christopher Wilson of Rigmaden.[1]

[1.] Boumphrey and Hudleston, 326.

Wanlass How (Waterhead, now Ambleside Park): for James Brenchley, 1841-2 (datestone I & M B), attributed to George Webster, a large gabled house perching on rocks above the head of Windermere. The terrace is one of Webster's 'fortified' battered-wall-and-bastion designs. The house was originally surrounded by an iron verandah. There is one good fireplace, but the barge-boarded gables and finials have gone.[1] The remaining plasterwork has ribs running from the corners to moulded central squares containing a single large pendant, like fan vaulting. None of that resembles other Webster work.

[1.] Photographs and lithograph in an album at the house.

Wansfell (Waterhead) (9): for Thomas Wrigley of Bury, paper-maker,[1] 1840-41, and almost certainly by George Webster. Another house of the 1840s near the head of Windermere, Jacobethan with barge-boards, gables, octagonal chimneys, and a three-arched greenhouse between the projecting wings on the south side, an arrangement similar to that at Conishead Priory. Good interiors and chimneypieces. The whole stands on a walled terrace.

[1.] Boumphrey and Hudleston, 332.

Waterhead (Waterhead): for Thomas Jackson, *c.*1840, attributed to George Webster. A slate house with projecting two-bay centre carrying a 'gable' pediment. The windows are mullioned and transomed and cylindrical chimneys are plentiful; in other words it is a Tudor house, although the ironwork balconies, railings, and verandahs are of Grecian design, straight from a pattern book.[1] Little original work has survived long use as an hotel but enough remains to show that the ceilings had Jacobethan plasterwork.

[1.] Probably from L. N. Cottingham, *The Smith and Founder's Director*, 1824, a book owned by Webster: see p. 326. There is a similar mixture in reverse at the Low Wood Hotel (1843), just down the lake.

Arkholme (L)

Lane House: a small Jacobethan farmhouse of *c.*1840, the model farm for the Storrs estate. All the details, including gate piers with stone balls and two handsome barns, suggest the Webster firm.

Storrs Hall (10): remodelled for Francis Pearson, 1848. There is a core of old masonry and much that suggests the Webster firm, and the work is probably by Thompson who was working from 1847 at Kirkby Lonsdale, close by. The 'pele' tower is a sham and in that resembles Whittington.[1]

[1.] VCH *Lancs.*, viii, 206.

Arnside (W)

Ashmeadow: for William Berry of Kendal, *c.*1810, attributed to Francis Webster. A three-bay villa with a simple verandah, standing on the shore; top-lit stairs, attached offices with cupola.[1]

[1.] *Lons. Mag.*, iii, 1822, illus. facing 321, 322-3.

Barbon (W)

Lowfields (now Underley Grange): *c.*1825, attributed to Francis Webster. Classical, three bays with a one-bay pediment. Pedimented tripartite door with windows on either side. Gate piers from Underley just across the river Lune. Edmund Tatham of Kendal, who later retired here, was a friend of Francis Webster, but the house was not built for him.

Whelprigg (**11**): for Joseph Gibson, 1834,[1] attributed to George Webster. An almost total rebuilding of a house of 1815, which had plain gothic windows to the east, as a square Jacobethan house of gabled, mullioned windows, canted bays, and a plainer service wing with plentiful finials. The centre is a large square saloon with the staircase climbing the outer walls. Good plaster-work and the library has original bookcases, but strangely no original chimneypieces. There is no known documentation, but few houses are more clearly by Webster.

[1] W. Whellan, *History and Topography of Cumberland and Westmorland*, 1860, 891; *The Websters of Kendal*, no. 24; Burke, *Visitations*, ii, 1853, 185.

Bardsea (L)

Bardsea Hall: restored for William Gale Braddyll at a date unknown. Of ancient origin with 18th-century work, it was 'much restored . . . in the Medieval style of domestic architecture', a reference to the tower with its restless crenellations in the manner of several Webster churches. Said to be 'now going to decay for want of an occupant' in 1850, so was the restoration after this?[1] Demolished in 1927.

[1] '*Sketches of Grange*, 1850, 100; Mannex, 1882, 275. In 1851 it was occupied by a Braddyll family servant: Mannex, 1851, 463.

Wellwood: *c.*1850, an Elizabethan house, probably by Thompson & Webster, for the Rev. Thomas Petty who was responsible for completing Webster's church.

Barrow-in-Furness (L)

Island House: with a centre of 1726 and later wings *c.*1792 when Robert Michaelson inherited it. It had angle-pilasters, a pedimented porch, and Venetian windows. The detail is reminiscent of Longlands at Cartmel, and Francis Webster was probably the architect of the later work. Demolished *c.*1914[1].

[1] *Barrow News*, 29 Aug. 1980; painting in Barrow Museum.

Beetham (W)

Beetham House: for the Rev. William Hutton, 1771-2 (datestone);[1] five bays of limestone ashlar; the links to one-bay pavilions with arched windows set under an arch are attributed to Francis Webster, 1792. Good chimneypieces. More alterations in 1882.

[1] W. Hutton, *The Beetham Repository, 1770*, ed. J. R. Ford, 1906, 123; B. C. Lee, *The Legacy*, 1997, 40.

Bolton-by-Bowland (YWR)

Bolton Hall: much rebuilding in a gothic style as befitted a house where Henry VI sheltered in 1464. Designed by J. M. Gandy for John Bolton of Liverpool and Storrs Hall *c.*1808, and 'carried into effect by Webster of Kendal'.[1] Demolished *c.*1959.[2]

[1] *Gentleman's Magazine*, 1841, i, 581; Burke, *Visitations*, ii, 1853, 137.

[2] E. Waterson and P. Meadows, *Lost Houses of the West Riding*, 1998, 8-9.

Bolton-le-Moors (L)

Eagley Village: a model village for the Philips family of Tean, Staffs. Thompson & Webster advertised for tenders in the *Bolton Chronicle*, 28 Jan. 1854. It included varied grades of cottages with shops, all near the mills but in a sylvan setting. The mills are closed but the village flourishes.[1]

[1.] Mr D. O'Connor of Bolton kindly drew the author's attention to this item.

Bolton-le-Sands (L)

Bolton Lodge: additions for Richard Sparling Berry, a friend of George Webster, *c*.1830, including a north wing and porch with panelled pilasters.

Hawksheads House (**12**): for John Coulston, 1856, attributed to Thompson & Webster. Coulston, of Wrightington Hall, bought the estate in the 1850s and soon afterwards built the new house,[1] standing high above the village, surrounded by woods. It is of 4 x 3 bays with a long service wing, classical in style and built of finely-weathered limestone blocks and articulated by pilaster strips and strings. The entrance is in a pedimented projection. There is a good white marble fireplace by the Websters. The lodge in the same style is dated 1861.

[1.] K. Entwistle, *From Bodeltune to Bolton-le-Sands*, 1982, 190-92.

Bolton-on-Eden (W)

Eden Grove (formerly Whitfield Brow) (**13**): for Richard Tinkler, 1844, by George Webster.[1] A large Jacobean addition to a farmhouse overlooking the River Eden, it is very much in Webster's 1820s manner, with a small tower, turreted porch, and mullioned windows. Inside there is good plasterwork in hall, dining and drawing rooms, and library. The lodge had a datestone, R.T. 1844. A classical tablet by the Websters to an earlier Richard Tinkler (d. 1831) in the church.

[1.] Kendal Library, sale catalogue, 1872, endorsed 'by the late Mr Webster of Kendal'.

Borwick (L)

Borwick Hall: an Elizabethan house, for some time a property of the Stricklands of Sizergh and neglected until 1812 (date on downspouts) when some repairs were carried out, probably by Francis Webster.

Linden Hall: 1839, for William Sharp, a Lancaster solicitor, extending a small square house which had belonged to Mr Sharp's wife's family. Two letters signed by Miles Thompson survive from a family scrapbook at the house, together with a ground plan of the 'proposed extension to Linden Cottage'. This shows the new work, notably the dining room and the delectable geometrically planned drawing room with its canted bay window, the design of which is referred to in one of the letters. Burke's view records the resulting *cottage orné* and the contemporary Loudonesque garden layout with its winding paths and small lake.[1] All this may be to George Webster's design; visually it is cousin to Eller How.

Early-20th century additions by Briggs, eliminating the original cottage, upset Webster's picturesque exterior and largely masked the pretty roof turret. The crenellated ruins, which may have been water-worn limestone (a large rockery heap of which was cleared by the present owner) are long gone, but the present orangery is on the ashlar footings of Webster's.

Otherwise the garden layout is intact and its character magnificently enhanced by Mr and Mrs Peter Sharp who bought back this family property.

1. Burke, *Visitations*, ii, 1853, 240. It is puzzling that the four Lancashire houses illustrated by Burke in what is essentially a literary survey – Arden Hall, Hyndburn, Linden Hall, and Graythwaite – appear to have George Webster as a common factor.

Bowness-on-Windermere (W)

The settlement of Bowness by strangers in search of views of lakes and mountains began in the 18th century. Thomas English who came first started building Belle Isle in 1774, but it was left for John Christian Curwen to complete it in 1781 and he was a Cumbrian. Sir John Legard built Storrs Hall *c.*1790, largely for the sailing; John Bolton of Liverpool enlarged it in 1808, and Francis Webster was his executant. After that many, usually less adventurous, small villas went up, some by the Websters. The following can be firmly attributed to them.

Belfield (or Belle Field): pre-1819[1] and modest enough, of three bays. It had a large square bay grafted on, mullioned and transomed, which is perhaps of *c.*1825 and by George Webster. The verandah has been clumsily replaced.

1. W. Green, *Tourist's New Guide*, 1819, i, 201. In fact, 1794 and built by Isabella Taylor, widow of Peter of Whitehaven, and daughter of Fletcher Fleming of Rayrigg: T. W. Thompson, *Wordsworth's Hawkshead*, 1970, 305-6, 378-9 [editor].

Belsfield (originally Bellefield) (**14**): for the Baron and Baroness de Sternberg, 1845, by George Webster, who had 46 working drawings, a photograph, and a watercolour at Eller How when he died.[1] Catherine Augusta Harrison married the mysterious Baron de Sternberg in 1836 and commissioned Webster to design an Italianate villa on the shores of Windermere in 1845. The house had a tower, splendid rooms overlooking the water below the cast-iron verandah, and a garden and magnificent greenhouse, partly of ridge-and-furrow design like that at Holker. The garden was laid out in arabesques like the garden at Nibthwaite Grange (1837). The staircase has an immensely tall window derived from Storrs Hall. The top floor of the tower has Italianate windows in groups of three.

   The house became an hotel *c.*1890 and the interior bears little resemblance to the original except for one or two chimneypieces. Externally much remains but it is soon apparent that an extra floor has been inserted, that the south wing is larger and has swept away both greenhouse and garden.[2]

   Webster met the Sternbergs, perhaps coincidentally, at Dover the following year and spent the day with them.[3] He probably met the Baron again later. In West Cumberland the Baroness owned 'an occasional residence', a three-bay square farmhouse, Acre Walls, four miles east of Whitehaven, in 1847,[4] and was a 'liberal patron' of the National school at Cleator (1854).[5] Webster worked in and around Cleator, rebuilding the church in 1841-2.

1. See p. 342.
2. J. Richardson, *Furness Past and Present*, ii, 1880, illus. facing 185; *CL*, 28 May 1987. The gardens at a later date were described in the *Gardeners' Chronicle*, reprinted in A. G. Banks, *H. W. Schneider of Barrow and Bowness*, 1984, 115-8.
3. CRO K, WDX 1315; see p. 86.
4. Mannex & Whellan, 1847, xii.
5. C. Caine, *Cleator Moor Past and Present*, 1916, 345. She had extensive interests in the West Cumberland iron industry: CRO K, WDX 7.

Burnside: for George Anthony Aufrere[1], *c.*1840, Jacobethan, attributed to George Webster. Only the front facing the lake, with its tripartite and canted bay windows, has survived the conversion to an hotel. Inside some reeded doorcases suggest a different style from the picturesque exterior.

[1.] Boumphrey and Hudleston, 13.

Crag Brow Cottage: has a tripartite studded door with panelled pilasters, and until recently an iron verandah like Belfield.

The Craig: for Admiral Sir Thomas Pasley, 1836-7, attributed to George Webster. The Craig was named after Pasley's Dumfriesshire home and took the place of rented houses at Rydal, Grasmere, and Bowness. A house of many gables, with mullioned and bay windows and tall grouped chimneys.[1] In October 1836 William and Mary Wordsworth advised the Pasleys on the layout of their garden, Wordsworth noting the fine views.[2] The family lived at The Craig up to August 1848 when they are found anxious to move out in order to let a waiting tenant take possession.[3] The house was eventually sold in 1867 to Lord Decies[4] and demolished in 1968. The Pasleys were waiting for the completion of their new house, *Craig Foot*, no more than a few yards below The Craig. There is no clue as to why this move was made.

[1.] The house is illustrated in L. and M. S. Pasley, *The Adventures of Madeleine and Louisa*, 1980.
[2.] A. G. Hill (ed.), *Letters of William and Dorothy Wordsworth*, vi, pt 3, 1982, 303-4. In Feb. 1836 the Pasleys had come 'to superintend the building of their house': *ibid.*, 175.
[3.] M. E. Burton, (ed.), *Letters of Mary Wordsworth 1800-1855*, 1958, 304.
[4.] Boumphrey and Hudleston, 29.

Ferney Green: a classical three-bay house with a full-height central bow and pedimented end elevations, probably for Joseph Pringle,[1] *c.*1800 and by Francis Webster. Behind the bow an oval drawing room and circular bedroom. In 1818 the verandah round the house was described as a 'light airy Piazza'.[2]

[1.] Green, *Tourist's New Guide*, i, 202.
[2.] *WG*, 14 Nov. 1818.

Holly Hill: the house of the Bellasis family – Edward Bellasis published *Westmorland Church Notes* in 1888. The house resembles Crag Brow and dates from before 1822.[1]

[1.] *Lons. Mag.*, iii, 1822, 39.

Old England: built as a private house but an hotel since 1859.[1] Begun before 1819 since William Green wrote in his *Guide* of a recent 'splendid addition' made by Joseph Greaves, probably the wing with tripartite windows and balcony seen in old photographs and for which Francis Webster was perhaps the designer.[2] There is a datestone of 1848.

[1.] C. Taylor, *Portrait of Windermere*, 1983, 154.
[2.] Green, *Tourist's New Guide*, i, 202.

Quarry How: for Thomas Ullock of the Royal Hotel, 1838, and probably designed by George Webster when he was remodelling the hotel. The two men were personal friends. The house is of 3 x 3 bays, with an east wing. It has a tripartite door. Altered as an hotel in 1869.

St Andrews: a small Italianate villa with a tower porch of 1843 (datestone, with initials F. and E. W.), no doubt by George Webster. It has a verandah of the same elements as Belsfield.

Bretherton (L)

Bank Hall (**15-16**): for G. A. Legh Keck, 1832-3, attributed to George Webster. As with so many other houses self-evidently by George Webster there are no supporting documents. What he had to work on was a small brick house of 1608 – the date appears on Webster's north porch. Little original brickwork now shows. New wings were built to east and west, the central tower was raised, and lodges and greenhouse added.[1] The roofs were of Burlington slate and the interior was 'almost wholly modernized'.[2] Webster reused the semi-circular motifs of the gables. Unhappily the house was shrouded in ivy thirty years ago and parts of it have recently collapsed. The good news is that there are now moves to restore it.

[1.] Twycross, i, 66.
[2.] VCH *Lancs.*, vi, 106-7.

Broughton (YWR)

Broughton Hall (**17-18**): altered for Sir Charles Tempest, 1838-41, by George Webster. Broughton has Elizabethan origins, was Georgianised *c*.1755, and in 1809 was given neo-classical wings by William Atkinson.[1] The stables of 1787-8 were designed by John Foss of Richmond.[2] George Webster extended the front, adding a *porte-cochère* with Ionic columns, and a stable clock tower.[3]

[1.] T. D. Whitaker, *History and Antiquities of the Deanery of Craven*, 1805, illus. facing 80.
[2.] Information from J. M. Robinson.
[3.] See pp. 33-4.

Broughton-in-Furness (L)

Broughton Tower: alterations for John Sawrey, 1839, attributed to George Webster. Broughton Tower was developed from a pele tower. In the 18th century a classical house was built across this with refined decoration but in 1777 the exterior was sensitively gothicised.[1] In 1837-9 (dates on downspouts) the dining and drawing rooms were remodelled and given new chimneypieces and Jacobean plaster ceilings. The one in the dining room survives and must be by George Webster. A white marble chimneypiece has gone but may be the gothic one now in the Judges' Lodging at Lancaster. A black and grey one has vanished.[2] After being used as a school, the house was recently converted to flats.

[1.] Robinson, *Country Houses*, 168.
[2.] For the house, see *North Lonsdale Magazine*, i, 1894, 92-5, 105-11; VCH *Lancs.*, viii, 403-4.

Burneside (W)

Tolson Hall: for William Whitwell, *c*.1840, attributed to George Webster. The core of Tolson Hall is of 1638, but additions and alterations have been made ever since. A watercolour of *c*.1800 shows a flat front symmetrical between gabled wings and with gothic detail probably done for the Batemans who owned the house until 1845.[1] They certainly put up the obelisk in the park to 'the pilot that weathered the storm' [William Pitt the younger] and the castellated entrance arch of *c*.1750. They were also generous donors to the new church at Burneside, built by George Webster in 1823.

William Whitwell MP leased the house about 1840, 'removed the battlements', and left the house very much as it is now, with barge-boarded gables and the fine timbered entrance porch, no doubt with Webster as his architect.[2]

James Cropper bought Burneside mills in 1845 and built *Ellergreen*, a large gabled house, in 1847, perhaps by Thompson & Webster. It lies between Tolson and the village. Tolson itself became Cropper property in 1876.[3]

[1.] The Batemans moved to Staffordshire where they created the famous gardens at Biddulph Grange.

[2.] For the house, see T. Jones and A. H. Willink, *James Cropper & Co. and Memories of Burneside 1845-1945*, 1945, 14-15.

[3.] *Ibid.*, 57-8.

Burnley (L)

Bank Hall: for the Revd John Hargreaves, 1796.[1] 7 x 5 bays with a bow on the long front, perhaps by Francis Webster, now engulfed in a hospital. There is a Webster tablet to Hargreaves in Holme (Cliviger) church.

[1.] VCH *Lancs.*, vi, 445.

Burton-in-Kendal (W)

Burton House: for William Atkinson, *c.*1795. One of the three-bay houses with links to wings which appear in the Morecambe Bay area. Of fine ashlar, it has an apsed principal room with good plasterwork and may be by Francis Webster. The plans are in Wellington, New Zealand.

Dalton Hall (L): for Edward Hornby, *c.*1812 and perhaps by Francis Webster. A five-bay classical house with a semi-circular porch.[1] Good gateposts on the main road. Engulfed in a grandiose design of 1859 by E. G. Paley,[2] overtaken by dry rot and demolished 1969, and rebuilt by Clough Williams-Ellis. The porch reused as a garden temple.

[1.] Twycross, i, 11.

[2.] J. Price, *Sharpe, Paley and Austin*, 1998, 73-4; photographs during demolition at National Monuments Record.

Cark-in-Cartmel (L)

Cark Villa (now Cark Manor): for James Newby, *c.*1820 and attributed to Francis Webster. A cruciform plan; broad angle pilasters.[1] Altered *c.*1900. A pretty lodge with octagonal window panes like those in Holker village just around the corner. Newby's elder brother Thomas had a house at Thorny Hills, Kendal, near that of George Webster.

[1.] *Lons. Mag.*, ii, 1821,162, where it is compared with Lunefield.

Holker Hall (**19-21**): remodelled for the 2nd Earl of Burlington, 1838-41, by George Webster. In 1838 the house was that built in 1783, possibly to designs by John Carr of York.[1] John Hird may also have been involved. George Webster added a suite of rooms in the Jacobean style; the offices and old stables are no doubt by Webster too. The cupola on the former exactly replicates those at Dallam Tower which date from 1826. The buildings are all classical here. The present estate office is also by Webster (1846).[2]

Burlington became the 7th Duke of Devonshire in 1858 and the following year summoned Caldecotts of Great Russell Street in London to Holker to make changes, largely internal. Windows were changed, ceilings lowered, and a grand staircase built. Work to the value of £3,968 was executed between 1859 and 1861, Paley of Lancaster being brought in to deal with the masonry work.[3]

In about 1861-2 Thompson built the model village at the gates, with its barge boards, timber porches, and fancy glazing, and in the same style in 1863 the new stable court with its slate-hung spire. In 1864 he built a school at the south end of the village.

On the morning of 10 March 1871 most of Webster's main block was destroyed by fire, after which a new one was built by Paley & Austin,[4] oddly reminiscent of Webster's, but using red sandstone rather than grey limestone. Perhaps it was the wish of the duke to retain some idea of the house which had been a memorial to happy times. The style is still Jacobean, the buttresses and turrets seeming like paraphrases of what was there in 1841, as does the copper dome. It is undoubtedly similar to the one at Eshton; perhaps there was such a one here too.

[1.] *Lons. Mag.*, i , 1820, frontispiece and 2.

[2.] See p. 40. Webster had the plans and ten working drawings at Eller How in 1864: see pp. 341, 342. For a note on the ridge-and-furrow greenhouse, see *CL*, 28 May 1987.

[3.] LRO, DDCa 13/328.

[4.] Price, *Sharpe, Paley and Austin*, 83.

Cartmel (L)

The centre of the Webster world for several generations but with few signs of their work except possibly the *Cavendish Arms* and *Priory Close* where George Webster's son Francis died in 1872. Their monuments predominate in the priory and further away there are several houses.

Aynsome Manor (**22-23**): alterations, 1842 (datestone), for the Rev. T. Machell Remington, vicar of Cartmel 1834-55, attributed to George Webster. In 1821 this house was classical, of five bays with single-bay pedimented wings so familiar in this district.[1] This essentially remains, but with a single wing. Remington added a porch with a figure-of-three head, a refined version of a vernacular feature (e.g. at Barwise Hall, Appleby).[2] Behind, a wing with a canted bay and pinnacles and yet more Jacobean detailing. The interior has more work of 1842 with a fine dining room with plasterwork like that at Rydal Hall and Abbot Hall, Kents Bank. The house is now an hotel.

[1.] *Lons. Mag.*, ii, 1821, illus. facing 361, 362-3.

[2.] Twycross, ii, 31.

Ivy Cottage (now Ivy House) (**24-25**): probably for the Lodge family of Preston, who have monuments in the churchyard, a three-bay cottage with large additions. The earliest has a fine tent-like drawing room with rich gothic decoration. About 1840 a tall Jacobethan gable with pinnacles was grafted onto the west front which looks as though it had drifted over from Holker and must be by George Webster.

Longlands (Broughton East) (**26**): one of a group of early 19th-century houses around Cartmel and in south Westmorland which share several characteristics. Five bays with a simple Doric porch; links to pedimented wings with tripartite windows under arches. Above it a narrow tripartite window squeezed between strings. Plain interior with good fireplaces, now removed, and handsome stables. Probably by Francis Webster and perhaps for Langdale Sunderland.[1] Now converted into flats following a long period of dereliction.

[1.] J. Stockdale, *Annals of Cartmel*, 1872, 419. His widow was the owner in 1821: *Lons. Mag.*, ii, 1821, 162.

Tanley: just outside the village and perhaps a Webster house. 3 x 3 bays but much altered whilst retaining some original early-19th century features, an arched porch, bracket eaves, and a very fine gothic chimneypiece.

Caton (L)

Elm Grove (now Croftlands) (**27-29**): for Richard Sparling Berry, 1833, by George Webster. Webster gave the house built in 1745 by Thomas Berry a new facade and the rooms behind it. Only three bays wide, it is of great elaboration and was formerly connected to the handsome gateway by an avenue of elms. Over the door is a tablet recording the transformation,[1] and above that is a small gable. The façade is flanked by octagonal ogee-capped turrets. Two rooms inside have good plaster ceilings set in black mouldings exactly like that over the stairs at Conishead Priory. The exterior detail and the gateway would later contribute to the design of the gothic alcove of 1840.

In the garden is the 'Abbot's Tomb' discussed in letters between Berry and Webster.[2] In Brookhouse church a gothic tablet for Thomas Berry of Liverpool and Elm Grove (d. 1832) is by the Webster firm.

[1.] E. Garnett, *The Dated Buildings of South Lonsdale*, 1994, 48.

[2.] CRO K, WDX 1315.

Claife (L)

Belle Vue (the Station): not strictly a house but a belvedere with dining and drawing rooms and kitchen as Father West tells us in his *Guide* (1800 ed.). Designed by John Carr of York, *c*.1799, for the Revd William Braithwaite. Bought by John Christian Curwen in 1801 and extended and castellated about 1805, probably by Francis Webster.[1] Ruinous.

[1.] Colvin, 225; CRO K, WDX 1315 contains a watercolour showing the extended state.

Lakefield (now Ees Wyke): for John Eccles, *c*.1820, attributed to Francis Webster, and for J. R. and F. Ogden, 1853 (datestone), by Thompson & Webster.[1] Originally a three-bay square house with a columned and pedimented door and sparing delicate cornice. The later extensions include a new wing with coupled arched windows and an iron verandah of slim fluted columns across the west front. A new dining room has typical late Webster decoration.

[1.] *WG*, 29 Oct. 1853, tenders invited.

Clayton-le-Moors (L)

Clayton Hall: the large additions to the Lomaxes' house of 1772 are traditionally attributed to George Webster, 1846, and details of the stone cantilever staircase, the joinery, and the marble fireplaces supported the tradition. Demolished.[1]

[1.] Twycross, i, 19; Burke, *Visitations*, ii, 1853, 218.

Cleator (C)

The Flosh: enlarged for Thomas Ainsworth, 1837 (datestone), attributed to George Webster.

The improvements were gabled with mullioned windows, a new entrance, and unmistakable Webster gate piers. Most of this was obscured by further additions of 1866.[1] Now the council offices. There is also estate housing in the same style, presumably also by Webster, who also rebuilt the church in 1840.

[1.] Caine, *Cleator Moor Past and Present*, 118.

Clifton-with-Salwick (L)

Clifton Hall (**30**): for Thomas Clifton of Lytham Hall, 1832, attributed to George Webster. 1832 was the year of George Webster's brick Jacobean houses in the Preston area and Clifton is in the same style.[1] The detailing is similar – mullioned and transomed windows, octagonal angle buttresses (here without the usual ogee caps), obelisk pinnacles. The string-courses crossing the gables are the same as those at Conishead Priory. The verandah is a clumsy addition, after 1855.[2]

[1.] Twycross, ii, 37.

[2.] There is an engraving of that date in C. Hardwick, *History of . . . Preston*, 1857, facing 554; Burke, *Visitations*, ii, 1853, 195; *ibid.*, 2nd ser., ii, 1855, 129.

Clitheroe (L)

Standen Hall: built 1757 in Palladian style.[1] Not long after 1847 John Aspinall added a large room which is probably by George Webster who provided a typical fireplace.

[1.] Twycross, i, 11.

Cliviger (L)

Ormerod House (**31-32**): altered for Col. John Hargreaves, 1833-4, by George Webster.[1] Webster added two tall towers, a Jacobean porch of fluted columns, one of which survives, and pierced balustrade,[2] and a version of an uncommon stepped arch linking house to stables seen at Barcroft Hall nearby (1636).[3] Judging from photographs (the house was demolished *c.*1922), he remodelled the interior with typical plasterwork and chimneypieces from designs used elsewhere. It was a case of 'renovation almost amounting to reconstruction' or 'interior almost entirely modern'.[4]

[1.] T. D. Whitaker, *History of the . . . Parish of Whalley*, 1876 ed., ii, 221 n.1, 'from designs by Mr Webster'.

[2.] Twycross, i, 30.

[3.] Others at Ordsall, Shuttleworth, and Martholme, all in SW Lancashire. Webster used the device in a similar position at Moreton.

[4.] T. Ormerod, *Calderdale*, 1906, 105; VCH *Lancs.*, vi, 485; Burke, *Visitations*, ii, 1853, 196; *The Websters of Kendal*, no. 23.

Cockermouth (C)

Cockermouth Castle: the outer bailey was modestly remodelled in 1805 for the 3rd Earl of Egremont when Webster & Holme supplied chimneypieces for all the rooms. They were later removed.[1] Two of them seem to have been installed in what is now the Trout Hotel.

[1.] G. Jackson-Stops, 'Cockermouth Castle', *CL*, 18 and 25 July 1974.

Colne (L)

Alkincoats (**33**): unexecuted additions for John Parker of Browsholme, 1820, by George

Webster. Alkincoats has recently been identified as Webster's earliest Jacobean house design[1], five years before Underley (1825), where his revived style was thought to have begun. The old house was Jacobean with many small gables and a central porch, but with inserted sash windows. Webster's plan was to enclose the front between two generously broad wings and create new rooms behind. The detailing of windows and balustrades appeared again at Eshton, Underley, Netherside, and elsewhere. One detail never repeated was the gothic niche set in the new gables. The VCH goes some way to suggest that Webster's west wing at least may have been built, dating it to the early 19th century 'with many of the characteristics of the revived Gothic of the period though that portion which is seen from the south carries out the design of the front in all its details'.[2] Demolished in 1958.[3]

[1.] LRO, DDB/80/30, plan and side elevation. The front elevation is at Browsholme: information from Simon Jervis.

[2.] VCH *Lancs.*, vi, 526.

[3.] RCHM, *Rural Houses of the Lancashire Pennines*, HMSO, 1985, 142; the house is illustrated in Robinson, *Country Houses*, 150.

Colton (L)

Bridgefield: for George or William Penny, *c.*1860, of slate with freestone details reminiscent of the firm. Porch and verandah removed. Probably by Miles Thompson.

Nibthwaite Grange: for Thomas Dixon, 1837, by George Webster. To a house of the early 18th century Webster added a suite of drawing and dining rooms and a slightly-projecting garden hall[1]. A simple glazed iron verandah follows this pattern, the supports carrying away water from the roof. The projection ties to a one-bay pediment. Inside, the new rooms have excellent chimneypieces and friezes. Webster also designed the garden, his only known design[2]. Dixon (d. 1856) has a tablet by Thompson in Colton church.

[1.] Plans at the house.

[2.] Belsfield had a similar plan of island beds.

Coniston (L)

Thurston Lodge: on the east side of the lake, n.d. but probably by Thompson. Now stripped of the picturesque architectural details which recalled Holker village.

Coniston Cold (YWR)

Coniston Hall (**34-37**): for J. B. Garforth, 1841, by George Webster. A classical ashlar house of 7 x 3 bays with heavy external detailing and plain interiors, not unlike Flasby Hall. The centre three bays to the south were pedimented and opposite on the north was a Greek Doric porch. The house was connected visually to the kitchen wing by an iron colonnade and beyond there were carefully-planned offices.

There are plans by both Webster (1841) and Thompson (1849).[1] In the latter's drawings the portico had outer square piers, but as built it had monolithic Doric columns, as has the surviving lodge. Did Garforth defer the execution of the plans and go ahead only eight years later? The house, long abandoned and derelict, was demolished in 1972 but the portico was left standing and was incorporated into the modern house.[2] Webster designed the church in 1846 and probably the school.

[1.] At the modern house.

2. Waterson and Meadows, *Lost Houses of the West Riding*, 7. A grand mahogany bookcase is now at Linden Hall, Borwick: information from J. M. Robinson.

Crackenthorpe (W)

Crackenthorpe Hall: not built, but plans and elevations for a new house and stables for Lord Lonsdale, *c*.1800, are attributed to Francis Webster.[1]

1. H. Colvin, J. M. Cook, and T. Friedman, *Architectural Drawings from Lowther Castle*, Society of Architectural Historians of Great Britain, 1980, nos. 204-5.

Crosthwaite (W)

Hill Top: Sir Daniel Fleming's 'favourite summer Residence'[1] – the 5th baronet presumably, since the house was 'modern built' in 1834.[2] Three bays with a Roman Doric porch and a yard surrounded by high walls with blocked windows and partly castellated. Perhaps by Francis Webster.

1. *WG*, 2 Oct. 1841, sale notice.
2. *Ibid.*, 25 Oct. 1834.

Dalton-in-Furness (L)

Bank House: for William Butler, 1851. An engraving of 1817 by G. Cuitt shows the castle with the colonnaded market buildings in front. Surprisingly at that date the western half had regular Tuscan columns. These buildings were demolished *c*.1850 and in 1851 a three-storey house-cum-office for the solicitor William Butler took their place. In a photograph of *c*.1860 the house is shown as gabled with mullioned and transomed windows and very much in the Webster mould. Two columns from the market colonnade were incorporated in the porch. Demolished in 1896.[1] Miles Thompson was probably the architect.

1. H. Gaythorne, 'Dalton Castle', *CW2*, x, 325, and illus. facing 323 and 325. William Butler's father Thomas organised the rebuilding of the parish church in 1825-30 and was one of the executors of Francis Webster's will in 1827.

Dalton Castle: Francis Webster made estimates for repairs in 1827, but his death in that year seems to have prevented their execution. Another plan by John Barnett, Philip Wyatt's clerk of works at Conishead, was proposed.[1]

1. *Dalton Castle, Cumbria*, National Trust, 1996, 14-15.

Skelgate: a terrace of houses facing the castle with Webster details and perhaps by George. Tripartite windows; no. 3 has wreaths and panelled pilasters on the doorcase.

Downham (L)

Downham Hall (**38-41**): for William Assheton, 1834-5, by George Webster. A remodelling of an old house retaining much of the masonry. Webster presented two sets of elevations, one Italianate, the other classical with a powerful Tuscan portico – the one selected with modifications.[1] Tripartite windows were intended for the north and east fronts but were abandoned, along with the south front verandah.[2] Inside, the library is an excellent Webster room and there are good chimneypieces. Other rooms were altered in the 1920s.[3] The nearby vicarage is in the style of the hall, and there is a Grecian Webster tablet in the church to Mary Assheton (d. 1832).

[1.] Designs at the house; *The Websters of Kendal*, no. 25.

[2.] Twycross, i, 9. Another version of the Storrs pattern.

[3.] G. Worsley, 'Downham Hall', *CL*, 5 Oct. 1989.

Edenhall (C)

Eden Hall (**42**): work for Sir George Musgrave, 1834-5, attributed to George Webster. The ancient seat of the Musgraves was demolished by Sir Philip Musgrave who had a new house designed by Robert Smirke, the architect of the new Lowther Castle not far away. Where Lowther Castle was gothic, Eden Hall (1821-5) was in Smirke's 'cubic' style.

Some of the subsidiary buildings at Eden Hall must have been built by George Webster. The church was restored in 1834. At about the same time the splendid entrance, at a cross-roads, was designed, marked by tall piers with a Greco-Italianate lodge, a near replica of the main lodge at Broughton Hall and very similar to one at Broad Oak, Accrington. The stables of 1842 can also be attributed to Webster and the pheasantries opposite are clearly by him. The house was demolished in 1934 and more recently a new one has been created from the stables.[1]

Between 1831 and 1836 Webster was rebuilding Whittington Hall. In the documents relating to that work, Sir George Musgrave is mentioned twice, once in connection with cast iron stoves from Whewell of Lancaster where his bills have been presented together with those for Whittington (1834).[2] When Webster went to Italy in 1836 he carried with him 'old' Lady Musgrave's card on which she had written an introduction to Gaggini, a sculptor in Genoa. There are Webster tablets to members of the family in the church.

[1.] Robinson, *Country Houses*, 105-6; *Websters of Kendal*, no. 26; Burke, *Visitations*, i, 1852, 264.

[2.] LRO, DDGr 6, accounts.

Egremont (C)

Rothersyke: for Henry Jefferson, 1853, by Thompson & Webster.[1] A red sandstone mildly Tudor house with a three-bay front and one-bay gabled projecting wings. The windows are not mullioned and the supply of finials is meagre. Another datestone of 1862 no doubt indicates additions.

[1.] *WG*, 5 Feb. 1853, tenders invited.

Egton-cum-Newland (L)

Penny Bridge Hall: the house came to the Machell family in 1788. What is seen now is the early-19th century five-bay, three-storey front with a simple verandah and immediately round the corner a fine Roman Doric porch. To the river a three-storey added bow with pilastered ground floor. The principal room has a screen of Ionic columns. It is possible that George Webster was the architect. The chimneypieces are probably from the marble showroom.

Ellel (L)

Ellel Hall: the seat of the Ford family *c.*1740-1898[1] and possibly by Francis Webster; three bays and three storeys with pedimented doorcase and a wing.

[1.] VCH *Lancs.*, viii, 100.

Finsthwaite (L)

Landing: a Greek revival remodelling of an older house for John Harrison, attributed to Francis Webster, *c*.1830. Much altered again *c*.1900, but even after use as a club and subsequent conversion into flats some interiors survived: staircase, hall, and notably the front door with wreaths. Demolished in 1991.

Forton (L)

Hay Carr (**43**): for Nicholas Lamb, *c*.1810, the Duke of Hamilton's agent. The early work could be by Francis Webster; there is an excellent inlaid chimneypiece among others. The enlargement of 1835 is no doubt by George Webster and includes gables, mullioned and transomed windows, and a porch of the same design as those at Howick and Clifton, of the same decade.[1]

[1.] A. Hewitson, *Northward*, 1900, 111-2.

Gargrave (YWR)

Eshton Hall (**44-49**): for Matthew Wilson IV (1772-1854), 1825-36, by George Webster.[1] Whitaker illustrates the house in 1805, low, classical, of 9 x 3 bays with tripartite windows under shallow arches.[2] The new building is Jacobean and of ashlar, not large but impressive. Columned porch with flanking bay windows, and a tower with an ogee cap. The service wing and stables are towered, pinnacled, and irregular, in contrast to the Jacobean formality of the house. The clock tower was built as late as 1840 by which time Flasby was going up across the valley. The coach house also has tall spired towers. *Kildwick Hall* was prepared as an interim residence while the new Eshton was building. This meant alterations including plasterwork in the same style as Eshton.[3]

[1.] The plans are in the library of the Yorkshire Archaeological Society, Leeds, MD 387, with building accounts, 1829-39, *ibid.*, MD 335; see R. W. Hoyle, 'The Bradfer-Lawrence Collection', *Yorks. Archaeological Soc. Transactions*, 1979, 166. George Webster had further plans or elevations at Eller How in 1864: see p. 341. Wilson's day-books, which record the work, are in Leeds University Library, MS 417.

[2.] Whitaker, *History . . . of the Deanery of Craven*, 1878 ed., facing 239.

[3.] See pp. 23-4, 25.

Flasby Hall (**50-51**): for Cooper Preston, 1840, additions by George Webster. Webster's Italianate villa retained the circular staircase from a house of *c*.1820. He encased and extended this nucleus using heavy, even brutal, detail and a tower. The known design[1] had giant angle pilasters which were replaced in execution by quoins. The tower was also re-thought, with panelled pilasters and a belvedere at the top. The house stood empty for many years and has recently been partly rebuilt.[2]

[1.] Plans and elevations survive but their whereabouts are unknown. The author only saw photocopies, signed and dated 'Geo Webster Archt Kendal 1840'.

[2.] Waterson and Meadows, *Lost Houses of the West Riding*, 9.

Sunnyside: reminiscent of nearby Broughton Hall, so perhaps by George Webster, *c*.1840. A small house with a front of only one generous bay of channelled rustication. Door with large consoles to the side.

Garstang (L)

Kirkland Hall: a classical house linked with John Carr of York, 1760. The remodelling and enlargement of the old wing at the back, *c.*1840, can be attributed to George Webster with two of his joke Pennine doors to accord with its supposed date of 1695. A fine pair of Grecian gateposts.

Giggleswick (YWR)

Bankwell: of several dates but the regular front to the garden and the rooms behind are early-19th century and probably the work of George Webster. Inside, the hall has the same design as Anley and Taitlands and in another room are friezes with laurel wreaths.

Catteral Hall: for John Hartley, 1830s and 1843.[1] A towered Italian villa with a staircase typical of George Webster. The Jacobethan porch is dated 1843. Now part of Giggleswick School.

[1.] T. Brayshaw and R. M. Robinson, *History of the Ancient Parish of Giggleswick*, 1932, 226.

Gleaston (L)

Gleaston Castle Farm: adjoining the ruins of the castle is a neat three-bay farmhouse with a datestone of 1830 on the porch. The house has Websterish details and, like Colt Park, is a farm built by George Webster for the 2nd Earl of Burlington's Holker estate.

Grange-over-Sands (L)

Several villas can be attributed to the Websters.

Bay Villa: for Robert Wright, *c.*1820, attributed to Francis Webster, and for Richard Wright, 1849 (datestone), by George Webster. In 1818 Robert Wright, master mariner, bought a property including two ruined cottages for £26. Soon afterwards he built a small house on the site, perhaps by Francis or Robert Webster. His son Richard became a prosperous merchant in Liverpool and built a grand villa contiguous with his father's and evidently chose his neighbour George Webster as his architect. Something like Black Rock would be just what he aspired to. The main rooms rise above a basement and have a canted bay on each floor. The handsome dining and drawing rooms have good plasterwork and typical Webster fireplaces.[1]

[1.] G. E. Collins, 'Notes on the early history of Bay Villa', 1987 (typescript); Bay Villa deeds.

Black Rock Villa (**52-54**): for himself, 1837-41 (datestones) and 1851, by George Webster. Grange is a place of villas, encouraged by the mild climate, and Black Rock is the most significant, being built on the shore behind a sea wall when the village was open to the sea. Webster's house at Eller How was no more than two miles inland, but he had become a partial invalid in the 1830s and began to travel to bathing establishments abroad and at home. The idea came to him that he could bathe both privately and daily if he built a house in a suitable place. Hence Black Rock with a lead-lined bath in the basement, fed by pipes directly from the sea at high tide. Above the basement rose the Italianate villa with good sea views through twin-arched windows. The balconies had standard Grecian ironwork and the whole made a 'picturesque object'. George's pleasure in Black Rock was ended by the building of the railway close by.[1] Today the house is just recognisable; inside nothing survives.

[1.] See p. 39. Twenty working drawings were at Eller How in 1864: see p. 342.

Blawith Cottage: 'the elegant country seat of Thomas Holme Maude . . . of Kendal',[1] *c.*1810. A cruciform design like Lunefield, Kirkby Lonsdale, and Cark Villa, with a 'Storrs' verandah across the front. The gardens ran down to Morecambe Bay. The Maudes and the Websters were close friends and Francis Webster was no doubt the architect here. Rebuilt by Willink and Thicknesse with much local detail in 1893,[2] and now the Netherwood Hotel. Webster's railings survive.

[1.] *Lons. Mag.*, iii, 1822, 323.
[2.] Pevsner, *N. Lancs.*, 131.

Eden Mount: Miles Thompson left an estate at Grange to his brother Marcellus who was described in the census of 1871 as a marble mason and landowner employing seven men and two boys. The estate seems to have been Eden Mount House which existed by 1863 when Thompson designed eight cottages for James Young[1] and probably the vicarage of 1864. Marcellus's son John was a stone mason and quarry owner of Eden Mount in 1882[2]. The unifying characteristic of all the villas, terraces, and semi-detached houses of the 1860s and 1870s is the use of natural limestone for detailing. *Oreton Villas* in Eden Mount Road are the most alarming, with stone mullions with tongues and pendants enclosing much of the plate glass windows. Stone was exported from Eden Mount to e.g. St George's Hall, Liverpool, 1854. The quarries were owned by the Thompsons until 1905 when they passed to Alfred Nelson.[3]

[1.] *WG*, 26 Dec. 1863.
[2.] Mannex, 1882, 339.
[3.] W. E. Swale, *Grange-over-Sands*, 1969, 52.

Eggerslack Cottage: for John Wakefield of Sedgwick,[1] 1841 (datestone), probably by George Webster. Of rough limestone blocks on a rocky, wooded site, it had a floor of larch logs laid honeycomb fashion. The verandah has been renewed.

[1.] *Sketches of Grange*, 16.

Holme Island House: *c.*1832 for John Fitchett of Warrington, and *c.*1844 for John Thompson, both attributed to George Webster. Fitchett (1776-1838), lawyer, poet, and bibliophile, bought Holme Island in 1828 when it seems to have had no building on it.[1] When it was sold the year after his death it had a 'Newly erected Ornamental Residence with Coach House etc'.[2] The stables of 1832 (datestone) were much larger than the house. Fitchett was a friend of Thomas Holme Maude of Blawith Cottage and it seems likely that George Webster, also a close friend, was responsible for the house, which was apparently very simple.[3] By November 1844, when Webster enquired in a letter home if 'Mr Thompson is settled to the Island',[4] it had passed to John Thompson. Twycross recorded that he had 'completed the Cottage Orné'[5] and on stylistic and other grounds George Webster would seem to have been the architect. Twycross showed an L-shaped, single-storey house with gothic windows, set on a terrace, and approached by flights of steps up from lawns and paths, the walls covered with trellises. The house, well-described in 1849,[6] when it was about to be sold, was bought in 1851 by John

Brogden, the engineer of the Ulverston-Lancaster Railway, shortly to be built close by.[7] When the railway was completed in 1857 the land behind was reclaimed and Brogden's son Alexander built the causeway that connects the island to the shore, thus removing the thrilling approach by boat, or across the sands at low tide.[8] The lodge at the mainland end of the causeway could well be by either Webster or Thompson. John Thompson also built in the grounds the ornamental circular temple with statuary by John Graham Lough.

[1.] Advertised for sale in *WG*, 16 and 30 Aug. 1828, 'well adapted for a scite for a villa'; CRO B, Z530, J. Melville, 'Holme Island', 2.

[2.] Melville, *op.cit.*, 3, and illus.

[3.] In a poem addressed to the 'Ladies of Blawith Cottage' (*Minor Poems*, 1836, 267), Fitchett called it a 'cot, a story high, whose structure may amuse the eye'. He was something of a collector and had much in common with George Webster: see the account of his library sale in *The Palatine Notebook*, Aug. 1882, 168-72. He is notable as the author of what is apparently the longest poem in any language; his 'King Alfred' had 131,238 lines.

[4.] See pp.85-6.

[5.] Twycross, ii, 17.

[6.] *Sketches of Grange*, 8-10.

[7.] J. D. Marshall, *Old Lakeland*, 1971, 191. Brogden or his son was probably responsible for the two-storey block with sash windows and heavy chimneys which looms over the more delicate ground floor.

[8.] P. Fleetwood-Hesketh, *Lancashire Architectural Guide*, 1955, 144; Swale, *Grange-over-Sands*, fig. 2.

Merlewood (**55-56**): for Alfred Binyon, 1853, by Thompson & Webster.[1] A late Elizabethan-style gabled house with timber porches and characteristic interiors, sometimes rudely handled. In a letter to Thomas Remington of Aynsome on 15 Mar. 1862, Webster wrote 'I made all the designs for Merlewood . . . after my retirement to oblige a neighbour . . . also for his lodge'. Miles Thompson was left with the 'constructive part'.[2] The garden had a serpentine ha-ha and the woods on the west show signs of landscaping. Some alterations were made in 1881 after the Millers bought the house.[3] Until 2003 a research centre of the National Environmental Research Council.

[1.] *WG*, 5 Feb. 1853, tenders invited.

[2.] CRO K, WPR 89/PR/2704/1.

[3.] See J. Beckett and A. Gardiner, *Merlewood, 1850-1950*, 1987; file in Kendal Library.

Slack (Lindale Road): a cottage on the Merlewood estate enlarged with a wing with windows using limestone clints as architraves. The porch is clearly related to that at Eller How but is all of timber. Probably by George Webster when he designed Merlewood itself. The house is linked to the hillside by a rocky wall with an arch flanked by niches.

Woodheads: bought by John Fitchett of Holme Island, in 1834,[1] and altered. A three-bay house, the centre projecting with a pediment. North wing with an Italianate window and a verandah across the front. Probably by George Webster.

[1.] Swale, *Grange-over-Sands*, 44.

Yewbarrow Lodge (**57**): for William Hargreaves, *c*.1840.[1] A square villa of water-worn limestone in a small park. The tower added later. Attributed to George Webster who had a lithograph of the house, made before the tower was added.[2] Demolished.

[1.] *Sketches of Grange*, 14.

[2.] Album in a private collection.

Grasmere (W)

Allan Bank: for John Gregory Crump, who may have bought plans from Liverpool, 1805.[1] Alterations and additions were made in 1834 (datestone), when a lodge, now *Glenthorne*, was built, perhaps by George Webster.

[1] Boumphrey and Hudleston, 92.

Craigside: for John Henry Tremenheere, and described as new in 1848. The site was recommended by Wordsworth[1] – was the architect also? It is certainly in a Webster mode, gabled, with diamond-set chimneys and wooden Tudor windows.

[1] Boumphrey and Hudleston, 299-300; Burton (ed), *Letters of Mary Wordsworth*, 304.

Forest Side: for Stephen Heelis, 1853, by Thompson & Webster who invited tenders for building 'a mansion house and offices' at Grasmere.[1] It was built under a steep wooded bank to the east of the village in a Jacobean style with barge-boarded gables and mullioned windows. Entry is by way of a timber porch of the same design as that at Merlewood. The staircase is of a Webster pattern rising in a less formal way than usual to an arcaded gallery. There are good Webster fireplaces. A tower was added later in the century.

[1] *WG*, 5 Feb. 1853. George Webster had a watercolour design at Eller How in 1864: see p. 340.

How Foot: for James Green, 1843, attributed to George Webster, with cylindrical windows and fossil 'marble' chimneypiece. Now an hotel.

Lancrigg: the 'beautiful little farm' bought by Mrs Fletcher in 1839 and enlarged on Wordsworth's advice,[1] probably by George Webster. The new work was on a larger scale, with cylindrical chimneys, thin Tudor mouldings round the doors, and a ribbed ceiling in the drawing room which had a Webster chimneypiece.

[1] *Autobiography of Mrs Fletcher of Edinburgh*, 1874, 211.

Moss Head Lodge (now the Wordsworth Hotel): for the 4th Earl of Cadogan, 1853.[1] Slate with barge-boarded gables, marble chimneypieces, and Websterish plasterwork. Attributed to Miles Thompson who was building Forest Side and enlarging the Hollens and Lowther Hotel in the same year.

[1] Boumphrey and Hudleston, 64.

Grayrigg (W)

Lambrigg Foot: enlarged perhaps for John Brunskill, *c*.1852, probably by Miles Thompson. Two canted bays with a plain verandah between and Webster fireplaces.

Great Harwood (L)

Allsprings: for James Lomax, brother to John of nearby Clayton Hall, 1839, probably by George Webster.[1] A Tudor-style house with a tall central tower rising high above the staircase hall. Websterish ceiling plasterwork.

[1] Twycross, i, 33; Robinson, *Country Houses*, 153.

Halton (L)

Halton Green: work possibly on existing buildings for Richard Sparling Berry, 1837, attributed to George Webster. Berry wrote to George Webster on 16 March 1837 to inform him that 'the barn will require about 6 rods 26 yards of slate or about 14 tons'.[1] The barn seems to have been in what Berry used as his mason's yard. It is large, with an inscription in a frame like that at Elm Grove.[2] There are gothic niches high in the gables.

[1.] CRO K, WDX 1315.

[2.] Garnett, *Dated Buildings of South Lonsdale*, 79.

Rectory: by William Coulthard of Lancaster, *c.*1832, in the Webster Jacobethan style with crestings, obelisks, mullioned and transomed windows, bay windows, and barge-boarded gables. George Webster had an engraving in his albums[1] and we know that he worked closely with Coulthard (e.g. at Helme Lodge, Kendal). The rectory could not have taken the form it did without Webster's very strong influence.

[1.] CRO K, WDX 1315, from E. Baines, *History of Lancashire*, 1835, iv, facing 584; Colvin, 273.

Haverthwaite (L)

Hollow Oak: In the autumn of 1767 John Hird was paid a total of 20 guineas by John Machell for 'sundry repairs to my house'. In the same year Robert Webster was paid £3 for a marble chimneypiece. Another was fitted in 1774 and paid for in July 1775, a total of £5.11s.6d.[1]

[1.] LRO, DDMc 28/1. The earliest, however, was recorded in 1760 and there was another in 1766.

Hawkshead (L)

Belmount (**58**): built in 1774 for the Rev. Reginald Braithwaite and bought in 1841 by the Rev. J. W. Whittaker, vicar of Blackburn. He installed chimneypieces from the Webster yard of which two remain.[1] It is possible that the first-floor and rear extensions of the western link block were by Webster.

[1.] CRO K, WD/GH, Belmount scrapbooks. For the house, see *Belmount, Hawkshead, Cumbria*, English Heritage Architectural Survey Report, 2000.

Esthwaite Lodge (**59**): for Thomas Alcock Beck, 1819-21, attributed to Francis and George Webster. Beck is best known as the author of *Annales Furnesienses*, which he wrote at the house. He was rich and disabled and the garden was designed for the use of a wheelchair.[1] Wordsworth noted that he had £2000 per annum.[2]

The design is dependent on Storrs, only a few miles away, more than any other house. Like Storrs it is gleaming white. It has a verandah of the same pattern, uses the same part-fluted order, has a domed staircase, and tripartite windows of similar design but in wood. The plasterwork in both houses is similar. The corners of the house have the giant panelled pilasters so often used by George Webster.[3] It is possible that he had also looked at Papworth's *Rural Residences*, which illustrates gate piers of the pattern of Esthwaite (and Broughton Hall), and a house façade with panelled pilasters.[4]

[1.] Armitt Library, Ambleside, ALMS 382.

[2.] M. Moorman and A. G. Hill (eds.), *Letters of William and Dorothy Wordsworth*, iii, pt. 2, 1970, 550.

[3.] Twycross, ii, 29.

[4.] J. B. Papworth, *Rural Residences*, 1818, pl. xx.

Field Head House (Outgate): the house of the Hardens of Brathay between 1836 and 1844, and best seen in John Harden's watercolours.[1] The verandah he shows is of the Storrs pattern so perhaps George Webster had a hand in the design. That and other details have gone.

[1.] D. Foskett, *John Harden of Brathay Hall*, 1974, 47, 53, and pl. xxix.

Ivy House: attributed to Francis Webster, *c*.1790, and probably when he was building the new Market Hall and Assembly Rooms nearby. A very pretty door of arch under arch and a staircase set in an apse. The door is repeated at the Fell house in Daltongate, Ulverston.

Hellifield (YWR)

Hellifield Green: the three-bay ashlar house of the Wilkinsons with a porch of coupled Ionic columns, perhaps *c*.1820 by the Websters. There are Webster tablets to the family in Slaidburn church.

Helsington (W)

Holeslack Farm: alterations by Miles Thompson, 1868, in the style of the original house, with cylindrical chimneys and mullioned windows.[1]

[1.] CRO K, WDX 140/45a.

Sizergh Castle: Francis Webster's father worked at the castle under John Hird in 1772 and later the Websters were always handy when work was needed. George Webster made alterations from 1820 to 1822, including a billiard room 'not yet completed' in the latter year. In the stone parlour is a columned chimneypiece of marble from the estate.[1]

[1.] *Lons. Mag.*, iii, 1822, 123-4.

Heversham (W)

Plumtree Hall (**60**): for Joseph Braithwaite of Kendal, mayor in 1820, *c*.1815, and probably by Francis Webster. One of the group of houses that included Longlands, Cartmel, and others. Fine ashlar limestone, the centre of three bays, porch with feathered capitals, links with arched windows under a projection to two-storey pedimented wings.

Woodhouse: for Robert Hayhurst, 1865, by Miles Thompson;[1] irregularly classical.

[1.] *WG*, 25 Mar. 1865.

Heysham (L)

Heysham Hall: for Thomas Rawstorne, 1839-40, by George Webster. George Webster had built Penwortham Priory for the Rawstornes, *c*.1830. A few years later this seaside home was constructed to Webster's designs. A rambling Jacobean design with a low tower, mullioned windows, gables, and so on. Projecting from a corner is a sort of cloister as there was at Penwortham. Datestone TRA 1839 for Thomas and Anne Rawstorne.[1] The house has been spoilt, shorn of its detail, a third storey added, and cut up into flats.

[1.] CRO K, WDX 1315, letter from Rawstorne to Webster, 6 July 1840; Twycross, ii, 29.

Hoghton (L)

Hoghton Tower: for Sir Henry Hoghton, 1835, unexecuted alterations by George Webster. The spectacular Hoghton Tower was neglected in the 18th century, the family preferring Walton Hall, near Preston.[1] Plans for rehabilitating Hoghton Tower had been commissioned from Lewis

Wyatt in 1816, but in 1835 the family obtained others from Webster. No elevations survive and there may have been none.[2] Nothing was done until the 1860s and then by Paley & Austin[3].

1. J. M. Robinson, 'Hoghton Tower', *CL*, 23 and 30 July 1992.
2. Both sets of plans are at the house.
3. Price, *Sharpe, Paley and Austin*, 83.

Holme (W)

Curwen Woods (**61**): for Thomas Dicey Cotton, *c.*1830, attributed to George Webster. Classical limestone ashlar, the recessed centre filled by a loggia of coupled square pillars. Large additions of the 1920s.[1]

1. Documents at the house.

Greenbank: a small T-plan house with fine barge boards and tripartite timber porch, possibly by Miles Thompson.

Trinity House: a handsome Websterish house with a timber porch, possibly by Webster or Thompson.

Hornby (L)

Hornby Castle (**62**): unexecuted design for John Marsden, 1823, by George Webster. In 1750 Bishop Pococke wrote that 'the old castle is almost all pulled down and a modern house built some time ago, but a tower in the middle is repaired, a turret added at the top and crowned with a fine gilt eagle'.[1] John Marsden bought the castle in 1789 and in 1810 it is said to have been 'chiefly rebuilt'.[2] He died in 1826 so his commissioning of a castle design from George Webster in 1823 suggests that he was in search of the picturesque.[3] If the plan was serious he had left it too late. Nor was Webster's design truly picturesque. Take away the old tower and the façade is symmetrical with a rather papery gatehouse at the centre. Everything is castellated and the windows all mullioned and transomed. It is worth remembering that George was embarking on a series of Jacobean houses at this time. The castle was eventually remodelled by Sharpe & Paley in 1849-52.[4]

1. J. J. Cartwright (ed.), *The Travels through England of Dr Richard Pococke*, Camden Society, NS, xlii, 1888, 44.
2. *Gentleman's Magazine*, 1800, i, 513; *Lons. Mag.*, iii, 1822, illus. facing 401.
3. Webster's designs are at the castle; Twycross, ii, 12; *The Websters of Kendal*, no. 8.
4. Price, *Sharpe, Paley and Austin*, 70.

Howick (L)

Howick House: for William Rawstorne, *c.*1835. Jacobethan with a verandah and diamond-set chimneys. No doubt by George Webster who was remodelling nearby Penwortham Priory, also in brick, in the 1830s.[1]

1. Hardwick, *History of . . . Preston*, 598; Twycross, i, 69-70, 'recently erected'; *The Websters of Kendal*, no. 29.

Hutton-in-the Forest (C)

Hutton-in-the-Forest (**63-65**): alterations for Francis Vane, 1826, by George Webster. An ancient house, but the 17th and 19th centuries dominate the view; the 18th century is seen only inside. Webster's most dramatic proposal – 'A Design for restoring . . .'[1] – would have removed the baroque facade of 1680 and recreated the medieval house as a screen of windows and turrets with no strong accent unless one counts the taller round tower almost off the picture, a raising of the gallery turret. In another version there is a deep square centre bay. A large new service wing, a new staircase, and other internal changes were proposed. In both versions the entrance has moved to the north side.

What was carried out in the end was the creation of a visible pele tower at the south-east corner, the real one being at the north-east angle. It is similar to that on the first plan but with a more varied skyline of battlements. An alternative to this was to bring in yet another layer of elaboration taken from Webster's design for Hornby Castle.[2] Before Webster took over the south front was altered in 1824 by William Nixon who died in that year. These no doubt were the 'great additions' commented on by James Losh on 30 August 1824.[3] Inside, the dining room with its Elizabethan ceiling and grey gothic chimneypiece will be Webster's. There are subsequent alterations by Salvin.

[1.] Designs at the house and in the RIBA, Drawings Collection, W8/1-2; *The Websters of Kendal*, no. 14. George painted a watercolour of the house in 1830: see p. 341.
[2.] J. Cornforth, 'Hutton-in-the-Forest', *CL*, 4, 11, and 18 Feb. 1965.
[3.] E. Hughes (ed.), *The Diaries and Correspondence of James Losh*, ii, Surtees Society, clxxiv, 1963, 13.

Ingleton (YWR)

Masongill House (**66**): enlargements for Brian Charles Waller, *c*.1832,[1] attributed to George Webster. Waller enlarged a rendered three-bay house by adding single-storey one-bay wings projecting to front and back. The centre bay of the old house was also raised into a gable with an arched window and supporting scrolls. The wings have pedimental gables and panelled pilasters and a canted bay on the return elevation. At the back a pilastered porch. The new rooms have enriched cornices and marble chimneypieces, one design also used at Holker Hall and Sand Aire House, Kendal.

[1.] *Dalesman*, July 1975.

Keighley (YWR)

Cliffe House (now Cliffe Castle): for Christopher Netherwood, 1833, by George Webster.[1] Netherwood was a Skipton banker and may have chosen Webster as his architect when Henry Alcock, also a banker, was making the same choice for Aireville. Alcock was part of the Birkbeck bank which was just then (1834) taking over the Chippendale, Netherwood, & Carr establishment.

The front of the house had a straight gable between curved ones, and three floors of mullioned and transomed windows. There were plenty of obelisks and ball finials. To the east a Venetian porch, a version of those at Eller How and elsewhere, continued by a 'Storrs' verandah.[2] When Henry Butterfield bought the house he made huge extensions by George Smith of Bradford and dubbed it 'Castle'. The interior was gutted and the exterior lost much of its decoration. There were more alterations, especially to the roofs, by Sir Albert Richardson in the 1950s.

[1.] '. . . an elegant specimen of architecture in the Elizabethan style built by the celebrated Mr Webster': Slater's *Commercial Directory*: *Yorkshire*, 1848, 1164.
[2.] Bradford City Art Galleries, photograph, CC/X/32.

Eastwood (**67**): for William Sugden.[1] A five-bay pedimented centre is probably the house dated 1819. The Grecian wings with Soanian ornament, panelled pilasters, and tripartite windows, the Doric porch, and the vanished lodges with Greek fret were probably later. The interior decoration, reminiscent of Esthwaite Lodge and Taitlands would go with a date of *c*.1825. All this work could be by the Websters. The Sugdens were later related to the Garforths of Coniston Cold, Mary Ann Sugden marrying Thomas Garforth in 1841. The Websters designed two Sugden tablets in Keighley church. Eastwood is now a sports centre.

[1] Whitaker, *History . . . of the Deanery of Craven*, 1878 ed., 203.

Kendal (W)

For houses in Kendal generally, see pp. 63-74.

Helme Lodge (**68**): for William Dillworth Crewdson, 1824-7, by Francis and George Webster. A square Grecian villa of great quality, built of limestone with freestone dressings and a service wing projecting to the east, it represents the retreat to the country of this Kendal banker. The Websters' designs are signed by Francis as titular head of the firm but the ideas are his son's.[1] The golden freestone is used for window architraves and the Ionic portico which was carved at Longridge Fell by William Coulthard who was paid £135 16s. 9d., and carried to the site by the Kendal-Lancaster canal which ran close by.

The designs show variations in planning within a fixed outline. The staircase moves around; the best design shows it leading to an Ionic gallery under a dome like that at Read Hall. The handrail is like those at Kendal Town Hall and Graythwaite Hall. There were excellent fireplaces throughout of local and imported marbles. Along the south front is a metal verandah. When repairs were carried out after a fire in 1915 the tripartite windows on the west were pushed forward to give balconies above them. Some subsidiary buildings like the stables and the gig house were by William Airey. Helme Lodge was divided into flats in 1988.

[1] CRO K, WD/Cr/4/192-200, 203; *The Websters of Kendal*, no. 9.

Keswick (C)

Lyssick Hall: for Abraham Fisher, 1845 (datestone), by George Webster.[1] Slate with characteristic detail without and within. Good staircase and marble chimneypieces.

[1] The author was told that Webster's plans exist.

Kirkby Lonsdale (W)

Cressbrook (now Cedar House) (**69**): perhaps for Humphrey Archer Gregg, *c*.1850, attributed to Miles Thompson. An Italianate villa with a tower and many projections and recessions. Bay windows, verandah, oriel window, terrace, and entrance gates are all typical.

Leyfield: a house of *c*.1845 with a gabled projection with a bay. The chimneys are paved squares. Perhaps by Miles Thompson who was busy in the town at this time.

Lunefield: for Roger Carus, 1815-16, attributed to Francis Webster. Roger Carus bought the Lunefield estate in 1812[1] and built his bijou classical residence soon afterwards. It was of Roman cement with stone dressings on a cruciform plan – unusual, as the *Lonsdale Magazine* pointed out,[2] its closest parallel being Cark Villa. At Lunefield the east and west ends of the cross were semi-circular. The drawing room bow had two windows, the other a porch of Ionic columns. To the north a service wing. Demolished 1869 to be replaced by Waterhouse's gothic house, demolished in its turn.[3] The original incised gate piers survive at the Devil's Bridge.

1. A. Pearson *et al.*, *Annals of Kirkby Lonsdale and Lunesdale Today*, 1996, 75.
2. *Lons. Mag.*, ii, 1821, illus facing 161, 161-4; Pearson, *op.cit.*, illus. facing 74.
3. CRO K, WDB 22, sale particulars, 1899, describe fireplaces of 'pilastered marble' and Carrara, which were perhaps from the old house; Pearson, *op.cit.*, 54.

Underley Hall (**70-78**): for Alexander Nowell, 1825-8, by George Webster. Hugh Ashton (d. 1753) of Croston (L) bought Underley in 1730.[1] The house was described as a 'neat white mansion' in 1789.[2] In 1808 Alexander Nowell, recently returned from India, bought the estate from Ashton's great-grandson, Joseph Burrow.[3] He was about to build Netherside to the designs of George Webster. In 1825 Nowell laid the foundation stone of a new Underley on a new site and by the same architect.[4] Jacobean, with two fronts; the entrance front with a frontispiece of paired columns in two tiers. The other has turrets, two canted bays, and a porch of Doric columns. A towering third storey was intended over the entrance front. The stables, as importantly large as the house, were destroyed by fire in 1873, and made way for enormous additions.[5] Webster's designs were praised by contemporaries like Henry Shaw and by modern architectural historians like Sir Nikolaus Pevsner.[6]

1. Pearson, *Annals of Kirkby Lonsdale and Lunesdale Today*, 47.
2. T. West, *Guide to the Lakes*, 4th ed., 1789, 239-40.
3. CRO K, WD/U/28/1.
4. Pearson, *op.cit.*, 57; see pp. 24. The designs and 96 working drawings, with elevations and a watercolour by Richard Stirzaker were at Eller How in 1864: see pp. 340, 341, 342. Two further Stirzaker watercolours belong to the present owners of the estate.
5. Price, *Sharpe, Paley and Austin*, 88; *The Websters of Kendal*, no. 11.
6. See pp. 23-4.

Lancaster (L)

Aldcliffe Hall (**79**): a new house of 1817-18 for Edward Dawson who married Anne, daughter of Christopher Wilson of Abbot Hall, Kendal. A plain house, now demolished, with minimal Tudor embellishments. Tower added after 1847. The lodge a characteristic Webster lodge of 1827 (datestone).[1]

1. *Lons. Mag.*, ii, 1821, illus. facing 422; Twycross, ii, illus. facing 19.

Springfield Hall: 'erected at the commencement of the present century' possibly by Francis Webster, and belonging to Richard Godson, MP, when illustrated in 1847.[1] Three-bay villa with 'Wyatt windows' flanking the semicircular porch. Demolished.

1. Twycross, ii, 21.

Langdale (W)

Elterwater Old Hall (now the Eltermere Hotel): for David Huddleston, *c*.1823, perhaps by Francis Webster. Three bays, the centre a porch of two columns supporting an upper bay. All windows are tripartite. Huddleston's partner, John Robinson, built a new *Elterwater*

Hall on a more commanding site just across the lane. A hard slate 3-bay house, the centre gabled with a porch in front. The windows are large sashes but with hood moulds. Perhaps as late as *c*.1850 and by Thompson & Webster. George Webster's son Francis married Sarah Huddleston in 1860.

Leck (L)

Leck Hall: a chaste classical house probably by John Webb for the Welch family, *c*.1800, and altered in the 1830s by George Webster. He inserted a new staircase and dark marble fireplaces.[1] The Jacobethan lodge must be by Webster too.

[1.] J. M. Robinson, 'Leck Hall', *CL*, 4 Aug. 1988.

Levens (W)

Heaves Lodge: remodelled for James Gandy, *c*.1818, attributed to Francis or George Webster.[1] A Grecian box, with a simple Ionic loggia flanked by tripartite windows. Inside, the central hall under a well acts as a saloon and gives access to rooms at both levels, as in other Webster houses. One chimneypiece is certainly from the marble yard. The unhappy mansard roof was added when Austin & Paley remodelled the house in 1932.[2] Now an hotel. The stable block under a central arch is also by the Websters. Francis Webster built Dockray Mills for Gandy in 1816-17 and 1825.

[1.] *The Websters of Kendal*, no. 2.
[2.] Price, *Sharpe, Paley and Austin*, 99.

Levens Hall (**80**): alterations and additions for Richard Howard, and for Fulke Greville and Mary Howard, by Francis Webster, *c*.1805-*c*.1820. Levens Hall is well known for its splendid late-Elizabethan rooms and its topiary garden. It is quite unknown for the work of Francis Webster because that work was designed to be obscure – one of his tasks at Levens was to repair and extend Elizabethan panelling. The panelling of the smoking room is 'obviously not Elizabethan but equally obviously intended to look Elizabethan'.[1] Other rooms, including some upstairs, are of the same character.

On 16 May 1805 Richardson the agent wrote to Richard Howard at Ashstead, Surrey: 'your orders for alterations at the hall were given to Mr. Webster who says he took them down in writing on the spot'. He reports what is done – folding doors in the Great Hall, a door 'where . . . you proposed a water closet being made', Mrs Howard's dressing room ready for papering. In 1808 Howard proposed to visit Levens 'where you will find the improvements . . . far greater than might be expected'. Mr Gillow's carpet for the drawing room has not arrived; Mr Webster's water closet has not materialised for which Richardson offers the excuse that he is 'an officer in the Kendal Volunteers on permanent duty at Penrith'. Ten days later a choice of WCs is available at Kendal and with them a plumber for the fitting which he had done in Lord Lonsdale's new house at Lowther to 'great satisfaction'.[2]

Something more substantial was initiated *c*.1807 when a suite of small private rooms and a library was conceived as a slim tower attached to the south-east corner of the house, the roof providing a belvedere. Work went slowly. It was probably not finished until 1820 by which time Col. Fulke Greville Howard and his wife Mary, the heiress, had inherited. It was still described as 'new' in 1822.[3] The ceilings of two of the rooms are a delicate reduction of that in the drawing room, another example of Francis's ability to absorb the unfamiliar. The lower half of the chimneypiece in the same room is suggestive of those by George Webster at Underley and Eshton in 1826 and one wonders if his interest in the late-Elizabethan-Jacobean style began with his father's work at Levens.

Francis Webster was paid for a plan and elevation of a new water closet in 1815 but a bath was delayed for Col. Howard's consideration. Webster eventually presented a bill of £20 for a Garsdale marble bath. Webster dealings with the Howards began before 1800. There is a receipt of 29 June 1799 from Webster & Holme for £210 for building a marble mill at Helsington Laithes for Webster's own use, where he developed water power for cutting and polishing local marble, and constant payments for rents, quarries, and land.

[1.] Pevsner, *Cumb. and Westm.*, 270.
[2.] The correspondence and accounts are variously in the archives at Levens Hall and in the Howard papers in the Surrey RO.
[3.] *Lons. Mag*, iii, 1822; *The Websters of Kendal*, no. 4. See also *CL*, 6 June 2001, 110-14.

Park Head: alterations, *c.*1840, including a fine barge-boarded porch, for John R. Yeates, attributed to George Webster who was related to the family. The two men met in Frankfurt in 1841.[1]

[1.] See p. 79.

Lindale (L)

Eller How (**81-85, 87**): for themselves, *c.*1818 *et seq.* by Francis Webster, and 1827 *et seq.* by George Webster. Francis Webster bought a property in a narrow valley north-west of Lindale, presumably as a retreat, an idea of much antiquity, a *cottage orné*. He died there in 1827 and it seems that George began further alterations and additions at about that time. As such buildings are, it is irregular, on differing levels, has a variety of window patterns, and chimneys, decorative but not always functional, perched on the barge-boarded gables. The distinguishing feature at Eller How is the rustic Palladian porch at the north-east corner. The four columns have narrow sunken bands at top and bottom and the voussoirs of the central arch are made of alternate stones, raised and sunk, under a barge board. There are several such designs in Papworth which may have suggested the idea.[1] Twycross[2] does not show the raised 'scissors' verandah at the south-west corner so it must have been added after 1847. It is similar to the many timber porches which appeared in the firm's work at that time.

Inside, the features are mixed Jacobean and classical with good chimneypieces, one of which seems to be constructed from ancient marbles, probably brought back by George from his travels. The garden has a small lake and had a weeping figure on a knoll (now lost) which commemorated Francis; a sundial has also disappeared. Behind the house the ground is steep and rocky with contrived paths and seats.[3] Higher still are two follies. One, fort-like and in ruins, is seen flying a flag in Twycross's view. Beyond the house is *Eller How Farm* (**86**) with a datestone G E W 1831, and lower down the valley is *Hunter's Fold*, the farm which George left to his daughter Margaret.

[1.] Papworth, *Rural Residences*, e.g. pl. x.
[2.] Twycross, ii, 31; *Sketches of Grange*, 63-4.
[3] Webster sent detailed instructions for the maintenance of the garden when he was abroad: see pp. 81, 83, 85. A watercolour of the house by Richard Stirzaker and some further views and photographs were at Eller How in 1864: see pp. 340, 341.

Little Mitton (L)

Little Mitton Hall: remodelled for John Aspinall, 1844, attributed to George Webster. When Aspinall bought the house in 1840 much of it was of timber construction.[1] He rebuilt it, retaining the hall of *c.*1500 and clearly using George Webster as his architect. He used rubble masonry and mullioned and transomed windows with ball finials throughout, though much of this exterior work has been concealed by later additions.[2] The lodge and the good entrance piers have been spoilt.

[1] Whitaker, *History of the ... Parish of Whalley*, 1818 ed., 256.
[2] VCH *Lancs.*, vi, 389-90; Twycross, i, 11.

Lowther (W)

Lowther Hall: for Sir James Lowther, Earl of Lonsdale (d. 1802), 1796-1801, by Francis Webster; for William Lowther, Earl of Lonsdale (2nd cr.), 1806-14 by Robert Smirke. After the destruction by fire of the mansion at Lowther in 1718 almost all the great 18th-century English and Scottish architects, including Gibbs and the Adam brothers, prepared their plans for a new house. Nothing was built.[1] The family lived in the surviving west wing. The last of these academic exercises was *c.*1800 when Harrison of Chester provided several sets of drawings on the basis of a site plan drawn by 'Mr Webster'.[2] Sir James seems to have ignored these too, and he set Francis Webster to work extending the west wing. At least he was paid for journeys from Kendal and for superintending the new work in 1799 when there are bills for masons, stone stairs, plastering, and lead. Even earlier there were bills for quarrying and lime-burning (1796-8). In 1800 sashes, architrave brackets, and glass are billed; in 1801 chimneypieces and gilding. For 1802-3 Webster was paid 'in full for drawing plans and journeys to Appleby, Whitehaven and many journeys and attendances at Lowther 8 Aug. 1796 to 1800 ... £67. 10.' He was paid a further £21 on account as 'architect' in June 1803, and the next month £25 for architecture and £128 for marble masonry work. In 1804 – and here we are in an interregnum – Webster was still working on the old wing, perhaps with renewed urgency to have something complete for the new lord, even if an altogether grander idea was already in Lowther's mind.

He asked George Dance (1741-1825), who made designs, but found the prospect of working 300 miles from home daunting. Webster then continued until 1805-6, after which there are no more payments to architects. Dance had recommended the young Robert Smirke to Lowther but he had been in Italy since 1801. He returned to England in 1805 and in April 1806 accepted a commission to design a house.[3] New stables were started in June which seems to show the adequacy of Webster's house and he became the executant architect. The last payment to Webster as architect was in 1807, but in 1808-9 there are large payments for chimneypieces and these continue to 1812 (£1,293 in the final bill). On 16 February 1812 Webster & Proctor were paid in full for masons' work in the period 1806-10, a grand total of £11,026, but given as £14,500 in Smirke's final account of £77,000 presented in June 1814.

At Lowther Smirke's gutted house is a grand eyecatcher, but you would look long and hard and find no more than a yard or two of walling to represent Webster's work on the site. In Lowther church there is a tablet to the Countess of Lonsdale (d. 1824) by the Websters.

[1] Colvin, Crook, and Friedman, *Architectural Drawings at Lowther Castle, passim.*
[2] *Ibid.*, no. 13.
[3] M. H. Port, 'Lowther Hall and Castle', C*W*2, lxxxi, pp. 122-36; *The Websters of Kendal*, no. 1.

Mansergh (W)

Rigmaden Park (**88**): for Christopher Wilson, 1825-8, by Francis and George Webster. Christopher Wilson of Abbot Hall, Kendal, bought the estate from the Satterthwaites of Lancaster in 1825.[1] On it, in a magnificent and rather exposed position, stood a 'superior newly built farmhouse', parts of which were retained according to a note on George's designs. It is easy to see the connections with Helme Lodge of the previous year but here Webster introduces the two-storeyed central saloon that he was using in his Jacobean houses, with a gallery at first floor level. The designs were modified in building and the colonnade for the south front was abandoned. In one drawing a pencil sketch shows that a dome was being considered over the saloon.[2]

The masonry is brilliantly done, particularly the east bow and its flanking pedimented tripartite windows. The entrance on the west is sheltered by a *porte-cochère* of coupled square columns. The Grecian plasterwork of the interior was lost when dry rot led to the house being reduced to a roofless shell in 1948. The chimneypieces were kept and a new interior was built in 1991-2. In 1852 Miles Thompson made two designs for stables and clock tower, the latter a splendid affair.[3]

[1.] Boumphrey and Hudleston, 322.

[2.] CRO K, WD/Rig/acc.1224/1-9. Webster had a design for the house at Eller How in 1864: see p. 341.

[3.] CRO K, WD/Rig/acc.1296/48; *The Websters of Kendal*, no. 10; Burke, *Visitations*, i, 1852, 253. Christopher Wilson was a partner in the Lowwood Company: A. Palmer, *The Low Wood Gunpowder Company*, Gunpowder Mills Study Group, 1998, 24-6.

Melling (L)

Crow Trees: for Reginald Remington, *c*.1815, probably by Francis Webster. A 3 x 2 bay house with a long east wing.[1] Tripartite windows flank a Tuscan porch on the west front. Remington's son inherited Aynsome.

[1.] *Lons. Mag.*, ii, 1821, 162.

Middleton (W)

Grimeshill (**89**): for William Moore, *c*. 1836, by George Webster.[1] On a most romantic bend of the river Lune, a late-17th century house was largely rebuilt by Webster with the usual display of gables, stepped windows, and finials. The door was arched and like the rest of the porch had a strongly classical flavour, comparable with Netherside and reminiscent of Thompson's bank at Kirkby Lonsdale. The contents were sold in 1938 just before the house was demolished. The sale catalogue[2] lists 'grotesque wooden fireplaces' and pieces dated between 1695 and 1702. The 'marble fireplaces . . . [with] . . . fluted columns' may be by Webster. Burlington slates certainly would be.

[1.] The working drawings were at Eller How in 1864: see p. 342.

[2.] CRO K, WBD 35/SP100. The house is illustrated in Robinson, *Country Houses*, 271.

Milnthorpe (W)

Dallam Tower (**90-91**): remodelled for George Wilson, 1826, by George Webster. The seven-bay brick house of 1720-22,[1] with hipped roof and door architraves pinched up in the centre as was then the fashion (there are two examples in Beetham), is still there forming the core of Webster's extensions of 1826[2]. He stuccoed the brick, scoring it as masonry, put a solid Tuscan *porte-cochère* in front of the door, and hid the basement behind an earth bank. He added low two-bay wings connected by one-bay links. Beyond on either side are stables and offices, making a very long façade.

Inside is a fine drawing room of 1720, but the library and dining room are Webster's although the latter has later plasterwork. Some mullioned windows from an even earlier house are retained as instructed in the basement. The fine greenhouse, once linked to the house by a glazed corridor, was supplied by W. & D. Bailey of Holborn, London.[3]

The court of farm offices was designed by Webster with detail partly derived from his designs for Wordsworth's house in the same year. As built, it was simplified, with much use of primitive orders and water-worn limestone, also seen in the park buildings like the substantial buck house of *c.*1851.

In Beetham church are tablets to several Wilsons by the Websters, including George Smyth (1782-1853), who changed his name to Wilson and was Webster's patron at Dallam.

[1.] *Lons. Mag.*, ii, 1821, illus. facing 281, 281-5.
[2.] The designs are in CRO K, WD/D/plans/4, and at the house; *The Websters of Kendal*, no. 13.
[3.] M. Woods and A. Warren, *Glasshouses*, 1988, 112.

Harmony Hill: for Capt. Joseph Fayrer (d. 1801), a partner in the Lowwood Company whose works were built by Francis Webster and William Holme.[1] A three-bay ashlar house with a pedimented Ionic doorcase, no doubt a Webster design, *c.*1800.

[1.] R. K. Bingham, *Chronicles of Milnthorpe*, 1987, 199; Palmer, *The Low Wood Gunpowder Company*, 26-9.

Morecambe (L)

The Elms (Bare): clearly of the same group and period as Hall Garth, Over Kellet, and probably by either Coulthard or George Webster. A recessed centre, angle pilasters, and good marble fireplaces. Lodge and gate piers with incised ornament. Much disturbed by enlargement as an hotel.

New Hutton (W)

Hill Top (**92-93**): extensions, *c.*1820 for Ralph Fisher, a Liverpool merchant who bought it 1818,[1] attributed to Francis and George Webster. New wings with tripartite windows to new dining and drawing rooms, the former with a curved inner wall with niches. Minor but attractive plasterwork and an excellent series of marble chimneypieces. The staircase is top-lit and has a handsome iron rail and a frieze with wreaths. Fisher gave £100 towards the new church of 1828 designed by George Webster.

[1.] *WG*, 8 and 15 Aug. 1818. The house said to have been built in the late 18th century by a Mr Nowell: Kelly, *Westm.*, 1934, 58.

Newton (Slaidburn), (YWR)

Knowlmere Manor: for Jonathan Peel, *c.*1849,[1] attributed to Thompson & Webster. Jonathan Peel moved from his large villa in Accrington, Hyndburn House, to his new Jacobethan country house in the Forest of Bowland in 1849. It has heavy detailing of gables, porch, and windows but many of them have forerunners in a lighter style, notably a stepped projecting chimney with a gothic niche as at Heysham Hall and Aireville.

[1.] Crossley, *Accrington Captains of Industry*, 17-18; Burke, *Visitations*, 2nd ser., i, 1854, 150.

Over Kellet (L)

Hall Garth: for the Rev. Gilbert Ainslie, 1826, by William Coulthard of Lancaster. At first sight a Webster house and of the same period as Helme Lodge, Kendal, of which it is a smaller version. It is a surprise to find that the designs are signed by William Coulthard,[1] the man who not only carved the portico of Helme Lodge to Webster's design but shipped it complete from Preston on the canal.[2] There were other links too. In one of his letter books George Webster stuck an engraving of Halton rectory[3] in his Jacobean style but wrote over it that William Coulthard designed it. Hall Garth is a square house in limestone ashlar of 5 x 4 bays. The centre is recessed on two fronts and in one of these a pedimented Greek Doric portico is set. At the angles of the house are giant plain pilasters, again as at Helme Lodge. There have been alterations inside and out. The authorship of the house remains something of a mystery.

[1.] Colvin, 273.
[2.] CRO K, WD/Cr/4/203/10.
[3.] CRO K, WDX 1315.

Patton (W)

Shaw End (**94-96**): for Arthur Shepherd, 1796-1802, by Francis Webster and William Holme. A plain seven-bay house with a three-bay porch of feathered capital columns. A tripartite door led to a hall with a screen of columns like those of the porch beyond which rose the staircase leading to a landing with another screen of Ionic columns. Some pretty inlaid fireplaces and delicate cornices. Behind is a court of offices. A handsome stable block is entered through an arch in a tower topped by an octagonal tempietto, the forerunner of such features at Dallam Tower (1826) and Holker (1838). On 7 July 1802 Shepherd noted that 'for £3735.13.5 I built my House, stables, 2 bridges, garden walls and a new road from Docker bridge'.[1] North lodge dated 1837. The house was severely damaged by fire in December 1983, but has since been rebuilt. Of the Websters' work only the porch remains.

[1.] CRO K, WD/SE, building accounts.

Pennington (L)

Conynger Hurst (now The Hurst): for Robert Francis Yarker, 1850-51, by Miles Thompson. A *cottage orné*, gabled and barge-boarded, four-centred porch with kings' heads on stops. Hall open to the roof, with a gallery.[1]

[1.] CRO B, BDX 96, plans, elevations, specifications.

Pennington House (formerly Shannon House): for the Park family, *c.*1860, probably by Miles Thompson. Marble chimneypieces but most conspicuously a large timber *porte-cochère*.

Penwortham (L)

The Oaks: for John Cooper, 1837, a Grecian villa of considerable size on a knoll above the River Ribble, directly south of the centre of Preston. Webster's hallmark of three discs heading each pilaster figures prominently in Twycross's detailed lithograph.[1] Demolished.

[1.] Twycross, i, 68.

Penwortham Priory (**97-98**): for Lt.-Col. Laurence Rawstorne, 1830-32, by George Webster. It is not easy to reconcile Buck's view of the house (1726) with Webster's house which incorporated a fragment of it. Webster used brick with stone dressings, curved and straight gables, crenellations, and mullioned and transomed windows. At the south-east corner was a powerful octagonal tower with larger gothic windows and at the south-west what appears to be a chapel with spired turrets and triple lancets, but in fact was the dining room. The tower had an octagon room with a groined ceiling and niches at the sides with statues executed in the studio of Canova. At the back was a large L-shaped gothic cloister of 11 bays.[1] This most picturesque of Webster's creations was demolished *c.*1922.

There are Rawstorne tablets by the Websters in the church and several buildings on the estate probably by George Webster, e.g. the school of 1839.[2]

[1.] Twycross, i, 47; LRO, DP 386/58, watercolour by John Weld, 1835. Rawstorne's diaries name Webster as the architect: *The Websters of Kendal*, no. 22. There are later plans in LRO, DDX 884/3-12.

[2.] A. Crosby, *Penwortham in the Past*, 1988, 117.

Preston Patrick (W)

Long Croft: *c.*1850. A stone gabled house looking very much like a Thompson vicarage such as that at Staveley, but possibly the 'Villa Residence at Crooklands' for which George Webster had plans and elevations at Eller How in 1864.[1]

[1.] See p. 342.

Preston Richard (W)

Summerlands (**99-101**): for John Harrison, 1846, attributed to George Webster or Miles Thompson, or both. A 5 x 4-bay Jacobethan house with a south front resembling Moreton of 1828, with two-storey canted bays with the same cresting.[1] The entrance side has square bays and a porch with ogee-capped turrets. Inside, the staircase, as at Whelprigg, rises round the walls of a large square saloon. Good chimneypieces and Jacobean ceilings. Excellent gate piers and 'rockery' stone lodge.

[1.] *The Websters of Kendal*, no. 38.

Read (L)

Read Hall (**102-108**): for John Fort, 1818-25, by George Webster.[1] Read was the seat of the Nowells and Alexander Nowell (d. 1772) ruined himself by his 'expensive and ill-judged alterations' left half-finished.[2] Richard Fort became the owner and his son rebuilt the house.

Read is strictly Grecian.[3] A central bow rising to a shallow dome in the centre of the main front is encircled by a colonnade of Ionic columns which also form the porch on the return front. All this, and the planning behind, appear to be based on Ingleborough Hall of 1814 by William Atkinson, perhaps Webster's teacher. The other striking feature is the giant panelled pilaster at each corner in place of the more usual quoins, and derived from Storrs Hall. Within, the 3-section hall and separate staircase hall introduce an unexpected grandeur of concept.

Pevsner found Read 'perfect externally, a little heavy internally',[4] and one sees what he meant in the drawing room in particular; the plasterwork is very elaborate. The glazed bookcases in the library compare with fittings at Netherside, which Webster designed in the same years.

[1.] Whitaker, *History of the . . . Parish of Whalley,* 1876 ed., ii, 40; VCH *Lancs.*, vi, 505.

[2.] Whitaker, *op.cit.*, 39.

[3.] Burke, *Visitations*, 2nd ser., ii, 1855, 169, VCH Lancs, vi, 503; Twycross, ii, 24; *The Websters of Kendal*, no. 3.

[4.] Pevsner, *N. Lancs*, 207.

Rusland (L)

Rusland Hall: for Charles Dickson Archibald, 1850 (datestone), attributed to Thompson & Webster. The five-bay, three-storey classical centre was the early-18th century house of the Rawlinsons. Wings of two bays and two stories were added in 1850 and Thompson was no doubt the designer. The east wing runs back to include the stables. The detail of window architraves and chimneys is characteristic of the firm at this time. The interior was also changed and here too are typical plasterwork, fireplaces, mouldings, and so on. A three-arched arcade opens the old house to the new wing.

Whitestock Hall: a plain rendered five-bay, two-storey house, *c*.1820, with a Tuscan porch, attached to one-bay pedimented pavilions by straight links. The Rev. John Romney, son of the painter, is said to have been his own designer here.[1] The detailing, however, suggests that Francis Webster's was the professional hand which carried out the design.

[1] A. B. Chamberlain, *George Romney*, 1910, 227.

Rydal (W)

Fox Ghyll: Robert Blakeney, an ex-customs officer from Whitehaven, lived here *c*.1813-19. Wordsworth wrote him a long letter about changing his windows to French windows so that he could see the views when seated.[1] The details of the interior suggest the Websters' hands.

[1] M. Moorman, *William Wordsworth: The Later Years*, 1965, 233.

Fox How: remodelled in 1833 for Dr Thomas Arnold. Gabled, with chimneys which were 'Wordsworth's "architectural creation and special care" (so the architect averred)' to Charlotte Brontë.[1] The interior details again suggest that he was George Webster.

[1] W. Gerin, *Charlotte Brontë*, 1967, 449.

Glen Rothay (formerly Ivy Cottage): for William Ball, *c*.1835, attributed to George Webster. A Cambridge academic, the Rev. Samuel Tillbrook, bought David's, an inn, and refurbished it in 1817 (datestone). It forms the south end of the present house (an inn again) with reeded doorcases to small rooms and could well be by Francis Webster. In 1831 it was bought by a Quaker, William Ball, who then obtained designs for additions on a larger scale, it would seem from George Webster, renaming it Glen Rotha.[1] Wordsworth, who never commented on the works at Rydal Hall by his landlady, wrote to his family on 25 June 1836 that 'the botched Ivy Cot[tage] . . . is just what I expected'.[2] Had he ever looked at it? Webster added new rooms with ribbed ceilings and large mullioned windows, a new entrance and hall, and a staircase like the one at the hall where he was then working.

[1] Boumphrey and Hudleston, 297; M. L. Armitt, *Rydal*, 1916, 434, 436-7.
[2] Hill (ed.), *Letters of William and Dorothy Wordsworth*, vi, pt. 3, 264.

The Rash: in 1826 the poet was expecting to be turned out of Rydal Mount by Lady le Fleming and bought a plot of land just below. He asked George Webster to make designs and the architect then made a second set with modifications prompted by the client whose views on how to build in the Lake District were strict. The house was never built but was important in Webster's career, introducing him to local vernacular elements which he thereafter absorbed into his style. In 1844 when Isabella Fenwick, the poet's amanuensis, wished to live nearer, a reduction of the plan was made, but again not built.[1]

[1] A. Taylor, 'The Lowly Dwelling of William Wordsworth Esqre', *Georgian Group Jnl*, vii, 1997, 43-55; see pp. 353-68.

Rydal Hall: alterations for Lady le Fleming, 1835-6, by George Webster. To the original vernacular hall Sir Michael's 'new front' was added shortly before 1796.[1] From Joseph Senhouse at Carlisle he received 'a plan and particulars of alterations to be made at Rydal'.[2] Could the stark plan with canted ends be this plan?[3] There is also a group of designs for the same position at Rydal, of different character and all from the end of the 18th century.[4] Sir Michael reigned from 1757, when he was nine, to 1806. There is an elevation with towered corners in the manner of Wilton and a plan with a circular drawing room between an oval eating room and a library, but with an oddly rough elevation. Lastly come two similar elevations, both of three storeys and both with a full-height centre bow. This is clearly the block that stands there now. One version has a three-bay arched loggia at the right hand side. None of the drawings is signed or dated.

John Hird was the architect of the 'new' front at Conishead Priory in 1777.[5] This was plain, of three storeys with three full-height bays and with a loggia almost exactly like that of the Rydal design. It is possible then that Hird built the carcass of the south wing, perhaps *c*.1780. Work, as correspondence between Jackson the agent and Sir Michael shows, was going on in 1805 and there are references to the 'Battlement' and 'roughcasting the library' which suggest old work rather than new.[6]

The earliest Webster bill is of 1818 and for a matter of shillings.[7] George Webster designed the new church at Rydal and there are bills for furniture, curtains, and so on in 1826, so some rooms must have been fitted up by then. In 1836 is a bill for the dining room fireplace from Websters and tacked onto this George Webster's 'account for plans and journeys, 12 gns'.[8] Comparing this with a bill of £25 for two designs for the Ulverston Savings Bank of the same time, twelve guineas would cover a good deal of 'architecture'. It is evident that most of the interiors of Rydal Hall are by Webster – dining and drawing rooms, the bow room, staircase, library upstairs, and part of the hall, together with their fireplaces and plasterwork can be authenticated by reference to other Webster houses.

[1] West, *Guide to the Lakes*, 6th ed., 1796, 79n.
[2] Hist. MSS Comm., 12th Rep., App. vii, *Rydal Hall Manuscripts*, 1890, 361 (26 April 1783).
[3] CRO K, WDY 56.
[4] CRO K, WD/Ry, additional records.
[4] *Lons. Mag.*, iii, 1822, illus. facing 201.
[6] CRO K, WD/Ry/5693.
[7] CRO K, WD/Ry/box 116.
[8] *Ibid.*

Rydal Mount: the Wordsworths and their landlady, Lady le Fleming, may have employed the Websters for e.g. the staircases. Two minor chimneypieces upstairs could be theirs.

Stepping Stones: a rebuilding of Lanty Fleming's cottage and a clear descendant of Wordsworth's unbuilt house with gables and circular and diamond chimneys, and with three fine marble chimneypieces inside. Probably by George Webster, *c*.1845.

Samlesbury (L)

Samlesbury Hall: bought by the Braddylls in 1678,[1] although they never lived there, acquiring Conishead by marriage. The house became an inn, the Braddyll Arms, beside the Preston-Blackburn turnpike in 1835.[2] When George Webster completed Conishead he quarried Samlesbury for woodwork, thus effecting alterations there. His additions were minor, but they include the large chimneypiece in the hall of 1845.

[1.] VCH *Lancs.*, vi, 307; R. Eaton, *History of Samlesbury*, 1936, 34.

[2.] A. Hodge, *Samlesbury Hall*, 1990, 16.

Satterthwaite (L)

Graythwaite Hall (**109**): for Myles Sandys, *c.*1840, alterations and additions by George Webster. A rambling house with much Webster detail in a plain style at the back. The south and west fronts are another matter. Here is his fully elaborated Jacobean style, with many gables, finials, and bay windows, but, oddly, an Italianate tower with mullioned windows. Inside, one or two ceilings possibly of this 1840 work. There is also a pretty lodge of this time.[1]

Alterations of 1874 with music and billiard rooms were designed by James Grundy of Ulverston but may not have been carried out.[2] Then about 1889 R. Knill Freeman introduced foreign red sandstone into a perverse pulling-about of Webster's south front. He also changed interiors.

[1.] Burke, *Visitations*, i, 1852, 121, illus; *ibid.*, 2nd ser., i, 1854, 227, illus. George had the designs at Eller How in 1864: see p. 341.

[2.] CRO B, Z/1179/3, plans.

Graythwaite New Hall (now Silverholme) (**110**): for John Job Rawlinson, *c.*1830, attributed to George Webster.[1] The Rawlinsons were seated at Low Graythwaite Hall, set in a hollow no more than a mile from Windermere but with no view of the lake. Probably at the time of his marriage in 1831 J. J. Rawlinson decided to build Graythwaite New Hall on a knoll above the lake with unrestricted views.[2] The ratio of glass to stone leaves no doubt that this was the objective. Very plain outside but the interior is another rich display of the decoration used by Webster at Read Hall and at his own house in Kendal. The staircase is also of the type used at Kendal Town Hall in 1859. The chimneypieces are some of the finest from the marble yard.

[1.] Rawlinson planned some alterations in 1844, which were undoubtedly by Webster: 'I told Mr Webster's clerk who travelled outside the Ulverston mail from Lindal to Levens Bridge to send the plans of my proposed alterations': CRO B, BD/HJ/90/33/6.

[2.] The house is on Rawlinson's Nab, 'a picturesque point, either for the eye or the pencil': West, *Guide to the Lakes*, 7th ed., 1799, 69.

Sedbergh (YWR)

Ingmire Hall (**111**): for John Upton, 1838 (datestone), attributed to George Webster. A large rambling house largely reconstructed in the early 19th century. In 1844 it was to let for seven years following Upton's death and was described as having 'undergone a state of complete repair, is newly furnished . . . the stables, coach houses and offices are quite new'.[1] More or less Jacobethan; behind its gables and chimneys rose a tower with square turrets rather like that at Whittington Hall but here hardly more than scenery with little depth. From a sale catalogue of 1922 we know that there were panelled plaster ceilings, black, red, and white marble chimneypieces, old oak, and modern staircases.[2] The house was severely damaged by fire in 1928, but has recently been partly rehabilitated.[3]

[1.] *W.G.*, 2 Jan. 1844.

[2.] CRO K, WDB 35/SP 277-8.

[3.] Waterson and Meadows, *Lost Houses of the West Riding*, 4-5.

Settlebeck: for John and Elizabeth Bousted, 1836 (datestone), probably by George Webster. Gabled, barge-boarded, with verandah and timber porch, no surviving interiors.

Sedgwick (W)

Sedgwick House: for John Wakefield, *c.*1810.[1] The house had a centre and wings, a semi-circular porch, and offices behind, and was comparable with Longlands.[2] The complex gates near Hawes Bridge survive from this building, which was probably by Francis Webster. A new house by Paley & Austen replaced it in 1868.[3]

[1.] *Lons. Mag.*, ii, 1821, 162.

[2.] CRO K, WDB/22, block plan.

[3.] Price, *Sharpe, Paley and Austin*, 86.

Selside (W)

Lowbridge House: for Richard Fothergill, *c.*1837, his own architect.[1] It is picturesque, large, gabled, with mullioned and transomed windows and varied chimneys. It is so completely Websterian that George must at least have given advice.

[1.] Colvin, 376.

Mozergh House (**112**): for J. and M. M[achell], 1835 (datestone), attributed to George Webster. A small but elaborate Jacobean house with barge-boarded gables, including that on the porch, and mullioned and transomed windows. The offices are contained in a north wing. The interior has ribbed ceilings and Webster fireplaces. Rescued from dereliction by the Aindow family, *c.*1970.

Settle (YWR)

Anley: for John Birkbeck, *c.*1818,[1] probably by the Websters. A handsome house in a small park. Ashlar, of 5 x 5 bays with a Greek Doric portico. Top-lit stairs, good plasterwork, and marble chimneypieces inside rather like Esthwaite Lodge. In the portico a band of decorative *guttae* seen in some Ulverston houses of the same period.

[1.] Brayshaw and Robinson, *History of . . . Giggleswick*, 176; R. Birkbeck, *The Birkbecks of Westmorland*, 1900.

Ashfield House: a large town house for William Birkbeck who married Rachel Gough of Kendal,[1] perhaps by Francis Webster. An early-19th century ashlar house of five bays and two-and-a-half storeys, with a semi-circular porch and a bow at the back. The attached wings are set back. The interior has been wrecked; the stairs have gone but led up to an oval landing.

[1.] Brayshaw and Robinson, *op. cit.*, 175.

Ingfield (now the Falcon Manor Hotel): for the Rev. Hogarth John Swale, first vicar of Settle,

1841 (datestone), by George Webster, who had 38 working drawings at Eller How in 1864.[1] A large freestone Jacobean house with gables and bay windows, set on a terrace bounded by a set of Webster walls and bastions. The plan is like Eshton with an imperial staircase in a central saloon from which the other rooms open. Here it has a glazed ceiling.[2] A billiard room was added in 1911 by C. Harrison Townsend.[3]

[1] See p. 342.

[2] Brayshaw and Robinson, *op. cit.*, 176; NYRO, ZXF M3/2/2, design for glazing in a traditional 17th-century style. The specification for carpenter's work 'for Mr Webster the architect', witnessed by Miles Thompson, 12 April 1841, is at the hotel.

[3] Designs at the hotel.

Langcliffe Place: additions probably for William Clayton, *c*.1839. The 18th-century house has an extension ending in a pilastered bow. The Jacobethan lodge of 1839 (datestone) is clearly a Webster design.

Terrace: nine houses with Greek ornament; a possible Webster design.

Whitefriars: altered in the early 19th century, perhaps by the Websters. The drawing room has a Jacobethan ceiling looking like a Webster design poorly executed, but there are some good marble fireplaces and the gates are like those at Nibthwaite Grange.

Silverdale (L)

Hill Top (now Hazelwood): for Leonard Willan of Kendal.[1] A classical villa with a matching lodge and a good farmhouse. Enough of the original build remains to suggest that it is a Webster house of the 1840s. Large extensions, and terraces by Thomas Mawson, *c*.1920.

[1] E. Baines, *History of Lancashire*, 1870, ii, 604.

West Lindeth: a rustic, early 19th-century house but with monumental Greek Doric columns as gateposts, and perhaps by George Webster. There is another pair, square in this case, at *Spring Bank* in the village.

Simonstone (L)

Simonstone Hall: refaced, 1818, in a Jacobethan style for Charles Whitaker, with mullions and obelisk finials.[1] George Webster started his first major commission just across the road at Read in the same year and may have been the architect here.[2]

[1] Robinson, *Country Houses*, 237.

[2] VCH *Lancs.*, vi, 498: 'very much modernised and of little architectural interest'.

Skelsmergh (W)

Dodding Green (**113**): altered for the Rev. Charles Brigham, *c*.1840-42 (datestones).[1] Jacobethan, with barge-boarded gables and diagonally-set square chimneys. The ceiling of the chapel marks it out as the work of George Webster, but all detail was lost in the philistine repairs of 1968.

[1] Sister Agnes, *The Story of Skelsmergh*, 1949, 68.

Gilthwaiterigg: a 15th-century hall house much altered, a property of the Rawlinsons of

Graythwaite.[1] Dormer windows in the form of those designed for Wordsworth's house at Rydal suggest that George Webster made the alterations.

[1] *Annals*, 119.

Skerton (L)

Ryelands Park: *c.*1836, may be attributable to George Webster. A rather heavy square classical house in a park, with several good marble chimneypieces of Webster design.

Skipton (YWR)

Aireville: for Henry Alcock of the Craven Bank, 1836, attributed to George Webster[1]. Harsh Tudor exterior; inside, the ceilings and other details survived the extensive alterations and additions of 1945 when the house became a school. The interior plasterwork is like that of Settle Town Hall and Ingfield.

[1] *The Websters of Kendal*, no. 28.

Slyne-with-Hest (L)

Beaumont Grange (Black Castle): for William Hinde of Lancaster, early-19th century,[1] visually linked to the work of Francis or George Webster. Three bays, the centre rising higher, long links to one-bay pavilions with battered walls, all castellated; marble chimneypieces. Webster tablets to members of the Hinde family in Lancaster church.

[1] Baines, *History of Lancashire*, 1870, ii, 597.

Slyne Lodge: alterations for R. B. Peacock, *c.*1830, by George Webster who had the plans in his portfolios at Eller How.[1] Three tall pedimented windows to the road, and a bow and Italianate window on the garden front. Enlarged in 1881 (datestone) and the interior altered.

[1] See p. 342.

Stainforth (YWR)

Neals Ing, for Pudsey Dawson, for some time resident at Hornby Castle, 1830-37. A large Elizabethan farmhouse in the style of George Webster's new Town Hall at Settle (1832). Stephen Wilman undertook to build the house and sent designs to Dawson. Edward Gibson of Kendal valued the house in January 1838 and on his recommendation Dawson added £10 'for plans'.[1] Wilman may have been Webster's executant.

[1] Leeds City Archives, Dawson of Langcliffe MSS, 7/DW/689.

Taitlands (**114**): for Thomas Redmayne, *c.*1835, probably by George Webster. Three bays wide with panelled angle pilasters and an Ionic porch. Rear elevation of four bays and more pilasters. An octagonal hall of the same design as that at Anley leads by way of an Ionic screen to the stairs in an apse. In the dining room an Ionic marble fireplace. A variety of datestones, 1831-41.

Stainmore (W)

Borrowthwaite: enlarged for Michael Ewbank, 1862, by Miles Thompson.[1] An Italian villa in a narrow valley in the Pennines. Thompson's designs were chosen in preference to those of Ross of Darlington. The house has a tower with a pyramid roof and arched windows, and a three-bay loggia with a datestone. The interior joinery is of high quality and resembles work at the Lancaster Bank in Ulverston of the same period.

[1.] The designs are in CRO K, WD/DE.

Staveley (W)

Bridge House: of slate and limestone, gabled, and very like Thompson's vicarage, so no doubt also by him, *c*.1860. Webster chimneypieces.

Staveley-in-Cartmel (L)

Townhead (**115**): a small house remodelled for William Townley, *c*.1800,[1] probably by Francis Webster. Wings were built set back behind colonnades of Tuscan columns and the windows were given architraves. The west front, looking out over Windermere, has a shallow bow lighting the drawing room which has a white marble chimneypiece. A grey fossil example in another room.

[1.] Sold in 1804 for £7,000, a 'new-built freehold dwelling-house': LRO, DDTy 1/2/25.

Threshfield (YWR)

Netherside (**116-119**): for Alexander Nowell, *c*.1820, attributed to George Webster. Alexander Nowell leased Netherside Wood on 10 March 1820 from the Atkinson family. The lease refers to his building an 'extensive mansion with suitable outhouses' soon after the death of William Atkinson in 1816. Assuming that the building followed the lease, a date of *c*.1820 seems probable.[1] Nowell had left the army in India to make a fortune in indigo dye, returning to England in 1805 to take a lease on Gawthorpe. Is this why he chose the Jacobean style?

Netherside is a severe stone house with straight gables and mullioned windows onto which a three-bay arched porch is fastened like an elaborate brooch.[2] Behind there is a large hall or salon lit from above by an octagonal dome. Decoration in other rooms is sparse but in the dining room is a sideboard very like that at Read Hall.

[1.] Information from Mrs S. P. Wrathnell of English Heritage, 9 Nov. 1988.

[2.] Illustrated in Whitaker, *History of . . . Craven*, 1878 ed., ii, 556. See also p. 24.

Troutbeck (W)

Briery Close: described by Charlotte Brontë in 1850 as 'of the local Westmorland stone with gables picked out in fretted wood', i.e. with barge boards.[1] Much enlarged or rebuilt. 'Newly built' when for sale in 1839.[2] It could well have been by George Webster.

[1.] Gerin, *Charlotte Brontë*, 444.

[2.] *WG*, 21 Sept. 1839.

Holbeck Cottage (**120**): a gabled house with fine arrays of cylindrical chimneys, possibly by Webster or Thompson. Entrance between wings under a balcony; plain interior.[1]

[1.] There is a garden plan of 1886: CRO K, WDB 35.

St Catherine's: a stone, brick, and slate *cottage orné* of *c*.1810 for Ann Parker of Park Nook and Hornby Hall, who sold to the Earl of Bradford in 1831.[1] It spanned the Wanlass Beck, had a verandah and balcony of intersecting arcs connecting drawing and dining rooms at first-floor level with stairs to the lawns and pleasure gardens. The chimneys were cylindrical, the chimneypieces of black marble, and Francis Webster was probably the designer. Crushingly enlarged upwards in 1895 and demolished *c.*1930.

[1] Boumphrey and Hudleston, 51.

Tunstall (L)

Aireville (now Greta House): attributed to George Webster. A stone Jacobethan house, gabled and barge-boarded, with chimneys like Larch How and a glazed porch; mullioned and tramsomed windows. Inside, simple moulded ceilings with rich cornices.

Summerfield: altered in 1841 for Edward Tatham by George Webster who had twelve working drawings at Eller How in 1864.[1]. The square house is a shadow of what was built. It was originally stuccoed, with angle pilasters. Side elevation with an open-based pediment over a balcony, and originally more panelled pilasters.

[1] See p. 342; Boumphrey and Hudleston, 290; Twycross, ii, 26.

Thurland Castle (**121**): restoration and additions for Richard Toulmin North, 1809-10 by Jeffry Wyatville and Francis Webster, and 1826-9 by George Webster. The medieval castle was destroyed in the Civil War although much walling and a 14th-century door are still visible. North took over the task of restoration and Wyatt, as he then was, exhibited designs at the R.A. in 1809, but Francis Webster was the executant architect.[1] Whitaker in 1819 considered the work 'very judiciously done on the old foundations'.[2] The tall tower was probably the model for Webster's Howard tower at Levens.

   In 1826-9 the castle was extended to the south when George Webster added a large drawing room but the work seems to have been left unfinished.[3] Between the castle and the moat Webster introduced the first of his bastioned terraces. Fire damaged the castle in 1879. It was restored by Paley & Austin and the interior is largely theirs.[4]

[1] VCH *Lancs.*, viii, 235 n. 81, 236, plan.
[2] *Ibid.*, 235.
[3] *Ibid.*, 235 n. 82, where Webster is said to have planned 'further additions' to extend the east wing to the south, *c.*1829. The designs were at Eller How in 1864: see p. 340.
[4] Price, *Sharpe, Paley and Austin*, 87-8.

Ulverston (L)

Conishead Priory (now the Manjushri Buddhist Centre) (**122-128**): for Col. Thomas Richmond-Gale-Braddyll, 1839-44, by George Webster. A priory of Austin canons existed on this site by 1184 but everything visible dates from after 1823. Dissolved in 1536, Conishead passed through several families to the Braddylls of Portfield, Whalley (L). Records of building are scant but by 1774 the north front was described by Father West as having 'a piazza supported by clustered gothic columns with three series of ox-eye windows' and battlements, the ox-eye windows suggesting a date in the mid-to-late 17th century.[1] According to the 11-year old William Fell in 1777 'one side is built anew by the Curious Architect Hird' in about 1775.[2] When Hird remodelled Sizergh about 1773 his mason was Robert Webster. Did he perform the same function at Conishead? Fell described the north front as 'of ancient form'. Hird's design of three plain classical floors was relieved by three-storey canted bays and an arched loggia at the north end.[3]

This was the house inherited by Braddyll and described as ruinous in 1821. Philip Wyatt was commissioned to rebuild, but was dismissed for lack of progress in 1828. George Webster's enormous gothic house was begun in 1838[4] and bankrupted its owner in 1848, after which both house and contents were put up for sale.[5]

George Webster also designed Bardsea church for Braddyll. There are several monuments to the Braddyll family in Ulverston church.

[1.] [T. West], *Antiquities of Furness*, 1774, xxvii.

[2.] W. Fell, *History and Antiquities of Furness*, ed. L. R. Ayre, 1887, 8.

[3.] *Lons. Mag.*, iii, 1822, facing 201.

[4.] There were 190 working drawings at Eller How in 1864: see p. 342. Surviving plans are in CRO B, BDX 53/10; copies showing the 'new Addition' in *ibid.*, Z1091, dated 1878 but in George Webster's name.

[5.] J. Park, *Some Ulverston Records*, 1932, 33-7. There is a priced sale catalogue in CRO B, Z3183. See pp. 34-5.

There is much charming and interesting building of the Websters' time in the 'London of Furness' including villas on the fringes of the town and much further out. John Wood's map of 1832 shows land owned by George Webster on both sides of Fountain Street and on the corner of Brewery Street and Union Street, a site now occupied by the Union Inn.

Belle Vue, Princes St: large additions at the front, probably by Francis Webster for William Dodgson J.P., *c.*1810. Porch with angled pilasters, very prettily decorated hall and staircase, and on the landing a Palladian opening of coupled Roman Doric columns with the curious use of *guttae* hanging like a fringe on the entablature, bereft of their triglyphs, which equally oddly figure on the stair-tread ends. Pattern books of the time encouraged the dismemberment of structural detail for purely decorative purposes.[1] The same details appear again at Springfield House, south of the town, and at Bigland Hall and Allithwaite Lodge.

[1.] C. and J. Paine, *Decorative Details*, 1795, 28n, is a case in point.

Daltongate, the Fell house (now the Lonsdale House Hotel): strictly a town house, of six bays and three storeys, the end bays recessed and the door of necessity off-centre. It is now round-headed and of the same design as Ivy House, Hawkshead. Plain interior with good Webster fireplace. At the end of the garden is a structure hard to describe. It is a façade only, a theatrical flat, but in rocky stone with castellations and blocked gothick openings. What can its date be? The house is doubtless by Francis Webster, *c.*1790.

Dykelands (**129**): further away from the town, a mixture of gothic and Tudor, gabled, with bay windows with pointed lights. Timber porch. Probably as late as *c.*1840 and by George Webster or Miles Thompson.[1]

[1.] To let in 1844: CRO B, Z/1531.

Fair View (**130-131**): for Charles Kennedy the ironmaster and said to be of 1817, which seems early for its style, perhaps by Francis Webster. It was certainly on Wood's map of 1832. Kennedy married in 1820. A classical five-bay house with a three-bay pediment and an entrance porch of Tuscan columns; on one side a blank window and a niche with statuary.

The house is of rockwork rustication throughout. The garden front has a bow with oval rooms behind; sparing decoration. A large greenhouse attached. In the same garden stood an Elizabethan-style house, *Kirklands*, much of the same date and said to have been built to house the overflow from Fair View.

Fountain Street, nos. 27-31 (**133**): a terrace of four three-storey houses with paired columned doorways and ground-floor windows under segmental arches. Built on land belonging to George Webster in 1832 and attributable to him. The houses are not mentioned in his will and must have been sold during his lifetime.

Hammershead Hill Villa: for the Rev. Bartholomew McHugh, 1835, attributed to George Webster. McHugh was the Roman Catholic priest at Ulverston and it was for him that the vaulted chapel was built in 1822. The house was built on the sea wall at the foot of the Ulverston canal. Its design was unusual. A Jacobean centre with barge-boarded gables, sets of chimneys, mullioned windows, and a north wing in the same style. Both ends of that had castellated structures, and these are all that remain.[1]

[1.] Twycross, ii, 32.

Heaning Wood: for Stephen Hart Jackson, 1866-7, by Miles Thompson who later added the stables. Hart Jackson married George Webster's daughter Ellen in 1863. Little trace of the Webster style except the chimneypieces.

Hill Top: outside the town and classical with porch, rendered with stone dressings. Inside plain but there is one good grey-veined columned chimneypiece. Enlarged on the south side. Before 1832 and probably by the Websters.

Hoad Cottage (now Ford House): a classical three-bay limestone house with projecting centre and north attached wing. A 'rockery' summerhouse in a small park. Tudor lodge of 1832. An uncomfortable design, probably by George Webster.

Princes St, no. 20: a three-bay house with a south wing. Of ashlar with windows set in a slight recess as many are in Kendal. It is very close to the Websters' no. 2 Thorny Hills there, and no doubt by them, *c*.1820.

Springfield (**132**): similar in plan to Belle Vue with a semi-circular porch and reeded doorcases; a Venetian screen to the staircase. Again probably by Francis Webster.

Stockbridge House: a three-bay, three-storey house. All front windows are tripartite with graceful attenuated brackets on the ground floor. Simple porch on columns. Another house apparently influenced by Storrs, *c*.1815, perhaps by Francis Webster.

Trinity House: built as the vicarage for Holy Trinity, *c*.1830, and now an hotel. Of ashlar with attached porch with off-centre pediment. There are fine Webster chimneypieces so perhaps George Webster was the architect, although Edward Gibson of Kendal, the builder of Salvin's church, is another candidate.

Underbarrow (W)

Hollin Bank: for Samuel Whineray of Kendal, 1853, attributed to Miles Thompson. A fine display of Webster motifs if at this late date actually by Thompson. Mullioned windows, gables, porches, finials, dominated by windows of all shapes. The interior is said to have been stripped. The approach is through fantastic gate piers with 'rockery' stones. Whineray (d. 1864) was a currier and leather dealer in Highgate, Kendal. He was mayor in 1843 and 1849.[1]

[1.] CRO K, WD/Cu 190; *Annals*, 301.

Larch How (**135**): for John Hudson, 1847 (datestone), the year after he sold Burneside mills to the Croppers. Italianate, with bay windows, an iron verandah, and characteristic chimneypieces. Miles Thompson, perhaps with George Webster, was probably the designer, and there is a garden plan of 1866 by him at the house. Hudson died in 1879 and has a handsome tomb at Underbarrow. Now within the Kendal borough boundary.

Low Gregg Hall: beautified *c*.1820 with a facade of three bays. The dining room had a fireplace between decorated arches and there is a typical Webster fireplace in the drawing room.

Thorns Villa: an 18th-century three-bay house enlarged *c*.1835, in a mild gothic, perhaps by George Webster, for Richard Wilson of Kendal, mayor in 1839 and the county coroner.[1] A wing was added but most surprising is the two-storey porch with the heads of Sir Walter Scott and the young Queen Victoria on drip-moulds.

[1.] *Annals*, 298, 300.

Upper Allithwaite (L)

The Height: for John Gibson, *c*.1830, and without doubt by George Webster. Three bays, rendered, with limestone dressings and facing a ha-ha. Like Nibthwaite Grange three rooms are added to an older house. The hall has an Elizabethan ceiling but the adjoining rooms are classical with good chimneypieces. An account book from the house lists payments for mason's work in 1787 to Robert Webster but they are probably nothing to do with this house.[1]

[1.] CRO K, WDY 462.

Upper Holker (L)

Backbarrow House or *The Mansion*: at some time, probably in the first half of the 19th century, a house was built close to the buildings of the cotton mill at Backbarrow, on the east bank of the river Leven. It is illustrated in a painting of 1848 by James Foley,[1] a gleaming white limestone gabled building with mullioned windows and conspicuous chimneys and must surely have been by George Webster. The Ainsworths who owned the mill were related to those of The Flosh, Cleator, which was largely rebuilt by Webster in 1837. The house was sold in 1870 when it was described as 'modern – suitable for a gentleman's family' and 'charmingly situated on the Leven amidst the choicest shrubs and evergreens',[2] but the proximity of the mill might have militated against its desirability. It is clearly shown on the 25" OS map of 1890 but was demolished in the 1930s. Only entrance gates remain.

[1.] The whereabouts of this picture are not known.

[2.] *Lancaster Guardian*, 7 July 1870.

Bigland Hall: a house of many periods. Designs of 1781 by John Hird seem to be for the front of the house except for the façade, three rooms, and the porch.[1] These are of 1809 (datestone) and almost certainly by Francis Webster.[2] These rooms are higher than those behind and are reached from the older work by three steps flanked by Roman Doric columns and pilasters. Groups of dentils are used decoratively, strung along string-courses. Good plasterwork at the front and fine chimneypieces. Limestone porch of Tuscan columns. The pedimented stables are probably by Hird.

[1.] Dr Peter Leach told the author that they were formerly at the house, but they cannot now be found.
[2.] *Lons. Mag.*, iii, 1822, 248; certainly by the architect of Belle Vue and Springfield in Ulverston.

Walton-le-Dale (L)

Walton Hall: rebuilt after a fire for the Hoghtons in 1830 in Jacobethan style, 'almost certainly to the designs of George Webster'.[1] Demolished in the late 19th century.

[1.] Robinson, *Country Houses*, 249.

Watermillock (C)

Hallsteads (now an Outward Bound School): for John Marshall of Leeds, 1815. A stuccoed house of 5 x 3 bays with Greek Doric porch and a wide canted bay round the corner.[1] Behind this a staircase with lyre railing. Good marble chimneypieces in the Webster style. Wordsworth's advice was sought by the Marshalls. Could he have recommended Francis Webster so early?

[1.] Robinson, *op. cit.*, 110.

Leeming House: the window frames in freestone look like those of e.g. Helme Lodge. One chimneypiece of Webster pattern; others go with the later high Victorian additions. Possibly by the Webster firm.

Whalley (L)

Moreton Hall (**134**): for John Taylor, 1828-9, by George Webster.[1] Moreton is the third in the trio of houses designed in a revived Jacobean style by Webster in the second half of the 1820s.[2] But there are differences. All three have a Jacobean frontispiece as entrance, Underley and Eshton combining it with horizontal balustrades. At Moreton the skyline is invaded by sharp gables and tall chimneys, a much more dramatic effect and one that puts style into reverse. It is Elizabethan rather than Jacobean[2]. In another two years, at Whittington, the frontispiece will disappear and a 'pele' tower and a bastioned terrace will push historical precedents further back still.

Unhappily the house was demolished in 1955, depriving this most beautiful stretch of country of its chief ornament. All we know of the interior is that it had a carved oak staircase.[3] A lodge and fragments of stables survive, and there are estate cottages nearby.[4] In the church at Whalley are tablets by Websters to Peggy (d. 1822) and John Taylor (d. 1829).

[1.] Burke, *Visitations*, i, 1852, 53; Whitaker, *History of the . . . Parish of Whalley*, 1876 ed., ii, 40-41. The designs were at Eller How in 1864: see p. 341.
[2.] Twycross, i, 20; *The Websters of Kendal*, no. 17; see p. 26.
[3.] VCH *Lancs.*, vi, 387.
[4.] T. Evans and C. Lycett Green, *English Cottages*, 1982, 96-7.

Parkhead: an old seat of the Kenyons, reduced to a mere farm on the Moreton estate. It shows signs of having been tidied up by George Webster in the 1830s.

Whitehaven (C)

Francis Webster's account for £67 10s. for 'drawing plans for buildings and journeys to Appleby and Whitehaven and many attendances and journeys to Lowther', between 8 August 1796 and 3 November 1800, are in the Lonsdale papers.[1] It is not clear what he was doing in Whitehaven, but his involvement on the Lowther estate there supports the attribution to him of a number of buildings.

[1.] *The Websters of Kendal*, no. 42; CRO, D/Lons/11/5/1.

Bransty House: a large house, plain and classical, of 7 x 3 bays and three storeys with a simple porch and a free use of tripartite windows under segmental arches. Attributed to Francis Webster.[1]

[1.] CRO, D/Lons/11/2/16-17, 9/31, plan and elevation; Colvin, Crook, and Friedman, *Architectural Drawings from Lowther Castle*, nos. 186-7.

Other houses in Whitehaven which may be by Webster are one in the Rope Walk, *c*.1794, no. 32 Queen St., and in Foxhouse Road, where Lord Lonsdale was releasing land from 1822.[1]

[1.] RCHM, *Whitehaven 1660-1800*, HMSO, 1991, 22.

Whittington (L)

Whittington Hall (**136-138**): for Thomas Greene of Slyne, 1831-6, by George Webster. Thomas Greene was buying land at Whittington from *c*. 1822 and purchased the hall in *c*.1830 from Thomas Sunderland, immediately instructing Webster to rebuild, retaining what he could of the structure. This amounted to keeping some masonry at the east end.

Webster's designs moved closer to the Elizabethan, even to the medieval.[1] For the first time he placed a major house, a house 'of great ambition' on a semi-medieval terrace like those at Wordsworth's house (1826) and Thurland Castle (1828). He went further, placing a powerful 'pele' tower behind the gables, a tower Pevsner thought most unlikely in 1831.[2] It seems that this was intended to suggest continuity of building over a long period. Was it Webster's idea, or Greene's? Inside there was handsome Jacobean decoration and chimneypieces, but there was interference about 1880 and again in the 1920s.

A narrow-gauge railway brought the golden freestone from a quarry at Docker, about a mile away; lead came from Liverpool via the canal to Burton Wharf. No other house by Webster has such complete accounts – details of craftsmen, lists of stoves required, all the sizes of plaster roses needed for one room. Who should make the bookcases? The unidentified 'man from Skipton who made those for Underley' is suggested.[3]

Webster tendered his ill-health as his excuse for slow work, or played one employer against another, assuring Greene that he was 'at present fully engaged designing for Lord Burlington at Holker'. He also designed the stables and two lodges, and the so-called 'Old Hall' in the village seems to have been tidied up at the same time. Did he also dispose the drives and park planting?

[1.] LRO, DDGr/Box P1; Twycross, ii, 9.

[2.] Pevsner, *N. Lancs.*, 262. Storrs Hall, Arkholme, nearby also has a 'pele' tower.

[3.] LRO, DDGr/6/34; for the building, see B. M. Copeland, *Whittington: The Story of a Country Estate*, 1981, 18-21, 59-72; Burke, *Visitations*, i, 1852, 155. There were 74 working drawings at Eller How in 1864: see p. 342, see also pp. 26-7.

Windermere (W)

The villas of Birthwaite, later Windermere, are a generation later than those of Bowness and date from the arrival of the railway in 1846. The railway company offered 'New and commodious dwelling houses for genteel families on Orrest Head' in the *Westmorland Gazette* on 27 May 1854. Many were almost certainly designed by Miles Thompson.

Elleray Bank: built as a private house in 1856, with barge-boarded gables and timber porch; probably by Thompson.

Fairhaven: for Richard Wilson of Thorns Villa, Underbarrow.[1] A large Italianate house with a tripartite door. In the country when built *c*.1850, but its gate piers are now in the next street.
[1.] L. Steele, *Windermere, its History and Growth*, 1928, 12.

Hazelthwaite (Ambleside Road): for R. M. Somervell, founder of K Shoes, Kendal, 1853. Italianate with a broad tower. All the land along the road to Ambleside belonged to Thompson who doubtless built many of the houses on it.

Tower House (off Ambleside Road, formerly The Grange): Italianate with a tower.

Willowsmere (Ambleside Road): again on Thompson's land and more Kendal-like than the other villas here.

Winster (W)

Winster House: a three-bay early19th-century house, attributed to Francis Webster, with good marble chimneypieces, and a stable block larger than the house.

Witherslack (W)

Halecat: probably for J. B. Wanklyn of Salford, *c*.1846,[1] whose architect must have been the Webster firm. The entrance front has a tripartite porch which incorporated the window above. The garden front has a canted bay window. Some recent internal remodelling by Francis Johnson.
[1.] Leaflet from the house.

Whitbarrow Lodge: a spectacularly sited house, acquired *c*.1840 by William Farrer, descended from a local Quaker family who had made a fortune in Liverpool. From 1896 the home of his nephew, also William Farrer, the historian and first editor of VCH *Lancs.*[1] A centre of *c*.1760 was added to at either end *c*.1840. There are enough Webster details to attribute the additions to the firm. A magnificent parade of cylindrical chimneys which the precipitous site brings to eye-level at the back.
[1.] Boumphrey and Hudleston, 112.

Yealand Conyers (L)

Beechfield: perhaps for John Proctor, *c*.1810. A 3 x 3-bay house with a two-storey bay on the garden front. Limestone rubble except the entrance front which is ashlar with a porch of two piers and two Tuscan columns. Probably by Francis Webster.

The Elms (now Wainmans House): a three-bay ashlar house behind a handsome *clair voie*.

The Larches: a house of several builds, including a drawing room with a marble chimneypiece, painted, and a pretty vaulted loggia on octagonal columns. Possibly by the Websters, *c.*1820.

CHURCHES AND CHAPELS

George Webster's churches are generally unambitious and formulaic, though his individual style is instantly recognisable with its monotonously repetitive geometric window openings and a general harshness usually mitigated in his domestic work. He rarely had money for more than a starved design, but nevertheless some are more ambitious. Oddly, his best church designs were for buildings that were not ecclesiastical, like the front of Conishead Priory and the deceptive 'chapel' at Penwortham. However, St George's, Kendal, with, before decapitation, its twin-spired front, and Holy Trinity and St George's, with its rich interior and sculpture, do form a valuable part of his output. Most of his simple unaffected designs were later compromised by the imposition of archaeologically correct gothic details or by substantial additions.

Appleby (W)
Gaols and Courts: Francis Webster made new designs in 1812 and was then asked to add a chapel.[1] Probably very simple, but its appearance is unknown.

[1] B. Tyson, 'An Architectural History of the Gaols and Court-Houses of Appleby, Cumbria', *Trans. Ancient Monuments Soc.*, xxxii, 1988, 101-39.

Arnside (W)
St James: 1864, by Miles Thompson, the foundation stone laid by Mrs Wilson of Dallam Tower.[1] So much extended that the original is hard to distinguish. Later additions by Austin & Paley, 1912-14.[2]

[1] *Lancaster Guardian*, 10 Sept. 1864; Kelly, *Westm.*, 1934, 28, where the date is given as 1869.

[2] J. Price, *Sharpe, Paley and Austin*, 1998, 92.

Bardsea (L)
Holy Trinity (**154**): 1843, by George Webster,[1] and built at the expense of the bankrupted Colonel Braddyll of Conishead. Work had to be suspended but was completed in 1853 by subscription and the energy of the Rev. Thomas Petty, the first incumbent. Of gleaming limestone and overlooking Morecambe Bay from a conspicuous height; nave and multangular apse, vestry, west tower, and spire on the model of Levens and Coniston Cold.

[1] *WG*, 9 Sept. 1843, plans at the office of Mr Webster; CRO B, BPR 34/7, subscription list, 'according to the plan by Mr Webster'; Mannex, 1882, 275.

Bolton-le-Sands (L)
St Michael: altered at various dates. Nave rebuilt 1813, north transept 1827, tower made into

entrance 1836, new chancel 1846.[1] Richard Sparling Berry of Elm Grove had a new pew built by George Webster in 1836 and he may have been responsible for other work.[2] William Coulthard made designs for pews over vaults in 1828-30, probably in the new transept.[3] There is a similar unsigned design and yet another of 1829 in the Greene of Whittington papers.[4] Little or any of this is to be seen.

[1.] VCH *Lancs.*, viii, 127-8; Lambeth Palace Library, ICBS files (Sir Howard Colvin kindly provided material from this source, here and below).
[2.] CRO K, WDX 1315.
[3.] Leeds City Archives, RD/AF/2/2a/52.
[4.] LRO, ARR 13/5/236; *ibid.*, DDGr, box P1.

Bowness (W)

Cemetery: consecrated 1856.[1] The lodge/chapel appears to be by Miles Thompson.
[1.] *Annals*, 303.

Broughton (YWR)

Broughton Hall: as part of George Webster's remodelling for the Tempest family in 1838-41 the Strawberry Hill gothic chapel, perhaps by Foss of Richmond, was redesigned but only exterior work was carried out.[1] Webster's design for the altar wall survives at the house.
[1.] C. Hussey, 'Broughton Hall', *CL*, 31 Mar., 7 and 14 April 1950; *The Websters of Kendal*, no. 87.

Burneside (W)

St Oswald: 1823-8, by George Webster. 'Already walled' in 1824.[1] Gothic, aisleless, with west tower and short spire.[2] Rebuilt by Ferguson in 1880-81.[3]
[1.] Lambeth Palace Library, ICBS files, including seating plan of 1828 by Webster.
[2.] CRO K, WPR 54, plan and elevation, dated 'Kendal 1823'.
[3.] Pevsner, *Cumb. and Westm.*, 236. The spire of the earlier church is said to have been transferred to the new one: Kelly, *Westm.*, 1934, 41.

Cartmel (L)

Cartmel Priory: Robert Webster was paid £5 12s. for freestone repairs to the west window in 1820, and 10s. for more work in 1823.[1]
[1.] B. Tyson, 'Francis Webster and the Market House at Hawkshead', *Quarto*, Oct. 1993, 11, n. 13.

Casterton (W)

Holy Trinity: 1833; part school chapel, part village church, Casterton was the brain-child of the Rev. W. Carus Wilson.[1] His experiences during the building were embodied in his *Helps to the building of Churches*, 1835, and the church as completed appears as the frontispiece. As at Holme, it seems likely that George Webster carried out Wilson's intentions here too.[2] Chancel added 1860; restored 1891.[3]
[1.] J. M. Ewbank, *Life and Works of William Carus Wilson*, 1959, 8-9.
[2.] However, the certifying architect was Thomas Garnett: CRO K, DRC10 [editor].
[3.] Pevsner, *Cumb. and Westm.*, 238; Kelly, *Westm.*, 1934, 44.

Cleator (C)

St Leonard: nave rebuilt, 1841-2, by George Webster, who was paid £9 8s. for two designs and specifications.[1] 'There was one extremely hideous feature . . . all around the church ornamenting the lancet windows was a series of monstrous heads very like mediaeval gargoyles.[2] Heavily restored in 1900.[3]

[1.] Lambeth Palace Library, ICBS files.
[2.] C. Caine, *Cleator Moor Past and Present*, 1916, 244.
[3.] *Ibid.*, 245-9.

Coniston Cold (YWR)

St Peter (**155**): 1846, for J. B. Garforth of Coniston Hall, by George Webster, whose designs, simplified in erection, are in the church. Similar to Levens and Bardsea.

Dalton-in-Furness (L)

St Mary: extended in 1825-6 by the addition of a north aisle, gallery, porch, and vestry to plans by either Francis or George Webster. Francis's executors were paid for plans and specifications in July 1829. The plans included a rare design for the east window, including the glazing. In 1830 George rebuilt the east end with three gables and the south aisle.[1] The church was rebuilt in 1883-5 by Paley & Austin, reusing three windows in the lady chapel.[2]

[1.] CRO B, BPR 1/C5/6 relate to this work, 1824-32. The earlier plans are dated 'Kendal 1825'; *ibid.*, BD/BUC/182. A copy of the faculty for rebuilding, 1825, is *ibid.*, BD/BUC/box 51/1/1, and there is an unsigned estimate of 1825 for £1,328 in LRO, ARR 13/5/234. The building is illustrated in E. Dent, *The Parish Church of Dalton-in-Furness*, 1985, facing 26.
[2.] Dent, *op cit.*, 38; Price, *Sharpe, Paley and Austin*, 81-2.

Dendron (L)

St Matthew: 1795-6, attributed to Francis Webster, for Thomas Greene of Slyne and Grays Inn, who had given £200 for the repair of the old church in 1774. The new building was church and school under one roof, classical, with tall arched windows set into arches, a form much used by Francis Webster, e.g. in the Hawkshead Assembly Rooms. The east end is in the form of a triumphal arch. The dividing wall between church and school was removed in 1833 when the new school was built[1]. Greene's son built Whittington Hall.

[1.] CRO B, BPR 31/C3/1-11; Boumphrey and Hudleston, 141.

Edenhall (C)

St Cuthbert (**156**): the medieval church was altered, probably by George Webster, for the Musgraves in 1834.[1] The extraordinary 'Norman' chancel arch of plaster must be his, as is the gallery with high windows to light it, and the vestry and balancing porch.

[1.] Pevsner, *Cumb. and Westm.*, 123; Kelly, *Cumb. and Westm.*, 1929, 142, gives the date 1836.

Egton-cum-Newland (L)

St Mary: rebuilt 1856 by Miles Thompson. Gothic, plate and geometrical tracery. Nave rebuilt 1864 and much later alteration.[1]

[1.] Pevsner, *N. Lancs.*, 117.

Firbank (W)

St John the Evangelist (**157**): 1841-2, attributed to George Webster. A small church with a bell tower and short chancel, on a magnificent site.

Flookburgh (L)

St John the Baptist: John Hird's church of 1776-7 had three bays of arched windows and a tiny apse.[1] It was 'greatly enlarged in 1836 at a cost of £350' by the addition of a gallery on the north side and new pews below,[2] but also perhaps by a fourth bay in the same style and a new entrance to the churchyard; probably by George Webster.[3] Replaced, on a different site, 1897-1900, by Austin & Paley.[4]

[1] Illustrated in J. Dickinson, *The Land of Cartmel*, 1980, plate 11, though the caption is incorrect.

[2] Mannex, 1851, 381; R. H. Kirkby *et al.* (eds.), *The Rural Deanery of Cartmel*, 1892, 55.

[3] Illustrated in Dickinson, *loc. cit.*

[4] Price, *Sharpe, Paley and Austin*, 93.

Garsdale (YWR)

St John the Baptist: rebuilt in 1861 by Miles Thompson.[1] Lancet style, bellcote, short chancel.

[1] CRO K, WPR 60, plans and specifications; *Church Builder*, i, 1862, 59.

Grasmere (W)

St Oswald: George Webster drew up plans for 'proposed improvements' in May 1840.[1] Included were a new roof, a new, or at least tidied-up, tower, new windows and doors. Neither roof nor tower were altered, but the windows and doors were replaced and a new floor laid. The cost of £300 was raised by subscription; Queen Adelaide, visiting the area, gave £50.[2]

[1] The designs are in Dove Cottage Library, and in CRO K, WPR 90/I29/1, I30-33; *The Websters of Kendal*, no. 86.

[2] M. L. Armitt, *The Church of Grasmere*, 1912, 149.

Grayrigg (W)

St John (**158**): 1837-8, gothic, aisleless nave and chancel, lancet windows, by George Webster.[1] Tower rebuilt in 1869 in a different style.[2]

[1] CRO K, WPR 5, plans, elevations, and sections; Lambeth Palace Library, ICBS files.

[2] Pevsner, *Cumb. and Westm.*, 248.

Great Urswick (L)

St Mary: gallery on two pairs of columns, 1826.[1] 'Renovated' in 1844 and 1848, including a new east window.[2] Perhaps by the Websters.

[1] VCH *Lancs.*, viii, 334.

[2] Mannex, 1882, 271.

Haverthwaite (L)

St Anne: 1824-5, and probably by the Websters. Lancet gothic with west tower; very close to Burneside of the year before.

Hawkshead (L)

Methodist chapel: 1862, a modest building, probably by Miles Thompson.

Holme (W)

Holy Trinity: 1839, a rustic lancet building by George Webster, whose signed plan survives, attached to the sentence of consecration.[1] Here, as at Casterton, he was carrying out the ideas of W. Carus Wilson. The church was identical, though rougher in execution, with Casterton, except for the top of the tower: 'it was determined to adopt precisely the same plan as at Casterton save that the steeple is wider and higher'.[2]

[1] CRO K, DRC 10.

[2] W. Carus Wilson, *Helps to the building of Churches*, 2nd ed., 1842, 24.

Irton (C)

St Paul: 1856-7 by Miles Thompson, and in the perpendicular style, unusual for the firm.[1]

[1] Kelly, *Cumb. & Westm.*, 1934, 177; Pevsner, *Cumb. and Westm.*, 143.

Kendal (W)

All Hallows, Fellside: 1864-6, by Miles Thompson. An unsympathetic gothic building.[1]

[1] CRO K, WSMB/K/Bk 1/103; *ibid.*, *Annals*, 304.64.

Castle Street Cemetery: lodge dated 1843, chapel 1845. The first is probably by George Webster.[1] The chapel, allegedly modelled on that of King's College, Cambridge, is by John Fisher junior, in the Webster style.[2]

[1] *WG*, 12 July 1845; Curwen, *KK*, 414-5.

[2] CRO K, *Annals*, 304.23.

Friends' Meeting House (**159**): 1816, by Francis Webster, on an old site. Plain, classical, two storeys externally, the lower windows arched. South front of ashlar 'inlaid with putty as being superior to lime mortar'.[1] The joinery, carried out by William Fisher, is more interesting than the building.[2]

[1] *Annals*, 163.

[2] D. M. Butler, *Quaker Meeting Houses of the Lake Counties*, 1978, 99-100, 119.

Holy Trinity: the old parish church of Kendal and its churchyard with a screen of stone piers and fine wrought-iron palisades of 1821-2.[1] Improvements in 1829, including the removal of limewash, perhaps with George Webster's advice.[2] In 1844-7 the senior churchwarden, Miles Thompson himself, advised on the removal of roughcasting, repairs to windows, and the demolition of the gallery.[3] The church contains more than twenty tablets by the Websters, classical, Grecian, and gothic.

[1] *Annals*, 295.

[2] *Ibid.*, 297. Richard Stirzaker recorded the church just after 1829: Curwen, *KK*, 224-5.

[3] *Annals*, 47. In the archives at Sizergh Castle is a plan for a window in the Strickland chapel by J. S. Thompson, 1855.

Holy Trinity and St George (R.C.) (**160-162**): 1835-7, by George Webster, the foundation stone laid by Walter Strickland of Sizergh on 10 Oct. 1835.[1] Gothic, nave and chancel, lancet windows; the facade to New Road with heavy pinnacles and a carving of St George and the dragon by Thomas Duckett.[2] Nicholson wrote that the church 'perhaps exhibits . . . the skill and taste of the architect more than any other of his numerous public buildings'.[3]

[1] *The Websters of Kendal*, no. 82.

[2] *Civil Engineer and Architect's Journal*, i, 1837-8, 57-8.

[3] *Annals*, 162. The church is illustrated in J. Macaulay, *The Gothic Revival 1745-1845*, 1975, plate 149.

Independent Chapel, Lowther Street: 'fronted with hammered limestone, and otherwise improved', 1828,[1] probably by George Webster. Now part of the South Lakeland District Council offices.

[1.] *Annals*, 297.

Inghamite Chapel, Beast Banks: rebuilt, 1844, by Miles Thompson.[1] An Italianate single-cell building with arched windows and broad eaves, now converted to flats.

[1.] *Annals*, 301. In 1856 the architect was presented with a Bible and Cruden's *Concordance* in recognition of his having planned the chapel 'some years since': CRO K, WDFC/1/2/14.

Parkside Road Cemetery: a chapel and lodge on either side of the road, gothic and Jacobethan. The chapels were erected in 1854, the cottages in 1855, all designed by Miles Thompson.[1]

[1.] CRO K, WSMB/K/box 21, burial board minutes, 1854-73.

St George (**163**): 1839-41, and George Webster's most ambitious church, built to replace St George's in the Market Place. The design was of major church mode with a façade of twin towers and spires 100 ft high, buttressed by porches. The triple lancet window between has good headstops by Thomas Duckett. Kendalians were given a preview in the *Westmorland Gazette*'s engraving by William Garside of Kendal after a drawing by Miles Thompson.[1] Inside, the timber roof structure obstructs the view of the plasterwork ceiling behind. Chancel of 1911 in a different stone and most insensitive. The towers have been progressively reduced in height since 1940.[2]

[1.] *WG*, 17 Nov. 1838; *Annals*, 77; *Civil Engineer and Architect's Journal*, i, 1837-8, 418; *WG*, 22 Sept. 1838, tenders to Mr. G. Webster.
[2.] *The Websters of Kendal*, no. 85. Twenty-six working drawings were at Eller How in 1864: see p. 342.

St Thomas (**164**): 1835-7, and Kendal's first 19th-century church, built at a cost of £3,200. Similar to Milnthorpe and by George Webster.[1] Aisleless nave and chancel, lancet windows. The tower was 95ft high but the pinnacles were reduced in 1970.

[1.] *Annals*, 76-7. The architect and his brother each subscribed £5: *WG*, 20 Dec. 1834; *ibid.*, 20 June 1835, plans at Mr. G. Webster's. Twenty working drawings for the church and school were at Eller How in 1864: see p. 342.

Kirkby Lonsdale (W)

St Mary: in 1807 Francis Webster made plans for alterations including a new roof, windows, buttresses, battlements, etc.[1] On 23 May an advertisement appeared in the *Newcastle Chronicle* 'to Plumbers, Carpenters and Masons. To be sold, the lead covering of Kirkby Lonsdale church, estimated at about 36 tons. Also to be let the new roofing, slating, ceiling, seating and pewing of the said church. Plans and specifications . . . may be inspected by application to Messrs. Buttle and Tomlinson'. 'This is when the leaden roofs, battlements, pinnacles and clerestory were removed to give way to an enormous sweeping roof of blue slate'.[2] The pillar in front of the pulpit was removed.[3]

[1.] LRO, ARR 13/5/108.
[2.] Curwen, *Rec. Kendale*, iii, 287.
[3.] A Pearson *et al.*, *The Annals of Kirkby Lonsdale and Lunesdale Today*, 1996, 109. The church, after all these alterations, is shown in an aquatint by Ralph Croft, *c.*1810: *ibid.*, facing 108.

Levens (W)

St John the Evangelist: 1826-8, by George Webster for F. G. Howard of Levens Hall.[1] Gothic, with lancets and west gallery and tower. The spire added 1831.[2]

[1] *Local Chronology*, 122.
[2] Surrey R.O., Howard MSS, 203/30/39.

Lindale (L)

St Paul (**165**): 1828-9, attributed to George Webster, but both father and son were clearly involved, Francis, just before his death, on the committee and George during the building. No fees to either are recorded and they probably gave their services free, although George was paid for the slate. Gothic, with lancets and west tower; it cost £500, of which Francis contributed £25, and George presented the font. After their father died, he and his sisters gave a further £50.[1] The Websters' local church when in residence at Eller How. The massive family mausoleum stands near the south door. North aisle added in 1912.[2]

[1] CRO K, WPR 99/I22-4, 33; Kirkby *et al.* (eds.), *Rural Deanery of Cartmel*, 68-9; Lambeth Palace Library, ICBS files.
[2] Pevsner, *N. Lancs.*, 168.

Longsleddale (W)

St Mary: church, school, and parsonage form a tight group. All have datestones of 1862, the year in which the old church was demolished.[1] The school is certainly by Miles Thompson[2] and it is probably safe to assume that the whole group is by him. The church is aisleless, with chancel, porch, bellcote, and coupled lancets.

[1] CRO K, *Annals*, 304.62.
[2] *Ibid.*, 304.49.

Mansergh (W)

St Peter (**166**): additions of 1829 by George Webster for Christopher Wilson of Rigmaden. Probably gothic but not clear from the plans.[1] Rebuilt in 1880 by Paley & Austin.[2]

[1] Leeds City Archives, RD/AF/2/2/10. In 1851 it was described as 'a neat building with a turret': Mannex, 1851, 356.
[2] Price, *Sharpe, Paley and Austin*, 85.

Milnthorpe (W)

St Thomas (**166**): 1835-7, by George Webster, a reduced version of St Thomas's, Kendal. Lancets in pairs between buttresses, west tower. The sentence of consecration names the architect.[1]

[1] R. K. Bingham, *Chronicles of Milnthorpe*, 1987, 224.

Morpeth (Northumb.)

Presbyterian Church: 1860, by 'M. Thompson'. Facing the street, 'perversely stepped-up W. tower, ending in an octagonal spirelet. The roof to the river goes very low down over the aisle'.[1] If the architect was Miles Thompson of Kendal one wonders how the commission came about.

[1] N. Pevsner, *Northumberland*, Buildings of England, 1957, 215.

Natland (W)

St Mark (**167**): 1825, by George Webster.[1] Gothic with lancets and west tower, and quite close to Haverthwaite in design. Rebuilt in 1910 by Austin & Paley.[2]

[1] Lambeth Palace Library, ICBS files.
[2] Price, *Sharpe, Paley and Austin*, 95.

New Hutton (W)

St Stephen: rebuilt 1828-9 by George Webster[1]. Lancet gothic, west tower with restless crenellations.

[1] CRO K, WPR 18/I8, unsigned plan of 1828 in George Webster's hand; *Annals*, 297; Lambeth Palace Library, ICBS files.

Pennington (L)

St Michael: of the rebuilding of 1826-7[1] only the tower survives. The Websters may have provided the designs and Colonel Braddyll and the Prince of Wales subscribed to the building fund. Chancel and porch rebuilt by Paley & Austin in 1924-6.[2]

[1] CRO B, BPR 24/I32, faculty and plan; Leeds City Archives, RD/AF/2/2/37.
[2] Price, *Sharpe, Paley and Austin*, 101.

Rusland (L)

St Paul: rebuilt on the old foundations in 1868 by Miles Thompson, except for the tower.[1] Aisleless nave and chancel.

[1] CRO B, BPR 30/C5/3/1-2.

Rydal (W)

St Mary: 1822-3, for Lady Fleming of Rydal Hall, and George Webster's first church.[1] Gothic, with pinnacled tower, originally covered in Roman cement. Wordsworth in general approved although he was critical of the lack of chancel and the ill-positioned font.[2] Chancel added and the lancets given tracery in 1884.[3]

[1] CRO K, WD/Ry/box 22, specifications.
[2] 'It has no chancel; the altar is unbecomingly confined; the pews are so narrow as to preclude the possibility of kneeling; there is no vestry; and . . . the font is thrust into the further end of a little Pew': quoted in M. Moorman, *William Wordsworth. The Later Years*, 1965, 421 n. 2.
[3] Pevsner, *Cumb. and Westm.*, 256.

Shap (W)

St Michael: letters of 13 and 19 February 1808 state that 'Webster has made a plan for rebuilding'.[1] Old photographs of the chancel show a Palladian window under a segmental arch as seen in Francis Webster's Lowther designs, but it is unclear what, other than the replacement of the pews, was done. The tower was rebuilt in 1828,[2] and the whole church restored and the chancel rebuilt in 1898-9.[3]

[1] CRO, D/Lons/L/1/3/55; J. Whiteside, *Shappe in Bygone Days*, 1904, 7, 10.
[2] CRO K, WPR 85, faculty; Lambeth Palace Library, ICBS files, plan of steeple.
[3] Whiteside, *op. cit.*, 209-54.

Skelsmergh (W)

Dodding Green: the centre of local Catholicism until the building of Holy Trinity and St George, Kendal, in 1835-7. George Webster restored the buildings here for the Rev. Charles Brigham, 1840-42 (datestones), giving the chapel a typical Jacobethan ceiling and frieze.[1] All details destroyed in 1968.

[1] Sister Agnes, *The Story of Skelsmergh*, 1949, illustration facing 43.

Ulverston (L)

Roman Catholic chapel: 1822, tower 1832, for the Rev. B. McHugh of Hammershead, on a very restricted site.[1] The great surprise here is the plaster rib vault with headstops. It is not unlike similar vaults at Lowther Castle, so Francis Webster may have been its designer.[2] Now a furniture showroom.

[1] Mannex, 1851, 441.

[2] The rib vault is a copy of the one in the infirmary chapel at Furness Abbey: A. C. Parkinson, *History of Catholicism in the Furness Peninsula*, 1998, 51-2 [editor].

Whalley (L)

St Mary: minor work paid for by John Taylor of Moreton Hall may be by George Webster. An inscription on St Anton's cage, a pew with dates 1534. 1610, and 1697, has another of 1830 with Taylor's initials, marking a restoration.[1] South porch of 1844.

[1] Pevsner, *N. Lancs.*, 258.

Windermere (W)

St Mary: 1848, gothic, by Miles Thompson for Dr J. A. Addison of Windermere College and his private property until bought by the parish and consecrated in 1856. Enlarged as the town grew. The south aisle of 1852 is by Thompson; extensions of 1857 and 1861 by J. S. Crowther, and of 1880 by Paley & Austin.[1]

[1] L. Steele, *Windermere, its Growth and History*, 1928, 12-14; information from Michael Bottomley.

Yealand Conyers (L)

St John: 1838, rustic gothic, attributed to George Webster. Altered in 1861 and 1882.[1]

[1] Pevsner, *N. Lancs*, 266.

PARSONAGE HOUSES

Francis and George Webster probably designed several parsonage houses such as Dalton (1825), but Miles Thompson and Thompson & Webster developed a wide practice in this field. The division of parishes with the growth of population presented opportunities and Thompson produced a basic design of T-plan with a gable in the centre upon which he worked variations, sometimes minimal classical, sometimes minimal Tudor, for about twenty years. He seems to have based the plan on the vicarage at Casterton (1837) which was probably by George Webster. Simple marble chimneypieces seem to have been normal provision.

Askrigg (YNR)

1850 (datestone); a large house with a central gabled projection with a canted bay window and small gables on either side. A handsome stable block behind. Attributed to Miles Thompson. Now Yorebridge House.

Burneside (W)

1856 (datestone); Elizabethan, with mullioned windows, cylindrical chimneys, and deliberately primitive three-bay loggia. Probably by Thompson.

Burton-in-Kendal (W)

1844 (datestone); a recessed centre between gabled bays. The porch has an entablature under a gable. Canted bay windows were an original feature.

Cartmel Fell (L)

1863 (datestone), by Miles Thompson.[1] Again the T-shaped plan with offices and stables; wooden mullions and hoodmoulds. Now Danes Court.

[1.] *WG*, 5 Dec. 1863, tenders invited.

Casterton (W)

1837, for the Rev. W. Carus Wilson and standing near his Clergy Daughters' School. He was responsible for the church as well but clearly had a competent designer, apparently George Webster, who probably made the plans for the other Casterton buildings. Carus Wilson illustrated the parsonage in 1842 in the second edition of his *Helps to the building of Churches*. Thinly Elizabethan with mullioned windows and barge-boarded gables, it is clearly the prototype for later parsonages by the firm, that at Staveley being particularly close. The plan is similar and the lower walls in both covered by a trellis pattern. Carus Wilson's intention was to provide simple, cheap plans for churches, parsonages, and schools.

Crosscrake (W)

1848, by Miles Thompson[1] (**168**); a fine example of the use of raw clints as door and window frames. The interior has Websterish detailing. Slightly altered in 1998 and now Sellet Lodge.

[1.] CRO K, acc. 706, 557, plans.

Dalton-in-Furness (L)

1825,[1] the year in which George Webster began his alterations to the church and probably by him or his father. Plain, three-bay house with a columned doorcase with an open pediment.

[1.] Mannex, 1882, 165.

Egton-cum-Newland (L)

1856.[1] The church was designed by Miles Thompson in the same year and the former vicarage may be his work, although his nephew John Strickland Thompson witnessed the agreement with the builder.

[1.] CRO B, BPR 26/I18/2, specifications; the document came from the office of 'Mr Thompson, Architect, Kendal'. Marcellus Thompson provided the chimneypieces: *ibid.*, I18/4.

Firbank (W)

1864, by Miles Thompson;[1] T-plan with porch and central bow. Marble chimneypieces.

[1.] *WG*, 30 April 1864, tenders invited; CRO K, WPR 32, plans and accounts.

Flookburgh (L)

1855 (datestone), at the expense of the 7th Duke of Devonshire.[1] Typical late Webster detail and no doubt by Miles Thompson.

[1.] J. Stockdale, *Annals of Cartmel*, 1872, 291.

Grange-over-Sands (L)

1864,[1] probably by Thompson. It has mullioned windows and a half-hipped roof. Enlarged by George Rigg of Kendal, 1872.[2]

[1.] Mannex, 1882, 337.
[2.] *WG*, 2 Mar. 1872.

Hardraw (YNR):

1863, by Miles Thompson[1] (**169**); again, his favoured T-plan with centre gable and porch to one side. Marble chimneypieces.

[1.] *WG*, 26 Dec. 1863.

Haverthwaite (L)

1847. The Websters may not have designed the building, described in 1851 as a 'handsome new parsonage', but they supplied marble chimneypieces.[1] Demolished.

[1.] Mannex, 1851, 388; R.H. Kirkby *et al.* (eds) , *The Rural Deanery of Cartmel*, 1892, 120; CRO K, WPR 90/79, receipts.

Helsington (W)

1850s, perhaps by Thompson;[1] hood moulds and an arched porch. Sold in 1930-31[2] and now Helsington Lodge.

[1.] Built by 1858: Kelly, 1858, 36.
[2.] CRO K, WPR 27/I40.

Heversham (W)

*c.*1843-4,[1] Miles Thompson found the old building (now part of the Blue Bell Hotel) unfit in 1843, but three working drawings were listed among George Webster's papers at Eller How in 1864, so the design must be by him.[2] Complete with marble chimneypieces and with some progressive detail like the corner-to-corner drawing room window. Now High Leasgill.

[1.] R. K. Bingham, *The Church at Heversham*, 1984, 115.
[2.] See p. 342.

Holme (W)

1845;[1] a simple three-bay house with a pilastered doorcase, later extended and given a bay window.

[1.] Mannex, 1851, 345. A house of this type illustrated in W. Carus Wilson, *Helps to the building of Churches*, 2nd ed., 1842, facing 24.

Ings (W)

1864, by Miles Thompson;[1] gabled, irregular, oriel window over the door, bay, mullioned windows.

[1.] CRO K, WPR 57/I22, plans; *Kendal Mercury*, 16 Jan. 1864, tenders invited.

Kendal (W)

St George, Castle Street: 1849;[1] a substantial gabled house with an Italianate window among sashes. No doubt by Thompson & Webster. Enlarged in 1885 by Daniel Brade,[2] and now subdivided and no longer the vicarage.

[1] *Annals*, 77.
[2] CRO K, WSMB/K/Bk 4/640.

St Thomas: 1854;[1] L-plan, projecting gable, sash windows, and typical Thompson detailing.
[1] *Annals*, 77.

Kirkby Lonsdale (W)

A large classical house of the early 19th century and perhaps by Francis Webster who remodelled the church in 1807. The top floor, with deep bracket eaves, was clearly added later.

Levens (W)

1828;[1] probably by the Websters who built the church in the same year for F. G. Howard of Levens Hall. No longer the vicarage.
[1] Levens Hall MSS, deeds.

Longsleddale (W)

1863 (datestone); part of a group with church and school, all by Miles Thompson[1]. Two-storey porch with an arched window over the door. No longer the vicarage.
[1] CRO K, acc.557, 706, plans.

Mansergh (W)

1866, by Miles Thompson, the porch of 1867.[1]
[1] CRO K, acc.706, plans.

Milnthorpe (W)

Formerly Belvedere Cottage, built for John Postlethwaite, one of the promoters of the church, *c.*1820, and bought as the parsonage house in 1844.[1] A neat, three-bay ashlar house, perhaps by Francis Webster. No longer the vicarage.
[1] R. K. Bingham, *Chronicles of Milnthorpe*, 1987, 230; J. F. Curwen, *History of Heversham with Milnthorpe*, 1930, 45-6.

Old Hutton (W)

1844 (datestone), by George Webster;[1] T-plan, central gable flanked by smaller ones. Sashes under hood moulds. Now Hutton View.
[1] Plans and elevations were at Eller How in 1864: see p. 342.

Rusland (W)

1857 (datestone);[1] L-plan, sashes under hood moulds, porch. Probably by Thompson. Now Romneys.
[1] CRO B, BPR 30/I3/6.

Staveley (W)

1859, by Miles Thompson;[1] T-plan, central gabled projections, side porch, slate construction. No longer the vicarage.

[1] CRO K, WPR 68, plans and elevations.

Thornton-in-Lonsdale (YWR)

1849, by Miles Thompson;[1] usual T-plan, central gable and small side gables with triangular-headed windows under central oriel.

[1] NYRO, PR/TNL 3-4, specifications.

Yealand Conyers (L)

Perhaps *c.*1860; central projection with gable, sash windows, bracket eaves, and gable. Probably by Thompson.

SCHOOLS

Bowness (W)

Girls' School: 1867, by Miles Thompson.[1] Slate with freestone dressings. The plaque from Webster's grammar school now fixed to the wall. No longer a school.

[1] CRO K, *Annals*, 304.73.

Grammar School: 1836, by George Webster. John Bolton of Storrs presented Bowness with this new building for both boys and girls, two schools under one roof and perched high above the village centre. He was too ill to lay the foundation stone, so Wordsworth took his place and gave his only recorded public speech. 'The building' he said, 'from the elegance of its architecture, and its elevated conspicuous situation, will prove a striking ornament to the beautiful country in the midst of which it will stand'.[1] It was the first of the firm's schools, Tudor in style with characteristic detail. The main gable carried a bell turret and had an oriel window between octagonal buttresses with ball finials as at Settle Town Hall. Became the boys' school in 1885 when a new grammar school was built, and demolished in 1973. An elaborate tablet by the Webster firm, in coloured marbles with a profile of Bolton, was set up inside, and is now on the former girls' school just below (**198**).

[1] *WG*, 16 April 1836, quoted in *Windermere Grammar School*, 1936, 34; *The Websters of Kendal*, no. 68; CRO K, WD/AG/box 111, building accounts. The working drawings were at Eller How in 1864: see p. 342.

Burton-in-Kendal (W)

Morewood School (**170**): 1867; very like Endmoor and Milnthorpe, and therefore probably by Miles Thompson.[1]

[1] CRO K, WPR 10, conveyance.

Cartmel (L)

Grammar School: built in 1789, four bays and two floors of arched windows. In 1861 the Duke of Devonshire and others, including George Webster, subscribed to a restoration and the addition of a master's house to the west and a boys' dining room to the east. Miles

Thompson made the designs but fell foul of a difficult headmaster. In 1862 George Webster, well into his retirement, wrote to Thomas Remington that having 'been a house prisoner' he had been 'trying to concoct some Plan of a Residence for the Master of the Grammar School' and seems to have made some 'rude sketches to show the committee' in order to prevent Thompson's plans 'from being again wrecked'.[1] The resulting slate, gabled house with a good timber porch is very much in Thompson's parsonage style. Chimneypieces remain inside. The western addition is also gabled but with arched door and windows with alternate rustication. No longer a school.

[1.] CRO K, WPR 89/PR/2704/1.

Casterton (W)

Clergy Daughters' School (Casterton School): 1833,[1] in the same style as the parsonage and presumably by George Webster. Three bays flanked by one-bay gabled projecting wings.

[1.] J. M. Ewbank, *Life and Works of William Carus Wilson*, 1959, 8.

Village School: 1841, across the road from the parsonage and the most picturesque of the group, with mullioned windows, pinnacled dormers, lozenged chimneys, and barge-boarded gables.[1] Again, probably by Webster. Now part of Casterton School.

[1.] Illustrated in G. Sale, *History of Casterton School*, 1983, 40-41. W. Carus Wilson, *Helps to the building of Churches*, 2nd ed., 1842, has a design for an infants' school with a room with a porch of rustic timber columns and a room for public meetings; Ewbank, *op. cit.*, 11.

Coniston (L)

Village School: 1853-4, by Thompson & Webster. Tenders, including those for a master's house, invited on 5 Feb. 1853.[1] Demolished in 1878 in order to enlarge the graveyard.[2]

[1.] *WG*, 5 Feb.1853; Mannex, 1866, 400; LRO, ARR/13/5/239, plans.
[2.] Mannex, 1882, 246.

Coniston Cold (YWR)

Village School: 1849 (datestone), and of a piece with the hall and church which are both by George Webster. Plain, Tudor, with mullions and hoodmoulds.

Edenhall (C)

Village School and Schoolhouse: 1847. The house dominates, two storeys against one. It had three bays with an oriel, mullioned and transomed windows, and diamond chimneys. Perhaps by George Webster or Miles Thompson.

Hackthorpe (W)

Village School: the old Lowther Grammar School, rebuilt by William, Earl of Lonsdale, 1810.[1] It has small four-centred windows and a hipped roof, very like Lowther farmhouses of the period; probably by Francis Webster.

[1.] *Gentleman's Magazine*, 1823, ii, 324.

Hawkshead (L)

Village School: 1863, and no doubt by Thompson. A small slate, three-bay building with a central projecting gable; across the road is its duplicate of ten years later.

Heversham (W)

Girls' and Infants' School (**171**): 1839, built at the 'sole expense' of James Gandy of Heaves.[1] Rubble walls, diamond chimneys, Gothic/Tudor windows with cusped lights, probably not by Webster. Nearby, the teacher's cottage, probably old, but with a one-bay gabled addition, dated MH 1841, for Mary Howard of Levens Hall, who paid for it. In the gable a mullioned window with a taller central light. The ground floor is a loggia with a lintel right across on irregular rustic columns, and this addition is probably by Webster. Changes made to the school in 1903 by Joseph Bintley of Kendal.[2]

[1] J. F. Curwen, *History of Heversham with Milnthorpe*, 1930, 25-6.
[2] CRO K, WPR 8.

Kendal (W)

Grammar School: On the north side of the churchyard, founded in 1525; donations of money and oak trees made in 1582-8.[1] What is seen now must be later, probably of 1843-4. The barge-boarded gables and cylindrical chimneys suggest that George Webster was the architect.

[1] *Annals*, 191.

Kirkland National Schools: 1861, by Miles Thompson, on the site of the former vicarage (a new vicarage was built in 1859) and its grounds. Tudor in style – the windows have pointed heads – and picturesque in composition, with gables and tall chimneys and constantly changing levels. Rubble and slate construction.[1] No longer a school.

[1] *Annals*, 205.

St George's Schools: 1852-3, Tudor, probably by Thompson.[1]

[1] *Annals*, 206, 302.

Kirkby Lonsdale (W)

Grammar School: rebuilt on its present site in 1848-50.[1] Three-bay, one-storey, with hood-moulded windows; an inscribed stone from the old school of 1628. Perhaps by Miles Thompson, or Thomas Garnett, his rival for the new bank. Large and unsympathetic additions.

[1] A. Pearson *et al*, *Annals of Kirkby Lonsdale and Lunesdale Today*, 1996, 157.

National Schools: 1857-8, by Miles Thompson, to replace the former 'subscription' school. The architect was said to have 'left nothing to be desired in the way of accommodation or comfort'.[1]

[1] CRO K, WPR 19; Pearson, *op. cit.*, 367-8.

Levens (W)

Village School: a school was built here by the 'munificence of F. G. Howard' of Levens Hall in 1819.[1] Francis Webster was probably the architect, but the building has not been identified.

[1] *Local Chronology*, 36; Parson & White, 1829, 626 gives the date as 1825.

Lindale (L)

Village School: *c.*1830, near George Webster's church, and much altered. Only the bellcote suggests his hand here too.

Longsleddale (W)

Village School: 1863, by Miles Thompson.[1]

[1.] CRO K, *Annals*, 304.49.

Lower Holker (L)

Holker: 1864, by Miles Thompson for the 7th Duke of Devonshire. Elizabethan, with gables, barge boards, and mullioned and transomed windows. The attached teacher's cottage is, like the rest of the village, rustic, with octagonal window panes.[1] No longer a school.

[1.] *WG*, 30 April 1864, tenders to Lowther St, Kendal.

Milnthorpe (W)

Village School: 1860; T-shaped plan, Elizabethan, with mullioned and transomed windows, and steep gables. So much a replica of the Burton school of 1867 that it must be by Thompson. No longer a school.

Preston Richard (W)

Endmoor: *c.*1865; a near-replica of Milnthorpe and attributable to Thompson. Partly demolished.

Tean (Staffs.)

Village School: perhaps the firm's most distant commission. Tenders were invited by Thompson & Webster for an 'extensive school' and three cottages for Messrs Philips of Tean Hall in 1854. On an H-plan, of red brick with blue brick diapering and stone trim. The windows are now very large, having been extended downwards. The roof is of hammer-beam construction. The cottages not identified.

[1.] *WG*, 9 Sept. 1854.

PUBLIC BUILDINGS

Public buildings listed here include those of the 18th and early 19th centuries – assembly rooms and the like – and run on to railway stations, a new type brought into being by advancing technology. Others, such as prisons and houses of correction, change totally in response to increasingly humane attitudes, and banks grow ever more dominating in the high street. The Websters had a share in all this, on the modest scale suited to the small towns of north-west England.

Appleby (W)

Gaols and Courts: the old gaol stood on the west bank of the Eden and the failure to accept Robert Adam's designs for a new building in 1766-7 (he was then working at Lowther and Whitehaven) on account of the cost led to Robert Fothergill's extremely modest building of

1771. Courts were added from 1773. In 1812 Francis Webster prepared plans to improve the building which were ready the next year when he was asked to add a chapel. He acted as surveyor for the building and brought in familiar tradesmen from Kendal. His new building was on the Panopticon principle of Jeremy Bentham, probably on advice from John Higgin of the gaol in Lancaster Castle. Further work began in 1818 and the facade of this was clearly based on Adam's earlier design, seven bays, the centre crowned with a pediment, but with none of Adam's finesse. Further alterations in 1822-3 and very substantial improvements in 1824. After his death in 1827 Webster's estate was paid £70 for plans. In 1830 William Coulthard, the Websters' associate, was paid for plans, including £20 from Levens Hall. His work at Appleby was one of Francis Webster's most extensive operations.[1]

[1] B. Tyson, 'An Architectural History of the Gaols and Court-Houses of Appleby, Cumbria', *Trans. Ancient Monuments Society*, xxxii, 1988, 101-39; *The Websters of Kendal*, no. 63.

Burneside (W)

Railway Station: 1847, of rock-work, limestone, 'of rough stones of irregular sizes, dark blue in colour, which harmonises well with the scenery'.[1] Very different from Windermere or Staveley stations, and attributed to Miles Thompson.

[1] J. Mellentin, *Kendal and Windermere Railway*, 1980, 12.

Burton-in-Kendal (W)

Market Cross: in the square of *c*.1810 and likely to be of the same date. Perhaps from the Websters' yard.

Carlisle (C)

Cumberland and Westmorland Lunatic Asylum: George Webster had three elevations at Eller How in 1864, but the present Garlands Hospital was not built until 1862. These elevations were probably for an earlier project at Lowry Hill, north of the town, for which architects were invited to submit plans in 1853. Three were selected but Webster was not one of them and, like the other unsuccessful applicants, he would have had his plans returned.[1]

[1] See p. 340; information kindly supplied by Susan Dench, Cumbria Record Office.

Cartmel (L)

Savings Bank: 1847, for the Rev. T. Remington of Aynsome; by Miles Thompson in the Tudor style and probably never built.[1]

[1] CRO K, WPR 83/PR/2718/10.

Giggleswick (YWR)

House of Industry: George Webster had two undated plans at Eller How in 1864.[1]

[1] See p. 342.

Hawkshead (L)

Market House and Assembly Rooms (**172**): 1790, a rebuilding of the earlier market for which subscriptions were raised in 1789. There may be reason to connect John Carr of York with the design of this building which features windows set in arches, a motif adopted about this time by Francis Webster.[1] He supplied chimneypieces and brought in his father and brother as part of the team of craftsmen – all the others were local. Enlarged by two bays in 1887.[2]

1. R. B. Wragg, *John Carr of York*, ed. G. Worsley, 2000, 113.
2. CRO K, WPR 83/25; B. Tyson, 'Francis Webster and the Market House at Hawkshead, 1790', *Quarto*, Oct. 1993, 8-11; T.W. Thompson, *Wordsworth's Hawkshead*, 1976, 130-31.

Kendal (W)

Castle Howe, Obelisk (**173**): 1788, to celebrate the Glorious Revolution of 1688, on the summit of the town's first castle's motte. So far as is known, it is Francis Webster's first work in Kendal.[1] William Holme was the builder and the monument was known as 'Bill Holme's Bodkin'.

1. *Annals*, 21; Curwen, *KK*, 85-6. For the Whig sentiments which inspired its erection, see J. Satchell and O. Wilson, *Christopher Wilson of Kendal*, 1988, 2.

Dowker's Hospital (**174**); established by the will of Dorothy Dowker (d. 1833) and designed in the same year by George Webster who was paid £5 10s. for plans and specifications and £7 10s. for supervision the following year. The almshouses were Jacobethan in style with a three-bay front of some complexity to Highgate. The centre projected as a porch with a small room over with an oriel with arched lights. On either side the ground-floor windows were mullioned and transomed, those above gabled into the roof space. Demolished 1965, the doorway re-erected in Webster's Yard, Highgate.[1]

1. Kendal Town Hall, sketch plans, etc.; *Annals*, 228; *WG*, 20 Feb.1987. Six working drawings and elevations were at Eller How in 1864: see p. 342.

House of Correction: built in 1785, Francis Webster's later partner William Holme being the waller and slater. Enlarged 1793-4 by Webster & Holme, and again in 1801 when it had become too small. Again deemed 'insufficient for the purpose' in 1817 and 'almost rebuilt'. Extended again in 1824. Closed 1894.[1]

1. CRO K, Quarter Sessions Minute Book, 1780-1804, *sub* 1793; Curwen, *Rec. Kendale*, iii, 95-7, 104.

Market Hall: 1855, by Thompson & Webster, on the site of St George's chapel in the Market Place, and an instructive contrast with that at Kirkby Lonsdale. There all was refinement, here, a year later, a coarse incoherent design of over-size elements, heavy pilasters, insensitive windows, and an overwhelming entablature. It became the public library in 1891. The façade was re-erected in Sandes Avenue in 1909. Originally built as a grain and butter market.[1]

1. CRO K, WSMB/K/Bk 1, plans; *Annals*, 157-8.

Moot Hall: the building in the Market Place which served as the Town Hall until 1859 and thereafter as the Moot Hall was built in 1729 when the Palladian window may have been installed. Alterations of 1801 were perhaps by Francis Webster who certainly carried out those of 1818 and 1824. Sold to Job Bintley, architect, 1859.[1] Badly damaged by fire in 1969 and rebuilt with the loss of such details as the unusual quoining.

1. CRO K, Quarter Sessions Minute Books; *Annals*, 304; Curwen, *KK*, 292-3; W. G. Wiseman, 'A Brief History of Kendal Petty Sessions', *CW3*, i, 105-22.

New Shambles: 1804,[1] running from the Market Place to Finkle Street in a gentle curve. Single-storey shops were divided by broad pilaster strips with groups of three discs on the capitals, as at Sand Aire House, George Webster's own house at Thorny Hills, and elsewhere, though these features speak of the 1820s. Perhaps by Francis Webster and John Fisher, since it is of timber construction.

[1.] *Annals*, 124.

Oddfellows' Hall (**176**): 1833,[1] attributed to George Webster. Classical, limestone, the ground floor with tripartite windows between wide arches. Above, four tall windows set into a pilastered segmental arcade. Entablature with the boldly lettered name and above it a pilastered attic. It became the Mechanics' Institute in 1857 and was reopened by Lord Brougham.[2]

[1.] *WG*, 21 Oct.1833.
[2.] *Annals*, 298, 304.

Sandes Hospital: founded in 1670 by Thomas Sandes. The houses behind the 17th-century front were rebuilt by Miles Thompson in 1852.[1]

[1.] *Annals*, 202; Curwen, *KK*, 137.

Wakefield's Bank (**175**): new premises in Stricklandgate were designed by Francis Webster in 1797. Austere and forbidding, with the bank on the ground floor and the family home above. Five bays and three storeys, with a smooth recessed door of a segmental arch on panelled pilasters, perhaps the earliest use of this motif.[1] Rebuilt.

[1.] Curwen, *KK*, 326, though he gives 1799; *The Websters of Kendal*, no. 55. The vellum foundation document is reproduced in Satchell and Wilson, *Christopher Wilson of Kendal*, 3.

Wash Houses and Baths: 1863-4, by Miles Thompson.[1] A three-bay centre block with a pedimental gable facing All Hallows Lane. Rustic ground floor with central arched door. Above are two arched windows between pilaster strips. The swimming bath added in 1883-4 when the corporation bought the building.[2] Now Shearman House.

[1.] CRO K, WSBM/K/94a; *ibid.*, *Annals*, 304.65.
[2.] R. K. Bingham, *Kendal: A Social History*, 1995, 311.

Westmorland Bank (now HSBC) (**177-178**): 1833-4, by George Webster who made five designs (one plan), all with attached colonnades. As built, it has five bays and a rusticated basement with two storeys above. The central three bays project to form an attached portico of square piers carrying an entablature which in turn supports a pedestal with flanking scrolls and a lion on top. The ground-floor windows are Egyptianising. The lion was cast in bronze by Felix Austin, painted to resemble limestone, and put in place in 1840. It is the oldest purpose-built bank of the HSBC; the door was unhappily brought forward in 1966.[1]

[1.] HSBC Head Office, plans; A. Taylor, 'The Bank of Westmorland Lion', *Quarto*, Jan. 1992, 16-19; *The Websters of Kendal*, no. 56; *Midland Bank, Kendal: 150 Years of Banking, 1833-1983*, [1983]. Twenty-four working drawings and a painting were at Eller How in 1864: see p. 342.

White Hall Assembly Rooms (now the Town Hall) (**179-180**): 1824-5, by Francis and George Webster. In 1824 buildings on the corner of Highgate and Lowther Street were demolished to make way for assembly rooms consisting of news room, library, ballroom, etc. The cost was £6,000, raised in shares of £55, and the mayor, Michael Braithwaite, laid the foundation stone on 1 July 1825. The architect was nominally Francis, as head of the firm, but the building was in the manner of George's new Grecian style, developed at Read Hall, just completed, and displayed in Kendal in his own house. The three-bay front has a ground floor of smooth rustication carrying an Ionic version of the gas meter house and forming a balcony with a pediment and cupola above. In 1859 the corporation bought the building and abandoned the former Town Hall to commerce. George Webster made plans to convert the suite of rooms into a new Town Hall. The cupola was replaced by a clock tower, 'designed by the original architect', which is descended from that of the Ulverston Savings Bank. The decoration of the interior with laurel wreaths and staircases of the same design as Graythwaite Hall largely survived the enlargements of 1893. The original building remains almost intact.[1]

[1.] Curwen, *Rec. Kendale*, iii, 97; *Annals*, 151-2; Curwen, *KK*, 41; *Local Chronology*, 62; *The Websters of Kendal*, no. 64. Thirty-five working drawings were at Eller How in 1864: see p. 342.

Working Men's Institute: the building, at the north-east corner of the Market Place, was largely rebuilt as a theatre in 1758. In 1820 the new Working Men's Institute was established there and the trustees, of whom George Webster was one, bought it in 1823. It was refronted by Miles Thompson in 1865.[1]

[1.] *Annals*, 294; Curwen, *KK*, 304.

Kirkby Lonsdale (W)

Market House (**181**): 1854, by Miles Thompson, who was paid £21. A subtle freestone façade turning the corner from Main Street to Market Street very gradually, bay by bay. Ground floor delicately rusticated with arches originally open. At mid-point, a massive chimney with the date, all now sadly removed. Interior structure of slim iron columns, otherwise altered.[1]

[1.] CRO K, WD/PP/Box 4, minutes; *The Websters of Kendal*, no. 69.

Trustee Savings Bank (**182**): on 18 Feb. 1847 Thomas Garnett of Kirkby Lonsdale was asked for plans. 'Differences arose' when they were received, and they were sent to Kendal to 'Mr Thompson, architect, as a guide to prepare plans and estimates' which were adopted unanimously on 19 April, a clock to be incorporated. Thompson's building fills the east side of the square very elegantly. Of three bays of freestone, it has a smooth rusticated ground floor with an arched projecting porch of paired pilasters, a feature that appears again on the first floor with the balcony on the porch in between. There is a window with twin arched lights and a bell turret above. Inside three Webster chimneypieces. The forecourt with piers and railings was removed in 1970 and should be reinstated to perfect the setting of this minor masterpiece.[1]

[1.] Lloyds TSB, TC/59/a/1; CRO K, WD/PP, Box 2/111, advertisement for tenders.

Milnthorpe (W)

Cross: 1823, a column with a ball, on steps, possibly by Francis Webster. Altered later.[1]

[1.] J. F. Curwen, *History of Heversham with Milnthorpe*, 1930, 49.

Workhouse (**183**): 1815, by Francis Webster. Tenders were let on 18 Feb. and the building cost £4,990; ten utilitarian bays, two storeys, centre canted bay. A long wing of 1869, with a verandah on columns.[1]

[1] CRO K, Quarter Sessions Minute Books; Curwen, *Rec. Kendale*, iii, 230; R. K. Bingham, *Chronicles of Milnthorpe*, 1987, 283-4 and illus. 285.

Preston (L)

Town Moor (**184-185**): enclosed in 1834 and Ladies' Walk laid out along the southern edge with lodges at either end in George Webster's Jacobethan style. A third lodge added on the north side in 1836. The east lodge has been demolished.[1]

[1] A. Hewitson, *History of Preston*, 1883, repr. 1969, 326-8.

Sedbergh (YWR)

Market Hall: 1858, a memorial to a headmaster of Sedbergh School. Of slate, with freestone dressings; the ground floor has open-shouldered arches and there is a mullioned and transomed window in the big gable. Possibly by Miles Thompson.

Settle (YWR)

Public Rooms (now the Town Hall) (**186**): 1832-3, by George Webster. The cost of £5,500 was raised in £10 shares, with the clock costing another £150. On an island site in the Market Place, the building, in Jacobean style, displays four façades of curved and straight gables, mullioned and transomed windows, four-centred doorways, and bold octagonal buttresses. Little of the interior survives except the south staircase. Originally it had a library, news room, bank, shops, and flats.[1]

[1] NYRO, DC/SET, plans; *Leeds Mercury*, 14 Sept.1833; *The Websters of Kendal*, no. 65.

Skipton (YWR)

Craven Bank (now Barclays): *c*.1834 and perhaps by George Webster. Originally the Chippendale, Netherwood & Carr Bank, taken over by the Birkbecks in 1834.[1] 4 + 2 bays, three storeys, of fine ashlar. Smooth rusticated base of arched windows, the upper floor scanned by Greek Ionic pilasters. George Webster built Cliffe House, Keighley, for Netherwood *c*.1830.

[1] W. C. E. Hartley, *Banking in Yorkshire*, 1975, 68, 143; *The Websters of Kendal*, no. 60.

Ulverston (L)

Kendal Bank: *c*.1825, probably by Francis Webster. Rendered, 5 + 2 bays and two storeys; an arched central door with angle pilasters. Now the District Council offices.

Lancaster Bank (now National Westminster) (**187**): *c*.1865,[1] attributed to Miles Thompson. Three bays and three storeys of ashlar limestone. Porch *in antis* of two columns and two piers of smooth rustication. First-floor windows pedimented, the centre one curved. Above the cornice a massive statement, BANK, flanked by consoles. Inside a fine original hall. Slightly overlapping the bank is the three-bay bank house with an overall pediment. The detail is nowhere quite the same as the bank itself. The upper windows are of that peculiar formation that the Websters derived from Storrs Hall.

[1] Mannex, 1866, 395, 'just erected'; *The Websters of Kendal*, no. 58.

Temperance Hall: 1851, for Hannah Goad, a Quaker.[1] Five bays and three storeys to Queen

Street, the centre projecting slightly and carrying a pedimental gable. Basement of rough stone, the rest rendered and quoined. Probably by Miles Thompson.

[1.] H. F. Birkett, *The Story of Ulverston*, 1949, 140.

Trustee Savings Bank (**188**): 1836, Greco-Italian, by George Webster, who offered an Elizabethan alternative, now lost. Three bays and two storeys with a rusticated ground floor and a porch of sturdy Tuscan columns. Above it, an Italianate twin-light window and a pediment; to either side an arched window. Behind, a tower was designed in 1844 with arched and coupled windows and a pediment. The tower was slightly altered quite recently. Nikolaus Pevsner thought it 'the best building in the town'.[1]

[1.] Pevsner, *N. Lancs.*, 252; CRO K, WDY 42, CRO B, Z1024/1-2, plans and correspondence; A. Taylor, 'A Bank and its Building: Ulverston Trustee Savings Bank', *CW2*, lxxiv, 146-58; *The Websters of Kendal*, no. 57.

Victoria Hall: 1850, a long building in a very narrow street, attributed to Miles Thompson. The main façade has five wide bays with a central pediment on pilasters over a twin-light window. Wreaths in architraves. At the south end, a two-bay pedimented extension with a rusticated ground floor of two arches.

Windermere (W)

Railway Station: 1846, by Miles Thompson, who advertised for tenders in October.[1] The terminus of the Kendal & Windermere Railway, with four functional parallel engine sheds and, to north and east, a slate and freestone reception building with arched windows. The elegant *porte-cochère* on slim cast-iron columns has survived the station's conversion to a supermarket.

[1.] *WG*, 31 Oct. 1846.

Workhouse: 1829-30. Several accounts survive so tradesmen's names are known, but not that of the architect.[1] However, Thomas Ullock, the moving spirit, was a friend of George Webster who built Quarry Howe and the Royal Hotel for him. The site has not been identified.

[1.] CRO K, WPR 61/O2.

INDUSTRIAL AND COMMERCIAL BUILDINGS

Are the unadorned mills of the early industrial revolution architecture? They will never be overlooked; their great bulk will see to that. Perhaps it matters little since, if a Webster designed a purely functional building, it will be noted here. There can be no safe attributions, since there are no suggestive details from which to work. The mills of the 1820s could have been designed by Francis Webster – if any architect was needed. He certainly designed Dockray Hall Mill for the Gandys but that has some distinction, a tower with what anyone will recognise as having architectural detailing. By the middle of the century mill-owners recognised an obligation to the public and the largest structures in Kendal were given just enough architectural ornament to be counted as public buildings, if not on the level of the banks.

Accrington (L)

Broad Oak Mill: the Broad Oak works of Thomas Hargreaves were expanding from about 1816 through the 1820s and '30s and as Hargreaves's sons grew up, it became Hargreaves Bros in 1836, and by 1846 had 850 employees. In the familiar way, the sons lost interest in manufacturing and leased out the works from 1854. During the expansion of the works a tall chimney began to lean to the point of collapse 'until Mr Webster, an architect of much repute at Kendal, being at Oak Hill suggested a plan . . . taking out two or three rows of bricks half-round the chimney and putting plates of iron with thin wedges between in place of the bricks removed . . . The wedges were knocked and the whole bulk of the chimney restored to its original position . . . a great feat of ingenuity and mechanical skill'.[1] This sounds like Francis Webster, with whom one associates ingenuity and practicality. He was perhaps involved in building the mill in the first place.

[1.] B. Hargreaves, *Recollections of Broad Oak*, 1882, 32.

Helsington (W)

Helsington Mills: the mill and perhaps the weir rebuilt 1799, partly as a marble mill for their own use by Webster & Holme for Lady Andover of Levens. The cost was £210, including some cottages. The Websters then rented back the marble mill.

[1.] Levens Hall MSS, box 7; J. Somervell, *Water-power Mills of South Westmorland*, 1930, 69.

Kendal (W)

Albert Buildings: from 1914 the Kendal Museum, but originally the new wool warehouse of Whitwell, Hargreaves & Co., a well-proportioned building of 1864 with arched openings carefully organised with rectangular ones. It had a handsomely-lettered name board between consoles.[1] Inside is a fine hammer-beam roof, just as Miles Thompson provided in schools (cf. Tean, Staffs., 1854), and churches (cf. Garsdale, 1861).

[1.] Illus. in J. Satchell, *Kendal on Tenterhooks*, 1984, 9.

Canal Head (**189**): the warehouses, wharves, cottages, and the Websters' marble showroom, all by Francis Webster for Kendal corporation, 1818, were the most complex of the family's industrial enterprises.[1] Though the canal has been drained many of the buildings survive. There were working drawings for the marble works at Eller How in 1864.[2]

[1.] P. N. Wilson, 'Canal Head, Kendal', *CW2*, lxviii, 132-50; J. Satchell, *Kendal's Canal: History, Industry and People*, Kendal Civic Society, 2001; see also pp. 50-51.
[2.] See p. 342.

Castle Mills: additions of 1855[1] singled out the centre bay. It projected slightly and contained the entrance. Over it is a row of three arched windows of even height and over them a circular window set in the gable. In the long wings on either side all is much as before. Thompson would be a likely candidate for this work.

[1.] *Annals*, 243; Satchell, *Kendal on Tenterhooks*, 59.

Dockray Hall Mills (**190**): for James Gandy & Sons, 1816-17 and 1825, by Francis Webster. 'The largest manufacturing building ever erected in the county',[1] of four storeys and thirteen bays, the centre projecting as a tower staircase with arched windows and ending in busy crenellations over 'arrow' slits and a quatrefoil. The mill race enters through a series of arches. The mill had a spectacular fire on 4 April 1824, but was at once rebuilt and fireproofed.[2] George Webster's rival in the marble business, Edward Bayliffe, built his mill here in 1830.[3]

1. Curwen, *KK*, 363; Somervell, *Water-power Mills of South Westmorland*, 56-7.
2. *Annals*, 295. The fire was the subject of a painting by Richard Stirzaker: Curwen, *KK*, 35.
3. *Annals*, 246-7.

Gas Light & Coke Co. (**191**): the meter house in the guise of a classical temple, 1825, by Francis and George Webster. Tetrastyle portico of Tuscan columns and outer piers carrying a pediment. The opening was marked by a 'glass of wine at the Town Hall where a beautiful gas star hung in front of the window'.[1] There were other buildings with angle pilasters, now demolished.[2] The façade of the meter house has been re-erected at Abbot Hall.

1. *Annals*, 158-9; *Local Chronology*, 62-3.
2. CRO K, WSMB/K/Bk 5/27, additions by Miles Thompson, 1859; *ibid.*, Bk 4/476, new manager's house by J. Thompson, 1878.

Highgate Brewery: built in the garden of William Whitwell's house in 1853, perhaps by Miles Thompson.[1]

1. Curwen, *KK*, 146.

Lowther Street: George Webster had two plans at Eller How in 1864 for a warehouse for 'Mr H. Airey', who is probably Henry Airey, corn and flour dealer and bacon curer in 1829, butter factor in 1851.[1]

1. See p. 342; Parson & White, 1829, 663; Mannex, 1851, 320.

Netherfield Works (K Shoes): started in 1825 by Thomas Wilson and sold in 1843. The site included 'two genteel . . . houses' and two cottages and there are still domestic premises near Nether Bridge which look very much like the work of George Webster.[1]

1. Curwen, *KK*, 197; R. Bingham, *Kendal: A Social History*, 1995, 241 shows the very extensive works.

Langdale (W)

Elterwater Gunpowder Works: for David Huddleston, licensed in 1824;[1] powder mills and magazines. Huddleston, a former clerk with the Kendal Bank, retired to Elterwater Old Hall in 1823. Francis Webster probably built or altered the hall and it seems likely that he planned the mills.

1. *WG*, 17 Jan. 1824.

Preston Richard (W)

Gatebeck Gunpowder Works: 1851-2, for Wakefield & Bainbridge, by Miles Thompson,[1] including refining and cooling houses, etc.

1. CRO K, WD/K/300, advertisement for tenders.

Sedgwick (W)

Gunpowder Works: 1790, for the Wakefields, perhaps by Francis Webster.[1]

1. CRO K, Quarter Sessions Minute Book, 1780-1804; Curwen, *Rec. Kendale*, iii, 235.

Skelsmergh (W)

Beck Mill: a malt kiln, 1796, for Lady Andover of Levens Hall. Webster & Holme were paid £121 1s. 1d.[1]

[1.] Levens Hall MSS, account books: information from Dr Blake Tyson.

Upper Holker (L)

Lowwood Gunpowder works: 1798-9, by Webster & Holme.[1]

[1.] A. Palmer, *The Low Wood Gunpowder Company*, Gunpowder Mills Study Group, 1998, 12-15.

HOTELS

Accrington (L)

Hargreaves Inn: 1834-5, Elizabethan-style, and attributed to George Webster as one of many works for the Hargreaves family.

Allithwaite (L)

Inn (Kents Bank): built *c*.1845 by Miss Lambert of Boarbank, whose rebuilt Abbot Hall is just across the road. Elizabethan in style, this 'inn of moderate dimensions'[1] is, like Abbot Hall, attributable to George Webster.

[1.] *Sketches of Grange*, 1850, 36.

Ambleside (W)

Salutation Inn (**192**): rebuilt 1821-2 by Francis Webster.[1] A three-bay entrance front with recessed centre enclosing an arched porch carrying a balcony, with a wing attached to the east side. All this is still recognisable. There is a view on a char dish in Abbot Hall Art Gallery and Museum, Kendal.[2]

[1.] *Westmorland Advertiser and Kendal Chronicle*, 2 June 1821.

[2.] *WG*, 27 May 1983.

Bowness (W)

White Lion (now the Royal Hotel): 1839, by George Webster, a rebuilding of the White Lion for Thomas Ullock, in readiness for the visit of Queen Adelaide in 1840. The tower-like south end was originally enclosed in a two-storey verandah as shown in an engraving owned by Webster, and endorsed by him as 'built under my direction'.[1] Grecian iron balconies survive and there is a timber porch to the street and a typical staircase inside. The Royal was no doubt the finest hotel in the area at this date.

[1.] CRO K, WDX 1315.

Clitheroe (L)

Starkie Arms: 1835, slightly grander than the White Lion, with Moreton Hall details, attributed to George Webster.

White Lion: 1835, Elizabethan, gabled and finialled, attributed to George Webster.

Coniston (L)

Waterhead Inn: 1849, for James Garth Marshall of Monk Coniston and Leeds, it replaced one on a different site.[1]. The architect was Miles Thompson. Elizabethan, of slate and freestone, and, Harriet Martineau claimed, 'one of the most comfortable . . . in England'.[2] A lithograph shows all the details of the H-shaped building – an iron verandah facing the lake, barge-boarded gables, mullioned, transomed, and bay windows, cylindrical chimneys, and a timber porch.[3] The latter and the staircase survive.

[1] *WG*, 1 June 1850, 'recently opened'.

[2] H. Martineau, *Complete Guide to the Lakes*, 1858, 28.

[3] F. Graham, *Picturesque Lakeland One Hundred Years Ago*, 1969, 30. George Webster had a copy at Eller How: see p. 339.

Grasmere (W)

Hollens and Lowther Hotel: originally a late-18th century villa, but an hotel by 1849, of which Edward Brown was the landlord.[1] Alterations by George Webster, probably with Miles Thompson in 1849 when the Italianate tower may have been added, and further additions by Thompson in 1851, with a 'carriage drive of 300 yards'.[2] In 1852 Edward Brown, 'late of the General Wolfe at Penrith', was admitted to the 'newly-built Hollins and Lowther Hotel'.[3] Inside are two white and one black marble chimneypieces from the Webster yard. Since 1990 the National Trust's regional office.

[1] Mannex, 1849, 266. A watercolour by William Green shows its original state: *Thomas de Quincey: an English Opium-Eater, 1785-1859*, Wordsworth Trust, 1985, 81.

[2] National Trust North-West Regional Office, letter from A. Taylor, 18 Feb. 1997; *WG*, 15 March 1851, tenders to be sent to Thompson.

[3] CRO, D/Lons/5/2/11/262.

Lake Hotel (now the Prince of Wales): 1855 (datestone), also for Edward Brown by Miles Thompson. Of enormous bulk, it sits between Dove Cottage and the lake shore. It was made yet larger, again by Thompson, in 1863[1]. The barge boards have gone, but the vast array of vernacular chimneys is still there, as is a typical staircase.

[1] *WG*, 21 Nov.1863.

Hawkshead (L)

Red Lion: the internal and external alterations, including barge boards, grotesque heads, a fine plaster Elizabethan ceiling, and a chimneypiece are all clearly the work of George Webster.[1]

[1] However, Ferdinando Taylor, who was the publican here and also a self-made architect, seems as likely to have made the alterations himself [editor].

Helsington (W)

Strickland Arms, Sizergh: older than it appears (note the blocked windows). The date of the remodelling could be anywhere between *c*.1840 and *c*.1850. It is clearly by George Webster who introduced the mullioned and transomed windows, the dormers, and the four-centred door.

Langdale (W)

Old Dungeon Ghyll Hotel: old indeed and humble, but with an abruptly-soaring wing of three storeys. Miles Thompson bought the inn in 1862[1] and this wing must have been his work. He left the hotel to his brother Robert in his will.[2]

[1] CRO K, WDX 40.
[2] *Ibid.*, WDX 708/T46.

Milnthorpe (W)

Cross Keys: rebuilt 1821. A 'town' hotel, probably by Francis Webster.[1]

[1] J. F. Curwen, *History of Heversham with Milnthorpe*, 1930, 70.

Patterdale (W)

Geldard's Family Hotel (now the Patterdale Hotel): a charming wing at the back with a verandah and pretty garden, all now subsumed in additions and alterations. Perhaps by Webster or Thompson.

Ullswater Hotel: c.1860 for Robert Bownass,[1] probably by Miles Thompson. An Italianate variant on the Windermere and Grasmere slate-built hotels and on a similar scale. Groups of one-, two-, and three-arched windows. Enlarged and much altered.

[1] W. P. Morris, *Records of Patterdale*, 1906, 59.

Preston (L)

Unicorn and *Moor Park*: c.1835, the first in the style of the Moor Park lodges, the latter Ionic; both attributable to George Webster.

Shap (W)

Shap Wells Hotel: built and owned by the Earl of Lonsdale in 1833. The original front was of seven bays with tripartite windows at the ends and a tripartite central door under a segmental arch. The Lowthers had over the years enough contacts with the Websters to make George's involvement a possibility and he did take the waters there in its early years.

Staveley (W)

New Hotel (now Abbey House): 1844-5 for the coming railway; the station was to have been next door. Built for J. H. Wilson of The Grange, Sussex, it was 'intended to be the best as it is undoubtedly the handsomest in the neighbourhood'.[1] Probably designed by Webster (with Thompson), although it is hard to find a parallel.

[1] *WG*, 27 Sept. 1845.

Troutbeck (W)

Low Wood Hotel (**193**): a large barn-like building here faced Lake Windermere in 1783.[1] Owned by Christopher Wilson of Abbot Hall, Kendal, it was advertised to let in 1824[2] and described a year later as 'recently improved . . . fitted up in the first style of elegance . . . new stables erected equal to any in the Kingdom'; no doubt by Francis Webster.[3] Some details of this work survive but there were additions in 1843 (datestone), with gothic detail and Grecian ironwork (south wing), undoubtedly by George Webster. A verandah was added to the centre *c.*1859 after a fire. Many later alterations and additions.

[1.] P. Crosthwaite, *Map of the Grand Lake of Windermere*, repr. in A. Hankinson, *The Regatta Men*, 1988.

[2.] *WG*, 13 March 1824.

[3.] *Westmorland Advertiser*, 28 May 1825.

Upper Allithwaite (L)

Coach and Horses (Low Newton): the landlord farmed the land and the barns are more interesting than the doll's house inn. The group is about a mile from George Webster's house at Eller How and everything suggests that he at least remodelled it all. The side door of the former inn has a mock 'Lancashire' lintel dated GG 1848 (George Gibson of The Height, Cartmel Fell) and a barn, with circular windows and crosses, is dated 1855. Now South View.

Windermere (W)

Rigg's Hotel: 1845-7, for Richard Rigg, again part of the railway promotion and here next to the terminus. Plans could be inspected and tenders presented at the offices of Webster & Thompson.[1] Rigg's is on a new scale and the term 'inn' would have been a misnomer. Of slate with freestone dressings and with an Italianate tower terminating the eight-bay, three-storey façade. The stables were of a size to cope with Rigg's fleet of liveried coaches which connected with the trains. By 1857 an extension was needed beyond the tower. The iron verandah is a replacement of the timber original. The plan is simple, each floor having a straight spinal corridor.

[1.] *WG*, 8 Nov.1845; L. Steele, *Windermere, its Growth and History*, 1928, 9.

BRIDGES

There are one or two larger and interesting bridges by the Websters and a minor work on a famous bridge which appears to be the first recorded building job by any member of the family. Most, however, are small, one-arched inconspicuous works, many part of the turnpike system. They include bridges for McAdam's newly aligned road over Shap Fell and for the Ulverston and Carnforth turnpike trust, of which Francis Webster was a trustee in the 1820s as were his friend T. H. Maude and many of his clients. George Webster was a trustee under the new act of 1850.[1]

[1.] J. L. Hobbs, 'The turnpike roads of North Lonsdale', *CW2*, lv, 271, 279. Thirty working drawings for county bridges were at Eller How in 1864: see p. 342.

Beetham (W)

Beetham Bridge (**194**): 1819-22, by Francis Webster, part of the turnpike improvements; three limestone arches with rounded breakwaters and embankments ending in pylons. Spoilt by road changes in 1969.[1] The toll house associated with the bridge remains as part of the school.

[1.] *Local Chronology*, 33; *The Websters of Kendal*, no. 74; Curwen, *Rec. Kendale*, iii, 250.

Kendal (W)

Miller or Mill Bridge (**195**): 1818, by Francis Webster,[1] a replacement of an ancient bridge to link all the activities at the newly extended canal with the town. Three arches of limestone with rounded breakwaters, over the mill race a bridge of three small arches.[2]

[1.] CRO K, WDY 42; CRO, DLons/L11/9/35; a design for the railings is at Kendal Town Hall; Curwen, *Rec. Kendale*, iii, 96; *The Websters of Kendal*, no. 73.

[2.] P. N. Wilson, 'Canal Head, Kendal', *CW2*, lxviii, fig. 2.

Stramongate Bridge: remodelled 1792-9 by Thomas Harrison who was rebuilding Lancaster Castle at this time. This is another case of Francis Webster and William Holme carrying out the designs of another. Harrison was paid ten guineas for plans, as was John Hird, on 16 July 1796. In 1797 Harrison was paid a further ten guineas for plans etc 'for amendment' on discovering that the old bridge was indestructible and would have to be accommodated. The result was two fronts of segmental arches with projections over the cutwaters containing niches with the date 1794. The material is large coursed rubble limestone.[1]

[1.] A. Taylor, 'Thomas Harrison and Stramongate Bridge, Kendal', *CW2*, lxix, 275-9; Curwen, *Rec. Kendale*, iii, 94.

Kirkby Lonsdale (W)

Devil's Bridge: in 1749 Thomas Webster of Kendal, Francis Webster's grandfather, made repairs at the bridge,[1] the earliest known work by a Webster in the field of building.

[1.] Curwen, *Rec. Kendale*, iii, 284; see p. 3.

Milnthorpe (W)

Dallam Tower Bridge (**196**): 1813, attributed to Francis Webster. The road from Milnthorpe to Arnside passed through the park of Dallam Tower until this bridge was built and the roadway realigned. There is a fine drawing of 1809 in George Webster's albums purporting to be by his son Robert. However, the new bridge was given its licence only in 1813.[1]

[1.] J. F. Curwen, *History of Heversham with Milnthorpe*, 1930, 74; Curwen, *Rec. Kendale*, iii, 228; *The Websters of Kendal*, no. 72.

Soulby (W)

Soulby Bridge: on the village green and almost identical in design with Beetham. Francis Webster was asked to view and prepare plan for a new bridge, Easter 1818; the tenders were out in 1819.[1]

[1.] *WG*, 1 May 1819; J. F. Curwen, *Later Records of North Westmorland*, 1932, 134.

Smaller bridges which were certainly by Francis Webster, including county bridges, turnpike, and other inconspicuous single-arched bridges, are at St Sunday's Beck (1819),[1] Farleton (1820),[2] Gilpin Bridge (1823),[3] Hucks Brow and Kitts How, Bannisdale (1826).[4] There are probably others.

[1.] *WG*, 10 July 1819, where the widening of the bridge at Crooklands is also mentioned; Curwen, *Rec. Kendale*, iii, 11, 121.

[2.] *WG*, 20 May 1820; Curwen, *op. cit.*, 11.

[3.] Over the Gilpin between Crook and Undermillbeck: Curwen, *op. cit.*, 165.

[4.] *Ibid.*, 132.

A curiosity is the wooden bridge on Gooseholme, Kendal, whose timbers were replaced on the old stone piers in 1875, by M. Thompson, woodwork, and Airey and Hill, masons.[1] This is Miles Thompson, nephew of the elder Miles, who appears in 1873 as building contractor, joiner, carpenter, and timber merchant at Beezon Lane saw mills.[2]

[1] *WG*, 25 Sept.1875.
[2] Kelly, *Cumb. & Westm.*, 1873, 927.

MONUMENTS

With one or two exceptions, the monuments listed here are inside churches. Only the earliest name on each stone is indicated.

Abbreviations: FW = Francis Webster; FWK = Francis Webster, Kendal; WK = Webster, Kendal; WsK = Websters, Kendal; D = Thomas Duckett; MT = Miles Thompson; ch. = chest; er. = erected; fig. = figure; n.s. = not signed; scr. = scroll; c = classical; g = gothic; G = Grecian; Gun. = known only from Gunnis

Accrington (L), St James	Thomas Hargreaves	WK	G	1822
	Benjamin Wilson (d. 1794)	WsK	G	er. 1829
	Nancy Hargreaves	FWK	G	1841
Addingham (YWR)	William C. Lister (**197**)	FWK	g	1841
Ambleside (W)	Richard Scambler	WK	c	1820
	Thomas J. Scales	FWK	G	1844
Askrigg (YNR)	Rev. John Lodge	FW	g	1853
Bampton (W)	Rev. John Bowstead (d. 1841)	FWK	c	er. 1843
	Sir Charles Richardson	FWK	G	1850
Barton (W)	Anne Wordsworth	n.s.	c	1815
	John Wordsworth	WK	c	1819
Bassenthwaite (C), St Bega	Sir Frederick F. Vane (d. 1832) [exterior]	FWK	ch	er. 1844
Beetham (W)	Rev. William Hutton	n.s.	urn	1811
	Daniel Wilson	FW	c	1824
	Sarah Wilson	n.s.	c	1831
	Sarah M. Wilson	FW	c	1843
	Rev. Joseph Thexton	FWK	g	1844
	Thomas Cartmel (d. 1785)	FW	G	er. later
	Richard Hadwen (d. 1779) *et al.*	n.s.	urn	er. later
Bolton-by-Bowland (YWR)	Rev. Thomas Wilson	n.s.	g	1813
Bolton-le-Sands (L)	Thomas Greene	n.s.	c	1810
	John Park	WK	c	1819
	Robert G. Bradley	FWK	G	1869
Bolton-on-Eden (W)	Richard Tinkler	WsK	c	1831
Bradford (YWR), Cathedral	Thomas Mann (d. 1811)	FWK	G	er. 1843
	Rev. John Crosse (d. 1816)	FWK	G	er. 1843
	George Anderton	n.s.	G	1817
Brookhouse (L)	Thomas Hodgson	WsK	c	1817
	Charles Gibson	WsK	G	1823

Brookhouse (L) [cont'd]	Thomas Berry	WsK	g	1832
	Edward Thurtell	FWK	c	1852
Brough (W)	John Dickinson	n.s.	G	1843
Broughton (Oxon)	Richard Haydon [Gun. 418]			1837
Burnley (L), St Peter	Nicholas Halstead	WK	G	1808
	James Holgate	n.s.	G	1810
	James Hargreaves	WsK	c	1830
	Rev. John Raws	WsK	G	1834
Burton-in-Kendal (W)	William Atkinson	WK	c	1825
	Thomas Dicey Cotton	WsK	c	1835
	William W. Atkinson	FWK	c	1844
Calder Bridge (C)	Joseph T. Senhouse (d. 1805)	FWK	c	er later
	Edmund L. Irton (d. 1820)	n.s.	G	er. 1850
Cartmel (L)	Catherine Gregg (d. 1781)	WK	G	er. later
	William Barrow	n.s.	c	1784
	John Robinson	n.s.	c	1788
	Robert Myers	WK	c	1793
	Robert Atkinson	n.s.	c	1794
	John F. Richardson	n.s.	c	1796
	Robert Webster [exterior]	n.s.	urn	1799
	Thomas Askew	n.s.	c	1809
	Edward Barrow	n.s.	G	1814
	Robert Michaelson	WsK	G	1822
	James Crosfield	n.s.	c	1826
	Thomas M. Machell	n.s.	G	1826
	Robert Webster [exterior]	n.s.	c	1828
	Agnes Atkinson	n.s.	c	1830
	John Walker	n.s.	g	1839
	Ann Redhead (**199**)	FWK	G	1845
Cartmel Fell (L)	John Gibson (d. 1834)	MT	c	er. 1859
Chester (Ches.), Cathedral	Capt. William Considine	FW	fig.	1841
Chorley (L), St Laurence	Sir Frank Standish, Bt	n.s.	c	1812
	Rev. Oliver Cooper	FWK	c	1825
	Thomas Coward	FWK	g	1840
	Frank H. Standish	FWK	G	1840
	John Thwaites	FWK	G	1846
Church (L)	Mary Halstead	WsK	c	1824
Clapham (YWR)	Elizabeth Clapham	FW	c	1831
Clitheroe (L), St Mary	John Oddie	FWK	g	1830
Magdalene	James Thompson (**200**)	FWK	G	1850
Cockerham (L)	Richard Atkinson	FWK	c	1843
	James Clarke	FWK	g	1845
Colne (L), St Bartholomew	Harry Bolton	n.s.	g	1842
	James B. Carr	n.s.	g	1843
Colton (L)	Edward Burns (d. 1787)	FWK	G	er. later

Colton (L) [cont'd]	Dorothy Rawlinson	n.s.	c	1828
	John Robinson	FWK	c	1842
	Thomas Dixon	MT	c	1856
Crosby Garrett (W)	Rev. William Bird (d. 1731)	n.s.	c	er. 1822
Crosthwaite (C), St Kentigern	Isaiah White	n.s.	c	1793
	William Brownrigg	FW	c	1800
	John Hodgson	n.s.	c	1807
	Rev. Isaac Denton	WK	G	1820
	Charles Denton	n.s.	G	1828
	John Edmondson	WK	G	1823
	John Jackson	WsK	scr.	1834
	Gen. William Peachey	WsK	c	1838
Crosthwaite (W), St Mary	Daniel Dickinson	WK	G	1792
	William Strickland	n.s.	c	1804
	William Pearson (d. 1856)	D	bust	er. 1857
	Ann Relph (d. 1825)	MT	c	er. 1865
Dalton-in-Furness (L) St Mary	William Postlethwaite (d. 1769)	n.s.	c	er. 1815
	Thomas Atkinson (d. 1779)	n.s.	g	er. 1817
	William Atkinson	WK	c	1821
	Thomas Ashburner	n.s.	c	1821
	James Atkinson	FWK	c	1846
Darlington (Co. Dur.)	Robert Botcherby	WsK	c	1838
Downham (L)	Mary Assheton	WsK	G	1832
Ecclesfield (YWR)	Thomas Parkin (d. 1808)	WK	c	er. 1825
Edenhall (C)	Sir Philip Musgrave	n.s.	c	1827
	Rev. Thomas Watson	WsK	G	1833
	Rev. Sir Christopher Musgrave	WsK	g	1834
	Lady Mary Musgrave	WsK	g	1838
	Sir George Musgrave	FWK	c	1872
	Lady Charlotte Musgrave	FWK	c	1873
Egremont (C)	Thomas Hartley	n.s.	G	1831
	Thomas Hartley	FWK	g	1855
Field Broughton (L)	Rev. Philip Knipe	WsK	G	1829
	John Atkinson	n.s.	c	1844
Finsthwaite (L)	George Braithwaite	n.s.	G	1814
	James King	WsK	c	1821
	Margaret Taylor (**201**)	WsK	G	1827
Garsdale (YWR)	James Haygarth	n.s.	c	1839
Garstang (L)	Rev. John Pedder	WK	c	1835
	Joseph Pedder	FWK	urn	1841
Gosforth (C)	Catherine Allen	n.s.	G	1825
Grasmere (W)	Octavia Kearsley	n.s.	c	1827
	Laetita Pritchard	n.s.	c	1827
Grayrigg (W)	Arthur Shepherd	FW	G	1816
	Henry Shepherd	MT	G	1850

Grayrigg (W) [cont'd]	Rev. George Wilson	MT	G	1860
Great Asby (W)	William Fairer	WsK	G	1811
	James Park	n.s.	c	1830
Great Harwood (L), St Bartholomew	John Dugdale	WsK	G	1835
Great Urswick (L)	Rev. William Ponsonby	FWK	g	1841
Gressingham (L)	Sarah Nelson	WsK	c	1831
Haverthwaite (L)	James McQuahe	n.s.	c	1819
	Thomas Catterall	n.s.	c	1825
	George W. Dickson	n.s.	c	1847
Hawkshead (L)	Anthony Gregg	n.s.	c	1807
	Rev. Reginald Braithwaite	n.s.	c	1809
	James Beck	n.s.	G	1812
	Rev. Thomas Bowman	WsK	c	1829
	Thomas A. Beck	FWK	g	1846
Heversham (W)	Rev. Alan Chambre	WK	G	1800
	Richard Nelson	WK	G	1804
	John Preston	WK	c	1816
	William Cragg	n.s.	urn	1820
	Benjamin Hunter	n.s.	G	1821
	Bateman Backhouse	n.s.	c	1823
	Rev. George Lawson	WsK	scr.	1842
High Bentham (YWR)	Hornby Roughsedge	MT	g	1859
Holme (Cliviger) (L)	John Hargreaves	WsK	c	1834
Holmes Chapel (Ches.)	Strethill Harrison	WsK	G	1823
Ings (W)	James Bateman	n.s.	c	1842
Keighley (YWR)	Mary A. Sugden (d. 1832)	WsK	G	er. 1834
	Martha S. Sugden	FWK	c	1841
Kendal (W), Holy Trinity	Reginald Remington (d. 1782)	n.s.	c	er. later
	Francis Drinkell	n.s.	G	1787
	Zachary Hubbersty	n.s.	c	1789
	Rev. Thomas Symonds	n.s	c	1789
	Rev. John Wilson	n.s.	c	1791
	John Braithwaite	n.s.	c	1792
	Sir John Wilson	n.s.	c	1793
	John Taylor (d. 1784)	n.s.	c	er. 1801
	George Romney	n.s.	urn	1802
	Joseph Maude	WsK	c	1803
	Elizabeth Carus	WsK	c	1804
	Jackson Harrison	WK	c	1804
	Christopher Wilson	n.s.	urn	1804
	Anthony Jackson[1]	WsK		1807
	James Wilson	n.s.	c	1807
	John Yeates	n.s.	c	1811
	George Dudgeon	n.s.	c	1814

Kendal (W), Holy Trinity [cont'd]	Rev. Matthew Murfitt	n.s.	c	1814
	Thomas Ireland (**202**)	WK	G	1817
	James Wilson	n.s.	c	1818
	Sir Alan Chambre	WK	G	1823
	John Jones	WK	G	1823
	Anne Moffett	n.s.	G	1828
	Thomas Atkinson	n.s.	g	1831
	Edward Burrell	WK	c	1837
	Agnes Yeates	n.s.	c	1837
	Rev. John Hudson	FW	g	1843
	Joseph Nelson (d. 1792)	FWK	c	er. 1848
	Christopher Robinson	FW	c	1850
Killington (W)	Robert Cooke (d. 1791)	n.s.	c	er. 1821
Kirkby Lonsdale (W)	Rev. John Wilson	n.s.	G	1797
	Janet Webster	n.s.	c	1805
	William Tomlinson (d. 1756)	FW	G	er. later
	John Parr	WK	G	1825
Kirkoswald (C)	Elizabeth Fetherstonhaugh	WK	c	1823
	Timothy Fetherstonhaugh (**203**)	FWK	g	1856
Lancaster (L), St Mary	Thomas Hinde	WK	c	1798
	Edward Suart	WK	G	1801
	Edward Buckley	WK	c	1817
	William Penny (d. 1716)	n.s.	c	er. 1818
	William Heysham	n.s.	c	er. 1818
	Thomas Hinde (d. 1798)	WK	G	er. 1819
	Frances Parke	WK	G	1822
	Rev. James Thomas	WsK	G	1824
	Agnes M. Hinde	WsK	G	1826
	Richard Thompson	WsK	c	1827
	Margaret Campbell	n.s.	c	1829
	Charles Gibson	n.s.	c	1832
	Thomas Bowes	n.s.	g	1833
	Ambrose Gillison (d. 1742)	FWK	G	er. 1841
Lancaster (L), St John	Corney Tomlinson	n.s.	G	1813
Ledbury (Heref.)	Richard Hankins (d. 1807)	W	c	er. 1829
Lindale (L)	Francis Webster	n.s.	c	1827
	George Webster	n.s.	c	1864
Llandaff (Glam.), Cathedral	Elizabeth Crawshay [Gun. 418]			1825
Long Marton (W)	Maria Rippon	n.s.	c	1798
	Richard Bellas	n.s.	G	1807
Lowick (L)	James Everard	FWK	c	1844
Lowther (W)	Mary, Countess of Lonsdale	WK	G	1824
	Rev. James Satterthwaite	WsK	G	1827
	Rev. William Burn	FWK	c	1852
Market Drayton (Salop)	William Steele	FW	G	1807

Market Drayton (Salop) [cont'd]	Richard M. Noneley (d. 1839)	FWK	scr.	er. 1852
Melling (L)	Rev. Sandford Tatham	n.s.	c	er. 1817
	Anne Parker	n.s.	c	1819
	David Murray	WsK	G	1822
	John Procter	FW	g	1831
	Thomas Smith	WsK	c	1831
Millom (C)	Rev. John Bolton	WK	c	1820
	John Myers	n.s.	c	1821
Milnthorpe (W)	Rev. Nicholas Padwick (**204**)	n.s.	scr.	1860
Natland (W)	Edmund Atkinson	MT	c	1857
	Thomas Read	MT	c	1876
New Hutton (W)	Ralph Fisher	WsK	G	1837
	Rev. Ralph W. Fisher	FWK	G	1849
Northallerton (YNR)	Susannah Rigge (**205**)	WsK	G	1828
	Francis P. Bedingfield	FW	g	1841
Orton (W)	Joseph Burn	WK	c	1818
	Margaret Holme	n.s.	g	1839
Otley (YWR)	Rev. Henry Robinson	WsK	G	1834
Over Kellet (L)	Lady Julia Barrie	WsK	c	1836
Penwortham (L)	Laurence Rawstorne	n.s.	c	1803
	Elizabeth G. A. Rawstorne	WsK	c	1823
	Laurence Rawstorne	FWK	c	1850
Ponsonby (C)	Edward Stanley	n.s.	g	1863
Poulton-le-Fylde (L)	John Hull	FWK	g	1843
	Giles Thornber	D	G	1860
Prestbury (Ches.)	Richard Orford (d. 1791)	WK	c	er. later
Preston (L), St John	William St Clare	WK	g	1822
	William Pritchard (d. 1803)	WK	c	er. 1829
	William Richardson	WsK	c	illeg.
	Thomas Hart [Gun. 133]	D		1861
Preston (L), St George	T. Lowndes [Gun. 133]	D		1854
	Rev. Robert Harris	D	effigy	1862
Preston Patrick (W)	Elizabeth B. Scott	WsK	c	1831
Richmond (YNR), St Mary	Rev. Christopher Goodwill	WK	G	1822
St John's-in-the-Vale (C)	Rev. Robert Hodgson (d. 1774)	n.s.	G	er. 1827
St Michael's-on-Wyre (L)	Edward Greenhalgh	WsK	c	1823
Sedbergh (YWR)	Thomas Swettenham	n.s.	c	1788
	Rev. Henry Wilkinson	n.s.	g	1838
	James Davis	n.s.	c	1837
Skipton (YWR), Holy Trinity	Oglethorpe Wainman	WK	c	1800
	Christopher Netherwood	WsK	g	1834
	Ann Metcalf	n.s.	G	1840
Slaidburn (YWR)	James Wilkinson (d. 1788)	FWK	g	er. later
	Robert Parker	n.s.	c	1808
	Richard Wilkinson	WsK	c	1826

Slaidburn (YWR) [cont'd]	Michael King	FWK	g	1832
	John Wilkinson	FWK	g	1839
	Thomas Wigglesworth	n.s.	c	1840
	Leonard Wilkinson	FWK	c	1848
Stand (L)	John Ramsbotham	n.s.	G	1818
Staveley (W)	Rev. Peter Strickland	n.s.	g	1837
Temple Sowerby (W)	Matthew Atkinson	n.s.	G	1789
	Joshua Marriot	n.s.	c	1827
Threlkeld (C)	Rev. Thomas Edmondson (d. 1797)	WK	G	er. 1822
Troutbeck (W)	Ann A. Parker	n.s.	c	1834
Tunstall (L)	Thomas Fenwick	n.s.	c	1837
	Rev. Robert Fenwick	FW	c	1868
Tyldesley (L)	William Higginson	WsK	G	1832
Ulverston (L), St Mary	Thomas Kilner	WK	c	1822
	William Dodgson	n.s.	G	1823
	Robert Fell	n.s.	c	1831
	John Fell	n.s.	G	1836
	Rev. John Sunderland	n.s.	g	1837
	Jane Sotheron	n.s.	G	1841
Ulverston (L) Holy Trinity	Charles Downard	n.s.	g	1838
	Thomas Fisher	FW	g	1840
Underbarrow (W)	Rev. Thomas Harvey	n.s.	c	1821
Walton-le-Dale (L), St Leonard	John Hindle	n.s.	G	1831
	Richard Geill	D	G	1841
Warrington (Ches.), St Elphin	Thomas Lyon	WsK	c	1818
Warton (L)	William Dawson	WK	G	1823
	William Taylor (d. 1819)	FWK	c	er. 1832
	Alexander Worswick (d. 1814)[2]	WsK	c	er. 1834
Whalley (L)	Alice Cottam	n.s.	c	1819
	Peggy Taylor	WK	G	1822
	Jane Smythe	FWK	c	1842
	Lady Jane Gardener	WK	c	1843
Whitehaven (C), St James	Isaac Foster	n.s.	G	1822
	Alexander Hammond	n.s.	c	1840
Windermere (W), St Martin	Barbara Fleming	WK	G	1817
	John Braithwaite	n.s.	g	1818
	Rev. William Barton	n.s.	G	1823
	Ann Barton	n.s.	c	1826
	Elizabeth Barton	n.s.	c	1830
	Henry G. Poulett Thomson	FW	c	1834
	John Braithwaite	FW	g	1854
Witherslack (W)	Anne Bownas	n.s.	c	1816
	Jane Walker	n.s.	c	1832
Wray (L, nr Hawkshead)	Margaret Dawson	n.s.	g	1862

| Yealand Conyers (L) | Lucy Rothwell | FWK | c | 1869 |
| | Thomas Wright | FWK | c | 1872 |

[1.] Removed in 1850: E. Bellasis, *Westmorland Church Notes*, ii, 1888, 36.

[2.] A note in one of the author's working notebooks, refers to a letter in the Suffolk RO which states that it was ordered from the firm by Richard Gillow.

Illustrations

Houses

1. *Accrington: Arden Hall*

2. Allithwaite: Allithwaite Lodge

3. Allithwaite: Boarbank Hall

4. *Ambleside: Croft Lodge*

5. *Ambleside: Croft Lodge, interior detail*

6. *Ambleside: Croft Lodge, exterior ironwork*

7. *Ambleside: Croft Lodge, interior detail*

8. *Ambleside: Croft Lodge, stables*

9. *Ambleside:Wansfell*

10. *Arkholme: Storrs Hall*

11. *Barbon:Whelprigg*

12. *Bolton-le-Sands: Hawksheads House, lodge*

13. *Bolton-on-Eden: Eden Grove, lodge*

14. *Bowness: Belsfield*

15. *Bretherton: Bank Hall in 1860 (Christopher Wood)*

16. *Bretherton: Bank Hall*

17. *Broughton: Broughton Hall*

18. *Broughton: Broughton Hall*

19. *Cark-in-Cartmel: Holker Hall in 1847*

20. *Cark-in-Cartmel: Holker Hall,* the old stables

21. *Cark-in-Cartmel: Holker, house in the estate village*

22. *Cartmel: Aynsome Manor, porch*

23. *Cartmel: Aynsome Manor, ceiling detail*

24. *Cartmel: Ivy Cottage*

25. *Cartmel: Ivy Cottage, music room*

26. *Cartmel: Longlands*

27. *Caton: Elm Grove*

28. *Caton: Elm Grove, chimneypiece*

29. *Caton: Elm Grove, ceiling detail*

30. *Clifton-with-Salwick: Clifton Hall*

31. *Cliviger: Ormerod House before c.1922*

32. *Cliviger: Ormerod House, gateway*

33. Colne: Alkincoats, unexecuted design, 1820 (Robert R. Parker)

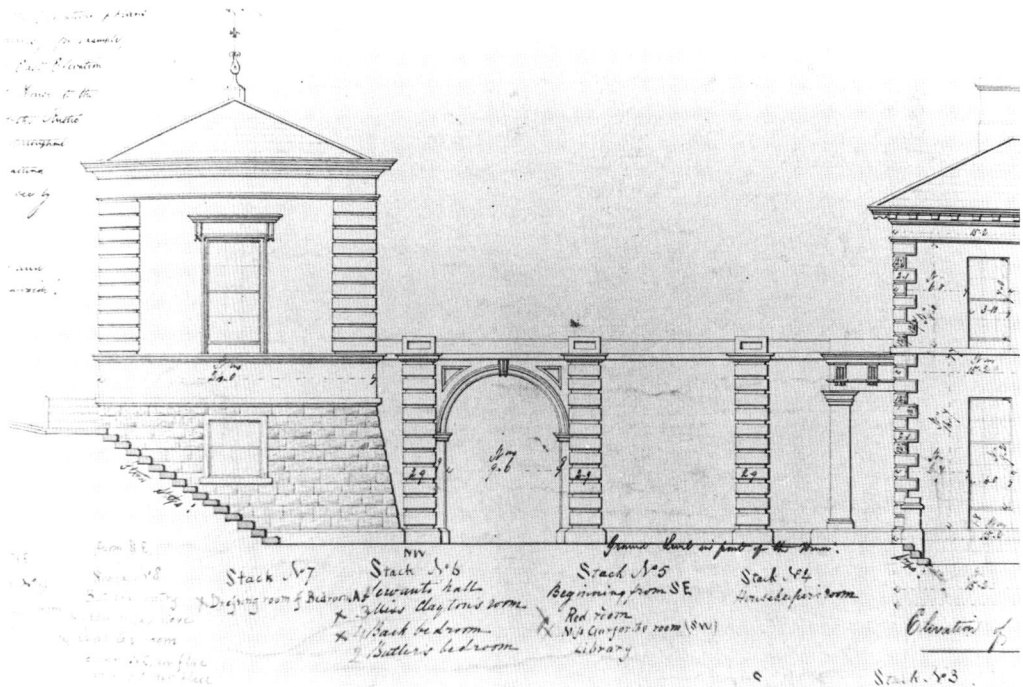

34. Coniston Cold: Coniston Hall, elevation, 1841 (Michael Bannister)

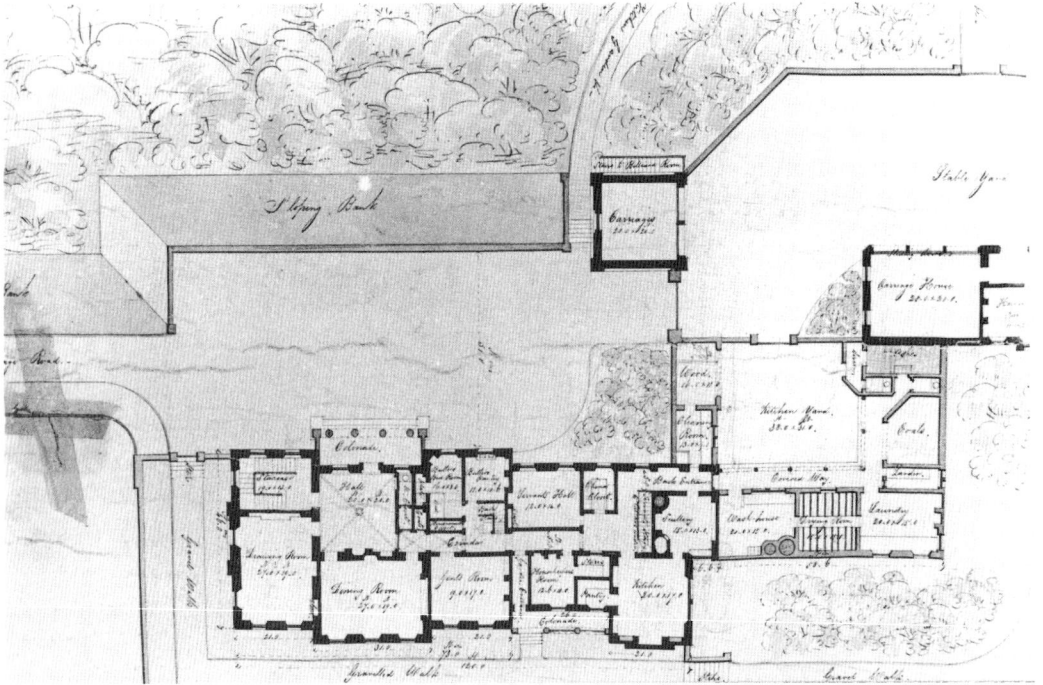

35. *Coniston Cold: Coniston Hall, plan (Michael Bannister)*

36. *Coniston Cold: Coniston Hall, portico*

38. *Downham: Downham Hall, portico*

37. *Coniston Cold: Coniston Hall, staircase detail*

39. *Downham: Downham Hall, elevations, 1834 (Lord Clitheroe)*

40. *Downham: Downham Hall, library*

41. *Downham: Downham Hall, ceiling detail*

42. *Edenhall: Eden Hall, south lodge*

43. *Forton: Hay Carr*

44. *Gargrave: Eshton Hall (Dare (Northern) Ltd)*

45. *Gargrave: Eshton Hall, library*

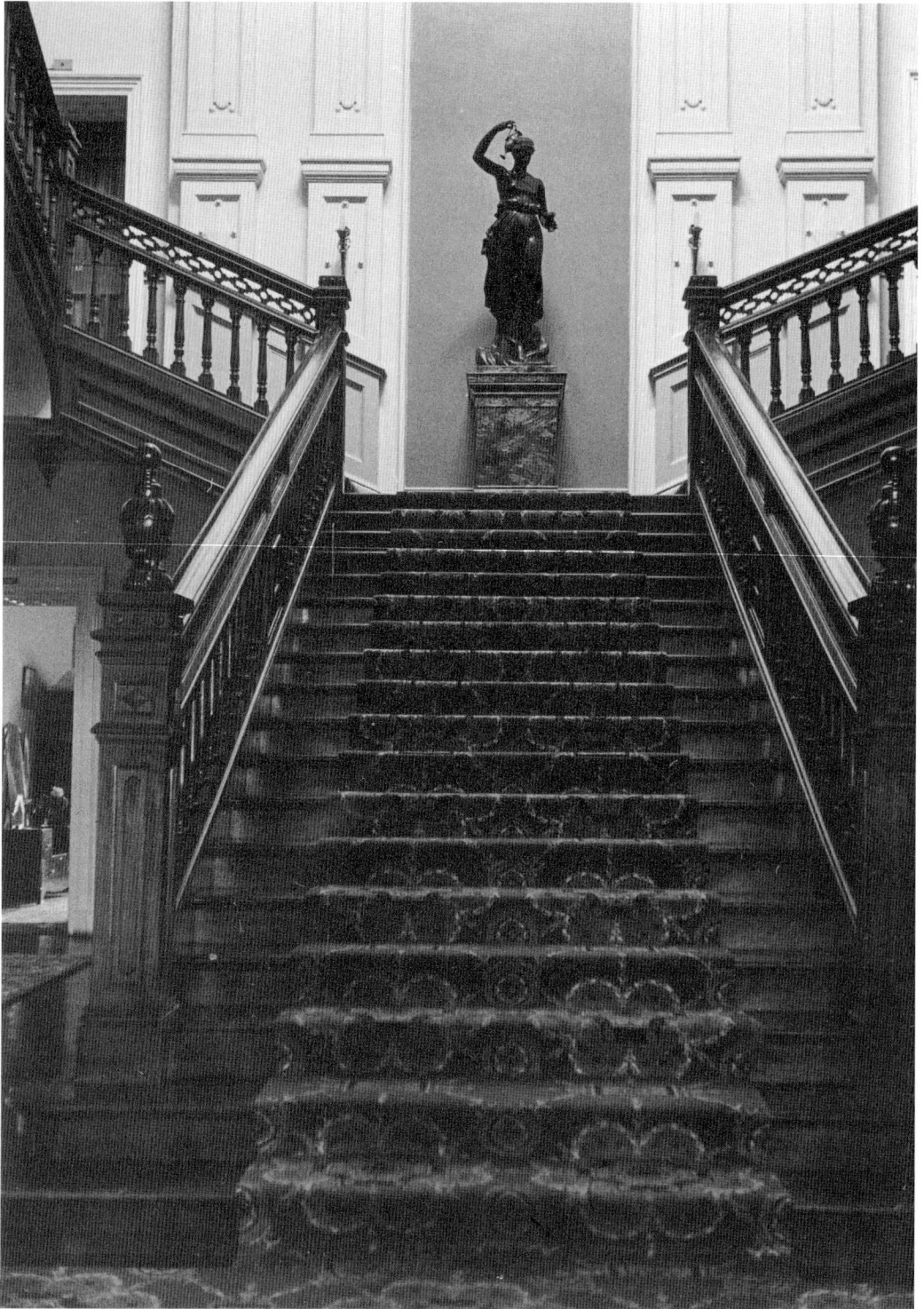

46. *Gargrave: Eshton Hall, staircase*

48. *Gargrave: Eshton Hall, staircase detail*

47. *Gargrave: Eshton Hall, staircase*

49. *Gargrave: Eshton Hall, library chimneypiece*

50. *Gargrave: Flasby Hall*

51. *Gargrave: Flasby Hall, main entrance*

52. *Grange-over-Sands: Black Rock Villa*

53. *Grange-over-Sands: Black Rock Villa, George Webster's drawing indicating the effect of the proposed railway, 1857 (Cumbria Record Office (Kendal))*

54. *Grange-over-Sands: Black Rock Villa, initials, 1841*

55. *Grange-over-Sands: Merlewood, porch*

56. *Grange-over-Sands: Merlewood, iron gate*

57. *Grange-over-Sands:Yewbarrow Lodge (Private Collection)*

58. *Hawkshead: Belmount, chimneypiece*

59. *Hawkshead: Esthwaite Lodge, verandah detail*

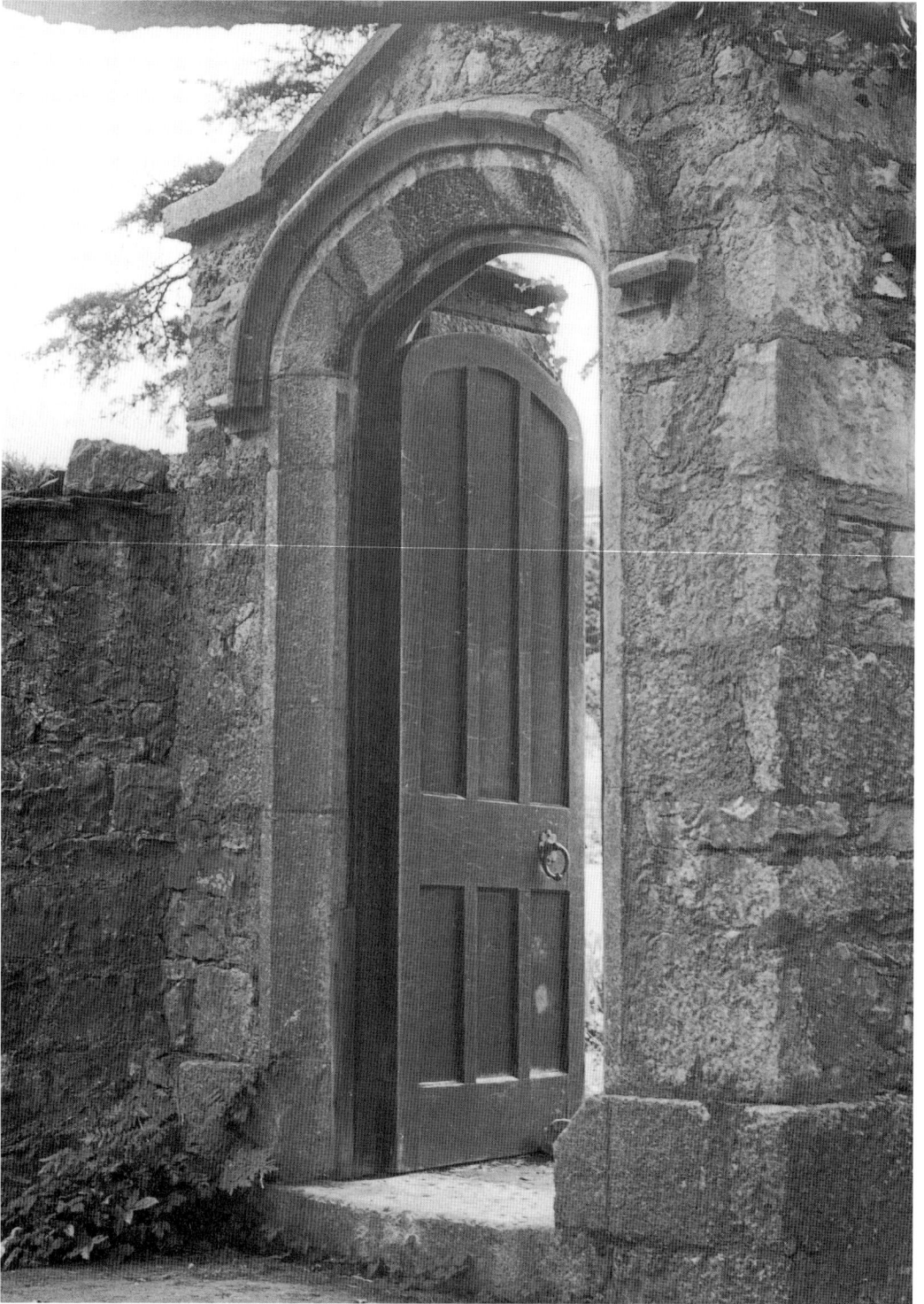

60. *Heversham: Plumtree Hall, garden doorway*

61. *Holme: Curwen Woods*

62. *Hornby: Hornby Castle, George Webster's unexecuted design, 1823 (David Battersby)*

63. *Hutton-in-the-Forest: Hutton-in-the-Forest, elevation of east front, 1826 (Lord Inglewood)*

64. *Hutton-in-the-Forest: Hutton-in-the-Forest, George Webster's tower*

65. *Hutton-in-the-Forest: Hutton-in-the-Forest, dining-room chimneypiece*

66. *Ingleton: Masongill House*

67. *Keighley: Eastwood*

68. *Kendal: Helme Lodge*

69. *Kirkby Lonsdale: Cressbrook*

70. *Kirkby Lonsdale: Underley Hall, elevation (Simon Pease)*

71. *Kirkby Lonsdale: Underley Hall, before 1873*

72. *Kirkby Lonsdale: Underley Hall, outside the main entrance*

73. *Kirkby Lonsdale: Underley Hall, frontispiece*

74. *Kirkby Lonsdale: Underley Hall,* garden front

75. *Kirkby Lonsdale: Underley Hall, entrance*

76. *Kirkby Lonsdale: Underley Hall, main gate*

77. Kirkby Lonsdale: Underley Hall, staircase ceiling

78. Kirkby Lonsdale: Underley Hall, detail of drawing room chimneypiece

79. *Lancaster: Aldcliffe Hall, lodge*

80. *Levens: Levens Hall, the Howard tower, from a print by Thomas Allom*

81. *Lindale: Eller How, Twycross's view of 1847*

82. *Lindale: Eller How, the romantic setting*

83. *Lindale: Eller How, garden front*

84. *Lindale: Eller How, porch*

85. *Lindale: Eller How, drawing room*

86. *Lindale: Eller How Farm*

87. *Lindale: Eller How, monument to Francis Webster*

88. *Mansergh: Rigmaden Park, the shell after 1948*

89. *Middleton: Grimeshill, before 1938*

90. *Milnthorpe: Dallam Tower*

91. *Milnthorpe: Dallam Tower, orangery*

92. *New Hutton: Hill Top*

93. *New Hutton: Hill Top, drawing room*

94. *Patton: Shaw End, c.1870*

95. *Patton: Shaw End, dining room recess*

96. *Patton: Shaw End, landing ceiling*

97. *Penwortham: Penwortham Priory, watercolour by John Weld, 1835 (Lancashire Record Office)*

98. *Penwortham: Penwortham Priory*

99. *Preston Richard: Summerlands, porch*

100. *Preston Richard: Summerlands, chimneypiece*

101. *Preston Richard: Summerlands, lodge*

102. *Read: Read Hall*

103. *Read: Read Hall, entrance hall*

104. *Read: Read Hall, library*

105. *Read: Read Hall, dining room ceiling*

106. *Read: Read Hall, drawing room ceiling*

107. *Read: Read Hall, staircase*

108. *Read: Read Hall, lodge*

109. *Satterthwaite: Graythwaite Hall, lodge*

110. *Satterthwaite: Silverholme, drawing room chimneypiece*

111. *Sedbergh: Ingmire Hall*

112. *Selside: Mosergh House*

113. *Skelsmergh: Dodding Green, before 1968*

114. *Stainforth: Taitlands, porch*

115. *Staveley-in-Cartmel: Townhead, from the garden*

116. *Threshfield: Netherside, porch*

118. *Threshfield: Netherside, dining room*

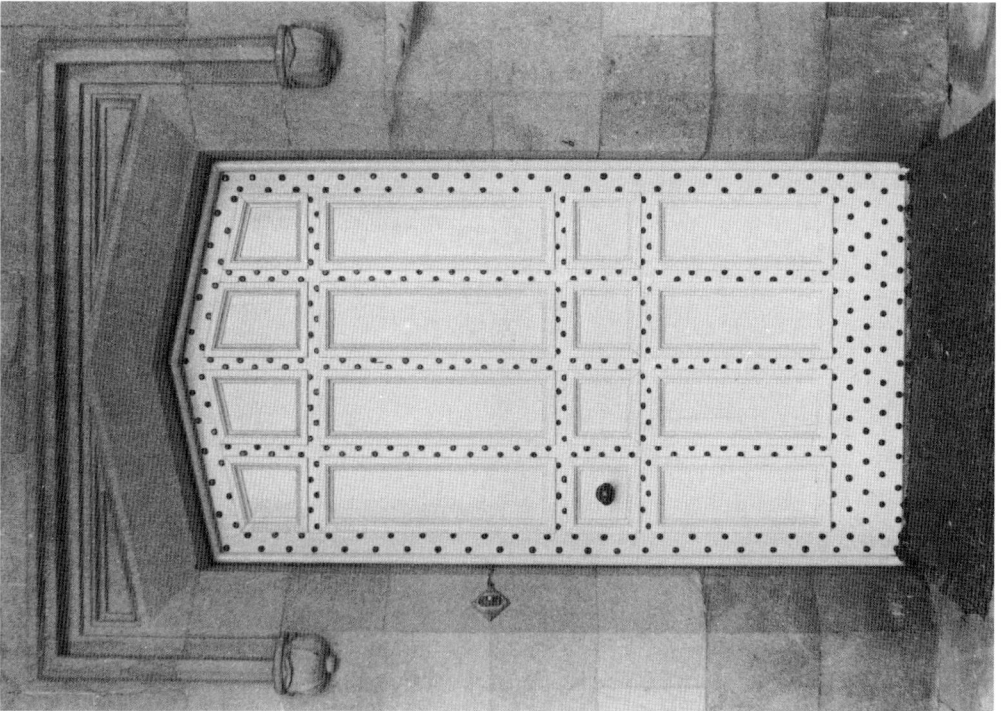

117. *Threshfield: Netherside, front door*

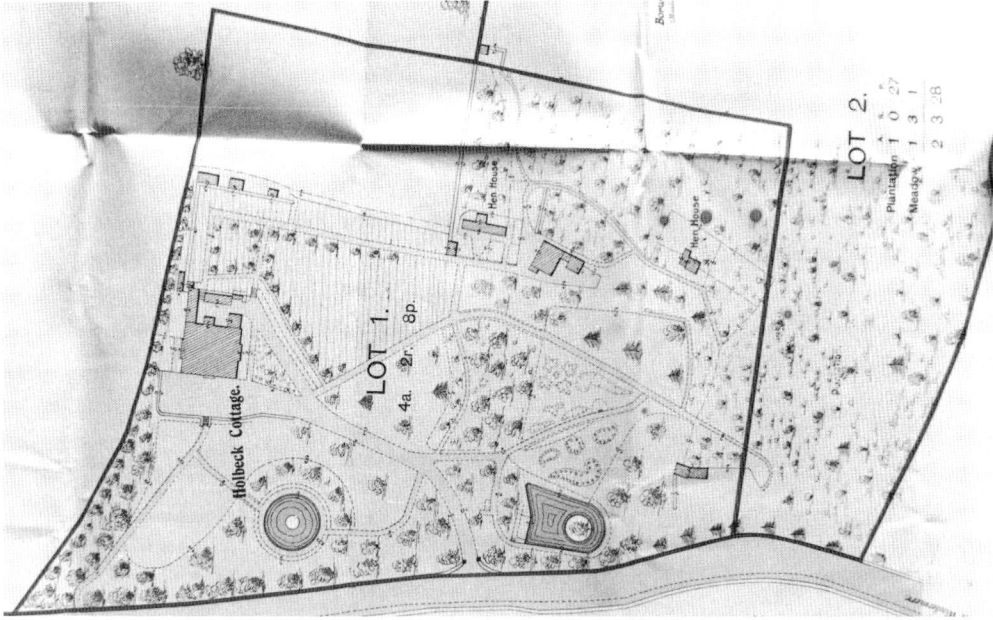

120. *Troutbeck: Holbeck Cottage, garden plan, 1886 (Cumbria Record Office (Kendal))*

119. *Threshfield: Netherside, hall*

121. *Tunstall: Thurland Castle, from a print*

122. *Ulverston: Conishead Priory*

123. *Ulverston: Conishead Priory, main entrance*

124. *Ulverston: Conishead Priory, south front*

125. *Ulverston: Conishead Priory, hall, about 1900*

126. *Ulverston: Conishead Priory, the corridor*

127. *Ulverston: Conishead Priory, ceiling detail*

128. *Ulverston: Conishead Priory, folly*

129. *Ulverston: Dykelands*

130. *Ulverston: Fair View*

132. *Ulverston: Springfield, hall*

131. *Ulverston: Fair View, garden niche*

133. *Ulverston: 27-31 Fountain St*

134. *Whalley: Moreton Hall, about 1900*

135. *Underbarrow: Larch How*

136. *Whittington: Whittington Hall, garden front*

137. *Whittington: Whittington Hall, bastion*

138. *Whittington: Whittington Hall, staircase*

Kendal

139. *Kendal: 134-6 Highgate*

140. *Kendal: 48-52 Stramongate, The Ladies' College*

141. *Kendal: Thorny Hills, general view from no. 1 (right) to no. 8 (left)*

143. *Kendal: 4 Thorny Hills, staircase*
(Geoffrey Berry Photographic Archive, Kendal Library)

142. *Kendal: 4 Thorny Hills, George Webster's house.*

144. *Kendal: 4 Thorny Hills, plasterwork in drawing room*
(Geoffrey Berry Photographic Archive, Kendal Library)

145. *Kendal: Stricklandgate, Farrer's shop*

146. *Kendal: 163 Highgate*

147. *Kendal: 24-8 Highgate*

148. *Kendal: Sand Aire House*

149. *Kendal: Sand Aire House*

150. *Kendal: Aikrigg End*

151. *Kendal: Spital*

152. *Kendal: Broom Close*

153. *Kendal: Birklands*

Churches and Chapels

154. *Bardsea*

155. *Coniston Cold*

156. *Edenhall, chancel arch*

157. *Firbank*

158. *Grayrigg, south elevation by George Webster, 1837 (The Revd Brian Pedder)*

159. *Kendal: Friends' Meeting House*

160. *Kendal: Holy Trinity and St George, interior*

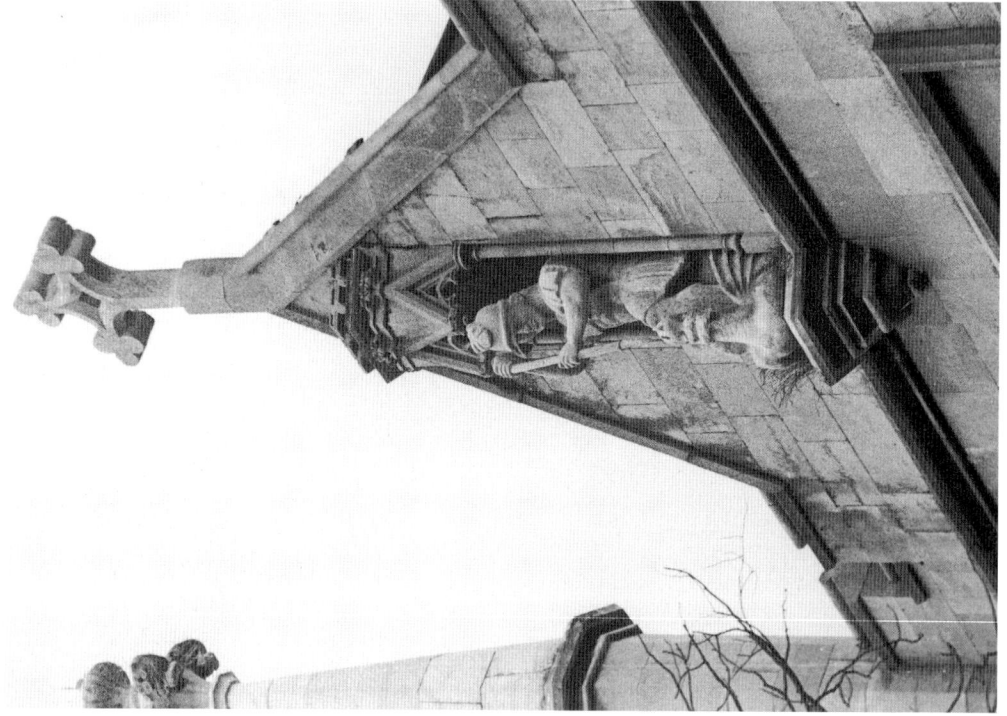

162. *Kendal: Holy Trinity and St George, Thomas Duckett's statue of St George*

161. *Kendal: Holy Trinity and St George*

163. *Kendal: St George, as completed*

164. *Kendal: St Thomas, before the galleries were removed*

166. *Milnthorpe*

165. *Lindale, showing the Webster tomb (at left)*

167. *Natland*

Parsonage Houses

168. *Crosscrake*

169. *Hardraw*

Schools

170. *Burton-in-Kendal*

171. *Heversham*

Public Buildings

172. *Hawkshead: Market House*

173. *Kendal: Castle Howe*

174. *Kendal: Dowker's Hospital*

175. *Kendal: Wakefield's Bank*

176. *Kendal: Oddfellows' Hall*

177. *Kendal: Westmorland Bank, George Webster's design, 1833*

178. *Kendal: Westmorland Bank, as built*

179. *Kendal:White Hall Assembly Rooms*

180. *Kendal: Town Hall, during the extensions of 1893*

181. *Kirkby Lonsdale: Market House*

182. *Kirkby Lonsdale: Trustee Savings Bank*

183. *Milnthorpe: Workhouse*

184. *Preston: Moor Park, north lodge*

185. *Preston: Moor Park, west lodge*

186. *Settle: Public Rooms*

187. *Ulverston: Lancaster Bank*

188. *Ulverston: Trustee Savings Bank*

Industrial and Commercial Buildings

189. *Kendal: Marble Works showroom*

190. *Kendal: Dockray Hall Mills*

191. *Kendal: Gas House portico*

Hotels

192. *Ambleside: Salutation Hotel, from an old photograph*

193. *Troutbeck: Low Wood Hotel*

Bridges

194. *Beetham*

195. *Kendal: Miller Bridge*

196. *Milnthorpe: Dallam Tower Bridge by Robert Webster (Private Collection)*

Monuments

SACRED TO THE MEMORY OF
WILLIAM CUNLIFFE LISTER ESQ^RE,
BARRISTER AT LAW,
AND M.P. FOR THE BOROUGH OF BRADFORD;
ELDEST SON OF ELLIS CUNLIFFE LISTER ESQ^RE
OF MANNINGHAM HALL, IN THE COUNTY OF YORK,
WHO DIED ON THE 19TH DAY OF AUGUST 1841,
AGED 31 YEARS.

IN THE PRIME OF MANHOOD,
AND THE MATURITY OF HIS TALENTS,
HE WAS TAKEN FROM A CAREER OF HONOUR, AND
FROM THE HOPES OF HIS SURVIVING PARENTS.

ALSO OF ELLIS, THIRD SON OF
ELLIS CUNLIFFE LISTER ESQ^RE M.P.
WHO DEPARTED THIS LIFE
ON THE 20TH DAY OF MAY 1833,
AGED 20 YEARS.

197 *Addingham: William C. Lister.*

198. *Bowness-on-Windermere: John Bolton, formerly on the grammar school*

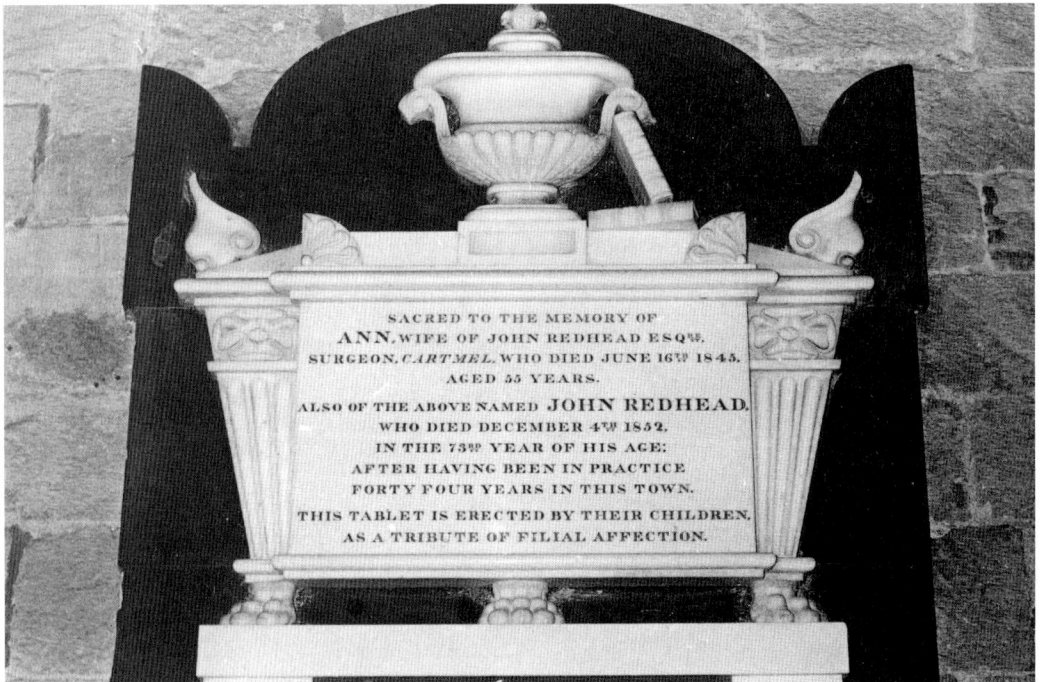

199. *Cartmel: Ann Redhead*

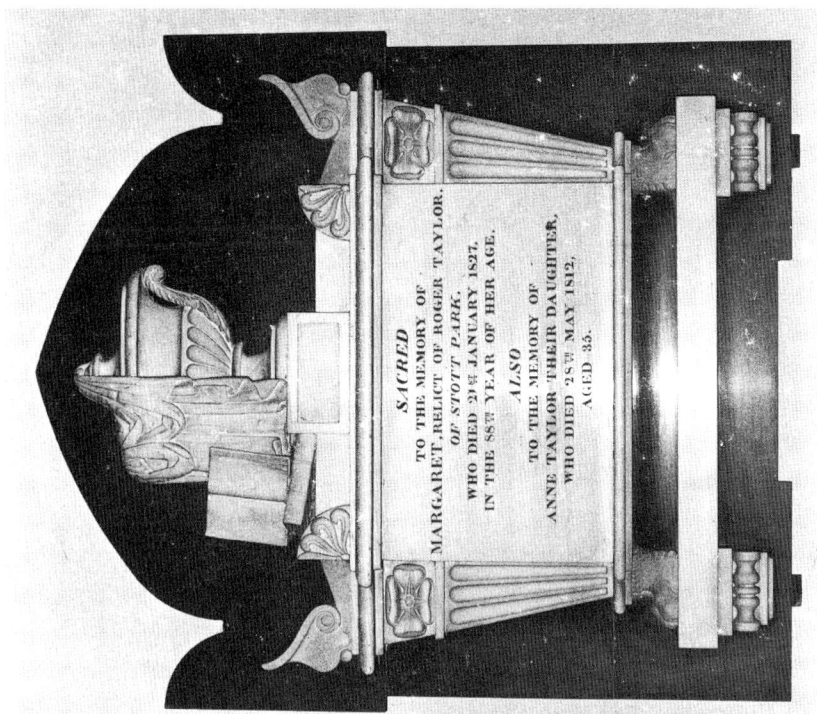

201. *Finsthwaite: Margaret Taylor*

200. *Clitheroe: James Thompson*

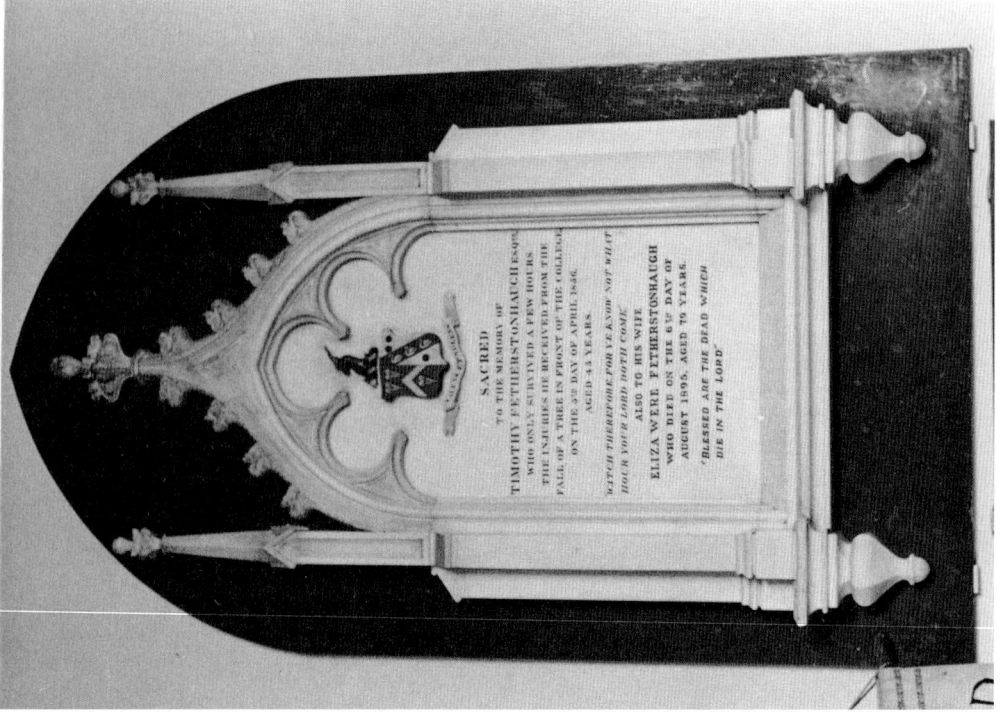

203. *Kirkoswald: Timothy Fetherstonhaugh*

SACRED
TO THE MEMORY OF
TIMOTHY FETHERSTONHAUGH ESQ.
WHO ONLY SURVIVED A FEW HOURS
THE INJURIES HE RECEIVED FROM THE
FALL OF A TREE IN FRONT OF THE COLLEGE
ON THE 3RD DAY OF APRIL 1846.
AGED 43 YEARS.

'WATCH THEREFORE FOR YE KNOW NOT WHAT
HOUR YOUR LORD DOTH COME'

ALSO TO HIS WIFE
ELIZA WERE FETHERSTONHAUGH
WHO DIED ON THE 6TH DAY OF
AUGUST 1895. AGED 79 YEARS.

'BLESSED ARE THE DEAD WHICH
DIE IN THE LORD'

202. *Kendal: Thomas Ireland*

SACRED
TO THE MEMORY OF
THOMAS IRELAND,
LATE OF KENDAL,
WHO DEPARTED THIS LIFE
NOV. 21ST 1817.
AGED 40.

Waiting for the Redemption of the Body

204. *Milnthorpe: Nicholas Padwick*

205. *Northallerton: Susannah Rigge*

Appendix I

Family Tree
by
Janet Martin

THE origins of the Webster family have been discussed in chapter one. It should be noted that there is an error on the memorial tablets in Lindale church, where Francis Webster is said to have been the youngest son of Robert Webster of Quarry Flatt and Ann Bare. Above is an undated tablet to 'Robert Bare of Wraysholme Tower esq. And his wife Margaret, daughter of Anthony Yeates of Hood Ridding [at Old Hutton], Westmorland'. In fact Francis's grandmother, Ann Bare (1706-32) married Robert Crosfield, wigmaker of Cartmel, in 1731. They were the parents of Francis's mother, Ann Crosfield. Ann Bare's brother Robert (b. 1705) married Margaret Yeates in 1728. This error must have been consciously committed by the Websters. Was it George, striving after gentility? An esquire does sound better than a wigmaker. Nicholas Cooper, in an article on Kendal [*CL*, 20 and 27 Sept. 1973], pays warm tribute to the work of both Francis and George but also suggests that George may have been 'torn between his architectural ambitions and those of founding a dynasty'. His impractical desire that Eller How and its contents should remain undisturbed in perpetuity was another manifestation of those ambitions.

Two other points may be made here. The Kendal registers give the birth dates of those of Francis's children who were baptised there, but George is said to have been born on 3 May 1797 and his sister Jane on 10 October in the same year, which must be an error for 1798. The family was never in a hurry to have children baptised. Francis himself was more than a year old and his daughter Margaret was eighteen months. The baptisms of his children Anne and Francis have not been traced at Kendal, Lindale, Kirkby Lonsdale, or elsewhere.

It is also noteworthy that George Webster married Eleanor, the daughter of his stepmother Margaret Lowry. She was married three times. She was a widow, Margaret Ashburner, when she married George Lowry in 1798 at Ulverston. George Lowry had a first wife, Sarah Hall, by whom he had four children born in Liverpool and in the middle of them a daughter Margaret in Ulverston. There was also another daughter, Ann, whose baptism has not been traced. When he died in 1805 it seems that only Ann and Margaret, of this first family, were living and they were placed in the guardianship of their maternal grandmother, Margaret Hall. Their mother seems to have died in 1798, soon after the birth of her son George. The guardianship of Eleanor, George Lowry's only child by his second wife, was

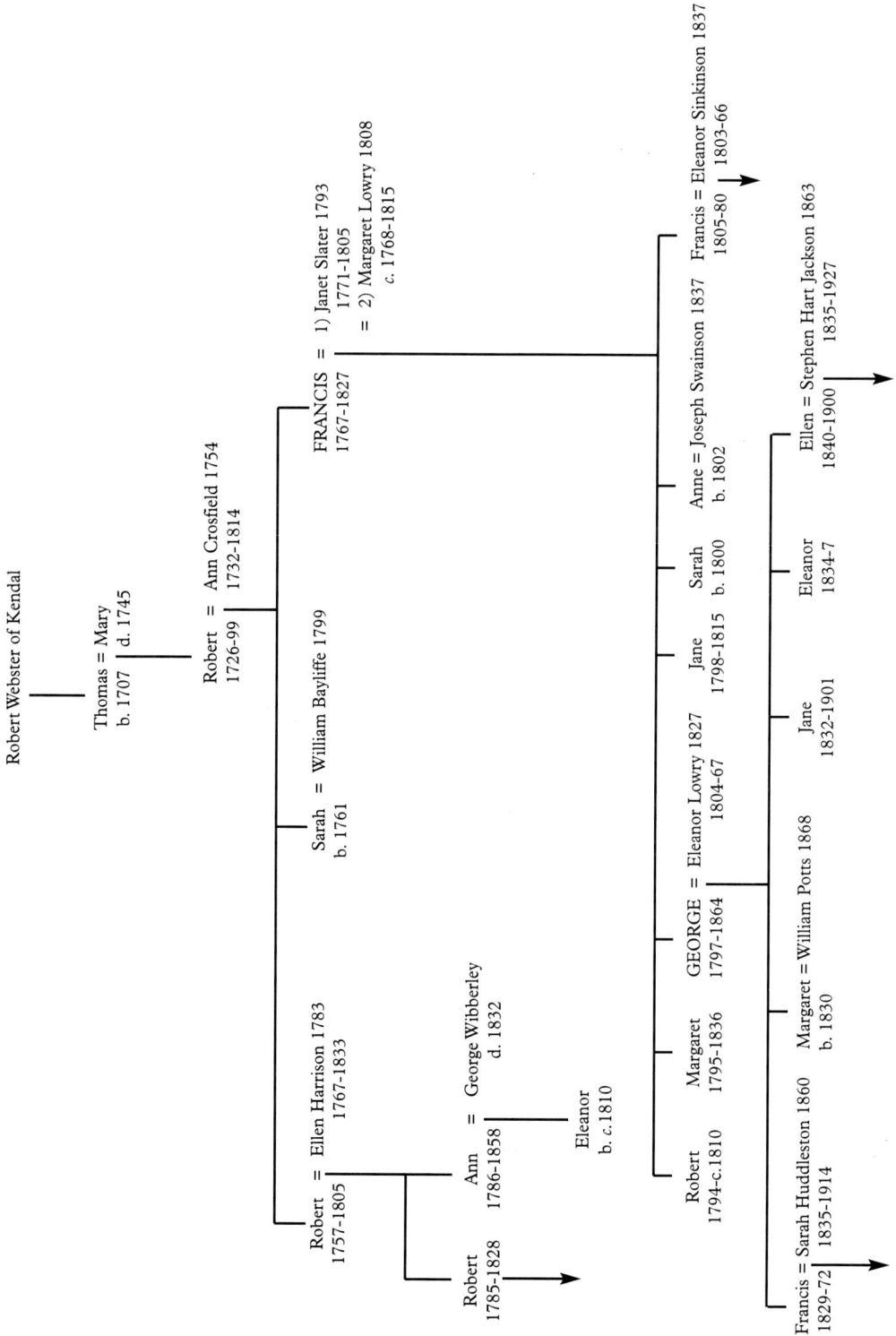

Robert Webster of Kendal

Thomas = Mary
b. 1707 | d. 1745

Robert = Ann Crosfield 1754
1726-99 | 1732-1814

Sarah = William Bayliffe 1799
b. 1761

FRANCIS = 1) Janet Slater 1793
1767-1827   1771-1805
= 2) Margaret Lowry 1808
c. 1768-1815

Francis = Eleanor Sinkinson 1837
1805-80   1803-66 →

Anne = Joseph Swainson 1837
b. 1802

Ellen = Stephen Hart Jackson 1863
1840-1900   1835-1927 →

Sarah
b. 1800

Jane
1798-1815

Eleanor
1834-7

GEORGE = Eleanor Lowry 1827
1797-1864   1804-67

Jane
1832-1901

Robert = Ellen Harrison 1783
1757-1805   1767-1833

Ann = George Wibberley
1786-1858   d. 1832

Eleanor
b. c.1810

Margaret
1795-1836

Margaret = William Potts 1868
b. 1830

Robert
1794-c.1810

Robert
1785-1828 →

Francis = Sarah Huddleston 1860
1829-72   1835-1914 →

given to her own mother, who became Francis Webster's second wife in 1808.

Francis Webster did not mention Margaret in his will, whether because she was already dead or because she had been sufficiently provided for by her first husband is unclear. However, she was probably the Margaret Webster of Kendal who was buried at Ulverston on 12 February 1815, aged 47. George Lowry died possessed of property at Oxen Park which later figures in George Webster's own will, but which he sold, according to the probate accounts, in his lifetime, and of a slate quarry at Smithy Hill, Kirkby Ireleth, of which George Webster was the owner in 1829 [Parson & White, 1829, 719]. Both pieces of property must have come to him through his wife.

Appendix II

George Webster's Inventory, 1864
by
Janet Martin and Jeffrey Haworth

T HE discovery, when the book was within a month or two of completion, of the inventory of George Webster's personal property at the time of his death enables us to amplify what Angus Taylor said on p. 76, that Webster's letters home from his travels are the only things that bring him near to us as a person. Something more can now be deduced from what he owned and valued.

The inventory was drawn up in accordance with a clause in Webster's will which specified that, apart from items specifically bequeathed elsewhere, his library, pictures and collections, plans and specifications, and all the household furniture should be attached to Eller How as heirlooms, and that a list should be made and kept with the title deeds. It was drawn up in May and June 1864 by John Burton, probably of Kendal, and survives among the probate papers in CRO K, WD/MM/box 113, as a board-covered book measuring 33 cm. x 21 cm. of which the inventory occupies some 90 pages. At the end is a statement dated 13 April 1866 and signed by Margaret Webster, with Joseph Swainson and Thomas Ullock as her father's executors, that it was a 'true list and Schedule of the . . . effects directed by the Will of the late George Webster Esquire deceased to remain at Eller How as heirlooms and to follow the entail'. Of the plethora of property listed only two books from the architectural library have been identified; some items of furniture have passed to descendants.

That George Webster lived in comfortable surroundings is undeniable. The furniture and fittings at Eller How may not be to everyone's taste in the twenty-first century, and they were not ducally luxurious, but everything points to a house which was very well appointed, and even cheerful, with its crimson and scarlet hangings in the two main bedrooms. The drawing room, with its drab (undyed) draperies and upholstery, may have presented a rather gloomy appearance, though efforts had been made to ensure good artificial lighting. Everywhere there were fitted Brussels carpets, probably protected by druggets to reduce wear, good beds, and well-stocked washstands. There was a sitz bath in the bathroom, though oddly there is no mention of portable tin baths and it is not clear from the inventory that the house had water closets, although a surviving bill among the probate papers indicates that one was installed not long before Webster died.

Furniture aside, the overwhelming impression is of a house stuffed with George's collections, pictures, prints, photographs, figures, what the Victorians knew as 'objects of vertu', drawers full of shells and geological specimens, especially and naturally marbles – the list is endless and the valuation of the collections by far the largest item in the inventory.

As in most country houses, there were mounted animal heads and some weapons and pieces of armour, but not everyone ran to a mailed knight and a 'Shell-fish woman of rare genus', both of which stood in the drawing room. George Webster had a certain amount of local seventeenth-century furniture, although it was given no prominent place in the main rooms and was with one exception confined to the kitchen quarters, and he had a few early books, including the sixteenth-century black-letter edition of Thomas's *Historie of Italie* of 1549. What was valuable to him was what he had brought back from his travels and which is mentioned in some detail in his will. But he brought more than pictures and statuary to adorn Eller How. The inventory reveals his touching habit of picking up stones and shards from the ancient sites he visited.

The library is listed in detail. It is quite exceptional to know what books a provincial architect collected in the early nineteenth century. The library includes as its foundation some of the principal architectural works of the eighteenth century – Leoni's *Alberti* (1739), Gibbs's *Book of Architecture* (1739), and Chambers's *Civil Architecture* (1791), leading forward to Soane's *Sketches in Architecture* (1798) and Schinkel's *Architectural Works*. With the library dispersed perhaps about a century ago, it is not possible to say whether book collecting and the earlier books started with Francis Webster.

It is fascinating to have the opportunity to observe how the appearance of Webster's buildings dovetails with the strong emphasis on architectural topography in the collection – how, for instance he would probably have seen the steel engraving of the frontispiece of three sets of classical orders at Browsholme Hall in Britton's *Architectural Antiquities* well before he prepared designs for improving the Parker family's other house at Alkincoats. This was the inspiration for similar eye-catching features invented by Webster at Underley and Eshton. He appears to have collected almost every book on Elizabethan and Jacobean architecture issued in the general period 1820-40, the decades when this very English brand of architecture was being rediscovered and publicised – and reinterpreted in a personal way by inventive architects. George Webster was interested to see how others were using this new material; it is no surprise to find most of Thomas Frederick Hunt's publications present, with their emphasis on small ornamental buildings – in which Webster himself excelled.

He would have found close parallels too between his own Grecian villas and those published by Francis Goodwin in 1833-5, but it was the rediscovery of purely English ways of building that seems to have fascinated him most. Webster owned most of John Britton's topographical works, including a complete run of his cathedral monographs. Here the ecclesiastical details do not seem to have rubbed off to the same extent.

As source material the volumes of William Green's beautiful line engravings would have combined utility for George Webster with the pleasure of local, predominantly Lake District, topography. 'Local history' was clearly an interest too, represented by Whitaker's histories of Craven and Whalley close at hand, as well as works on English counties further afield. Well-illustrated travel books about European countries abound, with particular emphasis on Italy, so often the destination of Webster's travels.

One may speculate that the more mundane and strictly practical books remained with Thompson and the practice. Though many of the books listed would, at least tangentially, be useful as architectural prompts in the day-to-day work of architectural practice, including the few engineering works or those relating to funerary monuments or sculpture (like Canova's works of 1824-8), or even gardening, the over-riding impression is rather of a gentleman's library with good bindings and quasi-armorial bookplates. These, which have been observed in J. C. Loudon's *Architectural Magazine* (1834) and John Britton's *Cathedrals* are spare and elegant – just a dragon's head crest with 'George Webster, Eller How'. Do the genealogical and heraldic books relate to the production of funerary monuments or do these 'boasting books' represent a refined fascination?

After two ambitious decades of book-buying, George Webster's library suddenly became complete a quarter of a century before his death. Were the Eller How shelves simply full (as one might suspect), or did Webster consider that his architectural books were essentially to inform his work? Or does a reduced income on quitting the practice explain it?

It is curious to observe, despite the fascination the lithographs must have had for him, that he appears to have bought only the first three volumes of Joseph Nash's *Mansions of England in the Olden Time* (1839-41), but not volume iv which completes this folio set. Isolated in date were Hood *On Warming Buildings by Hot Water* (1844) – perhaps for practical consideration in his own houses – and Edward Twycross's *Mansions of the Northern Division of the County of Lancaster* (1847), two volumes which not only illustrate 'Eller How, the seat of George Webster, Esq' but, equally gratifying to him, so many houses he had seen built or improved to his designs. Again, the third volume, featuring the hundreds of West Derby and Salford which have no Webster buildings, is not in the library. These rare and evocative tinted lithographs commemorate not only an idealised Lancashire, which has never again since looked so picturesque and elegant, but memorialise a lifetime of achievement for the milieu whose ranks George Webster had joined. He must have expected his dynasty and renown to be perpetuated for centuries.

Of the other books, the list reveals, as one might perhaps expect, a certain solemnity of outlook. There were very few novels; only *Nicholas Nickleby* represents Dickens, for example. There was some poetry, although no Wordsworth later than 1807. Perhaps Eleanor and the daughters owned more. Books of travel figure largely and were perhaps his favourite reading, although he had an evident interest in the Napoleonic Wars. Some books and some of the statuary and pictures indicate a solid, but possibly not a burning, adherence to the Church of England. Webster bought very few books in the last ten years of his life. Of those dated in the 1860s only the revised edition of Nicholson's *Annals of Kendal* of 1861 is mentioned, apart from three medical works which must reflect his continuing preoccupation with his health. In that context the 'Ebonised Easy Chair with elevating movement' in his dressing room may be noted.

When he was well George may have been something of a sportsman. He had a gun and a game-bag and a run of *The Sportsman's Magazine*. How much of his own gardening he did is not clear, but we know from his letters that the garden was one of his enthusiasms. Many plants were grown in pots and two items are listed which were evidently part of the statuary which is known to have been in the garden, a five-foot figure of Francis Webster and a terracotta statue of Sir Jeffrey Hudson, Charles I's dwarf, which George mentioned in a letter from the Mediterranean in 1843. Lavish provision was evidently made for sitting outside when the weather was good.

George Webster was not a man who bought clothes on any large scale. His wardrobe was very limited, considering his undoubted prosperity – only three coats and four pairs of trousers, for instance, and seven pairs of assorted shoes. The bills among the probate papers indicate that he had had one of his two cloaks, a hat, two morning coats, and two pairs of trousers turned by a tailor in Liverpool in the month before he died, so he was evidently careful with his clothes. He had a gold watch and one gold ring.

In spite of his express wishes, George's collections were dispersed at some later and unknown date, and indeed it was would have been impracticable to preserve everything in the house as it had been in his day. Some of the items, principally the articles of vertu, are numbered at the side, possibly as lots in a sale. If so, no trace of such a sale has been found. When Eleanor Webster made her own will not long before her death in 1867, she made mention of those items in the inventory which had been specifically bequeathed to her. She left her son Francis half the table silver. Margaret, as yet unmarried, was her executrix, and received the James Ward portraits of George and his father, George's watch, silver tankard, and journal. Jane had the remaining table silver and other items, and the marble bust of her father. The horse, pony wagonette and phaeton were left in trust to Margaret to be sold for the payment of any debts and a legacy of £10 to Eleanor Wibberley, George's cousin who had been a member of the household for so long.

Eller How itself was sold in 1916 [CRO K, WDB 35/SP236], but the sale particulars make no reference to the contents, which may have been dispersed earlier, nor to the seller. In 1949 the portraits of Francis and George were presented to Kendal Town Hall, and most unfortunately George's can no longer be found. Some other articles and pictures may well survive unrecognised. One wonders what happened to the garden statuary. Were Francis Webster and Jeffrey Hudson broken up? And the caryatid sideboard in the dining room? And the Roman biga which was left to Thomas Ullock? And the 'Sportive Lizzards in Bronze'? By far the greatest loss, however, are the architectural drawings, nearly two thousand of them, over and above those which the appraiser assigned to particular houses. The list does serve to confirm some of Angus Taylor's attributions and to indicate George Webster's connection with some buildings of which we had no previous knowledge, like the Giggleswick House of Industry, and it implies rather more. His output was evidently greater than has been realised. We offer this transcription of the inventory as an appendix to Angus Taylor's work. He would have been delighted to have come upon it himself.

Inventory & Valuation of the Household Furniture

Plate, Linen, China,
Books, Prints, Pictures,
and
Articles of Vertu;
Wearing Apparel,
Jewels, Trinkets, & Ornaments of the Person;
Wines & Other Liquors;
Horses and Carriages;
and Other the Effects personal,
late of
George Webster,
of
Eller How,
in the
County Palatine of Lancaster
Esquire, deceased

Made May & June 1864
by me

John Burton
Appraiser

Inventory, &c
Household Furniture and Effects

Attic Sitting Room

Perforated Brass-mounted Fender with Ash-plate
Set of Polished Fire-irons
Brass-bound Ash-receiver and Kettle-stand
Fancy Bellows & Hearth-Brush
Sundry Mantel-piece Ornaments (7)
Rope-back Hearth-rug
Carpet-covered Foot-stool
Piece of Printed Drugget
Brussels Carpet, as planned to floor
Crimson Damask Window Drapery with Painted & Gilt pole Cornice
Roller Window Blind & fittings
Mahogany framed Sofa, in Hair-seating with loose Cushion &c in Black Damask
Maple American Rocking Chair in Black Cloth
Four Maple Cane-seated Chairs with loose Cushions
Mahogany Writing-desk with two drawers &c
Mahogany Pembroke Table (small) and Printed Damask cover

Painted Writing Desk, with Chest of three drawers and glazed Bookcase
Maple Writing-Table with Morocco Cloth top & two drawers
Tea Caddy and Ink-tray
Mahogany-Pole Fire-screen on tripod
Printed Circular Occasional table on turned supporters
Chimney Looking-glass (broken) $29^1/2$ x $17^1/2$ Gilt frame

South-West Attic Bed-room

Painted tray-top Toilet Commode
Printed Dimity Window Curtain
Oak-painted Tray-top Washstand
Earthenware Toilet Service – 7 pieces
Painted Towel-rail
Oak-painted 42 in. Chest of five Drawers
Mahogany-framed Toilet Looking-glass
Mahogany Wardrobe with Chest of four drawers & four sliding tray-shelves
Three Rosewood-stained Cane-seated Chairs
Japanned Rush-seated Arm Chair with loose hair-cushion
Chintz-covered Box-Ottoman
Oak French Bedstead
Flock Mattress
Two Feather Beds, two Bolsters, and four Feather Pillows
Two Blankets
Marseilles Counterpane
ditto Toilet Cover
Kidderminster Carpet, as planned

Corridor Bed-room, West

Perforated Brass-bound Fender with Ash-plate
Set of Polished Fire-irons
Brass-bound Ash-receiver
Wire-wrought Fire-guard
Pair of Tunbridge Hand-screens and a Scent-Bottle
Small Painted Table
Maple-painted $41^1/2$ in. Chest of five drawers
Mahogany-posted Bedstead, with Painted Cornice & Watered Crimson Drapery
Paillasse [sic] in two parts
Curled Horse-hair Mattress
Woollen-Flock Mattress
Blanket
Marseilles Counterpane
Two Maple Cane-seated Chairs
Painted tray-top Washstand with extra loose Marble top
Earthenware Toilet Service, 12 pieces, & Water-bottle & Craft

Painted Towel-rail
Deal Dressing-table with figured muslin apron
Two Marseilles Toilet-covers
Mahogany-framed tray Looking-glass $9^1/_2$ x $13^1/_2$
Painted Window Cornice and Moreen Valens
Scotch Cottage Carpet as planned to floor
Rope-back Hearth-rug
Roller Window-blind & fittings

Quinquangular Bed-room

Baize-covered Bedsteps & Night-Commode
Two Rush-seated attiring stools
Chintz-covered Box-Ottoman
Birch-posted Bedstead with upholstered Foot-board, moulded Cornice, & Chocolate-coloured Moreen Drapery
Spring Mattress in two parts
Flock Mattress
Feather Bed, Bolster & two Pillows
Two Blankets
Coloured Bolton Counterpane
Marseilles Counterpane
Mahogany 46 in. Chest of five Drawers
Two Marseilles Toilet-covers
Painted tray-top Washstand with drawer
Painted Dressing-table with two drawers and Garsdale marble top
Mahogany-framed tray Looking-glass $8^3/_4$ x $13^1/_2$
Painted Towel-rail
Earthenware Toilet-service, 10 pieces
Two Rosewood-stained Cane-seated Chairs
Japanned Rush-seated Chair
Oak-painted 47 in. Chest of four drawers
Oak 35 in, Chest of five drawers on Elizabethan frame with three drawers
Eel-trap Clothes-Basket
Kidderminster Carpet as planned to floor

Back Passage

American Clock in Mahogany Case
Cocoa-fibre Floor-Matting

Servant's Bedroom

American Alarum Clock
Japanned Rush-seated Chair
Oak Stump-Bedstead & Paillasse

Two Feather Beds, Bolster & two Pillows
Blanket & Coloured Bolton Counterpane
Three slips of Carpet, various
Chocolate-coloured Curtain screen
Mahogany-framed Toilet Looking-glass

S.E. Attic Bed-room

Perforated Brass-mounted Fender with ash-plate
Equestrian Time-piece
Oak French Bedstead with Painted Canopy & Striped Damask Drapery
Mahogany Corner Washstand and sundry pieces of Toilet-ware
Painted Towel-rail
Woollen-flock Mattress
Feather Bed & three Bolsters
Four Blankets
Bolton Counterpane
Two Marseilles Toilet-covers
Oak-painted 33 in. Chest of five drawers
Mahogany framed Tray Looking-glass
Muslin & Damask Window Curtains
Two Rosewood-stained Cane-seated Chairs
Clothes-basket with Cover [deleted]

Corridor & Stairs

Brussels Carpet as planned to Landing & stairs
Eleven Brass Carpet-rods
Two Rope-back Door-rugs
Painted Chinese Hall Lantern
Two pieces Chinese-painted Clock

Vestibule

Octagon-framed Chinese Lantern
Bracket Lamp with Reflector
Four Antique Mahogany Chairs with Crimson Damask Seating
Brown Sheep-skin Rug & two Cocoa-fibre Foot-mats
Mahogany two-flap Dining-table on turned & reeded supporters

Ante-room

Three-light suspending Bronze Lamp
Dinner Lamp on Bronze Pillar
Three French Moderator Lamps
Palmer's Patent Candle Lamp
Bronze Tea-urn

Hand-Bell
Curled Oak Tea Caddy
Painted Panelled Cupboard with Garsdale-Marble top 34 x 45
Two-flap Circular Oak Table on turned frame-work supporters with two drawers
Mahogany-framed Hall-Table on turned pillar & supporters – Beetham Marble top 74 x 24
Two antique Oak Chairs with panelled Backs inscribed "A.G."
Perforated Brass Fender with Ash-plate
Set of Polished Fire-irons
Two Wire-wrought Fire-Guards
Cast Bronze Door-parker
Oil Floor-cloth – 7 yards
Brussels Carpet as planned to floor
Four-leaved Screen with Chinese Decorations – painted
Mahogany Writing-desk with 49 in Chest of six drawers & Panelled fronted Bookcase
Scotch Damask Table Cover
Writing Apparatus
Painted Window Blind – "group of Flowers" – and fittings
Mahogany Bracket
Painted & Gilt pole Window Cornice
Two Brown Sheep-skin Mats
Cocoa-fibre foot-mat

Spare Bedroom
(Ground floor)

Chintz-covered Ottoman plate Chest
Mahogany Wardrobe with 49 in Chest of four drawers
Two Maple Hair-seated Chairs
Two Mahogany Hair-seated Chairs
Tray-top Toilet Table (Cupboard & drawer) with extra Veined marble top
Earthenware Toilet Service, 14 pieces
Hall Table – ebonized frame with Veined marble top 62 x 25
Chintz-covered Ottoman Tidy
Italian-Marble Circular Table 24 in Diameter on Ornamental Bronze stand
Brass & Bronze Fender with Ash-plate & Iron-supporters
Set of super-polished Fire-irons
Wire-wrought Fire-guard
Time-piece on pillar supporters with Thermometer
Sundry Mantel-piece Ornaments
Mahogany $38^{1}/_2$ in. Chest of five drawers with fluted corners
Mahogany framed Tray Looking-glass $15^{1}/_2$ x $21^{1}/_2$
Mahogany Oval Tray table on pillar and tripod
Mahogany framed Tray-Looking-glass $13^{1}/_2$ x $14^{1}/_2$
Glass Shade $15^{1}/_2$ x $8^{1}/_2$
Palmer's Patent Candle-Lamp

Mahogany Bidet on turned supporters with Queen-ware pan
Mahogany Night Commode with patent apparatus
Needle-wrought Hearth-rug
Scotch Cottage Carpet as planned to floor
Two small Rope-back Hearth-rugs
Japanned Rush-seated Arm Chair
Chintz-covered Sofa with loose Hair Cushion &c &c
Mahogany-posted Bedstead with upholstered foot-board, Painted Cornice & Crimson Moreen Drapery
Two Tasselled Bell-pulls
Two Oak pole Window Cornices with Brass rings
Cocoa Matting [*deleted*]

Balcony

Marble-top Table, 28 x 21, on painted frame
Iron Chair with loose Cushion
Iron-wrought three-tier Flower-stand

Dressing Room

Painted Nest of eight shelves
Ebonized East Chair with elevating movement – loose Cushions in Black Hair-cloth
Painted Deal Wardrobe 98 x 48
Circular Iron Table 26 in. diameter on Ornamental supporter
Japanned Oval Waiter
Painted Pedestal Dressing Table, two cupboards & two drawers
Rosewood-stained Cane-seated Chair
Mahogany Smoking Chair
Two painted Towel-rails
Painted Tray Washstand with drawer and Veined-marble top
Queen-ware Foot Bath & supply Jug
Painted 47 in. Chest of five drawers
Mahogany Shoe-rack
Oak-painted Deal Cupboard and Drawers 23 x 48
Perforated Brass-bound Fender with Ash-plate
Set of Polished Fire-irons
Sundries on Mantelpiece
Gilt Window Cornice & Valens
Chubbs' Fire-proof Safe

Passages

Black Leather Port-manteau
Cocoa-fibre Floor-matting [*deleted*] 6 yds
Ditto Ditto [*deleted*] 7$^{1}/_{2}$ yds

Japanned Rush-seated Arm Chair
Mahogany Brass-bound Clothes Chest on framed stand with turned supporters
Painted Deal Clothes-Box
Three Cocoa-fibre Ditto

West-end Bed-room
Ground floor

Perforated Brass-mounted Fender with ash-plate
Set of polished Fire-irons
Pair of Tonbridge Hand-screens
Five Rosewood-stained Cane-seated Chairs
Japanned Rush-seated Arm Chair
Slip of Oil Floor-cloth
Mahogany reeded Posted Bedstead with panelled & upholstered Footboard, painted & Gilt
   Cornice & Scarlet Moreen Drapery
Flock & Hair Mattress in two parts
Two Blankets
Marseilles Counterpane
Feather Bed, Bolster, & Pillow
Birch inlaid Wardrobe with 44 in. Chest of four drawers
Painted tray Washstand with drawer & veined-marble top
Chintz-pattern toilet Service 12 pieces – including Slop Jar, Foot-bath & Supply Jug
Water Bottle and Craft
Painted Towel-rail
Mahogany Dressing-table with two drawers & Marseilles Toilet Cover
Mahogany tray Looking-glass $13^{1}/_{2}$ x $14^{1}/_{2}$
Brussels Carpet as planned to floor
Rope-back Hearth-Rug
Painted Frieze Window Cornice & Scarlet Moreen Drapery
Roller Window Blind & fittings

Dressing Room

Barometer & Thermometer by Davis in Mahogany Case
Painted pannelled fronted Wardrobe with three sliding tray shelves – 45 x 52
Mahogany Writing-desk with 45 in. Chest of five drawers
Antique Robing-glass in Mahogany & gilt frame with supporters on tray
Painted Tray Washstand with loose veined-marble top
Earthenware Chamber Service 8 pieces
Painted Towel-rail
Painted 44 in. Chest of three drawers with Garsdale marble top
Mahogany framed Toilet Looking-glass $9^{1}/_{2}$ x 13
Two Rosewood-stained Cane-seated Chairs
Japanned Rush-seated Arm Chair
Chintz-covered Box-ottoman

Perforated Brass-mounted Fender
Rope-back Hearth rug
Brussels Carpet
Painted Moulded Window Cornice with Bullion fringe Valens
Roller Window-Blind & fittings
Two Muslin Dwarf Blinds

House Keeper's Room

Mahogany Sandwich-Tray
Butler's Mahogany tray & stand
Papier-maché Tea-Tray
Four Rush-seated Chairs – Various
Painted deal two-flap Table
Painted Cupboards (3) & Drawers (4) 55 x 91
Painted Cupboard & four drawers 48 x 96
Eight-day Clock (by E. Burton, Kendal) in Mahogany Case
Two glazed Lanterns & small Magic Lantern
Painted Lined Press (screw) with Drawer
Four Brass Chamber Candlesticks
Four Brass pillar Candlesticks
Four Dwarf Ditto
Britannia-metal Teapot & Waterpot
Three painted Tin Canisters
Masticating Machine

Pantry

Divers Sweeping Brushes, Baluster-brushes, Dusters, &c, &c
Forty-eight pieces Brown Earthenware Various
Twenty-one Wedgwood Moulds – Various
Thirty White potting-pots
Four Fish-pots
Willow-pattern Dinner-Service 84 pieces
Four Hot-water Steak-Dishes
Earthenware Dinner-Service Sahara pattern 150 pieces
Wedgwood Stilton Cheese-tray and Cover
Twelve pieces Brown Ware, Various Stillage and two Brass taps

Kitchen

Covered Oak Chest 1695
Six Japanned Waiters
Six Common Knives & two forks
Two Buck-handled Carvers & forks
Bread-Knife, Steel, & small Rotary Knife sharpener

Two pairs Ivory-handled Game-Carvers & Forks
Nineteen Ivory-handled Dinner-Knives
Nineteen ditto small Ditto
Steak Tongs, Meat-hooks, & Skewers
Five Tin Dish-covers
Two Brawn-Moulds, Toddy-Kettle and sundry Tin-ware
Three Japanned Hot-water Cans
Iron Fountain-Kettle with Brass tap
Stock Coffee-mill
Salter's Patent Weighing Machine
Hot-water Plate, Bread grater, and Sundry Egg-spoons
Sundry Crockery – 20 pieces
Copper Bed-warming Pan
Circular painted Deal Table
Six rush-seated Chairs
Tall-leaf Side-table
Parrot-Cage
Circular Hard-wood Table
Two-flap Deal table
Broad sliding-barred Fender
Large Provender Chest

Scullery

Painted Towel-Rail
Three Water-Cans
Two Zinc Slop-pails & two Zinc Coal Boxes
Two Oak Washing-Tubs & Buckit [sic]
Meat-saw, Cleaver, & Chopping-Knife
Iron Digester
    "   Round of Beef-Pan
    "   Leg of Mutton-ditto
Tin Pudding-Pan
    " Fish-Pan and Drainer
Large Dripping-Pan & Baster
Two Iron Frying-pans & Grid-iron
Ten Iron Sauce-pans
Three Brass-pans
Three Copper Sauce-pans
Dutch Oven
Small Copper Tea-Kettle
Tin Tea-Kettle & Tin Coffee-Boiler
Four Baking and Cutting-boards

Dairy

Sundry Bottles & Crockery [*deleted*]
Bottle Rack
Six dozen Wine Bottles – various [*deleted*]

Nursery

Cast Fender with ash-plate
Polished Fire-irons
Wire-wrought Fire-guard
Rush-seated Smoking Chair
Two Mahogany Hair seated Arm-Chairs & six others
Set of D. end Mahogany Dining Tables
Japanned Plate-Warmer
Garsdale-Marble Slab 70 x 14
Child's Mahogany Table
Bottling-stool and two Carpet-covered Foot-stools
Horizontal Piano-forte by Broadwood & Sons in Mahogany and Rosewood Case
Printed Drugget & Cocoa-fibre Matting as planned to floor [*deleted*]
Fancy Bellows
Hand-Bell and Sundries
Roller Window Blinds & fittings
Cocoa-fibre Foot-mat

Man-Servant's Bed-room

Stump Bedstead & Paillasse
Feather Bed, Bolster, and two Pillows
Sundry Bedding

Store-room

Painted Towel-rail
Sundry Crockery – 50 pieces
Crimson Baize-covered Folding-screen
Ironing-Board
Six Boxes – various
Large Leather Portmanteau
Two pieces Oil Floor-cloth
Six pieces (slips) Carpet [*deleted*]
Large Japanned Oval Tea-tray
Two Japanned papier-maché Tea Trays
Large Painted Baize-lined Plate Chest
Oak Night-Commode
Old Leather Portmanteau
Japanned Foot-pan

Oak Foot-rest
Large Deal Corn-Chest
Dinner-Bell
Bird-Cage
Japanned Rush-seated Chair
Tin Refractor
Dutch Oven
Copper Coal-box & Zinc Coal-box
Sundry pieces Cocoa-matting
Black-tin Tea-Pot, Coffee-Pot, and Chocolate-mill [*deleted*]
Three Britannia-metal Teapots [*deleted*]
Deal Dresser (8 ft. 6 in. long) with two Cupboards and three drawers (3 ft. 1 in. high)

Bath-room

Painted Hat & Cloak stand
Twelve Chair-Cushions
Large Carpet Travelling-bag
Japanned Sitz-bath
Chamber-ware – 4 pieces
Looking-Glass (swing)
Sundry pieces of Carpet

Laundry

Oak Chest-bench (or "Settle")
Provender Chest
Oblong Deal Table
Carved Oak Almery
Oblong Deal Ironing-Table
Carved Oak Chest 1673
Mangle and Appliances
Twelve Flat Irons
Two Iron-stands
Broad-barred Fender
Sundry Fire-irons
Three Wooden-seated Chairs
Rush-seated Chair
Three-leaved Clothes-Horse
Three large Clothes-"swills"
Three folding Clothes-horses

Wash-house

Three Water-Cans
Two large Washing Crocks
Seven Deal Washing-troughs

Wringing Tub
Washing & Wringing Machine
Two large Iron Boiler-weights

Entrance Hall & Porch

Two Painted Wooden Benches
Two Iron Foot-scrapers
Hand-Bell
Mahogany Hat & Umbrella-stand
Ebonized Hall-table with Garsdale-marble top 42 x 21
Small Garsdale-Marble slab
Veined-marble Tray
Suspending Hall-Lamp
Two pieces painted Chinese Cloth
Painted Perforated Pedestal 11 in. square, 45 in. high
Oak framed Table with twisted Supporters & Kendal-marble top 27 x 22
High scoop-backed Arm Chair
Hall-Table – painted frame – Italian-marble top 54 x 22
Carved-fronted Flemish Oak Cabinet 64 x 46 – dated 1633 – on turned pillars & frame
  supporter
Patent Iron Stove
Veined-Marble Slab
Two Brown sheep-skin Rugs
Three Cocoa-fibre Foot-mats
Cocoa-fibre Floor Matting, 9 yds
Four pieces Oil Floor-cloth

Dining Room

Carved Oak Side-board Bookcase in three compartments with Veined-Marble Back & top –
  7 ft. 2 in. long – and Caryatide supporters
Oak framed Looking-glass in two compartments – 59 x 28
Mahogany Circular Pedestal Commode with Italian-marble top
Oak-framed Portfolio stand
Circular Rosewood Loo-Table 5 ft. diameter on richly carved Block & supporters
Crimson Damask Drapery for two Windows, with Brass Cornices and Rings
Two Roller Window-Blinds & fittings
Oak Bookcase in three compartments with Flemish carved frieze & figure supporters – 7. 4
  in long – with Garsdale-Marble top
Chimney Looking-glass – 46 x 24 – in ornamental Gilt frame on Oak bracket supporters
Maple Cabinet & Bookcase 42 in. high with Beetham Marble top 47 in. by 22 in.
Flemish Carved Oak Cabinet with Sienna-Marble top 50 x 22$^{1}/_{2}$ on turned framework
  supporter extreme height 5 ft.
Oak Pedestal Bookcase with Verde-antique top 23$^{1}/_{2}$ x [blank]
Circular Sienna-Marble Table on Bronzed Iron-supporters

Wicker-wrought Fire-screen

Two Mahogany-framed Needle-wrought Foot-stools

Oak Pole Fire-screen with ancient carved panel

Segmental Fender of Brass & steel with radiating bars

Set of Fire Brasses

Mahogany framed Reclining-Chair with moveable back & loose Cushions in Maroon Morocco

Child's Table Chair of carved oak dated 1657

Oak-carved Bookcase-bench (or "Settle") 53 in. long – 64^1/$_2$ extreme height

Twelve Mahogany Hair seated Chairs including two Arm Chairs – with carved backs & reeded supporters

Mahogany Dwarf Bookcase 46 front 66 back with White Marble top

Mahogany Urn-stand with Needle-wrought top

Set of Mahogany Dining Tables on Pillars and Claws

Three Rhenish Wine Bottles with Plated holders & stoppers

Two Or-molu pillar Candlesticks richly ornamented

Four-light Bronze & Or-molu Chandelier

Flemish Carved Oak Cabinet 30 in. wide 49 in. high with Dove-Marble top

Crimson Damask Screen Curtain with Oak pole & Rings

Brussels Carpet as planned to floor

Scotch Drugget, 24 yards

Rope-back Hearth Rug

Piece of Indian Matting

Balcony

Circular Marble Table on Iron Supporter

Iron Chair

Drawing Room

Polished & Bronze Fender with Ash-plate & Iron-supporters

Set of Polished Fire-irons

Chimney Looking-glass 50 x 44 in Rosewood & gilt frame

Two Glass Candelabra with rich prismatic lustres & White Marble pedestals

Pair of Fancy Feather Hand screens

Rosewood & Brass pole Fire screen

Mail Figure in Snail armour

A Shell-fish Woman of rare genus

Two frosted Flower-holders

Glazed Oak case & gilt bracket

Three-light Pendent Lamp

Circular Inlaid work-Cabinet with Brass rim

Rosewood Chiffonier 38 x 37^1/$_2$ with Bardiglio-Marble top

Two Mahogany Foot-stools with Needle-wrought covers

Ten Rosewood Chairs with Drab Damask-covered Hair seats

Rosewood-framed Sofa with loose Cushion & Pillow in Drab Damask
Rosewood brass-inlaid Sofa Table on squared pillar & block
Two Rosewood Card-Tables en suite
Gilt carved Window Cornice and Drab Damask Drapery
Four figured-Muslin Curtains
Roller Window-Blind and fittings
Brussels Carpet as planned to floor
Rope-back Hearth-rug

Breakfast-Room

Two Portfolio Cases of Curled Oak 8¼ broad 23½ deep 38½ high
Two Semi-circular Oak Brackets
Pair of Cornucopii
Flemish Carved Oak Cabinet 55 in. long 44½ high on Carved frame supporters
Two Carpet-covered Foot stools
Carved painted Oak Book-case 49in long 47½ in. high with Garsdale-Marble top 14 in. broad
Mahogany Occasional Table 21½ x 16½ on turned pillar Block & Claws [deleted]
Mahogany-framed Easy Chair in Black Damask with cushioned Seat
Five Antique-fashioned Oak Chairs with upholstered seat & back in Hair-cloth
Mahogany Library-Table 49 x 35 on squared pillar & block with sliding ends
Small Oak framed Couch upholstered in Black Hair-cloth with loose cushion
Italian Marble-table 24 in. diameter on Bronzed Iron supporter
Perforated Brass Fender with ash plate
Set of Polished Fire-irons
Japanned Hearth-brush
Patent-carved Fancy Bellows
Japanned Coal-box with Painting of "a Distinguished Member of the Human Society" after Landseer
Rope-backed Hearth Rug
Brussels Carpet as planned to floor
Scotch Cottage Carpet
Four Bronze Candlesticks
Parisian Time-piece in Or-molu with French glass shade & Rosewood stand
Two Taper-stands
Chimney Looking-glass 37½ x 27½ in. Flemish Carved Oak frame
Two German Flower Vases
Oak Window Cornice & Crimson Moreen Drapery
Roller Window Blind & fittings

Offices

Carved Oak Chair 1679 1680
Small Stamping Press
Letter Weighing Apparatus
Pocket Taper stand

Pocket Lantern
Leather-covered Trunk
Carved Oak Cradle 1666
Small Step-ladder
Three long-shafted Pruning Chisels
Nail-box & sundry Tools

*Set of Polished Fire-irons
Perforated Brass-mounted Fender
Deal Table 43 x 30
Five T Squares
Case of Mathematical Instruments
Pentagraph in Mahogany Case
Tortoise Case, silver mounted with Extensions & Ivory parallel ruler
Extensions in Roan Case
Three Rules, various
Turtle silver-mounted Pencil Case
Two Mahogany Colour Boxes <u>empty</u>
Two Japanned Moist-colour Boxes
Photogenic Drawing Apparatus
Levelling Apparatus
Office Stool
Two-flap Drawing Table – 48 x 31 – with two drawers
Circular Table – painted
Oval Deal Table
Five Bamboo-painted Rush-seated Chairs
Painted Wooden Stool
Ebonized Hair-seated Arm Chair
Mahogany two-flap Drawing table on turned frame-work supporter with four drawers
Baize covered Drawing Desk on ebonized frame &c &c
Two Mahogany Drawing Boards
Five Deal Drawing Boards
Hinged Mounting Boards
Cocoa Matting as planned to floor
Brass-mounted Fire-guard
Three Dwarf Candlesticks
Hand Bell & sundries

At Kendal

Desk with drawers & Drawing-Table
Marble-topped Table
Two Port-folios
Fender & Fire Irons*
Valued at £424 19 6
[*items between * and * marked* specifically bequeathed F.W.]

Plate, Linen, & China

Plate

[*all items in this section were silver*]

*Soup Ladle
Fish Knife
Gravy Spoon
Four Sauce Ladles
Twelve Dinner Spoons
Twelve   "   Forks
Seven-holed Cruet Frame
Six Salt Spoons
Mustard Spoon
Two Wine Strainers
Two   "   Labels
Whiskey Label
Nineteen Dessert Spoons
Fourteen   "   Forks
Tea Pot, Coffee Pot, Sugar-basin & Cream Jug
Twelve Tea Spoons
Nine Ditto
Sugar Tongs
Ditto
Butter Knife
Cheese Scoop
Two Pickle Fork [*sic*]
Drinking Cup
Three Toddy Ladles

Plated Articles

Four-holed Sauce Basket
Salt, Pepper & Mustard Stand
Mustard-pot
Four Knife rests
Meat Skewer
Gravy Spoon
Marrow Scoop
Two Dinner Forks
Two Vase Salts
Four Shell ditto, gilt
Grape Scissors
Seventeen Ivory-handled Dessert Knives
Nineteen ditto ditto Forks
Two Small ditto Knives

One " ditto Forks [*sic*]
Four Nut-cracks
Nut-cracks & Salt-spoon
Four Bottle-Coasters
Four Gilt Cigar-trays
Coffee Pot
Six Tea spoons
Toast Rack
Egg-stand with four Cups and four spoons gilt
Six Telescope Pillar Candlesticks
Three Snuffers and trays

German Silver

Twelve Dinner Forks
Six Dessert Spoons
Twelve Dessert Forks*
[*items between* * *and* * *marked* specifically bequeathed Mrs. W]

Linen

Eighteen Pairs of Sheets
Nine Bolster Cases
Twenty-four Pillow Cases
Forty-eight Towels
Sixteen Table Cloths
Twenty-four Damask Napkins
Sundry Tray Cloths &c &c &c

China

Green, Gold, and Painted Tea Service – comprising Eighteen Saucers, Sixteen Tea Cups, Ten
  Coffee Cups, Slop Basin, Sugar box, Two Cream Jugs, and Sic Bread and Butter Plates
  [Closet in Passage *in pencil below*]
Gilt Sea-weed Pattern Breakfast Service – comprising Twelve Cups, twelve saucers, Two Milk
  Jugs, Slop Basin, Two Meat Dishes, Eleven Plates, & Four Bread & Butter Plates [Closet
  in Passage *in pencil below*]
Old Chelsea Ware – Tea Pot, Eight Saucers, Two Coffee Cups, Two handled Loving Cup
  [Closet in Passage *in pencil below*]
Portions of Divers Breakfast Services – one hundred pieces [Housekeeper's Room *in pencil
  below*]
Six Dishes – Various [Housekeeper's Room *in pencil below*]
Three Wedgwood Jugs, various [Housekeeper's Room *in pencil below*]
Two Worcester Vases, small [Corridor Bedroom *in pencil below*]
Two Smaller Worcester Vases
Three Oriental China Cups & saucers

Three Nankin Basins
Antique Delft Dish

Cut Glass

Two quart Decanters
Two pink ditto
One quart ditto different
One pint ditto ditto
Claret Jug
Spirit Square
Six Water Bottles
Water Jug
Fourteen Wine glasses
Fourteen Ditto different
Six ditto ditto
Five ditto ditto
Four ditto ditto
Three ditto ditto
Six ditto various
Eighteen Hock-glasses
Twelve Tazza Champagne Glasses
Four tall " ditto
Twelve Goblets
Seven Tumblers
Celery Jar
Two Pickle Jars
Butter Cooler, stand, & Cover
Two Sweetmeat Dishes
Seven Small Trifle Dishes
Butter Cooler
Eight Custard glasses
Three ditto different

Plain Glass

Twelve Finger glasses
Ten tall Champagne Glasses
Three Jelly glasses
Three Pepper Casters
Mustard glass
Six Hyacinth Glasses

Pressed Glass

Massive Sugar Basin

Three Soda-water Tumblers
Two Dessert Dishes and stands
Sugar Basin and Cream Jug
Four Salt Cellars – various
Three Pickle-shells
Two Shrimp-pots
Two Schiedam Bottles
Valued at £104 8 0

Books, Prints, & Pictures

Books
Architecture, Archaeology, Fine Arts, and Topography

Adams' Geometrical & Geographical Essays – 2 Vols, 8vo, $^1/_2$ Calf, 1813

Alberti's Architecture, Painting, & Statuary, by Bartoli & Leoni, 3 Vols, folio, in one, Calf, 1739

Allason's Picturesque Antiquities of Pola in Istria, folio, $^1/_2$ Calf, 1819

Antiquarian Itinerary, 7 Vols, 12mo, $^1/_2$ Calf, gilt, 1815-18

Arabesque Ornaments of [*blank*], Outlines in Lithograph, by Engelmann, Imperial 4to, No date

Architecture Moderne (chiefly in the style of the Renaissance), large folio, 12 plates, sewed

Arnold's Magazine of the Fine Arts, 4 Vols, 8vo, Cloth, 1833-34

Art-Union Journal, Vols 4 & 5, 4to, $^1/_2$ Calf, 1843-43

Ashmore's Views in Scotland (24), Oblong 4to, sewed, n.d.

Atkinson's Gothic Ornaments, Lithograph, 4to, $^1/_2$ Calf, no Title

Barlow's Trip to Rome in 1835, 12mo, Cloth, 1836

Barr's Anglican Church Architecture, 12mo, Cloth, 1832

Barry's (Sir Charles) Traveller's Club House, 4to, large paper, $^1/_2$ Morocco, 1829

Batty's (Capt.) German Scenery, Imperial 8vo, Cloth, 1823

Batty's (") Hanoverian and Saxon Scenery, Imperial 8vo, Cloth, 1829

Berry's Encyclopedia of Heraldry, 3 Vols, 4to, large paper, boards, n.d.

Blore's Monumental Remains of Noble & Eminent Persons, Imperial 8vo, Calf, gilt, 1826

Bloxam's Principles of Gothic Ecclesiastical Architecture, 12mo, boards, 1838

Brayley & Britton's History of the Ancient Palace and late Houses of Parliament at Westminster, 8vo, $^1/_2$ Calf, gilt, 1836

Breaks' (Thos.) System of Land-Surveying, 8vo, Calf, 1778

Bree's (S. C.) Railway Practice, 2 Vols, 4to, Cloth, 1838

Brewer's Palaces & Public Buildings, by Gill, 4to, Calf, 1821

Britton's Architectural Antiquities of Great Britain, 4 Vols, 4to, large paper – Original impressions of the Engravings – boards, 1807-14

Britton's History & Antiquities of the Cathedral Church of Winchester, 4to, India proofs, $^1/_2$ Russia, 1817

Britton's Cathedral Antiquities of Great Britain, 7 Vols, 4to, Russia – gilt, 1821-31

Britton & Pugin's Illustrations of the Public Buildings of London, 2 Vols, 8vo, Calf, gilt, 1825

Britton's Chronological History of Christian Architecture in England, imperial 4to, 1/2 Morocco, 1835

Britton's Dictionary of Architecture & Archaeology of the Middle Ages, 4to, large paper, 1/2 Morocco & Cloth, 1838

Brooks' Designs for Cottage & Villa Architecture, 4to, 1/2 Calf, 1839

Brown's Principles of Practical Perspective or Scenographic Projection, 4to, boards, 1815

Bunning's Designs for Tombs & Monuments, royal 4to, sewed, 1839, and Reilley's Monumental Designs, oblong 4to, n.d.

Canova's Life & Works, with Engravings in Outline by Moses, 3 Vols, Imperial 8vo, Calf, gilt, 1824-28

Catton's English Peerage, 3 Vols, 4to, 1/2 Calf & (the Vol. of Plates), Calf, 1790

Chadley on the Formation of Flues of Chimneys, 8vo, Cloth, n.d.

Chambers' (Sir W.) Treatise on the Decorative Part of Civil Architecture, Imperial folio, Calf, 1791

Chippendale's Cabinet Maker's Director, folio, Rough Calf, 1754

Civil Engineer's and Architect's Journal, Vols 1 & 2, Cloth, 1837-39

Clark's Domestic Architecture of the Reigns of Elizabeth & James 1st, 8vo, Cloth, 1833

Clark & Wormull's Introduction to Heraldry, 12mo, Calf, 1781

Collection of 'Scraps' from Provincial Excursions, chiefly Norfolk & Essex, 12mo, Morocco, 1819

Coney's Fifty-six Architectural Sketches in France, the Netherlands &c. &c., 4to, sewed, n.d.

Cooke's Topographical Description of the English Counties, 28 Vols, 12mo, 1/2 Calf, n.d.

Clerk (vide Hogarth)

Conder's Description of Palestine & the Holy Land, 12mo

Cottingham's (L. N.) Collection of Architectural Ornaments and Decorations, Lithographs by Hullmandel, Atlas folio, 1/2 Calf, 1824

Cottingham's Smith & Founder's Director for Ornamental Iron & Brass Work, Lithographs by Hullmandel, 4to, 1/2 Russia, 1824

Chesy's Illustrations of Stone Church Kent, folio, Cloth, 1840

Cumbrian Tourist, 12mo, Calf, gilt, 1821 & divers Pocket Guides thro' Wales

Davy's Builder's Constructive Manual, 8vo, Cloth, 1839

Davy's Architectural Precedents &c, 8vo, 1/2 Calf, 1841

Debrett's Baronetage of England, 2 Vols, 8vo, Cloth, 1828

Derick's Views &c. of Staunton Harcourt Church &c, folio, sewed, 1841

Designs for Gates &c. of the Royal Parks by various Architects, Imperial 4to, Cloth, 1841

Dibden's Bibliographical, Antiquarian, & Picturesque Tour in the Northern Counties of England & Scotland, 2 Vols, royal 8vo, boards, 1838

Donaldson's (T. L.) Collection of Doorways & Sketch of the History of Italian Architecture, 4to, sewed, 1836

Doyle's Practical Gardening, 12mo, Cloth, 1836

Dugdale – vide post

Duncan's Artist's Portfolio, 2 Vols in one, 4to, 1/2 roan, 1837

Elmes's Topographical Dictionary of London, 8vo, $^1/_2$ Calf, 1821

Elmes's Memoirs of Sir Christopher Wren, 4to, $^1/_2$ Calf, 1823

Elsam's (Richard) Essay on Rural Architecture &c, Imperial 4to, $^1/_2$ Calf, 1803

Englefield's (Sir H. C.) Collection of Antique Vases, Engraved by H. Moses, 4to, boards, 1819

Evelyn's Compleat Gardn'er, from de la Quintinye, folio, Calf, 1693

Faulkner's Designs for Mural Monuments & Tombs, first series, 4to, 1805

Fellowes' Xanthian Marbles – their acquisition & transmission to England, Imperial 8vo, sewed, 1843, with M.S. note by G.W.

Fellowes' Journal in Asia Minor in 1838, Imperial 8vo, sewed, 1843

Fisher – vide post

Forbes' (Alex) Hints on Ornamental Gardening, 12mo, boards, 1820

Ford's Guide to the Lakes, 12mo, 1845, with Pencil Sketch of "the Lion & the Lamb", Grasmere, by G.W.

Forsyth's Beauties of Scotland, 5 Vols, 8vo, Calf, 1805

Forsyth's Remarks on Antiquities, Arts & Letters in Italy, 12mo, Calf, 1824

Furniture Designs, Fifty, 4to, Coloured, anon, n.d.

Gandy & Bands' Windsor Castle &c, folio, $^1/_2$ Russia

Gandy's (Joseph A. R.A.) Designs for Cottages & other Rural Buildings, 4to, $^1/_2$ Calf, 1805

Gastineau's North & South Wales Illustrated, 2 Vols. in one, 4to, Calf

Gell's (Sir W.) Pompeiana, 2 Vols, Imperial 8vo, Boards, 1832

Gibbs' Book of Architecture and Ornament, folio, Calf, 1739

Gilpin's Hints on Landscape Gardening, Imperial 8vo, boards, 1832

Godwin & Britton's Churches of London, 2 Vols, 8vo, Cloth, 1838

Goodwin's (Francis) Domestic Architecture, 3 Vols, 4to, $^1/_2$ Calf , 1833, 4, 5

Graphic Illustrations of the French Capital, Atlas 4to, $^1/_2$ roan, n.d.

Green's (William) Guide to the Lake and Mountain Scenery of Cumberland, Westmoreland, and Lancashire, 2 Vols, 8vo (No map & no plates), Calf, 1819

Green's (W) "Sixty" (only 52) small Etchings of Scenery in the District of the English Lakes, oblong 4to, $^1/_2$ Calf, 1814 a copy probably unique – each Etching being carefully and most artistically tinted in Indian Ink

Green's (W) Thirty Views in the District of the English Lakes – aquatint – (No title & several plates wanting) oblong 4to, $^1/_2$ Calf, 1804

Green's (W) Forty Etchings, chiefly of Old Buildings in the District of the English Lakes (No title nor letter-press) Oblong 4to, $^1/_2$ Calf, 1822

Gregson's (Matthew) Port-folio of Fragments relating to the History & Antiquities of the County Palatine & Duchy of Lancaster, folio, (Parts 1, 2, & 3), Russia, Gilt, 1817

Griffiths' History of Cheltenham, 4to, large paper, Proof Illustrations on India paper, boards, 1826

Guillim's Display of Heraldrie, Written title, preface wanting, no end, arms coloured & some extra Drawings inserted, folio, Calf (1660 ?)

Habershon's Half-Timbered Houses of England, Imperial 4to, $^1/_2$ Morocco, 1836

Hakewill's Views in the Neighbourhood of Windsor, 4to, boards, 1829
Hakewill's Picturesque Tour in Italy, 4to, Cloth, 1820
Hakewill on Elizabethan Architecture, 8vo, Cloth, 1825
Hand-Book of Furness Abbey, 8vo, $^1/_2$ Morocco, 1845
Hand-Book to Holland, Belgium, & Northern Germany, 8vo, 1845
Harrison's Floricultural Cabinet, 11 Vols (3 & 4 wanting), 8vo, Calf, 1833-43
Herve's Residence in Greece & Turkey, 2 Vols, 8vo, Cloth, 1837
Historical Gallery of Portraits and Paintings, 2 Vols (only), 8vo, Calf, 1807-8
Hoare's (Sir R. C.) Classical Tour in Italy & Sicily, 2 Vols, 8vo, Cloth, 1819
Hogarth's (William) Life and Works by Clerk, 2 Vols, Imperial 8vo, Calf, gilt, 1821
Holland – vide Guide Books, Travelling Maps &c. "Miscellaneous"
Hood on Warming Buildings by Hot Water &c, 8vo, Cloth, 1844
Hosking's Treatise on Architecture and Building, 4to, boards, 1832
Hoppus's Practical Measurer, 8vo, C[al]f, 1792
Hunt's Half a dozen Hints on Domestic Architecture, 4to, boards, 1825
Hunt's Designs for Parsonage Houses, Alms Houses &c, 4to, boards, 1825
Hunt's Designs for Lodges, Gardener's Houses &c. in the Italian Style, 4to, boards, 1827
Hunt's Exemplars of Tudor Architecture, 4to, $^1/_2$ Calf, 1820
Hutchinson's History of Cumberland, 2 Vols, 4to, Calf, 1794

Imison's School of Arts &c, &c, 8vo, Calf, n.d.
Ingram's Memorials of Oxford, 2 Vols, 8vo, Cloth, 1837
Inwood's (W. H.) Erechtheion at Athens, Imperial folio, $^1/_2$ Calf, gilt, 1827
Iron Roof of the New Houses of Parliament, 4to, sewed, 1836

Jackson's Detached Enrichments in papier-maché, 4to, sewed, 1836
Jackson & Andrews' Illustrations of Bishop West's Chapel in Putney Church, 4to, $^1/_2$ Calf, 1825
Jamieson's Dictionary of Mechanical Science, 2 Vols, 4to, Calf, 1827
Jolimont's Most Remarkable Monument in the City of Rouen, Lithograph & Letterpress, folio, $^1/_2$ Russia, 1822
Jones vide post

Kennett's Antiquities of Rome, 8vo, Calf, 1786
King's Shop Fronts & Exterior Doors, Oblong folio, board, n.d.
Knight's Analytical Inquiry into the Principles of Taste, 8vo, $^1/_2$ Calf, 1806
Knight's (H. G.) Architectural tour in Normandy, 8vo, boards, 1836

Lancaster, History of the Town of, 8vo, boards, 1811
Laing's Plans, Elevations, & Sections of Buildings Public & Private in various parts of England, Imperial folio, $^1/_2$ Russia, gilt, 1818
Langley's (Batty) Architecture (no title & otherwise imperfect, 4to, Calf, 1741
Lawrence's (Richard) Elgin Marbles from the Parthenon at Athens – Fifty Etchings, no Letterpress, Oblong folio, boards, 1818
Leigh's New Picture of London, 12mo, Russia, 1822

Lewis's Topographical Dictionary of England, 4 Vols, 4to, Cloth, 1831

Loudon (J. C.) On the Construction of Hot Houses, 4to, boards, 1817

Loudon's (J. C.) Encyclopedia of Cottage, Farm, & Villa Architecture, 8vo, Calf, 1833

Loudon's (J. C.) Architectural Magazine, 5 Vols, 8vo, $^1/_2$ Calf, 1834-38

Loudon's (J. C.) Encyclopedia of Gardening, 8vo, Calf, 1835

Lugar's Plans & Views of Buildings in England & Scotland, 4to, Cloth, 1823

Lugar's Villa Architecture – coloured – folio, large paper, $^1/_2$ Russia, 1828

Mackenzie & Pugin's Ancient Buildings of Oxford, 4to, $^1/_2$ Calf, n.d.

Mannex's History, Topography, &c. of Westmoreland, 8vo, $^1/_2$ Calf, 1849

Mawe's Complete Gardener, 12mo, Cloth, 1839

McAdam on Road Making, 8vo, boards, 1821

McGregor's Picture of Dublin, 8vo, Roan, 1821

Meyrick & Smith's Costume of the Original Inhabitants of the British Islands, 4to, large paper, Coloured, 1815

Meyrick's Ancient Armour, 3 Vols, folio, $^1/_2$ Morocco, 1824

Minton's Old English Flooring Tiles, 4to, Cloth n.d.

Moller's Memories of German Architecture – large Engravings – folio, Leipsig, 1836 – and Text in English by W. H. Leeds, 8vo, Cloth, 1836

Monuments of Edinburgh on Canvas folded, for Priket, 12mo

Morceau's Fragments of Architectural Ornaments – drawn from the Antique at Rome, Paris n.d.

Morey's Cathedral of Messina – richly illuminated illustrations – folio, $^1/_2$ Morocco, 1841

Morton's Monastic Annals of Teviotdale, 4to, Cloth, 1832

Mosses' (H) Outline Illustrations of Modern Costume, 4to, $^1/_2$ Russia, 1823

Moule's essay on Roman Villas &c, 8vo, Cloth, 1833

Milner on the Ecclesiastical Architecture of England during the Middle ages, 8vo, Calf, 1811

Murphy's Plans, Elevations, & Sections of the Church at Batalha, folio, $^1/_2$ Morocco, 1841

Nash's (Joseph) Mansions of England in the Olden-Time, 1st, 2d, & 3d Series, 3 Vols, $^1/_2$ Morocco, folio, Cloth, 1839, 40, 41 [M.W. in margin]

Neale & Le Keny's Collegiate & Parochial Churches of Great Britain, 2 Vols, 8vo, Cloth, 1841

Neale's (J. P.) Views of Seats of Noblemen & Gentlemen in England, Wales, Scotland & Ireland, 11 Vols, 8vo, (Vols 2, 3, 7, 8, 9, 10 incomplete), Calf, gilt, 1822-29

Nelson's Hand-book to Scotland: & twenty-three other Guide-Books of various dates &c.

Nicholson's (Cornelius) Annals of Kendal, 8vo, Cloth, 1832

Nicholson's (Cornelius) Annals of Kendal, a New edition – with Portrait – 8vo, Cloth, 1861

Nicholson's (Peter) Principles of Architecture, 3 Vols, 8vo, $^1/_2$ Calf, 1809

Nicholson's (Peter) Dictionary of Architecture, 2 Vols, 4to, Calf, 1819

Nicholson's (Peter) Course of Pure Mathematics & Key to Ditto, 2 Vols, 8vo, Sheep, 1822

Oblong Scrap Book with Drawings, Wood-cuts &c, 8vo, Calf, n.d.

Ornamental Fragments – Anonymous – Lithograph, Oblong folio, Calf, n.d.

Ornamental Gates, Lodges, &c. Part 1, 25 Engravings, 4to, boards, 1839

Ottley's Guide to the Lakes, 12mo, $^1/_2$ Calf, 1823, with M.S. note by G.W.

Parker's Villa Rustica selected from Buildings near Rome & Florence, 2 Vols, 4to, boards, 1832-33

Parker's Glossary of Terms used in Architecture, 8vo, Cloth, 1838

Parker's Glossary of Terms used in Architecture, 2 Vols, 8vo, Cloth, 1840

Partington's Builder's Guide, 8vo, $^1/_2$ Calf, 1825

Pasley's Observations on Limes, Cements, Mortars, &c, &c, 8vo, Cloth, 1838

Patterns of Metal Work – various – 4 numbers, sewed

Pilkington's Dictionary of Painters by Fuseli, 4to, $^1/_2$ Calf, 1810

Pocock's Modern Finishings for Rooms, 4to, 1811

Prout's Twenty-six Sketches in France, Switzerland & Italy, Lithographs, folio, $^1/_2$ Morocco, n.d. [M.W. *in margin*]

Pugin's (Augustus) Specimens of Gothic Architecture in England, 3 Vols, 4to, $^1/_2$ Calf, 1823 &c

Pugin's (Augustus) Examples of Gothic Architecture in England – second series – 2 Vols, 4to, $^1/_2$ Calf, 1830 – & Letter-press to Ditto, sewed, 1836

Pugin's (Augustus) Examples of Gothic Architecture in England – third series – by T. L. Walker, three parts, 4to, $^1/_2$ Cloth, 1836, 37, 38

Pugin's (Augustus) Examples illustrated by Nash & Leeds, 4to, $^1/_2$ Calf, 1830

Pugin's (Augustus) Gothic Ornaments from Buildings in England & France Lithographs by J. D. Harding, 4to, $^1/_2$ Calf, 1831

Pugin's (Augustus) Ornamental Timber Gables in England & France, Imperial 4to, Cloth, 1839

Pugin & Le Keux's Specimens of the Architectural Antiquities of Normandy by Britton, 4to, Cloth, 1828

Pugin & Heath's Paris & its Environs, 2 Vols in One, 4to, Cloth, 1830-31

Pugin's (A. W.), Designs for Gothic Furniture, 4to, Cloth, 1835

Pugin's (A. W.) True Principles of Pointed Architecture, 4to, Cloth, 1841

Reilley's Monumental Designs &c. vide Bunning, ante

Report of the Warming, Ventilation, & Transmission of Sound, with notes by Inman, 8vo, Cloth, 1836

Repton's Design for the Pavilion at Brighton, atlas folio, $^1/_2$ Calf, 1806

Richardson's Architectural Remains of the Reigns of Elizabeth and James 1, vol 1, folio

Richardson's Studies of Old English Mansions, their Furniture &c, Lithograph folio, Cloth, 1841

Richardson's Old English Mansions, third series, 4to, Cloth, 1835

Richardson's Observations on the Architecture of England during the reign of Elizabeth & James 1, 4to, $^1/_2$ Morocco, 1837

Rickman's Attempt to discriminate the Styles of Architecture in England, 8vo, $^1/_2$ Calf, 1825

Rider's Principles of Perspective, 8vo, Cloth, 1836

Robinson's Rural Architecture, 4to, $^1/_2$ Calf, 1823

Robinson's Designs for Ornamental Villas, 4to, $^1/_2$ Calf, 1827

Robinson's History of Hatfield House (New Vitruvius Britannicus) Folio, $^1/_2$ Russia, 1823

Robinson's History of Castle Ashby (Ditto), Folio, $^1/_2$ Russia, 1841

Rome Ancient & Modern – a series of Views – Outline – Oblong 4to, $^1/_2$ Calf, 1831

Roe – Views of the Palaces, Churches, and Public Buildings during the Papacy of Alexander VII, 3 Vols in 1, Oblong Folio, ¹/₂ Calf, 1665

Schinkel's Architectural Works a Series of Outline Engravings – large atlas, 4to, ¹/₂ Morocco No Title, no Letter-press, n.d.

Scraps from the Continent – Lithograph – Oblong 4to, ¹/₂ Calf, n.d.

Seven Various Books of Views of Windsor Castle, English Lakes, &c. &c. Small

Sharpe's General Peerage of the British Empire with Arms drawn & engraved by Williams, 3 Vols, 12mo, Cloth, n.d.

Sharpe's (Ed.) Architectural Parallels from Examples in England in the 12th & 13th Centuries, 2 Vols, Folio, ¹/₂ Morocco, 1848

Shaw's Metal Ornaments, 4to, ¹/₂ Calf (no Title & otherwise imperfect), 1825

Shaw's Specimens of Ancient Furniture, coloured, 4to, ¹/₂ Calf, 1836

Shaw's Illuminated Ornaments of the Middle Ages (Illustrations only), small 4to, ¹/₂ Calf, 1830

Shaw's Details of Elizabethan Architecture, 4to, ¹/₂ Calf, 1839

Shepherd's Modern Athens (Edinburgh) in the Nineteenth Century – a series of Views, 4to, ¹/₂ Calf, 1829

Simm's Treatise on Levelling, 8vo, Cloth, 1837

Simpson's Ancient Baptismal Fonts, Imperial 8vo, Cloth, 1838

Simson's Elements of Euclid, by Wright, 8vo, Calf, 1803

Smith's History of the County of Warwick, 4to, large paper, India proofs, boards, Birmingham, 1836

Smyth's Monuments & Genii of St. Paul's & Westminster abbey, 8vo, calf, gilt, 1826

Soane's (Sir John) Sketches in Architecture, folio, ¹/₂ Calf, 1798

Soane's (Sir John) Union of Architecture, Sculpture & Painting, 4to, Boards, 1827

Souvenir of the North – a Selection of Views in Scotland, 12mo, Cloth

Souvenir de la Suisse (100 Views in Switzerland), lithograph, Morocco, gilt, Genève, n.d.

Starke's Guide through Italy, 8vo, ¹/₂ Calf, Paris, 1828

Starke's Travels in Europe, 12mo, ¹/₂ Calf, [Paris], 1834, with MS memoranda by G.W.

Strickney's Contrasts, lithographed by George Smith, 4to, Sewed, 1832

Strickland's Reports on Roads, Railways & Canals, oblong folio, ¹/₂ Calf, Philadelphia, 1826

Stuart's Dictionary of Architecture, Vols 1 & 2, 8vo, ¹/₂ Calf (the Vol of Plates wanting)

Taylor's Designs for Shop Fronts, 4to, boards, n.d.

Taylor's Builder's Price Book, 8vo, ¹/₂ Calf, 1822

Thompson's Retreats, a series of Designs for Ornamental Cottages &c, coloured, 4to, boards, 1827

Tod's Plans, Elevations & Sections of Hot-houses, Green-houses &c., Imperial 4to, board, 1823

Tomlinson's Views on the Rhine, 4to, ¹/₂ Calf, gilt, 1823

Transactions of the Institute of British Architects, Vol. 1 pt. 1, 4to, Cloth, 1836

Transactions of the Institute of Civil Engineers, Vol. 1, 4to, Cloth, 1836

Traveller's Guide through Scotland, 12mo, Calf, 1805 & twenty others of various dates &c.

Travelling Sketch & Memorandum Books, pocket size with M.S.S. & Drawings by the late

Mr. W., thirteen various

Travelling Maps – various British & Continental, folded, in cases – <u>Twenty</u>

Tredgold's Elementary Principles of Carpentry, by Barlow, 4to, boards, 1820

Tredgold's Elementary Principles of Carpentry, by Barlow, 4to, boards, 1840

Trendell's Designs for Cottages and Villas, 4to, Cloth, 1831

Treys's Modern Churches, large 4to, $^1/_2$ Cloth boards, 1831

Tunnicliffe's Survey of the Counties of Stafford, Chester & Lancaster, 8vo, $^1/_2$ Calf, <u>Nantwich,</u> 1797

Twycross's Mansions of the Northern Division of the County of Lancaster, 2 Vols, Imperial 4to, $^1/_2$ Morocco, 1847

Unedited Antiquities of Attica by the Society of Dilettanti, Imperial folio, Calf, gilt, 1833

Union Atlas of all the Empires, Kingdoms & States in the known World, 4to, $^1/_2$ Calf, 1812

Views on the Grand Canal, Venice, oblong 8vo, boards, 1834

Vignettes from Bowyer's Edition of the History of England, comprising Coins, Medals, Portraits, &c, Atlas 4to, $^1/_2$ Russia, <u>n.d.</u>

Vulliamy's Architectural Ornaments – Outline – by H. Mosses, Oblong Folio, $^1/_2$ Calf, 1825

Waistell's Designs for Agricultural Buildings & Labourers' Cottages by Jopling, 4to, $^1/_2$ Calf, 1827

Walford's Baronetage & Peerage, 12mo, Cloth

Walker's Architectural Precedents, 8vo, Cloth, 1841

Wallen's History & Antiquities of the Round Church at Little Maplestead, 8vo, Cloth, 1836

West's Antiquities of Furness <u>Original Edition</u>, 4to, Calf, 1774

West's Antiquities of Furness by Close, 8vo, $^1/_2$ Calf, <u>Ulverston</u>, 1805

Whewell's Architectural Notes on German Churches, 8vo, Cloth, 1835

Whitaker's History of Craven, 4to, Second edition, large paper, Boards, 1812

Whitaker's History of Whalley, 4to, Third edition, boards, 1818

Whittock's Topographical & Historical Description of the University & City of Oxford, 4to, $^1/_2$ Calf, 1828

Wilkey's Wanderings in Germany, 8vo, Cloth, 1829

Wilkins's Civil Architecture of the Middle Ages, especially in Italy, 8vo, Cloth, 1835

Weale's Quarterly Papers on Architecture, 2 Vols, 4to, boards, 1844

Windsor Castle, Architectural Illustrations of, by Gandy & Band, with descriptions by John Britton, folio, $^1/_2$ Morocco

Wickles' Cathedral Churches of England & Wales, 3 Vols, Imperial 8vo, Cloth, 1838 [*deleted*]

Wood's Letters of an Architect from Italy & Greece, 2 Vols, 4to, Cloth, 1828

Working Drawings of Gothic Ornaments, on Stone by L.N. Cottingham, Atlas Folio, <u>n.d.</u>

Wright's (G.N.) Tours in Ireland, 3 Vols in One, $^1/_2$ Calf, 1822-3

Wright's (G.N.) Scenes in Ireland, 12mo, boards, 1834

Omissions

Dugdale's History of St. Paul's Cathedral, London, by Sir H. Ellis, folio, Calf, gilt, 1818

Jones' (Inigo) Designs for Public & Private Buildings, by Kent, 2 Vols, folio, in one, Calf, 1777

Fisher's National Portrait Gallery with Memoirs by Jerdau, 5 Vols, Imperial 8vo, $^1/_2$ Calf, 1830-34

History, Voyages & Travels, Personal Narrative, the Belles-Lettres, Miscellaneous Literature

Adams' Voyage to South America, 2 Vols, 8vo, $^1/_2$ Calf, 1807

Aikmann's Buchanan's History of Scotland continued to the Union, 4 Vols, 8vo, Calf, 1827

Arundel's Visit to the Seven Churches of Asia &c, &c, 8vo, $^1/_2$ Calf, 1828

Athenian Letters, translated by Lord Hardwicke, 2 Vols, 4to, Boards, 1810

Baines' History &c. of Cumberland & Westmoreland, 8vo, Calf, n.d.

Baines' History &c. of Lancashire, 2 Vols, 8vo, Calf, n.d.

Baines' History &c. of Yorkshire, 2 Vols, 8vo, Calf, n.d.

Baines' History &c. of Durham and Northumberland, 2 Vols, 8vo, Calf, n.d.

Baines, Maps & Plans to illustrate the foregoing series, 4to, $^1/_2$ Calf

Baker's Chronicle of the Kings of England, folio, Calf (portrait of Charles II inserted), 1684

Barnes on an Infirmary at Carlisle, 8vo, Cloth, 1831

Beckford's Recollections of an Excursion to Alcobaca & Batalha, 8vo, Cloth, 1835

Bell's Geography &c. &c, 6 Vols, 8vo, Calf, 1832

Blair's Lectures on Rhetoric & Belles Lettres, 2 Vols, 8vo, $^1/_2$ Calf, 1819

Bourienne's Memoirs of Napoleon Bonaparte, 4 Vols, 12mo, Cloth, 1831

Bourn's Gazetteer, 8vo, 1815, & Bradshaw's Continental Railway Guide

Bracken's (H.) Farriery &c, 12mo, Calf, Lancaster, 1742

Briggs' (John – Editor of the Lonsdale Magazine & Westmorland Gazette) Remains, 12mo, boards, 1825

Bubbles from the Brunnens of Nassau, 12mo, boards, Frankfort, 1835

Bubbles from the Brunnens of Nassau, 8vo, $^1/_2$ Calf, 1834

Buchan's Domestic Medicine, 8vo, Calf, 1805

Bulwer's (Sir E. L.) Athens, its Rise & Fall, 2 Vols, 8vo, $^1/_2$ Calf, 1837

Bunyan's Pilgrim's Progress – Memoir &c; & Illustrations by H. C. Selons, oblong 4to, $^1/_2$ Calf, 1854

Burton's (Richard) Historical Remarks on London & Westminster, small 4to (reprint), 1810

Burke, Life of the Rt, Hon. Edmund, 8vo (no title), $^1/_2$ Calf, 1798

Bygone Times & Latecome Changes, 12mo, boards, 1811

Callcott's Treatise on the Deluge, 8vo, boards, 1761

Campbell's Lives of the Lord Chancellors &c, Vols. 4 & 5, second series, 8vo, Cloth, & $^1/_2$ calf, 1846

Carey's Experiments in Chemistry, 12mo, $^1/_2$ Calf, 1825

Chambers' Edinburgh Journal, second series, 11 Vols, 4to, Cloth, 1844-49

Chart of the Kings & Queens of England to William IV, folded in case

Chesterfield's Letters to his Son, 3 Vols, 18mo, Calf, gilt, 1810

Chronology of the History of France — abridged – 8vo, Calf, 1747

Clark on the Shoeing of Horses, 8vo, Calf, Edinburgh, 1782

Clarke's (Hewson) History of the Wars in Europe from the commencement of the French

Revolution to the Peace of 1815, 3 Vols, 4to, Calf, <u>n.d.</u>
Coleridge's (H. N.) Six Months in the West Indies in 1825, 12mo, Calf, gilt, 1832
Cooper's Lionel Lincoln & The Spy, 8vo, ¹/₂ Calf, 1838-9
Culpepper's English Physician and Herbal, 4to, Calf, 1809
Cumberland's Lives & Portraits of Public Characters, 3 Vols, 12mo, Calf, 1828
Cunningham's Lives of Illustrious Englishmen, 16 parts, 8vo, Cloth, 1837

Davenport's History of the Bastile, 12mo, Calf, gilt, 1838
Dear (Dr.) & Garnett (Dr.) on the English spaw & Mineral waters of Harrogate,8vo, ¹/₂ Calf, 1736, 1792
De Moleville's Private Memoirs of Louis XVI, King of France, 3 Vols, 8vo, ¹/₂ Calf, 1797
Dickens' Nicholas Nickleby, 8vo, Cloth, 1838
Dobbs' Universal History, 9 Vols. In 6, 12mo, ¹/₂ Calf, 1788
Dover's New General Atlas of the World, small folio, Gilt, Morocco, 1842
Dryden's Virgil, 18mo, Morocco, 1825

Edgeworth (Maria) Tales & Romances, 18 Vols, 12mo, Cloth, 1832-33 [M.W. *in margin*]
English Encyclopedia, 10 Vols, 4to, Calf, 1802
European Magazine, Vol. 7, ¹/₂ Calf, 1805

Farey's Agriculture & Minerals of Derbyshire, 3 Vols, 8vo, Boards, 1811
Fellowes' Paris in July 1815, 8vo, ¹/₂ Calf, 1815
Fielding's History of Tom Jones, 3 Vols, 12mo, Calf, Edinburgh, 1780

Gerroud's Practical & Prose Works &c, 12mo, Boards, <u>Leith</u>, 1815
Goldsmith's History of Rome, 2 Vols, 8vo, ¹/₂ Calf, 1826
Goodfellow's Lectures on Diseases of the Kidney & Dropsy, 8vo, Cloth, 1861
Grant's Sketches in London, 8vo, Cloth, 1840
Guardian (The), 2 Vols, 12mo, Calf, 1754

Hall's Dictionary of Arts & Sciences, 3 Vols, folio, Calf, <u>n.d.</u>
Hanger – Life &c. of Colonel George, 2 Vols, 8vo, ¹/₂ Calf, 101
Hart's History of Gustavus Adolphus King of Sweden by Stockdale, 2 Vols, 8vo, boards, 1807
Hayes' Treatise on Fluxions, folio, Calf, 1704
Herbert's (Sir Thomas) Memoirs of the last two years of the Reign of King Charles I, 8vo, ¹/₂ Calf, 1813
Heron's Scotland described, 12mo, 1797 & six Guide Books – various
Historic, Military, & Naval Anecdotes &c, of the late War, 4to, ¹/₂ Morocco, Coloured, 1815
Holy Bible &c, 4to, Calf, <u>Dublin</u>, 1752
Holy Bible, with reference notes, &c, 8vo, Morocco, Gilt, 1838
Holy Bible, with Scott's Explanatory Notes & Practical Observations, 3 Vols, Imperial 8vo, Calf, 1834
Hooper's History of the Rebellion & Civil Wars of England during the Reign of Charles I, folio, Calf, 1738
Hudibras (a very rare edition) 8vo, Calf, 1704

Hudibras (Butler's, by Dr. Zachary Grey) 2 Vols, 8vo, Calf (Grey's Original Edition) 1744
Hughes (Jabez) Lives of the Caesars, 12mo, Calf, 1717
Hulme, Smollett, Cormick, & Lloyd's History of England, 25 Vols, 12mo, Calf, 1794
Humphrey Clinker, with Rowlandson's Illustrations (No title), 8vo, Calf

Illustrated London News, 1842 to 1856 & 1862, Cloth, gilt
Irving's (Washington) Salmagundi, 12mo, Calf, gilt, 1839
Irving's (W.) History of New York from the beginning of the world, 12mo, Calf, Gilt, 1836

Johnson's (Dr. S.) Journey to the Western Islands of Scotland, 8vo, Calf, 1775
Johnson's (Dr. S.) Dictionary of the English Language, 8vo, Calf, 1799
Johnson on Diseases of the Kidney, 8vo, Cloth, 1832

Kelly's History of the Battle of Waterloo, 4to, $^1/_2$ Calf, 1829
Kliman's Journey to the World under ground, 8vo, Calf, 1742

La Perouse's Voyage round the World 1785 to 1788, 3 Vols, 8vo, Calf, 1807
Langhorne's Plutarch's Lives, 8vo, Boards. 1828
Lax's Latitude & Longitude at Sea, 8v, $^1/_2$ Calf, 1821
Leti's Life of Pope Sixtus V, 8vo, Calf, 1704
Lettres sur l'Education, 3 tomes, 12mo, 1807
Life in Paris (no title) 8vo, Calf, <u>n.d.</u>
Lowthion's (John) Jerusalem and Palestine in 1843-44, 12mo, Cloth

Macfarlane's Constantinople in 1828, 2 Vols, 8vo, $^1/_2$ Calf, 1829
Macgillivray's Manual of Geology, 12mo, Cloth, 1840
Marryat's Japhet in Search of a Father, 12mo, Cloth, 1838
Martial Achievements of Gt. Britain & Her Allies from 1799 to 1815, 4to, Coloured, $^1/_2$ Roan
Martin's Philosophical Grammar, 8vo, Calf, 1738
Matthew's Diary of an Invalid, 12mo, Cloth, 1835
Mawe's Lessons on Mineralogy & Geology &c, 8vo, Cloth, 1828
McGowan's Informal Conference, 12mo, $^1/_2$ Calf, 1816
McPherson's Poems of Ossian, 8vo, Calf, 1792
Mears's Voyages &c. &c, 2 Vols, 8vo, $^1/_2$ Calf, 1791
Melmoth's Letters on Pliny, 2 Vols, 12mo, Calf, gilt, 1810
Memoirs of Don Miguel de Godoz by Himself, 2 Vols, 8vo, boards, 1836
Milner's Church History, by Haweis, 8vo, Cloth, 1833
Montagu's (Lady Mary Wortley) Letters & Works, 3 Vols, 8vo, Cloth, 1857
More's (Mrs H.) Sacred Dramas, 18mo, Calf, <u>no date</u>
Muller's Elements of Mathematics, 2 Vols, 8vo, Cloth, 1748

Natural History of Quadrupeds, Birds, Fishes, & Insects, 3 Vols, 8vo, Calf, <u>Edinburgh</u>, 1791
Naval Achievements of Gt. Britain from 1793 to 1817 – Coloured – Imperial 4to, $^1/_2$ Morocco
New Week's Preparation for the Lord's Supper, in two parts, 8vo, Calf, <u>n.d.</u>
Note-Book of an Oxonian, 12mo, boards, 1831

Ovid's Art of Love, 8vo, Calf, 1759 and Metamorphoses by Garth, 12mo, Morocco, 1812
Osbaldiston's British Sportsman, 4to, ¹/₂ Calf, 1792

Paley's Principles of Moral and Political Philosophy, 4to, ¹/₂ Calf, 1786
Papal Usurpation and Tyranny, folio, ¹/₂ Calf, 1712
Payne's Universal Geography, 2 Vols, folio, Calf, 1791
Penny Magazine, 9 Vols, 4to, Cloth, 1832 to 1840
Phillip's Poems & Life by Sewall, 12m, Calf, 1726
Pigot's Directory &c, 3 Vols, 8vo, Calf, & Vol. of Maps &c, 4to, 1826-27
Pope's Homer's Iliad & Odyssey, 4 Vols, 12mo, Morocco, 1824
Principles of Hydropathy (Ben Rhydding) 8vo, Cloth, 1861
Public Charities of Lonsdale North of the Sands, 12mo, ¹/₂ Morocco, 1852 with <u>M.S.</u> notes
    by G.W.
Pulszky's Algeria & the French Conquest, 8vo, Cloth, 1854
Portlock's Voyage round the World, 4to, ¹/₂ Calf, 1789

Raffald's English Housekeeper, 8vo, Calf, 1795
Robertson's Treatise on regimen and Diet, 12mo, Cloth, 1838

Salmon's Critical Review of State Trials & Impeachments for High Treason, folio, Calf, 1738
Scott's (Elizabeth) Selections of British Poetry, 8vo, ¹/₂ Calf, 1823
Scott's Explanatory Notes &c, <u>vide</u> Holy Bible <u>ante</u>
Select Criminal Trials &c, Vol. 1, 8vo, ¹/₂ Calf, 1803
Select British Poems &c, &c, 12mo, Morocco, gilt, 1825
Shakespeare's Dramatic Works with Notes & Life, 8vo, Calf, 125
Spectacle de la Nature, 7 Vols, Calf, 1760-70
Spectator – complete in one Vol, 8vo, Calf, 1823
Sporting Anecdotes, 12mo, ¹/₂ Calf, <u>n.d.</u>
Sporting Magazine, Vols 1 to 54 (wanting 20 & 21, & otherwise imperfect) 8vo, ¹/₂ Calf,
    1792-1819 [Frank got them *pencilled in margin*]
Sterne's (Lawrence) Sentimental Journey, 12mo, Calf, 1754
Storey's (Robert) Lyrical Ballads, 12mo, Cloth, <u>n.d.</u>
Struther's History of Scotland from the Union to 1748, 2 Vols, 8vo, Calf, 1827
Sturm's Reflections on the Works of God, 2 Vols, 18mo, Morocco, 1824
Summer Rambles in the North Islands, 12mo, Calf, 1825
Symons' Practical Gager, 12mo, 1777

Tatler & Guardian, complete in One Vol, 8vo, Calf, gilt, <u>n.d.</u>
Taylor (Jeremy) Great Exemplars of Sanctity & Holy Life, folio, 1792 – Cave's Lives, Acts,
    & Martyrdoms of the Holy Apostles, folio, 1702, bound in One Volume, Calf
Thomas's Historie of Italie, 8vo, Calf, <u>Black Letter</u> (some leaves wanting at the end) 1549
Thompson's Sentimental Gleaner, 8vo, Boards, 1823
Tibbins's French & English Dictionary, 12mo, Morocco, 1839
To-day in Ireland (the Carders &c.), 3 Vols, 8vo, ¹/₂ Calf, 1827
Tuck's Shareholder's Manual, 12mo, Cloth
Two large 4to Cases with divers Pamphlets &c

Universal Magazine,8vo, 1799, No Plates

Valpy's Greek Testament, 12mo, Morocco, 1838 [*marked* Frank]
Vaux's Mathematics for Young Students, 3 Vols, 8vo, Calf, 1709
Voyages of Travels of Parry, Franklin, Ross & Belzoni, 8vo, Calf, 1829
Voyage Pittoresque et Historique de l'Istrie et de la Dalmatie par Cassas et Lavallée, Imperial
    folio, ¹/₂ Calf, Paris, 1802
Voyage Pittoresque de Paris, 3 tomes, 12mo, Calf, 1768-70

Walker's Pronouncing Dictionary of the English Language, 8vo,boards, 1826
Walpole's Catalogue of Noble & Royal Authors of England, 2 Vols, 8vo, ¹/₂ Morocco,
    Edinburgh, 1792
Walsh's Treatise on Diseases of the Heart &c, 8vo, Cloth, 1862
Watkins' Memoirs of Frederick Duke of York and Albany, 8vo, ¹/₂ Calf, 1827
Waverley Novels (Sir Walter Scott), 48 Vols, 12mo, Cloth, 1829-33 [M.W. *in margin*]
Wellington – Life of, 8vo, Cloth, n.d.
Whewell (Professor) on the Principles of English University Education, 8vo, Cloth, 1837
Whiston's Historical Preface to Christianity reviv'd, 8vo, Calf, 1711
Whitelaw's Casquet of Literary Gems, 4 Vols, 12mo, Calf, 1828-29
Whole Duty of Man (The) 8vo, Morocco, Gilt, 1704
Whole Duty of Man (The), 8vo, Calf, 1733
Williams's Life of Alexander the Great, 12mo, Calf, gilt, 1829
Wordsworth's Poems, 2 Vols in one, ¹/₂ Calf, 1807

Young's Night Thoughts, 8vo, Calf, 1768

Zorhlin's Recreations in Geology, 12mo, Calf, 1839

Prints &c. Principally in Painted Frames
(1. Framed. 2. Varnished & framed. 3. Framed & Glazed.)

Large Etchings by Piranesi –
The Capitol, Rome (1)
Castle & Bridge of St. Angelo (1)
The Colloseum (1)
The Vatican &c (1)
Basilica &c (1)
Theatre of Marcella (2)
Portico of Octavio (2)
Ruins of the Amphitheatre (1)
Piazza Monte Cavallo (1)
St. Peter's (1)
Quirinal Palace (1)
Piazza del Popolo (1)
Church of St. Paul (1)

Temple of Bacchus (1)

Palace of the French Academy (1)

The Forum of Nerva (1)

St. Peter's & the Vatican (1)

The Rotunda (1)

Campo Vaccino (2)

Fountain of Michael Angelo (2)

Very large view of the City of Rome by G. V. Conte, 1829 – line – (on twelve sheets), varnished, Oak & gilt frame

Plan of the City of Rome, 1832, on Canvas & Roller

Plan of Venice, 1838, on Canvas & Roller

Costume of Italian Peasants after Pirelli, Coloured (1)

Carnival Ditto ditto (3)

The Pantheon & Trajan's Pillar, Rome – line, by Boydell (1)

Interior of the Pantheon – line – by Boydell (1)

The Bay of Naples near Ginelini (1)

Roman Remains, after Panninni by Major, line (1)

Jupiter & Europa, after Claude, by Vivares, line (3)

Lincoln Cathedral after Burgess by Burgess – line (2)

Ely Cathedral after Burgess by Burgess – line (2)

The Lady Chapel, St Saviour's, Southwark, Exterior by Hawkins, lithograph (1)

The Lady Chapel, St Saviour's, Interior, by Hawkins, lithograph (1)

Return from Labour, after Wheatley by Earlom, Mezzotint (2)

Conjugal Affection after Smirke by Thew, Stipple (2)

St. George's Hall, Liverpool, Lithograph, gilt frame

Balmoral, printed in Colours, small, gilt frame, glazed

Conishead Priory after Harwood, small – line (3)

The Houses of Parliament: outline after Sir Charles Barry, maple & gilt Frame, glazed

The Scott Monument, Edinburgh, line, gilt frame, glazed

Holker Hall, Lithograph, gilt frame glazed

Westmorland Society's School, Lithograph, gilt frame, glazed

Ilam Hall ditto ditto

The Village Festival, after Teniers by Thelot, line (3)

The Jealous Husband, after Teniers by Major, line (1)

The Labratory [sic], after Teniers by Major, line (3)

The Chemist, after Teniers by Major, line (3)

The Cottagers, after Dusart by Brown & Woollett, line (3)

The Jocund Peasants, after Dusart by Brown & Woollett, line (3)

The Misers, after Quintin Matsys, Mezzotint (2)

A Country Attorney & his Clients after Holbein, by Walker, line (3)

A Dutch School, after Jan Steen, by W. Ward, Mezzotint (2)

The Fishery, after Richard Wright by Woollett, line (2)

Installation of Alderman Newnham after Brown by Smith, Stipple (1)

Pointers & Fox &c, Lithograph, Satin-wood frame, glazed

Lucerne – aquatint, coloured, gilt frame

St. Mark's, Venice – two views in one frame – aquatint coloured

Views on the Rhine, three coloured Lithographs, small

Royal Institution, Manchester, line, gilt frame, glazed

The Houses of Parliament, outline, gilt frame, glazed

Waterhead Inn, Conistone, Lithograph (3)

Plan of Liverpool on Canvas & Roller

Peacock's Key to the Scenery surrounding Morecambe Bay, Canvas & Roller

Bradshaw's Map & Sections of British Railways, Canvas & Roller

Richardson's Plan of Westminster Hall & adjacent Public Buildings, Canvas & Roller

Gillies' Plan of Blackburn, Canvas & Roller

Plan & View of Paxton's Palace for the Exhibition of 1851, Canvas & Roller

Whittock's Panoramic View of Jerusalem (3)

Wood's Plan of Kendal, varnished, Canvas & Roller

Hodgson's Map of Westmoreland 1823-25, varnished, Canvas & Roller

Binns' Map of Lancaster, 1821, varnished, Canvas & Roller

Wood's Plan of Ulverstone, 1832, varnished, Canvas & Roller

Maritime Flags of all Nations, varnished, Canvas & Roller

View of the Principal Mountains & Rivers of the World, Canvas & Roller

Joshua commanding the Sun to stand still, after Martini, Mezzotint (2)

Balshazzer's Feast, by J. Martin, Mezzotint (2)

The Deluge by John Martin, Mezzotint (2)

The Passage of the Red Sea, Mezzotint (2)

Moreby Hall near York, lithograph, Coloured, frame gilt & Glazed

The Holy Family, after Raphael, in Colours, frame gilt & glazed

Portrait of Queen Victoria, anaglyptograph, maple gilt & glazed

Prince Albert, Lithograph by R. J. Lane, Oak & Gilt frame, glazed

Sir Robert Clayton, full length, after Illidge by Ward, Mezzotint, Gilt Frame, glazed

John Bolton Esqre Storrs Hall, Lithograph, Maple & Gilt

Adam Cotton Esqre after Illidge by Geller, Mezzotint, Maple & Gilt

The Duke of Devonshire, lithograph, Maple & Gilt

The Earl of Lonsdale when Viscount Lowther, after J. Ward by W. Ward, Mezzotint, Gilt

The Earl of Lonsdale, as above, Oak frame

John Wakefield Esquire, after Bowness by Bellini, Mezzotint, Gilt

Bishop Watson after Romney by Meyer, Stipple (2)

The Rent-day, after Sir D. Wilkie by Jazet, Mez[zotint] (3)

Blind Man's Buff, after Wilkie by Jazet, Mezzotint (3)

Village Politicians after Wilkie by Raimbach, line (3)

The Rabbit on the Wall, Wilkie by Burnet, line (3)

View in Lombardy after Prout, Coloured (3)

Portfolio containing 220 Engravings, various, comprising Architectural, Historical, Portrait
   & Landscape Subjects – mounted on leaves, $^1/_2$ Calf

Portfolio containing Forty-six plans of various Cities of the World and Fifty Maps & Plans,
   various

Portfolio containing divers Subjects from the "Illustrated London News" – two Views of

Scarborough, lithograph, two photographic Views of Scarbro' – Photographic & Lithographic Views of Eller How &c. &c – also thirty-seven various drawings by Francis Webster &c. &c. &c.

Portfolio containing numerous Select cuttings from the "Illustrated London News" – fifty-six Topographical Engravings, twenty-one various Etchings – four Engravings after Teniers, & three small port-folios – also fifty Pencil Drawings, early studies of the late Mr. W. &c. &c. &c.

Water-colour Drawings

Perspective Elevation of Underley Hall by Richard Stirzaker, $43^1/2$ x $29^1/2$, varnished in Painted & Gilt Frame

Ditto ditto ditto, $43^1/2$ x $29^1/2$, Varnished in Painted & Gilt Frame

Ditto ditto ditto, 25 x 16, Gilt frame

Ditto ditto ditto, 25 x 16, glazed in Rosewood & Gilt Frame

Distant View of Underley Hall & Park by Richard Stirzaker, 19 x $13^3/4$, glazed in Rosewood & Gilt Frame

Lancaster Castle, by Richard Stirzaker, 26 x 19, varnished – Gilt Frame

The Acanthus, oak painted Frame – glazed

The Islands on Derwent-Water, Skiddaw &c, by Robert Webster, glazed, painted frame

Thirlmere by Robert Webster, glazed, painted frame

Loughrigg Tarn & Windermere by Robert Webster, painted frame

Design for Mansion for Richard North, Esquire, $26^1/2$ x 8, gilt frame

Ditto ditto, $26^1/2$ x 11, gilt frame

Ditto ditto, 24 x 10, gilt frame

Ditto ditto, $25^1/2$ x $11^1/2$, gilt frame

Ditto ditto, 26 x 11, gilt frame

Design for Thurland Castle, 24 x $9^1/2$, gilt frame

Ditto ditto, $25^1/2$ x 10, gilt frame

Design for Castellated Mansion, 19_ x 10, gilt frame

Ditto ditto, $27^1/2$ x $11^1/2$, gilt frame

Design for a Mansion, $20^1/2$ x $6^1/2$, gilt frame

Design for Castellated Mansion, $15^1/2$ x 9, gilt frame

Ditto ditto, $27^1/2$ x $11^1/2$, gilt frame

Ditto [Thurland added in pencil], 25 x $11^1/2$, gilt frame

Ditto [Thurland Castle added in pencil], 25 x $12^3/4$, gilt frame

Ditto [Mansion added in pencil], $19^1/4$ x 9, gilt frame

Ditto [Richard North added in pencil], $13^1/4$ x $7^1/2$, gilt frame

Design for Cumberland & Westmorland Lunatic Asylum – East Elevation – $26^1/2$ x $13^1/2$, gilt frame

Ditto ditto – South Elevation, 38 x 13, gilt frame

Ditto ditto – West Elevation, $26^1/2$ x 14, gilt frame

Design for the Bank of Westmoreland, $7^1/2$ x $10^3/4$, gilt frame

View of Bellefield, Windermere, $18^1/4$ x 8, gilt frame

View of Forest-Side, Grasmere, 13 x 9, gilt frame

Design for Thurland Castle, $25^1/2$ x 9, gilt frame

Ditto ditto, 24 x 7^1/$_2$, gilt frame
Ditto ditto, 25 x 15^1/$_2$, gilt frame
View of Harrington House, Kensington Palace Gardens, 13 x 11, gilt frame
View of Eller How (general view) by Richard Stirzaker, Rosewood (Ser.) frame
Interior of a Crypt, 5^1/$_2$ x 3^3/$_4$, Oak frame, glazed [Indian Ink, Black Lead &c *added in pencil*]
The Braddyll Arms, Emblazoned, gilt frame, glazed

Design for Rigmaden Park, 18^1/$_2$ x 9^1/$_2$, gilt frame [Indian Ink, Black Lead *added in pencil*]
Design for Hutton Hall, Cumberland (G.W. 1830), gilt frame
View of Water Eaton House, Oxfordshire, by J. Buckler, 10 x 7^1/$_2$, gilt frame
Evercreech Park House, Exterior, by J. Buckler, 11^1/$_2$ x 8^1/$_4$, gilt frame
Ditto ditto, Interior, by J. Buckler, 11^3/$_4$ x 8^3/$_4$, gilt frame
Bramshill House, by J. Buckler, 12^1/$_4$ x 8^1/$_2$, gilt frame
The Terrace at Bramshill, after Nash, 15 x 11^1/$_2$, gilt frame
View of Eller How, on tinted paper, 12 x 7^1/$_2$, gilt frame
Ditto ditto ditto, 12 x 8^1/$_2$, gilt frame
Venetian Palace & Roman Ruins in circular twin mounts, 17^1/$_2$ x 10^1/$_2$, gilt frame
Constantinople (Water Colour), 12 x 7, maple frame
Mosque & Tomb (Water Colour), 9 x 5^1/$_2$, gilt frame
Neapolitan Peasant family (1846) by Jane Preston, 12 x 9^3/$_4$, gilt frame
Design for a Country Church (pen & ink), 8^3/$_4$ x 11, gilt frame
Ditto ditto ditto, 8^1/$_2$ x 12, gilt frame
Ditto ditto ditto, 9 x 10^3/$_4$, gilt frame
View of Eller How, pen & ink, 13^1/$_4$ x 9, gilt frame

Port-folio containing seventeen large Pencil Drawings – Views in the Lake District – by Robert Webster
Large bound Portfolio containing Plans, Elevations, & Sections of Mansions, Churches, &c. &c. designed by the late Mr. Webster – including Eshton Hall, Underley Park, Holker Hall, Moreton Hall, &c. &c. – 54 leaves, Mounted both both [*sic*] sides – ^{1}/$_2$ Calf & Cloth – labelled "Architectural Tracings"
Large Bound Portfolio containing Plans, Elevations & Sections of Mansions, Villas, &c. &c. designed by the late Mr. Webster including Graythwaite Hall, Underley Hall, &c. &c. & numerous engraved Views – 48 leaves mounted both side – ^{1}/$_2$ Calf & Cloth, with leather straps & buckles – labelled "Architectural Drawings"
Large [bound *deleted*] Portfolio containing Sketches, Plans, & Details of various Buildings designed by the late Mr. Webster – 416 – also 40 others by Sir Jefrey Wyatville and Sir Robert Smirke
Large Portfolio containing 222 Plans & Details of Buildings erected under the Superintendence of the late Mr. Webster
Portfolio containing 113 Plans & Details of divers Churches, Chapels, Schools, & Prisons designed by the late Mr. Webster
Large Portfolio, ^{1}/$_2$ bound in Calf containing 201 Plans and Elevations designed by the late Mr Webster, mounted on 110 pages
Large bound Portfolio containing 480 Plans, Elevations, & Details of various Buildings

designed by the late Mr. Webster, mounted on Cartridge Paper – $^1/_2$ Morocco with straps & buckles

Large bound Portfolio containing 435 of Plans, Elevations, & Details of various Buildings in the North of England designed by the late Mr. Webster, mounted on Cartridge Paper, $^1/_2$ Rough Calf with straps & buckles – Labelled "Architectural Tracings 4"

Box containing 30 Plans & Elevations &c. of various Asylums and Workhouses by the late Mr. W.

Hair Trunk containing Sketch-Books, Architectural Correspondence, Specifications and Estimates – Family Pedigrees & Portfolio with thirty Architectural Drawings in Pen & Ink

Twenty-two Working Drawings of Sand Area, Kendal, with Boards and <u>two</u> ditto for Singleton Park

Ten Working Drawings for Holker Hall – Earl of Burlington – with Boards

Seventy-four Working Drawings, Elevations &c. of Whittington Hall – Thomas Greene Esquire – with Boards

Thirty-eight Working Drawings of Ingfield, Settle – Revd. H.J. Swale – with Boards

Twenty-four Working Drawings &c. Bank of Westmoreland, Kendal, with Boards

Six Working Drawings & Elevations Dowker's Hospital, Kendal, with Boards

Nine Working Drawings &c. &c. Bowness School, Windermere with Boards

Twenty Working Drawings, Elevations & Sections – St. Thomas's Church & School, Kendal with Boards

One hundred & ninety-three Working Drawings &c. &c. – Conishead Priory – T. R. G. Braddyll Esq. – with Boards

Twenty-six Working Drawings &c. St George's Church, Kendal with Boards

Forty-six Working Drawings &c. Bellefield, Windermere – the Baroness de Sternberg with Boards

Thirty Working Drawings &c. &c. Divers County Bridges with Boards

Thirty-five Working Drawings &c. Whitehall Buildings, Kendal with Boards

Ninety six Working Drawings &c. &c. Underley Hall, Westmoreland – Alexander Nowell Esquire with Boards

Twenty Plans, Sketches, Working Drawings &c. – Black Rock – with Boards

Twelve Working Drawings &c. &c. Summerfield, Kirkby Lonsdale with Boards

Three Working Plans, Elevations &c. Heversham Vicarage – with Boards

Four Working Drawings & Elevations for Farm House &c. at Murley Moss, Kendal – Alderman Thompson, with Boards

Four Plans, Elevations &c. of Villa Residence at Crooklands – with Boards

Two Plans, Elevations &c. for old Hutton Parsonage, with Boards

Two Plans &c. &c. – House of Industry, Giggleswick with Boards

Two plans &c. for alterations at Slyne R. B. Peacock Esquire – with Boards

Two plans, Elevations &c. – Marble Works &c. Kendal with Boards

Two Plans, Elevations &c. Mr. Webster's House, Kent Terrace with Boards

Two Working Drawings &c. &c. another House – Kent Terrace with boards

Two Plans, Elevations & Working Drawings for Warehouse in Kendal – Mr. H. Airey with Boards

Two Plans & Elevation Cottages, Angel Inn Yard, Kendal with Boards

One Sheet of Working Drawings Grimeshill, Westmoreland W. Moore, Esquire with Boards

Paintings – Oil

Noah & his family sacrificing after the Deluge (of one of the Schools of Italy) artist unknown – 48^1/$_2$ x 39^1/$_2$ Gilt frame

Head of King Lear (artist unknown) (Query Barrow of Eccleston?) 12 x 15 painted frame

Holy Family after Baroccio, 10 x 12 (on panel) Gilt frame

Virgin & Child after Baroccio 10 x 12 (on Copper) Gilt frame [M.W. *in margin*]

Watts' Field, on the Kent, near Kendal (Query Mason?) artist not known

An Italian City – not known – Painted & Gilt frame

Portrait (^{3}/$_4$) of George Webster Esq. By James Ward, 25 x 30, Gilt frame

Portrait (^{3}/$_4$) of Francis Webster Esq. By James Ward 1823, 25 x 30 Gilt frame

[*last two items marked* specifically bequeathed Mrs. W; M.W. *in margin*]

Peasant Girl, full length. Unknown (Query Hurlstone?) 33 x 48 Gilt frame

Portrait (^{3}/$_4$) of – Lowry, Esquire by William Higgins, 1799, 25 x 30 Gilt frame

Portrait (^{3}/$_4$) of Mrs. Lowry by W. Higgins – 25 x 30. Gilt frame

[*last two items marked* specifically bequeathed Mrs. W]

Gale at Sea by J. W. Carmichael painted in 1840 – 36 x 24 Gilt Frame [M.W. *in margin*]

Dead Calm by J. W. Carmichael painted in 1840 – 36 x 24 Gilt frame [M.W. *in margin*]

Miniature Portrait of Henry VIII, on Copper, unknown, gilt frame

Head of an Old Woman, 13^1/$_2$ x 18 By Jacob Jordaens – Gilt frame

Portrait of Pope Sixtus V. ^{1}/$_2$ <u>length</u> after Raphael by Mazzolini of Rome – 33 x 41. Gilt frame

Judith with the Head of Holfernes by Guercino 38 x 50 Gilt frame

Il Fornarini after Raphael 34^1/$_2$ x 40^1/$_2$ Gilt frame

Head of Christ crowned with Thorns after Coreggio 21 x 26 Gilt frame

St. Cecilia – after Romanelli. 16 x 21 Gilt frame [M.W. *in margin*]

Roman Ruins with Infant procession Floral wreaths & goat 19 x 24 Gilt frame

The Rabbit – Flowers &c. 54 x 34 Oak & Gilt frame

Head of a Madonna after Sasso Ferrato painted in the school of the Carracci – 14 x 18 Gilt frame [M.W. *in margin*]

Interior of Hall, Conishead Priory by Joseph Tuer – gilt frame [M.W. *in margin*]

View of Conishead Priory by Joseph Tuer – gilt frame [M.W. *in margin*]

Rape of the Sabine Women after Lucca Giordano 30 x 25 Gilt frame

View of the City of Bath 39 x 28 after Linton ? – painted frame

Portrait of Beatrice Cenci. 20 x 24 after [*blank*] Gilt frame [M.W. *in margin*]

Portrait of Mrs. Robinson in Black Mantle &c. by Romney. 20 x 30. Gilt frame [M.W. *in margin*]

Moonlight Scene. Coast of Scotland 8^1/$_2$ x 6^1/$_2$. Gilt frame

Moonlight Scene. Coast of Scotland (Companion Picture) 8^1/$_2$ x 6^1/$_2$ gilt frame

Magdalen after [*blank*] 23 x 29 gilt frame

Portrait of Raphael from a Picture painted by himself in 1518. 23 x 29. Gilt frame

Tempera

Entrance to the Great Harbour at Malta by Louis Taffien – maple & gilt frame – glazed

View in Switzerland 29 x 21^1/$_2$ maple & gilt frame

View of the City & Bay of Naples <u>three</u> – each 25 x 16 painted & gilt frames

Five Views in the Bay of Naples each 9 x 6. Painted & Gilt frames
Eight Views near Naples – each 11¹/₂ x 7³/₄ in two frames
Two Neapolitan Scenes 8¹/₄ x 5³/₄ painted & Gilt frame
Eruption of a Volcano 25 x 17 Painted & Gilt frame
Eruption of Vesuvius – surrounded by sixteen other Views – small – Painted & Gilt frame

Glass

Two painted-glass pannels – Views on the Rhine
Stained glass – Knight at Devotion
Two other paintings on glass
Two specimens of Stained glass

Articles of Vertu &c. &c

Head of Raphael – S.T. Porcelain
Virgin, Infant Saviour & St. John – S.T. Porcelain
Head of Christ after Guido – S.T. Porcelain
Age after Greuze – S.T. Porcelain
Youth Ditto – S.T. Porcelain

Bronzed Plaster Bust – "Inigo Jones"
Head of "Canova's Venus" – plaster
Ditto of Ditto's "Paris" – ditto
Bust of General [blank] – plaster-bronzed
Antique Head of Roman Vestal in Terra Cotta
Figure of a Water Nymph – plaster bronzed
Bas-relief Tablet "the Last Supper" plaster-bronzed

Miniature Bust – George Webster Esq. Of Statuary Marble – sculptured in Rome [specifically bequeathed Mrs. W; M.W. *in margin by this and next three items*]
Bust of Sir Walter Scott, 31in. high after Chantry [*sic*] – in Statuary Marble
Bust of George IV. (30 in. high) after Chantrey – Statuary Marble
Antique Bust. Roman Emperor 30 in. high. Statuary Marble, on Dove Pedestal 46 in. high
Florentine Statuette of Napleon Bonaparte (broken) 8 in. high
Statuette Group "Roman Gladiators" of Florentine Marble on Pedestal with black marble plinth – extreme height 18 in. & Florentine glass shade
Florentine Statuette Group of "the Graces" supporting Flower Basket – on fluted pedestal – extreme height 21 in.
Model of the Tomb of [blank] of Sienna Marble [M.W. *in margin*]
Model of the Tomb of Scipio
Antique Roman Sculptured Monument of Marble (with incised Inscription) 24 x 15
Ditto ditto 12 x 13
Modern Sculptured Monumental Figure of Statuary Marble "To F.W." 5 ft.6 in. high

Four Veined Marble Vases 31 x 26
Two Ditto 33 x 28

Two ditto 28 [*sic*]
Two ditto 30 [*sic*]
Six ditto 22 x 18

Barberini Vase – Iron – 33 x 23
Sculptured Pedestal (Sandstone) and Sun Dial
A Triton of sculptured marble
Terra Cotta Statue "Sir Jeffrey Hudson"
Painted Plaster Figure "Pomona"
Mutilated figure – Terra Cotta

Two Verde-antique Vases with sculptured vine-leaf wreaths $16^{1}/_{2}$ x 10 – on white pannelled
  pedestals with Black Plinths [M.W. *in margin*]
Verde-antique Tazza – $9^{3}/_{4}$ x 10 – on White Statuary Pedestal 9 in. high [M.W. *in margin*]
Cup & Dish of Verde-antique
Classical-shaped Cup of Black Marble $7^{1}/_{4}$ x $5^{1}/_{4}$ with White Marble Plinth
Lava Tazza on various Marble Pedestal
Oval-shaped Verde-antique Tazza with Sculptured ornaments $13^{1}/_{2}$ in. high
Circular Verde-antique Tazza 10 in. high – $12^{1}/_{2}$ diameter – on Pedestal & Plinth – extreme
  height 20 in.
Two Small Sculptured Dogs
Fluted Oval-shaped Verde-antique Tazza with Birds – on White marble plinth – extreme
  height $14^{1}/_{2}$ in.
White Marble Vase on pannelled Pedestal with Black Plinth – extreme height $21^{1}/_{2}$ in. $7^{1}/_{2}$
  diameter and glass shade
Sienna Laver on tripod and various Marble Pedestal & Plinth [M.W. *in margin*]
Tazza of Derbyshire Spar 16 in diameter on Black & White Marble Pedestal – extreme height
  16 inches
Italian Marble Tazza. 8 in. high 11 in. diameter on Black marble Pedestal $6^{1}/_{2}$ high [M.W. *in
  margin*]
Two Sculptured Florentine Vases with Birds – $10^{1}/_{2}$ x 11. And two French glass shades
Mosaic Table 22 in. diameter on carved Rosewood Pillar & Block
Scagliola Table (Italian Fisherman) $33^{1}/_{2}$ diameter on inlaid Mahogany Pillar & Block
Mosaic Table 34 in diameter on carved Rosewood Pillar & Block [M.W. *in margin*]
Mosaic Table on Oak with twisted pillar, block & claws
Sienna Marble Table $23^{1}/_{2}$ diameter on ornamental Iron Supporter
Large Statuary-Porcelain Jug with group of "Silenus & Bacchus" in alto relief
Smaller ditto ditto ditto [M.W. *in margin by last two items*]
Three small sculptured Dogs on various marble plinths
 Portland Vase – copy in plaster
Two large Acanthus Brackets – plaster – painted
Ancient Carved Cherubim Bracket
Two Bacchanal Brackets plaster – painted
Two Virgin Ditto ditto
Two other Ditto Ditto

Two other Ditto ditto

Two ditto Ditto (smaller) ditto

Portion of an Antique Grecian Sculptured Capital

Piece of Ancient Roman Tesselated Pavement 19 x 19

Cast from an Ancient Egyptian Tablet

Specimen of Mural Decoration from the Alhambra – a large Painted & Gilt Panel

Another Panel – small – from the same Palace

Another Panel – Drab painted in gilt frame – from the same

Carved Oak Group "Christ & the Maries" – 24 in. high – in full relief [M.W. *in margin*]

Carved Oak Group "The Entombment" 22 in. high in full relief [M.W. *in margin*]

Bust of W. Hogarth – Plaster – Bronzed

Bust of Virgil Plaster. Bronzed

Portion of a Carved antique Frieze

Architectural Ornament in Cast Iron

Bronze Lizzard

Two Small Tazzi of Derbyshire Spar

Antique Bronze Incense-Burner on Various-Marble Pedestal extreme height $8^{3}/_{4}$ in.

Stork, Tortoise, & Snake – Bronze – on Various-marble Pedestal

Small Bronze Vase

Pair of small Bronze Lachrymatories on Marble Pedestals

Bronze Laver with carved Rosewood stand

Chinese Bronze Dog

Model of Temple of Tivoli Bronze

Sportive Lizzards in Bronze

Two Imitation Bronze Incense Burners

Two Derbyshire Paper-weights with Landscape Etchings after Sir Francis Chantrey

Antique Roman Cinerary Urn

Ancient Bronze Medallion – Birkeymer

Ditto Medal Albert Durer

Ditto ditto Henry IV &c.

Ditto ditto Charles V

Mahogany framed glazed Case containing Fifty specimens of various Marbles and precious stones

Ditto ditto containing Sixty specimens of British and Foreign Marbles – various

Thirty-nine specimens of Marbles various

Eight gilt Frames containing two hundred & fifty two specimens of Marbles from all parts of the world

Drawer (contents of) in Maple Cabinet Bookcase viz. Twenty-six Fossils from various geological formations; five pieces of Roman Tessera; pot of divers pebbles; & twenty recent Shells, univalve & bivalve

Ditto Fifty Fossils, various, & fifteen pieces of Silica, various

Ditto Forty Fossils, various, principally from Chalk

Ditto Thirty Fossils, various, principally from Coal

Ditto One hundred & fifty Fossil Shells from Chalk & Oolite

Ditto Fifty-four Fossils, various, principally from Limestone

Ditto about Sixty Fossils, various, from Limestone, & Chalk

Ditto Forty-six Fossil & Recent Teeth of animals

Ditto Twenty specimens of Marbles from Greece, Asia minor, &c

Ditto Thirty-five Pebbles, Flints, Granites, Stone from the Tomb of the Kings of Jerusalem, & Fossils from Ryde

Ditto Twenty-seven various Marbles from Africa & divers specimens of Mica, Flints, & Ores

Ditto Five Specimens of Marbles various

Ditto Forty various Pebbles from Cairo, Athens, Malta &c. Crystals from Brazil &c. Hematite Iron Ore; and Relics from from [sic] the Palace of the Caesars, & the Circus of Romulus at Rome

Ditto Fifteen Specimens of Marbles

Ditto Fifty stones from Egypt, Asia Minor, and Rome

Drawer, Contents of, – Fourteen fragments from the Temple of Jupiter Tonans &c. &c. at Rome

Ditto Ninety various Ores & Crystals

Ditto Eighteen Marbles & Crystals

Ditto Six Pebbles, Stalactites, & numerous Fossil Shells

Ditto Sixteen "samples" of Carrara Marble

Glazed Oak Case in three compartments $86^{1}/_{2}$ x 10 in. containing Seven Egyptian Household Deities, Ten Etruscan & Roman Vessels, Numerous Roman Tessera stones, Mosaic Shield, Twelve specimens of Marbles, Black Marble Paper Weight curiously engraved, Three Intaglio Seals, Four Small Bronze Trays

Two other Egyptian Household Deities

Twenty Various Fossil Formations

Tooth of Hippopotamus

Beautifully preserved Head of Roe-buck

Deer's foot Snuff-box

Deer's hoof Snuff-box

Mauchline Snuff-box with Portrait of George IV

"Hindoo Deity" – and a "Holy Friar"

Snuff-box of Oak from York-minster with Silver Medallion Inscription

Small glazed Oak Case containing divers specimens of Conchology (Cones, Cowries, Razors &c. &c.) and six specimens of Foreign marbles

Small glazed Oak Case – containing Fossil & Recent Shells & sundry specimens of Granite & Flint

Glazed Case – containing numerous English & Foreign Birds & Quadrupeds

Preserved Weasel & Robin

Numerous specimens of Septaria, Crystallized Spar, Fossil Plants, Ores, & other Mineral and Geological formations

A few specimens of Conchology including Bulla, Cama, Cone, Murex, Pearl Oyster (with curiously engraved representation of "the Nativity") Spider &c.

Specimens of Coral, Madripore, and Sundry Zoophytes

Mahogany Camera Obscura

Gothic carved Oak Panel (Hearts & Darts)

Five Grecian Running Mouldings in ebonized frames

Four Ditto ditto unframed

Specimen of Leather Moulding

Twelve Papier-maché Ornaments, various

Large Alto-relief Tablet "The Fall of Phaeton" – Painted & Gilt frame

Sculptured Medallion (Roman Emperor) Sienna on Black ground [M.W. *in margin*]

Sculptured Medallion (Roman Empress) Sienna on Black ground [M.W. *in margin*]

Medallion of Napoleon & Marie Louise gilt frame

Bas-relief Monkey & Cats

Mosaic Tablet. Fox & Hounds in gilt frame

Collection of 200 Casts from Gems illustrating the History of Rome – four Cabinet Cases ¹/₂ bound Vellum [M.W. *in margin*]

Collection of 96 Medallions of Illustrious Men in four Cabinet Cases ¹/₂ bound Vellum [M.W. *in margin*]

Collection of 174 Casts from Gems Antique & Modern – five Cabinet Cases ¹/₂ bound Vellum [M.W. *in margin*]

Photograph, large size. Articles of Vertu gilt frame

Ditto Birthwaite Church

Ditto Bellefield

Ditto Eller How

Ditto Ditto

Ditto Mansion of [*blank*]

Ditto Late Mr. Webster

Ditto Ditto

Ditto Ditto

Ditto Mrs. Webster

Ditto Late Mr. Webster [*last five items marked* specifically bequeathed Mrs. W]

Daguerreotype The Pantheon

Rosewood Stereoscope on Brass stand

Fifty Stereographs in Mahogany Case

Eighteen Ditto in Ditto

Musical Box

Compound Microscope

Telescope

Double-barrelled Pistol

Single dito

Gun [*this section marked* specifically bequeathed F.W.]

Bronze Model of Ancient Roman Biga on Marble Plinth [*marked* specifically bequeathed T.U. Esq.

Small Cabinet of Coins & medals principally third Roman Brass and English provincial Copper Tokens

Small Cabinet of Gems & antiquities – fragments collected by the late Mr. Webster on travelling abroad [*last two items marked* specifically bequeathed J.S. Esq.]

Glazed Cabinet with Cameo Heads (Imitations by Wedgwood) of ancient authors &c [*marked* specifically bequeathed R.M. Esq.]

Stone Weapon of the Ancient Britons
Ancient Stone Axe
English Bow & Arrow
Ancient Iron Mace
Pole-axe or Ancient Battle-Axe
Ancient Halbert
Pair of Steel-plate Gauntlets
Gorget richly ornamented with Battle-piece in bas-relief
Three Ancient Scottish Swords
Ancient Short-sword
Two pairs of Spanish Pistols
Persian Sword & Scabbard
Small Cannon
Hazel Walking-stick with damascened Rapier
Indian Bow and Arrows
Four long Bush Arrows
War axe from New Zealand

Swiss Mountaineering Companions (<u>Leather & Tin</u>)
Four Tyrolese Pipes
Turkish Pipe and two flexible smoking tubes
Curious Neapolitan Drinking-Vessel of baked clay
Hunter's Knife with ornamental Ivory handle
Game-bag & two Leather Satchels

Pair of Horns of the Ibex
Two large Buffalo-horns polished

Large Orbicular Mirror
Valued at £766 11s. 6d.

Wearing Apparel

Three Coats
Five Waistcoats
Four Trousers
Two Overcoats
Two dressing-gowns
Twelve Shirts & sundry Linen
Gloves, Hose, and Flannels
Silk Pocket Handkerchiefs
Sundries

Three Hats & divers Caps
Boots, Shoes, and Slippers, seven pairs
Valued at £8 10s. 0d.
[*this section marked* specifically bequeathed Mrs. W]

Jewels, Trinkets, and Ornaments of the Person

Gold Watch & Appendages
Three Pins – various
One Gold Ring
Gold & Cornelian Seal
Derbyshire Card tray & sundry Amulets
Pocket Compass by Watkins & Hill
Reading Lens
Card Rack & Pencil Case
Valued at £16 1s. 0d.
[*this section marked* specifically bequeathed Mrs. W]

Wines & Other Liquors

Two & a half dozens Port Wine
Two dozens Sherry
Six bottles Moselle
Three bottles Champagne
2 Bottles Brandy
18 Gallons Ale
Valued at £7 16s. 0d.
[*this section marked* specifically bequeathed Mrs. W]

Horses & Carriages

Black Horse – aged [*blank*]
Dun Pony – aged 20 years [*marked* specifically bequeathed Mrs. W]
Covered Car
Pony Phaeton and Harness [*marked* specifically bequeathed Mrs. W]
Carriage "set"
Set of Carriage Harness
Hackney Saddle
Side Saddle
Two Bridles
Sundry Saddles & Harness
Divers Stable Implements
Valued at £39 12s. 0d.

Farming Stock & Implements of Husbandry and Gardening

Live Stock – <u>Nil</u>
Husbandry Cart
Field Roller
Two Sets of Husbandry Harness
Hand Water-cart
Two Ladders
Provender Chest
Sundries

Three three-sheet Hot-bed frames
Two one-sheet Ditto
Twenty-six large Garden Pots with Plants
Two Brass Syringes
Four-hundred Plants & Pots
Twelve Tubs with Plants
Two Ornamental Iron Garden Chairs
Fifteen Iron Hurdles
Garden Roller
Four Chair-seats on folding Iron frames
Plain Iron Chairs
Wooden-framed Garden Chair
Painted Table & Garden Seat
Iron Foot-scraper
Four Wire-wrought Flower Baskets

Boat & pair of Oars
Bucket & Baling Pot

Two Wheelbarrows
Three Garden Spades
Four Bill-hooks
Two Wire-riddles
Two Garden-spades
Two   "   forks
Three Scythes &c.
Two Daisy-rakes
Six Iron & wooden Rakes
Hoes, Forks, Trowels & sundries
Three Pick-axes
Mattock
Cross-cut Saw
Three Hand-saws
Pruning Hook

Two pairs Pruning Scissors
Two   "   "   Shears
Three "   Hedging Shears
Three Pruning Hooks
Two felling axes
Two Gavelocks
Hammers, Pincers, & divers Tools
Nest of Nine seed-drawers
Six long Ladders
Four tall folding Step Ladders
Short Deal Step-ladder
Three long Hooks
Six Watering Cans – various
Two gross Earthenware Pots
Dog Kennel
Sundries not otherwise named including all remaining Garden moveables
Valued at £65 18s. 6d.

Abstract of the foregoing Valuation

Household Furniture & Effects p.p. 1 to 23   Valued at 424. 19. 6
Plate, Linen, & China &c. p.p. 24 to 28   Valued at 104. 8.
Books, Prints, Pictures, and Articles of Vertu p.p. 29 to 83   Valued at 766. 11. 6
Wearing Apparel p. 84   Valued at 8. 10
Jewels, Trinkets, & Ornaments of the Person p. 84   Valued at 16. 1
Wine and Other Liquors p. 85   Valued at 32. 12.
Farming Stock & Implements of Husbandry & Gardening &c. &c. &c.
p.p. 86 & 87   Valued at 65. 18. 6
                                                                                  _____
                                                                                  Total Valuation £1433. 16. 6

(One Thousand, four hundred and thirty-three Pounds, sixteen shillings, and sixpence)
                                                                                                    John Burton
                                                                                                    Appraiser

Appendix III

The Lowly Dwelling of
William Wordsworth Esq[re]
by
Angus Taylor

Reprinted by kind permission and with a few corrections, from The Georgian Group Journal, vii, 1997, pp. 43-55.

I N 1825, at the age of fifty-five, William Wordsworth decided to build a house for his family at Rydal in Westmorland. For twenty-five years they had lived in Grasmere searching for a piece of land on which to build. They acquired several, but built on none, and for the last twelve years had lived comfortably at Rydal Mount, Rydal, a house rented from Lady le Fleming of Rydal Old Hall. In 1825 there were rumours that the Mount was needed for Mrs Hudleston, Lady le Fleming's sister. Wordsworth's reaction was to commission designs from George Webster of Kendal for a new house to be built on an adjacent plot known as The Rash. These designs were unknown until 1973 when a group of four was lent by the Wordsworth Trust to *The Websters of Kendal* exhibition held at Abbot Hall, Kendal. What follows is an attempt to show how the poet's passionately held views on building in the Lakes is exemplified in these designs[1] and how Webster's co-operation with the poet affected his future practice.

In the twelve years after he left Hawkshead Grammar School for Cambridge in 1787 Wordsworth was in the lakes briefly and infrequently. In 1799 he came with Samuel Taylor Coleridge and his brother John on a walking tour. When the party reached Grasmere he at once decided to build a house. 'You will think my idea a mad one but I have thought of building a house by the lakeside' he wrote to his sister Dorothy on 8 November. In the same letter he mentioned 'an empty house . . . which we might take'.[2] This was Dove Cottage, where they were indeed installed two months later. The ideal of building remained, however, and in the next four years he acquired three small estates.[3] No building materialised. In 1802 Wordsworth married Mary Hutchinson and soon Dove Cottage became too small for family and friends.[4] The only available house was Allan Bank which they had execrated daily as it rose over the church tower.[5] In 1811 its builders, the Crumps,[6] were ready to move in and the Wordsworths moved to the restored Rectory – the Rector living in Langdale.[7] This was disastrous; in the two years they were here they lost two children.[8] Then in 1813 Rydal

Mount became vacant.[9] Taking it meant leaving Grasmere, but from the first they liked the house, its garden and surroundings.[10]

In these years the Wordsworth had considered building four times.[11] They had looked at four houses from Troutbeck (Julius Caesar Ibbetson's)[12] to the village of Bouth between Lake Windermere and Morecambe Bay.[13] Had Wordsworth's 'mad' plan of 1799 been realised what would the cottage have been like? At this time he had formulated no principles about building in Lakeland and it may have been the dismay he felt on returning after a long absence which led to his doing so. It was Coleridge's first visit, but they both excoriated the new buildings. They were 'much disgusted with the New Erections and objects about Windermere'.[14] The whiteness of Rydal Hall was 'a trespass on the eye' and 'Mr Law's White Palace – a bitch'.[15] The smart Assembly-Room at Hawkshead 'perk'd and flair'd with wash and roughcast'.[16] The list suggests what Wordsworth's house would *not* have been like. The writings which present his ideas most completely on how best to build in the Lake District are *Select Views* of 1810, an album of generalised views by the Rev. J. Wilkinson for which Wordsworth wrote a commentary (towards which he later felt disgust),[17] and the *Guide through the District of the Lakes in the North of England* which evolved from it in 1820.[18] A letter to his friend Sir George Beaumont of 17th October 1805,[19] the *Poetic Epistle* dedicated to Beaumont of 1811[20] and the letters of the family and their friends provide further evidence.

Wordsworth's own experience of building was limited to slight timber constructions in his gardens.[21] He made grassy terraces. He had given advice on planting at Allan Bank to his landlord[22] and designed the Winter Garden at Coleorton, Beaumont's seat in Leicestershire.[23] The Beaumonts spent much of their time in the Lakes[24] and when Sir George Beaumont bought Loughrigg Tarn and planned a summer residence there,[25] Wordsworth saw a vision of the house, 'such a residence as is alluded to in the *Epistle*'.

> . . . the few grey cabins rose
> That yet disturb not its concealed repose
> . . . one chimney smoking and its azure wreath,
> . . . a glimpse I caught of that Abode, by Thee
> Designed to rise in humble privacy,
> A lowly dwelling here to be outspread,
> Like a small hamlet with its bashfull head
> Half hid in native trees . . .

The poem continues 'Alas 'tis not, nor ever was'[26] and in a note of 1841 Wordsworth regretted that 'local untowardness', emanating from Sir Michael le Fleming of Rydal Hall (who did not want a rival baronet or knight in his 'Lordship') prevented further progress,[27] for Wordsworth would have known that Beaumont would seek his advice at every turn in building an example for others to follow. Thus he lost the opportunity to demonstrate 'how building with all the accommodations modern Society requires might be introduced into the most secluded parts of this country without injuring their natural character'.[28]

The nucleus of Rydal Mount is an old gabled farmhouse, Keens, with a version of Wordsworth's favourite chimney, a cylinder on a square base. To this Michael Knott, married to a le Fleming and agent to the Rydal estate, added a wing with sashed windows in the mid-eighteenth century, turning it into a gentleman's resident and renaming it High House. A Liverpool family, the Norths, bought it in 1803 and called it Rydal Mount. They left in 1813 having sold the house to Lady le Fleming.

Just below the garden of the Mount was a field called the Rash. In 1825 the owner would sell it for £300, 'three times its value',[29] which Wordsworth was able to raise through a new edition of his poetry. He then wrote to his landlady asking if the rumours were true, telling her that, if they were, he must 'make preparations for building – that his family may not be without a house to remove to'.[30] Lady le Fleming replied verbally that Mrs Huddleston was coming in 1827.[31] Others were less gloomy. Sara Hutchingson told Edward Quillinan that Wordsworth was 'resolved to build a house rather than quit Rydal – but we have hopes that . . . we may be permitted to stay to prevent the erection of another "genteel cottage" a thing very obnoxious to the dignity of the "Lady of the Manor" '.[32]

In the discussion following the ultimatum from the hall the female household would as ever defer to William, the acknowledged authority on local building. His daughter Dora could draw and we may assume that 'the dwelling which Dora has already sketched upon paper'[33] was the visible synthesis of their ideas. By April Dorothy wrote 'for my part I can as little endure the thought of building as of quitting Rydal Mount'.[34] In the same month Henry Crabb Robinson had read in 'the public prints' that Wordsworth intended to 'exchange the happier occupation of building the lofty rhyme for the more vulgar architecture of bricks and mortar'.[35] But when Wordsworth undertook to direct the alteration to the rectory at Grasmere in 1810 Dorothy wrote 'you know how unfit he is for anything of that kind'.[36]

He did not have to look far for a professional architect. George Webster of Kendal was building the new gothic chapel for Lady le Fleming below Rydal Mount from 1822-24.[37] This was Webster's first church and in 1822 Wordsworth had written a poem, dedicated to Lady le Fleming, *On seeing the Foundation Preparing for . . . Rydal Chapel.*[38] The Websters had already worked for Lady le Fleming at Rydal Hall; there are bills from 1818 to 1836 in the Rydal papers.[39] There was a direct connection between the two men in 1824. Jemima Quillinan, staying at Lanty Fleming's cottage, Stepping Stones, in 1822, was severely burnt and later died.[40] The Wordsworths undertook to see to the installation of a memorial table to her by Sir Francis Chantrey, and George Webster was involved in ways that are not completely clear, but at least included setting it up in Grasmere Church.[41] Francis Webster, George's father, rebuilt the Salutation Inn in the centre of Ambleside in 1821-22.[42] It was passed by Wordsworth on his way to and from his official place of work, the Stamp Office.[43] Francis was also responsible for the Assembly Rooms at Hawkshead of 1790,[44] for which the poet had expressed his dislike in 1799.[45] In the one known letter from poet to architect of 18th February 1826 Wordsworth invited Webster to Rydal Mount ('I have a bed at your service') 'for the benefit of your plans and judgement in respect of the House I design building . . . bring as many plans as you think may be of use to me'.[46] The use of 'design' here is ambiguous. Does Wordsworth mean 'intend' or is it a recognition of his own part in the conception of the house?

In 1825 Webster had begun his first two 'classic' Elizabethan houses, Underley and Eshton Halls,[47] with Longleat and Audley End amongst their models. Wordsworth's views would have been sharpened by Beaumont's failure and the obligation he must have felt to take over his friend's role and follow 'ancient models' and the 'grace and dignity of traditional building'.[48] As he wrote to Beaumont, 'internal architecture seems to have arrived at great excellence in England but . . . I scarcely see the outside of a new house that pleases me'.[49]

In April Webster submitted a set of three elevations and three plans entitled 'A residence

North Elevation of a Residence.
designed for William Wordsworth Esqʳᵉ

FIGURE 1. *George Webster, proposal drawing for the Rash, Rydal, Westmorland, 1826.*
Wordsworth Trust, Grasmere.

FIGURE 2. *George Webster, proposal drawing for the Rash, Rydal, Westmorland, 1826.*
Wordsworth Trust, Grasmere.

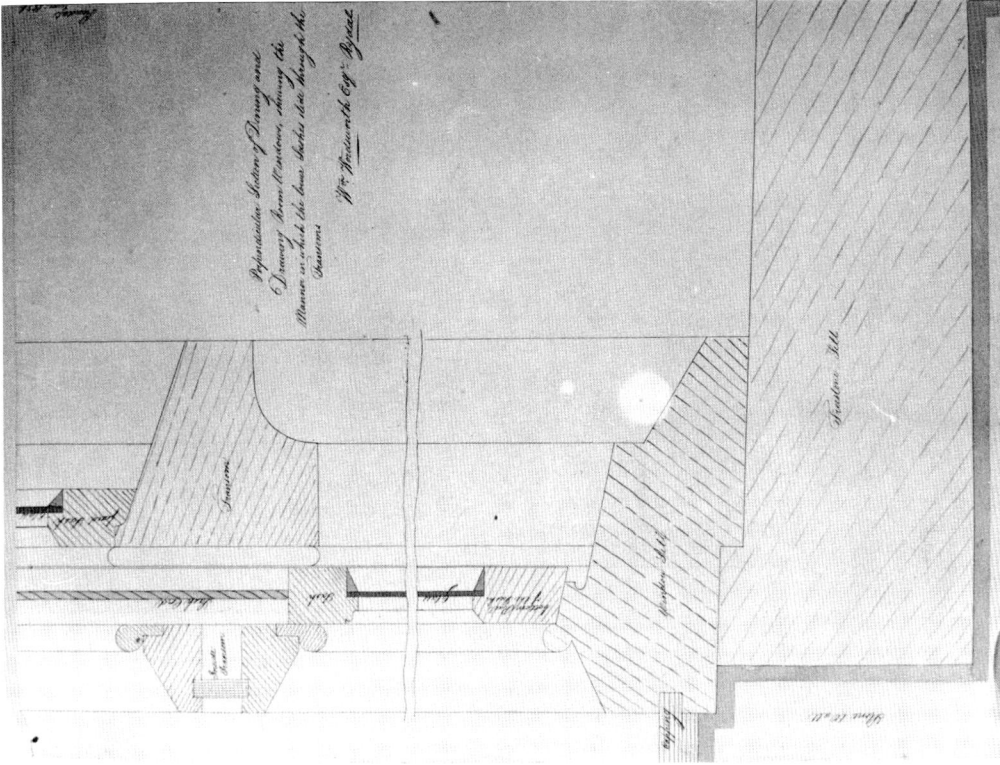

FIGURE 4. *George Webster, proposal drawing for the Rash, Rydal, Westmorland, 1826.* Wordsworth Trust, Grasmere.

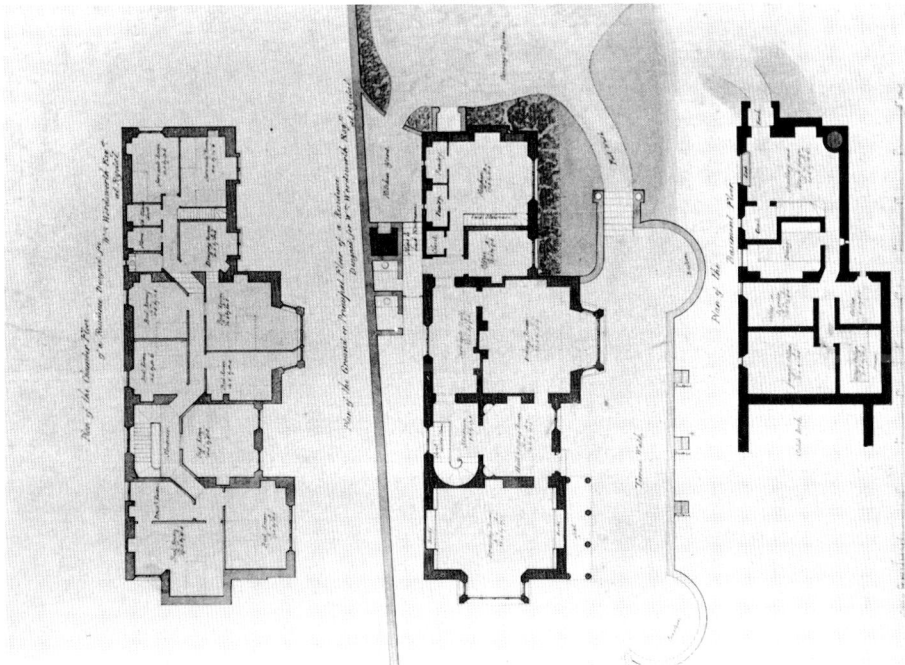

FIGURE 3. *George Webster, proposal drawing for the Rash, Rydal, Westmorland, 1826.* Wordsworth Trust, Grasmere.

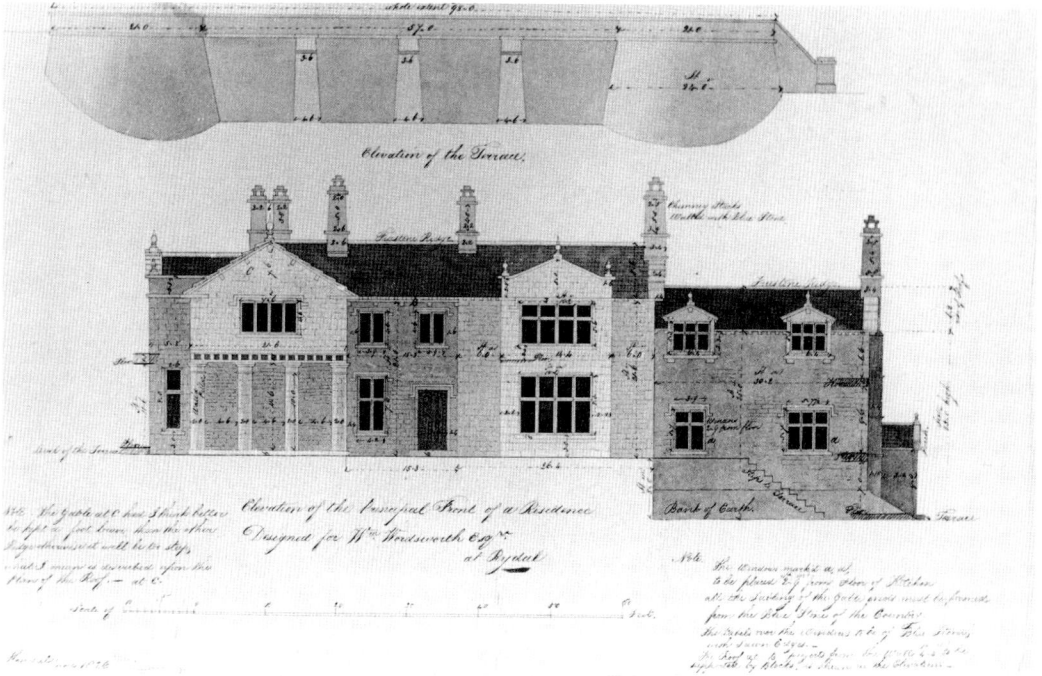

FIGURE 5. *George Webster, working drawing for the Rash, Rydal, Westmorland, 1826.*
Wordsworth Trust, Grasmere.

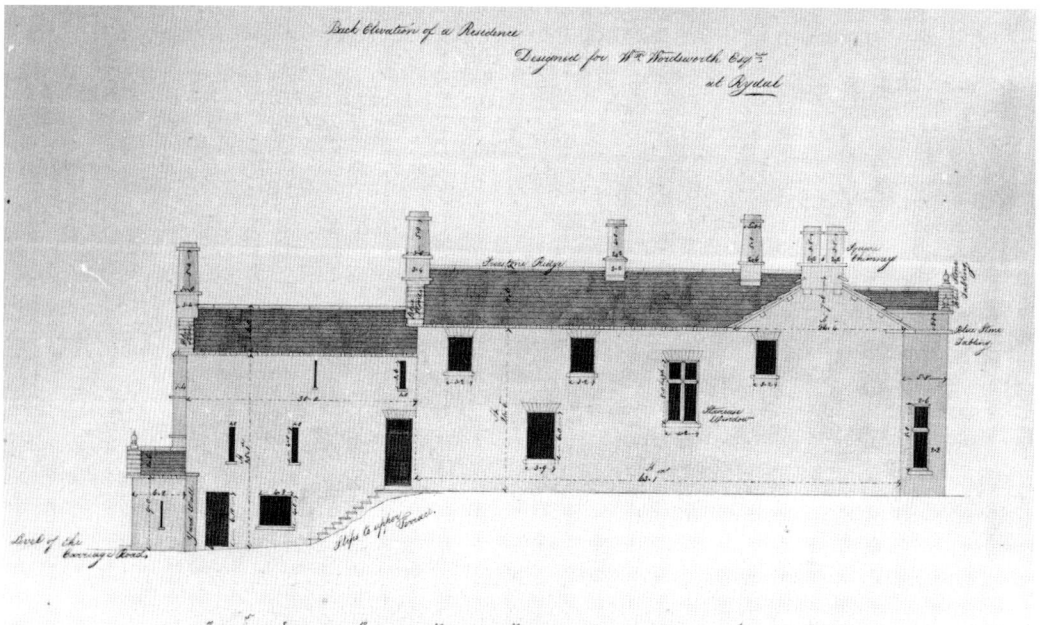

FIGURE 6. *George Webster, working drawing for the Rash, Rydal, Westmorland, 1826.*
Wordsworth Trust, Grasmere.

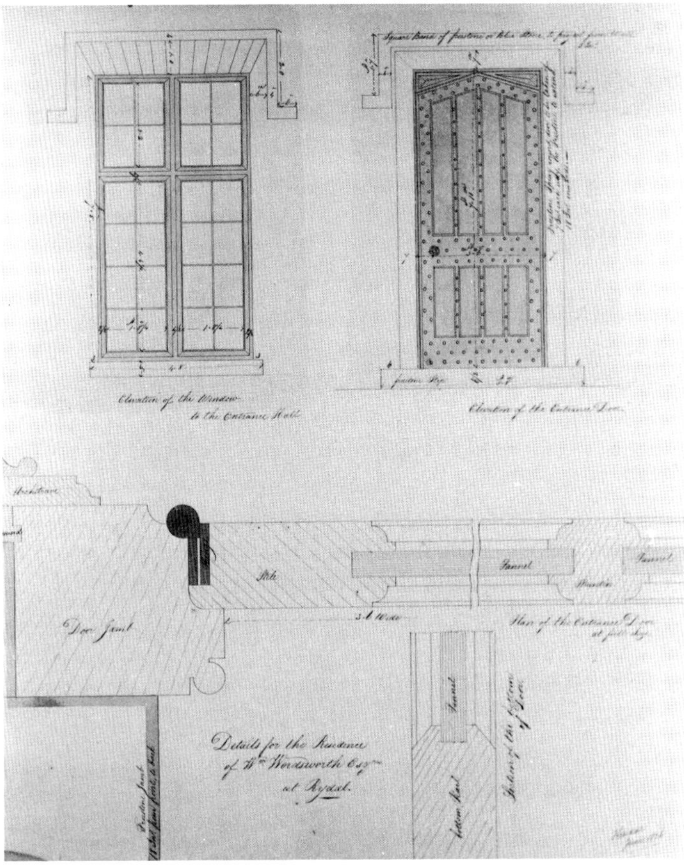

FIGURE 7. *George Webster, working drawing for the Rash, Rydal, Westmorland, 1826.* Wordsworth Trust, Grasmere.

for William Wordsworth Esqre at Rydal'; all survive except for the front elevation (Figs. 1, 2 and 3). They show a long narrow house with none of the formal style of Underley or Eshton. It is asymmetrical, with a sequence of changing levels, gables of varying sizes, a bay window and groups of cylindrical chimneys. The windows to the main rooms are shown mullioned and transomed with, apparently, casement openings. There is a subterfuge here for, despite appearances, they are sash windows, the sashes passing through the transoms (Fig. 4). 'Ancient models' outside meet the 'great excellence' of new inventiveness inside.

Pencil markings on the April drawings show alterations no doubt agreed between client and architect. The projecting kitchen chimney is redesigned with more set-offs; the dining room chimney is shown corbelled out and with its 'pipes' fused into one mass. These vernacular refinements were transferred to working drawings dated May and June (Figs. 4, 5, 6 and 7). A more conspicuous alteration was made by Webster alone for technical reasons, as the architect explained in a covering letter with specifications. He had changed the canted bay of the dining room to a square one 'from the conviction that your Valley would never be able to execute it without the use of freestone', and there was very little of this available in south Westmorland. Most of the house was to be of 'the stone of the country', that is from the le Flemings' own quarry. Freestone of good quality for the front windows and door frame was to be brought from the quarries at Hutton Roof,[50] some twenty miles to the south. Other minor modifications include one design for all finials, a pierced ball.

This rich anthology of local detail is drawn from buildings which Wordsworth knew well and praised in his writings. They can be visualised as he knew them through contemporary drawings, like the volumes of naturalistic etchings by William Green, such as *Studies from Nature* of 1809[51] (Fig. 8). Wordsworth was 'fond o' steans and mortar' and 'chimneys square up haufway and round t'other' and 'so we built 'em that road', local builders recalled after his death.[52] In the *Guide* he writes of 'the singular beauty of the chimneys . . . sometimes a low chimney . . . is overlaid with a slate supported on four slender pillars . . . others [are] quadrangular . . . surmounted by a tall cylinder, giving the most beautiful shape which is ever seen'. He noted 'the pleasing harmony between chimney . . . and the living column of smoke ascending from it through the still air'.[53] Cylindrical chimneys, built so because of a lack of good building stone, are widespread in south Westmorland and Furness (Fig. 9). They tend to be massive and single but are sometimes grouped. They are difficult to date and were still built 'naturally' into the nineteenth century. There are no less than ten circular chimneys in the Rash design, each with a formalised adaptation of the cap on four slender pillars. Traditional chimney construction includes stacks through the roof, stacks, corbelled out and stacks rising from ground level. In the Rash designs all three find a place.

There are three types of gable finish used in Lakeland, crow-stepped, continuous freestone slabs or the latter laid so that the slabs or slates overlap (Fig. 8). The last is the method formalised for the Rash. A continuous edging was proposed on both bays and was called

FIGURE 8. *William Green, view of Lakeland farm, 1809 from* Studies from Nature.

FIGURE 9. *Peter Crosthwaite, view of Coniston Hall, 1810, from his map of Coniston Lake.*

FIGURE 10. *William Green, view of The Cross, Ambleside, 1809, from* Studies from Nature.

FIGURE 11. *Lancrigg, near Grasmere*. Angus Taylor.

FIGURE 12. *Birklands, Kendal, Westmorland, by George Webster, 1831*. Angus Taylor.

FIGURE 13. *George Webster, working drawing for cottage, court of farm offices, Dallam Tower, Milnthorpe, Westmorland, 1826.* Cumbria Record Office.

FIGURE 14. *Birket Houses, Winster, by Dan Gibson, 1907.* Angus Taylor.

'tabling', usually the term for the flat stones built into chimney stacks to deflect rain. In the specifications all copings are called tabling and here Webster referred to his plans, adding 'but for better examples reference must be had to some of the old houses in the neighbourhood'. He proposed windows which were mullioned and transomed, of timber not specifically local. They were to have plain stone labels. He proposed doors which were vertically panelled and oak studded (Fig. 7). The semi-dormer windows of the kitchen wing, pushed forward on corbels (Figs. 2 and 5), have precedents, for example at Coniston Hall (Fig. 9), a particular favourite of Wordsworth's and essentially what he was recreating at Rydal.[54]

In both houses the main entrances is modest and far from prominent, although at first sight the Rash has a four-columned porch (Fig. 5). This turns out to be a verandah or 'piazza with seat', as the plan has it. Its four baseless columns support the gabled room above and reflect the form of the chimneys. Apparently without domestic precedent, it seems to derive from public buildings like the Cross House in Ambleside (Fig. 10), where rough square piers support an upper floor.[55] The Cross House was visible from the Stamp Office, Wordsworth's place of work. Webster must have known of the 'primitive hut' as the origin of the Greek temple, if only from a standard book like Chamber's *Treatise* of 1759,[56] and this may have suggested the idea of baseless columns.

A terrace was a necessity at the Rash and the steep site explains its massive structure, its semi-circular bastions, its battered and buttressed walls (Figs. 1, 2 and 5). Although Wordsworth had made terraces, these were no more than broad grassy paths. Webster probably contributed this feature, which no doubt derives from his years of training. Over the drawing-room window, where a datestone or armorial device might have been expected, is the only purely decorative feature of the design, the framed relief carving of a harp (Fig. 1). Is it the poet's 'harp of yore'[57] marking his house, or is it a talisman against the drying up of poetic inspiration? Wordsworth wrote little in the early eighteen twenties. Later in life, when the problem was more acute, he wrote he 'hoped to retouch a harp which I will not say with Tasso, oppressed by misfortune and years, has been hung upon a cypress but which has however for some time been set aside'.[58]

On 18 May 1826 Wordsworth wrote to Robert Jones, 'I have no hope of visiting Wales this spring or summer I am entangled in preparing to build a house'.[59] A week later Sara Hutchinson wrote 'the timber is brought – the plan and the elevation all upon paper etc. and he is eager to begin in good earnest!'[60] Webster's reference to 'the floor now staked out' in the specifications shows work in progress, yet in July Wordsworth declared his 'text was to build or not to build'.[61] Mrs Hudleston visited Rydal and declined the Mount. She wrote to her son 'the Wordsworths are all ready for building just below the chapel though not without hopes of remaining on as your cousin must consider a building so near her quite a nuisance'.[62]

Lady le Fleming did relent and no more is heard of building on the Rash until 1844. Webster's designs were brought out then, when Isabella Fenwick wished to be near the Wordsworths. Various cottages were concocted from them and a surviving drawing shows a plan of a reduced version of the original.[63] There was talk of asking Anthony Salvin, Miss Fenwick's cousin, for his opinion, or even a plan of his own.[64] On 14 August 1844 'there were 50 men looking at the marked out ground before bidding for jobs',[65] when a letter was put into Wordsworth's hand by Lady le Fleming's attorney to the effect that 'no new house had been erected except on an old house stead, in the memory of man on the Rydal Manor' and this would continue to be the case.[66] Wordsworth rejected a courteous offer from Lady le

Fleming to buy the land on the grounds of his daughter Dora's 'attachment to this country is so strong that she lives in the hopes at some future date to build a cottage on some site interesting to her affections'.[67] His suggestion that the Rash field could be exchanged for the Wishing Gate field at the Grasmere end of the estate was rejected.

Wordsworth must have felt that the ideal of providing a paradigm begun with Beaumont's dreams at Loughrigg had died at Rydal on the Rash Field. Nevertheless the Rash designs had their effect on client and architect. Wordsworth gained an understanding of how buildings were put together and embarked on a career of advising friends on their houses, in the process no doubt promoting Webster's interest. When Dr. Arnold of Ruby began his house at Fox How in 1833 Wordsworth 'set forth his ideas'.[68] When Charlotte Brontë visited the Arnolds she saw 'the chimneys . . . which were Wordsworth's "architectural creation and special care" (so the architect averred)'.[69] The architect may well have been George Webster. Mrs Fletcher of Edinburgh read *Lyrical Ballads* (1789) and determined to move to be near the poet. In 1835 he was looking for a suitable house for her and four years later they met at Lancrigg near Grasmere to discuss alterations to the farmhouse (Fig. 11). These were on a larger scale, but entirely rustic and it is impossible to identify the new chimneys 'like those at Troutbeck . . . Mr Wordsworth thinks they are the best for this country'.[70] Lesketh How at Ambleside of 1844 is perhaps by Webster. It is a crisp design of slate with its share of tidied-up local features like the Rash designs.[71] The Knoll of 1845, nearby, was, Harriet Martineau claimed, of her own planning whilst admitting to Wordsworth's help.[72] The semi-circular bastion in front must be a memory of the Rash terrace.

For the architect the collaboration opened his eyes to the vernacular. Details from the Rash entered his vocabulary, as, for instance, at Birklands, Kendal (1831) (Fig. 12); and others were added or reconsidered. Features accepted only for the office wing at Eshton came round to the façade at Moreton Hall (1829) and Whittington Hall (1831).[73] Part of Webster's reconstruction of Dallam Tower (1826) was a 'Court of Farm Offices' with a cottage exactly copying the columns, porch and chimneys of the Rash[74] (Fig. 13).

With the arrival of the railway in 1845 the crowds predicted by Wordsworth duly arrived at the terminus at Birthwaite, the hamlet which consequently developed into modern Windermere town. The station was designed by Webster's draughtsman and new partner Miles Thompson.[75] The adjoining Rigg's (now Windermere) Hotel, Italianate with a tower, and on a new scale for the Lakes, was designed by both the partners.[76] Where they used a post-Rash local style, as at the Lake Hotel and Posting House, later the Prince of Wales, on the Lake at Grasmere[77] which has banks of Rash chimneys, the detail barely alleviates the great bulk of the slate masses. Ironically the Prince of Wales stands where the young Wordsworth contemplated building a cottage in 1799, half a century before.

Had the Rash been built would the example of such a house lived in by a man of Wordsworth eminence have had imitators? Did the failure in 1826 in effect postpone a domestic vernacular revival to the end of the century, when Voysey and Baillie Scott built their splendid houses on Windermere? Looking at an example by a lesser contemporary, Dan Gibson, at Birket Houses (1907)[78] (Fig. 14), it is hard not to conclude that he knew Webster's designs in Wordsworth's library.

NOTES

1. Grasmere, Wordsworth Trust, drawings and specifications; catalogue of *The Websters of Kendal* exhibition, Abbot Hall, Kendal, 8 September to 14 October 1973. The house was never named but referred to as the Rash, after the site.

2. C. L. Shaver (ed.), *The Letters of William and Dorothy Wordsworth*, I, Oxford, 1967, 271.

3. Applethwaite, near Keswick, the gift of Sir George Beaumont, Bart., 1803 [Mary Moorman, *William Wordsworth, A Biography,* Oxford, 1966, II, 137], Broad How, Ullswater, bought with the secret help of Lord Lonsdale [*ibid.*, 60-61], and an estate near Keswick, bought by Wordsworth on the repayment of a debt and the receipt of a legacy [*ibid.*, 241].

4. Shaver, *op. cit.*, 506.

5. *Ibid.*, 533, 536, 635.

6. The Crumps were from Liverpool where he was an attorney and merchant. They built a house on a hill-top near the village of Grasmere and only too visible from Dove Cottage. To the Wordsworths and their friends it seemed to sit on top of the church tower.

7. Mary Moorman (ed.), *The Letters of William and Dorothy Wordsworth*, II, Oxford, 407.

8. Moorman, *op. cit.*, 228.

9. *Idem.*

10. K. Coburn (ed.), *The Letters of Sarah Hutchinson, 1800-1835*, London, 1954, 53.

11. On the sites in notes 2 and 3 above.

12. Shaver *op. cit.*, 468.

13. Moorman, *op. cit*, 394.

14. Shaver, *op. cit.*, 271.

15. K. Coburn (ed.), *The Notebooks of Samuel Taylor Coleridge*, I, London, 1957, 511.

16. Stephen Parrish (ed.), *The Prelude 1798-99*, 1977, 55, lines 37-8; Blake Tyson, 'Francis Webster and the Market House at Hawkshead', *Quarto*, xxxi (3) 1993, 8-11.

17. Moorman, *op. cit.*, 404.

18. Ernest de Selincourt (ed.), *William Wordsworth, A Guide Through the District of the Lakes in the North of England,* Oxford, 1978, *passim.*

19. Shaver, *op. cit.*, 622.

20. E. de Selincourt and H. Darbishire (eds.), *William Wordsworth, The Poetic Works*, Oxford, 1940-49.

21. Russel Noyes, *Wordsworth and the Art of Landscape*, New York, 1973, 127, 130.

22. *Idem.*

23. Moorman, *op. cit.*, 159.

24. *Ibid.*, 112.

25. Shaver, *op. cit.*, 490.

26. de Selincourt and Darbishire, *op. cit.*, 142-150.

27. *Ibid.*, 151.

28. *Idem.*

29. E. Morley (ed.), *Correspondence of Henry Crabb Robinson with the Wordsworth Circle*, I, Oxford, 1927, 79.

30. A. G. Hill (ed.), *The Letters of William and Dorothy Wordsworth*, III, Oxford, 1978, 415.

31. *Ibid.*, 411.

32. Coburn, *op. cit.*, 1954, 314.

33. Hill, *op. cit.*, 411.

34. *Ibid.*, 431.

35. Morley, *op. cit.*, 78.

36. R. Gittings and Jo Manton, *Dorothy Wordsworth*, Oxford, 1985, 189.

37. Kendal, Cumbria Record Office (hereafter CRO), Rydal papers, WD/Ry, Box 22; Howard Colvin, *Biographical Dictionary of British Architects, 1600-1840*. New Haven and London, 1995, 1034.

38. de Selincourt and Darbishire, *op. cit.*, 155-68.

39. CRO, *loc. cit.*, Box 16.

40. Moorman, *op. cit.*, 427.

41. A. C. Taylor, 'The Wordsworths, the Websters and Chantrey's Quillinan Monument', *Quarto*, xxxi (2), 1993, 12-14.

42. Colvin, *op. cit.*, 1033.

43. In 1813, through the influence of Lord Lonsdale, Wordsworth became Distributor for Stamps for the Westmorland part of the Inland Revenue. The Salutation Inn lay on the route from his office to Rydal Mount [Moorman, *op. cit.*, 244].

44. Tyson, *loc. cit.*

45. Parrish, *op. cit.*, 37-8.

46. A. G. Hill (ed.), *The Letters of William and Dorothy Wordsworth: A Supplement of New Letters*, Oxford, 1993, 191.

47. Colvin, *op. cit.*, 1034.

48. de Selincourt, *Guide . . ., cit.*, 74.

49. Shaver, *op. cit.*, 497.

50. A. C. Hyelman, *The Development of Quarrying in Rural Areas of Lonsdale and South Westmorland*, unpublished thesis, 1984 (copy in CRO). Hutton Roof quarries had a 'wide variety of stone' including 'fine creamy-white sandstone' [*ibid.*, 228]. George Atkinson contracted to supply fine dressed stone to George Webster at Underley and Whittington Halls, [*ibid.*, 242].

51. William Green, *Studies from Nature*, Kendal, 1809, n.p. A Manchester surveyor, Green settled as a topographical artist in Ambleside. Wordsworth bought a drawing of Glencoyne with its cylindrical chimneys and stepped gables from his friend in 1808.

52. H. D. Rawnsley, *Reminiscences of Wordsworth among the Peasantry of Westmorland*, London, 1968, 39.

53. de Selincourt, *Guide . . ., cit.*, 63.

54. W. J. Owen and J. W. Smyser (eds.), *William Wordsworth, Prose Works*, II, 308. 'Coniston Hall is the most interesting piece of architecture these Lakes have to boast of'.

55. Green, *op. cit.*.

56. Sir William Chambers, *A Treatise on the Decorative Part of Civil Architecture*, London, 1862 ed, f.p. 78; Angus Taylor, 'George Webster, The Education of an Architect: a Proposal', *Quarto*, xxxi (1), 1993, 13-16.

57. de Selincourt and Darbyshire, *op. cit.*, 270.

58. Moorman, *op. cit.*, 11, 560.

59. Hill, *op. cit.*, 448.

60. Coburn, *op. cit.*, 1954, 318.

61. Hill, *op. cit.*, 480.

62. Moorman, *op. cit.*, 422.

63. With the Webster drawings at Grasmere.

64. A. G. Hill (ed.), *The Letters of William and Dorothy Wordsworth*, VII, Oxford, 1988, 571.

65. Wordsworth Trust, MS. Letter, Dora Wordsworth to Isabella Fenwick, 21 August 1844.

66. *Idem.*

67. Hill, *op. cit.*, 571.

68. Moorman, *op. cit.*, 485.

69. Winifred Gerin, *Charlotte Brontë*, Oxford, 1967, 449.

70. Elizabeth Fletcher, *Autobiography*, private, 1875, 217.

71. For Dr. Davy, Mrs Fletcher's son-in-law.

72. Harriet Martineau, *Autobiography*, 3rd. ed., London, 1887, 235.

73. E. Twycross, *The Mansions of England and Wales*, Lancaster, 1847, I, 20 (Moreton Hall); II, 9 (Whittington Hall).

74. CRO, WD/D plans, /4.

75. *Westmorland Gazette*, 31 October 1846.

76. *Ibid.*, 8 November 1845, 'Plans at the offices of Webster and Thompson, Kendal'.

77. Lake Hotel and Posting House, datestone 1853, almost certainly by Thompson. The extension is in the same style, ten years later, by Thompson [*Westmorland Gazette*, 21 November 1863].

78. CRO, WDX/400, Birket Houses for Myles Higgin Birket.

Select Bibliography

The bibliography contains, besides the works listed under Abbreviations (p. xvi), the printed books most frequently consulted or cited in the text and footnotes.

Barker, P., 'The Websters' Marble Works in Miller's Close', *Quarto*, xxviii, Jan. 1991

Bellasis, E., *Westmorland Church Notes*, 2 vols, Kendal, 1888

Bingham, R. K., *Chronicles of Milnthorpe*, Milnthorpe, 1987
     Kendal, A Social History, Milnthorpe, 1995

Boumphrey, R. S., Hudleston, C. R., and Hughes, J., *An Armorial for Westmorland and Lonsdale*, CWAAS, Extra Series xxi, 1975

Briggs, J. (ed.), *Lonsdale Magazine*, 3 vols, Kirkby Lonsdale and Kendal, 1820-22

Burke, B., *Visitation of Seats and Arms of the Noblemen and Gentlemen of Great Britain and Ireland*, 2 vols, London, 1852-3; 2nd series, 2 vols, London, 1854-5

Colvin, H., *Biographical Dictionary of British Architects, 1600-1840*, 3rd ed., New Haven and London, 1995

Colvin, H., Crook, J. M., and Friedman, T., *Architectural Drawings from Lowther Castle, Westmorland*, Society of Architectural Historians of Great Britain, 1980

Curwen, J. F., *Ancient Parish of Heversham with Milnthorpe*, Kendal, 1930
     Kirkbie-Kendall, Kendal, 1900
     Records relating to the Barony of Kendale, iii, CWAAS, Record Series vi, 1926

Fleetwood-Hesketh, P., *Murray's Lancashire Architectural Guide*, London, 1955

Green, W., *Tourist's New Guide* [to] *Cumberland, Westmorland, and Lancashire*, 2 vols, Kendal, 1819

Gunnis, R., *Dictionary of British Sculptors, 1660-1851*, 2nd ed., London, n.d.

Hall, M., *Artists of Cumbria*, Newcastle-upon-Tyne, 1979

Hudleston, C. R., and Boumphrey, R. S., *Cumberland Families and Heraldry*, CWAAS, Extra Series xxiii, 1978

Kirkby, R. H. *et al* (eds), *Rural Deanery of Cartmel*, Ulverston, 1872

Local Chronology, London and Kendal, 1865

Mannex & Co., *History, topography and directory of Westmorland and of the hundreds of Lonsdale and Amounderness*, Beverley, 1851

Mannex & Whellan, *History, gazetteer and directory of Cumberland*, Beverley, 1847

Nicholson, C., *Annals of Kendal*, 2nd ed., London and Kendal, 1861

Parson, W., and White, W., *History, directory, and gazetteer of . . . Cumberland and Westmorland with . . . Furness and Cartmel*, Leeds, 1829

Pevsner, N., *Cumberland and Westmorland*, Buildings of England, London, 1967; also *North Lancashire*, 1969, *Yorkshire, North Riding*, 1966, *Yorkshire, West Riding*, 1959

Price, J., *Sharpe, Paley and Austin: A Lancashire Architectural Practice: 1836-1942*, University of Lancaster, 1998

Richardson, J., *Furness Past and Present*, 2 vols, Barrow-in-Furness, 1880

Robinson, J. M., *Guide to the Country Houses of the North-West*, London, 1991

Satchell, J., *Kendal's Canal: History, Industry and People*, Kendal Civic Society, 2001

Sketches of Grange and the Neighbourhood, Kendal, 1850

Somervell, J., *Water-power Mills of South Westmorland*, Kendal, 1930

Stockdale, J., *Annals of Cartmel*, Ulverston, 1872

Taylor A., works listed on p. 0

Thompson, T. W., *Wordsworth's Hawkshead*, ed. R. Woof, London, 1970

Twycross, E., *Mansions of England and Wales: County Palatine of Lancaster*, 3 vols, London, 1847

Tyson, B., 'Francis Webster and the Market House at Hawkshead, 1790', *Quarto*, xxxi, Oct. 1993

Victoria History of the County of Lancaster, ed. W. Farrer *et al*, 8 vols, London, 1906-14

Websters of Kendal, Abbot Hall Art Gallery, Kendal, 1973

West, T., *Guide to the Lakes*, London and Kendal, 1778; ten further eds to 1821

Whitaker, T. D., *History and Antiquities of the Deanery of Craven*, London, 1805; 3rd ed. Didsbury and Skipton, 1878

Whitwell, J., *Old Houses of Kendal*, Kendal, 1866

Index